To Joshua and Anna.
You keep me young.

WHAT I REALLY WANT TO DO ON SET IN HOLLYWOOD

WHAT I REALLY WANT TO DO ON SET IN HOLLYWOOD

Brian Dzyak

Back Stage Books
An imprint of Watson-Guptill Publications
New York

First published in 2008 by Back Stage Books, an imprint of
Watson-Guptill Publications, Nielsen Business Media,
a division of The Nielsen Company
770 Broadway, New York, NY 10003
www.watsonguptill.com

Library of Congress Control Number: 2007936521

ISBN-13: 978-0-8230-9953-5
ISBN-10: 0-8230-9953-9

Watson-Guptill Publications books are available at special discounts when purchased in bulk for premiums and sales promotions, as well as for fund-raising or
educational use. Special editions or book excerpts can be created to specifica-
tion. For details, please contact the Special Sales Director at the address above.

First printing 2008

Printed in the United States of America

1 2 3 4 5 6 7 8 / 14 13 12 11 10 09 08

Contents

Acknowledgments

Just like a movie, this book couldn't have been completed without the help and cooperation of many skilled and knowledgeable people. Information has come from a large variety of sources both on and off set, and, for a variety of reasons, the list is not inclusive of everyone who has contributed. I specifically want to thank the following, who generously gave their time to help make this a useful and valuable resource:

Dean Cundy, Director of Photography, A.S.C.; Matt Jenson, Director of Photography; Peter Hapke, Camera Operator; C. E. Courtney, Gaffer; Dennis White, First Assistant Director; Mike Demerrit, Assistant Director; Leigh Killberg, Production Coordinator; Marissa Pollack, Production Assistant; Jerry Henry, Transportation Coordinator; Gabriella McKenna, Standby Painter; Tasha Oldham, Director and Script Supervisor; Philip Hoffman, Production Designer; Meredith Korn, On-Set Dresser; Carrie Urzua, DGA Trainee; Todd Russell, Boom Operator; Keith Campbell, Stuntman/Coordinator; Dominique Jaramillo, On-Set Medic; Zade Rosenthal, Unit Still Photographer; Greg Kawecki, Second Assistant Director; Evan Nesbitt, Director of Photography/DIT; Joel Harlow, Special Effects Makeup Artist; Greg Sanger, Leadman; Tom Acosta, Greens; Ron Bolanowski and Darrell Burgess, Special Effects; Nancy Sykes and Leah Amir, Crafts Service; Charlene Amateau, Costume Supervisor; Josh Stickler, Production Assistant; Sherri Perry, Hair Stylist; Josh Elliot, On-Set Dresser; Tommy Tomlison, Property Master; Lori Harris, Costumer; Ross Addielo, Dolly Grip; Ben Younger, Director; Steve Pink, Director; David Linck, Publicist; Ernie Malick, Publicist; Mary Vogt, Costume Designer; Bob Roe, First Assistant Director/Producer; John Lowe, Locations; Lisa Blond, EPK Producer; Patty Foy, Studio Teacher; Mark Yacullo, Transportation Coordinator; and Tom Wilson, Actor.

A very special thank you to Producer Sean Perrone for believing in this and helping me to the next step.

Special thanks to my literary agent, Lilly Gharemani of Full Circle Literary, for also believing in *What I Really Want to Do*. Thank you for your patience in guiding me in my first time through the publishing process.

Thank you to my editors at Watson-Guptill, Bob Nirkind and Gary Sunshine, for helping me bring the book into focus.

Thanks to everyone at Watson-Guptill for taking a chance on this book and this concept.

A very special thank you to Susan Greenawalt Joba for your countless hours of editorial input and for providing a much-needed outsider's perspective. Not only would this book have been far less without your love, dedication, generosity, and support for me and for this project, but it might not have been finished at all. Your strength is a continued inspiration. You always told me how much you loved my words. Let's hope that there will be much more to come for both of us.

Thank you to my parents for always believing in, encouraging, and never giving up on me.

Thank you to Karen, for having patience through the ups and downs that define this tumultuous industry. If I (we) had only known even half of what is in this book before we moved from Ohio... Thank you for believing in me, not only with this book.

Part I

THE BUSINESS...REALLY!

What I Really Want to Do

What I Really Need to Know

Where I Really Need to Go

What I Really Need to Have

What Am I Getting Myself Into?

Chapter 1

What I Really Want to Do

I want to make movies! What else is there to talk about?

Okay, let's cut to the chase. If you're reading this, you really want to know how to get a job in the entertainment industry, be it in movies, television, music videos, or commercials. You want to know where to go, what to do, and who to meet. Fair enough. You need answers to these questions if this is the field you believe you want to enter.

But there's one question that most people who want to be in the business fail to ask themselves before jumping in: "Do I *really* want to do this?" Success can bring great prestige at your next class reunion and perhaps even lots of cash. But there's more to a career in the entertainment business than just showing up and making movies. Breaking in takes enthusiasm and perseverance. *Maintaining* a viable career begins by being realistic about what you're really getting yourself into.

Every year, millions of people watch the glamour of Hollywood from the comfort of their own homes and dream of sharing in a piece of that fantasy. And every year, thousands of those people pack their bags and head west, with little more than dreams and enthusiasm, intent on finding a job that will make them rich and famous. Some hit upon the success they are looking for, but many more do not. The expectations are almost always different than the harsh reality of life in the "biz." However, with just a little guidance, you can increase the odds of building a successful career and finding that fame, fortune, and artistic outlet you crave.

What is this book really all about?

What I Really Want To Do on Set in Hollywood gives you a taste of the *experience* of working on a movie SET by explaining the nuts and bolts of the industry, the various departments, the jobs within the departments, and how they all interact with one another on a shot-by-shot basis. With this detailed information in your hands, you will then have a very good idea of how the industry really functions, how you can find a way in for yourself, and what your own life will be like while doing it.

Whether you are a college grad in the Midwest, a thirty-something parent of two along one of the coasts, or an already established member of **IATSE, SAG,** the **DGA,** or the TEAMSTERS in Los Angeles, knowing more about the minutia of how movies are really made will enable you to embark on a career path in a much wiser fashion.

So where do I start?

To get your career search going, you first have to figure out what it is you really want to do. It isn't enough for you to say that you just "want to make movies." That kind of general ambition is fine when you're young and just having fun, but creating an actual career that pays your bills and affords you the lifestyle you're looking for requires you to be more specific. All of the jobs done on a small student film are still involved in making a big-budget project—only when more money is available, more people can be brought in to help. Consider Hollywood as the major league of the entertainment business, where art and commerce are merged within the world of high finance. It's the ultimate playground, where big kids get to play make-believe with the best toys at the highest level.

The exact process that occurs to get an idea from script to screen is fairly simple.

THE IDEA

An idea occurs to someone such as a Writer, Director, Producer, or Actor. In this competitive industry, ideas need to be fresh and marketable. Whether the idea moves forward from this point, and how quickly, depends on who comes up with it.

DEVELOPMENT

An idea has to be evaluated before any significant money is spent on developing it into a full-fledged screenplay. The idea has to be original yet have an air of familiarity to be marketable to a broad spectrum of people. The budget is taken into account at every point of the process. If the idea manages to jump successfully through all the requisite hoops, a writer is hired under the **WGA** contract and a TREATMENT of the story is completed.

The treatment may go through many committees and studio executives before the process is allowed to continue to the actual screenwriting stage. Typically the writer who pitched the idea and worked up the treatment is hired to do at least the first draft. The screenplay usually goes through the same obstacle course that the treatment did. Major rewrites may continue right up to the first day of shooting, and daily rewrites throughout production are a common occurrence.

PREPRODUCTION

Once all the ABOVE-THE-LINE people are reasonably happy, the project moves into official preproduction. It is during this stage that any additional above-the-line personnel are hired. As the production start date becomes imminent, BELOW-THE-LINE crew are called. More often than not, the Director and at least one A-LIST star are asked to commit during development. Most films, both studio and independent, have a difficult time being financed without the interest of a major corporate or financial entity. As momentum for the project builds, schedules are created and a "realistic" budget is calculated. If not enough time is spent or shoddy work is done during preproduction, all efforts later on, during production and beyond, will undoubtedly suffer.

PRODUCTION

Assuming that the story and screenplay are strong and that plenty of time and money have been spent on preproduction, then PRODUCTION should be the easiest and most enjoyable part of the process. It is during this twelve-week period that the words on the page are turned into pictures and sound by a cast and crew of over one hundred skilled, and typically union (IATSE, DGA, SAG, Teamsters), employees. Every shot featuring the principal cast is filmed by the FIRST UNIT crew. If additional photography is needed that doesn't necessarily involve the main cast, such as stunts or elaborate special effects, a SECOND UNIT and/or SPECIAL EFFECTS UNIT is assembled to shoot simultaneously at a different location.

POSTPRODUCTION

Postproduction is usually considered the period when all of the film is edited. The truth is that during actual production, an Editor has been cutting the DAILIES continually. By the time the shooting schedule ends, the Director will have a nearly complete movie to look at. Some Second Unit and effects work may continue far into the postproduction schedule. The Director and Producers will alter the Editor's work as they please until they are happy. Location sound is fixed with ADR, SOUND EFFECTS are added, and a music score is married to the completed picture.

MARKETING

A publicity campaign is designed for the project during preproduction. Behind-the-scenes footage is coordinated by the Unit Publicist during production, as are any interviews that newspapers, magazines, and television outlets request. Prior to release, a PRESS JUNKET is held at a hotel with the principal players and reporters from around the world.

RELEASE

The red-carpet premiere, a marketing tool in the guise of a party to help sell the movie to the public, is a staple for many films. Journalists from around the world are invited to take pictures and ask questions of the movie stars.

It all sounds pretty exciting! What kinds of jobs are available?

If you already have a job outside of the movie business, there very well may be a parallel existing position inside the industry or a trade in which you can apply your current skills. The real trick is finding your way in and learning the specific protocols that apply to film production.

The key to building a successful career is to put some careful thought into what part of the process really suits you best. Some people really enjoy building models (fabrication) while others like blowing them up (pyrotechnics). If camera work excites you most, you need to decide whether it is the directing portion (camera placement) that is best or if it is the lighting and operating (which falls under cinematography). Some people aren't necessarily creatively inclined but like to be involved in other ways (executives and agents). What follows is an overview of the most common jobs involved in making a movie. It is important to note that while there are some differences in creating a feature motion picture as opposed to a television show, commercial, or music video, all of the jobs described here are done nearly exactly the same way, regardless of the project.

JOBS OFF SET

Jobs done primarily away from the set during actual production include the following:

- **Writer** — changes intangible ideas into words, providing a blueprint for every aspect of production
- **Studio Executive** — part of the financing and distribution arm of the industry; oversees production of a project as a whole from the development stage to exhibition
- **Producer** — oversees *all* aspects of production
- **Agent** — secures work for those with creative and technical talent... and takes 10 percent of the earnings
- **Manager** — much like an agent, but gives more personal attention to the client for 15 percent of the earnings
- **Unit Production Manager** — in charge of all logistics including, but not limited to, day-to-day planning, production scheduling, terms of employment for cast and crew, supplies, equipment, locations, permits, travel, transportation, and financial considerations for production
- **Studio Accountant** — handles the financial considerations of a studio
- **Production Accountant** — manages the day-to-day financial details of a specific production
- **Production Coordinator** — handles the logistics of scheduling and paperwork
- **Production Designer** — translates the ideas expressed in the script into the elements that will be seen

- **Art Director** — working under the Production Designer, coordinates the Art Department
- **Construction Coordinator** — plans and coordinates the construction schedule and crew requirements
- **Construction Foreman** — supervises construction work
- **Visual Effects Supervisor** — coordinates the various effects requirements
- **Visual Effects (CGI)** — uses computers to create any number of illusions that are impossible to achieve practically on set or are simply less expensive to create digitally
- **Editor** — syncs sound and image and then cuts shots into a logical order to tell the story
- **Assistant Editor** — maintains editing equipment and deals with related paperwork
- **Postproduction Sound** — "sweetens" (improves sound quality) and edits dialogue, sound effects, and music tracks
- **Film Lab** — processes the shot negative then checks it for damage or exposure problems
- **Composer** — creates a musical score to accompany images onscreen
- **Musician** — performs instrumentals to help create the musical score

JOBS ON SET

Jobs done primarily on set during actual production include the following:

- **Director** — generally in charge of the creative decisions made throughout production
- **Script Supervisor** — keeps a detailed log of each shot and tracks continuity
- **Actor** — performs a character as written in the screenplay; generally has lines of dialogue to speak
- **Extra** — an Actor without dialogue; fills in the background to support the principal action
- **Stand-in** — placeholder for a principal Actor while the crew lights the set
- **Stunt Coordinator** — coordinates and designs sequences or actions considered dangerous
- **Stunt Performer** — skilled and trained performer capable of executing dangerous actions
- **First Assistant Director** — coordinates each department on a shot-by-shot basis to keep the production on schedule
- **Second Assistant Director** — assists the First Assistant Director and completes necessary paperwork
- **Second Second Assistant Director** — lends assistance to the Second Assistant Director

- **DGA Trainee** — an on-set Assistant Director trainee
- **Production Assistant** — generally runs errands for any number of department personnel
- **Director of Photography** — responsible for technical and creative decisions regarding lighting and camera setup
- **Digital Imaging Technician (DIT)** — video engineer specializing in HIGH-DEFINITION cameras
- **Camera Operator** — points the camera and frames the shot using a variety of tools
- **First Assistant Camera/Focus Puller** — responsible for technical upkeep of camera and keeps subjects in focus during each take
- **Second Assistant Camera/Clapper** — assists the First Assistant Camera in camera setup and keeps track of all camera equipment
- **Loader** — loads and keeps track of all film used throughout production
- **Camera PA** — trainee who assists the rest of the camera department
- **Aerial Pilot** — flies a variety of aircraft with camera mounted onboard
- **Stabilized Camera Operator/Technician** — operates a gyroscopically stabilized camera system, usually attached to an aircraft
- **Key Grip** — coordinates all grip personnel in working with the Electric Department to set lighting and with the Camera Department to move and secure camera equipment.
- **Best Boy Grip** — keeps track of all paperwork and equipment used by the Grip Department
- **Company Grip** — provides safe rigging for lighting and camera equipment
- **Dolly Grip** — lays track or flat surface on which to push a dolly-mounted camera
- **Gaffer** — coordinates the actual nuts and bolts of lighting the set
- **Best Boy Electric** — prepares and tracks all lighting equipment
- **Electricians** — run electrical cable and set lights
- **Generator Operator** — maintains correct electrical output for set lighting and power
- **Location Mixer** — maintains proper sound levels during a take
- **Boom Operator** — holds a microphone over the action, out of sight from the camera
- **Cable Puller** — assists the Mixer and Boom Operator during setup and each shot
- **Costumer** — assists the Wardrobe Supervisor and dresses Actors
- **Wardrobe Supervisor** — organizes and maintains costumes and also tracks costume continuity

- **Costume Designer** — designs and/or buys clothing that the Actors should be wearing per the script
- **Makeup Artist** — applies cosmetic makeup in accordance with the requirements of the story
- **Hair Stylist** — designs and styles hair in accordance with the requirements of the story
- **Property Master** — acquires, maintains, and tracks all props
- **Set Decorator** — in charge of all furnishings seen on set
- **Leadman** — coordinates physical set decoration with the Set Decorator and the Set Dressers
- **Set Dresser** — works with the Set Decorator to place items on the set
- **Standby Painter** — creates signage and touches up damaged painted surfaces during production
- **Greensman** — creates and maintains any vegetation and/or landscaping on a film set
- **Crafts Service** — provides a table of snacks that is close to the set throughout the day
- **Catering** — provides at least one or two hot meals per shooting day at location
- **Special Effects** — constructs on-set rigging of props to perform a variety of real effects (not computer graphics) and is usually a specialist in creating explosions, fire, and bullet hits
- **Transportation Coordinator** — supervises the transportation of personnel, equipment, and vehicles
- **Transportation Captain** — assists the Transportation Coordinator
- **Truck Drivers** — trained and licensed to operate a variety of large vehicles
- **Crew Cab Driver** — primarily assigned to drive crew passenger vans
- **Location Manager/Scout** — finds suitable locations for filming and secures proper permissions and permits
- **Set Medic** — trained Registered Nurse (RN) or Emergency Medical Technician (EMT) who is on set just in case of illness or injury
- **Set Teacher** — on-set schoolteacher when child Actors are present
- **Unit Publicist** — coordinates all elements required for successful marketing of the film
- **Unit Still Photographer** — obtains photos to be used primarily in the marketing of the film
- **Behind-the-Scenes Cameraman/Videographer** — shoots behind-the-scenes footage and interviews for Electronic Press Kit (EPK) or DVD use
- **Security** — maintains a secure work environment for cast and crew and keeps watch over sets and equipment after wrap

What sorts of productions might I get to work on?

While distinctions are made between the various types of production work, the truth is that the specific functions of your particular job won't really change much from one to another. For example, a Makeup Artist on a feature film will essentially do the same exact job on a sitcom or music video. You will get paid more on a TV commercial, less on an independent film, work more hours on a music video, and be employed longer term on a feature film, but the basics of your own job don't change. A typical movie schedule is around twelve weeks, a series TV show is nine months, and commercials and music videos are a day to a week or two of work.

Here is an overview of the various and most common types of production.

Feature films (shot on film or high-definition video)

A feature film is generally narrative fiction, typically having a running time of between ninety minutes and two hours. A standard shooting schedule for a Hollywood feature is several weeks of preproduction, twelve weeks of production, and ten weeks of postproduction. A feature is usually distributed to movie theaters first, but cable television and home video have provided filmmakers with alternative methods of getting their work out into the marketplace.

Independently financed features (features not financed or distributed by a major Hollywood studio) vie for attention through various means, such as film festivals and, to some extent, the Internet.

Documentaries (shot on film and tape)

A documentary is a nonfiction film whose running time depends on its ultimate distribution outlet. They are usually independently financed or produced with the support of mainstream media, like PBS's *Frontline* series. Production schedules are as varied as the topic matter and can fluctuate wildly as funding comes and goes. Film festivals tend to be primary outlets for documentaries as their creators try to catch the attention of distributors.

Movie of the Week (shot on film)

A Movie of the Week (MOW) is essentially a feature film produced on a smaller scale with less money and in less time. Although the production process is pretty much identical to a feature, as a crewmember you will work at a faster pace, with longer hours, and with a little less pay than you would make on a feature film.

Episodic Television (shot on film)

One-hour episodic television is most like a feature film in production protocol but is done with a smaller budget and in less time. It is narrative fiction typically shot in one-camera "film" style on film stock. Nearly without exception, the exposed film stock is immediately transferred to videotape or digital format for quick editing and broadcast. A typical shooting schedule is five to seven days.

Situation Comedies (shot on film and tape)

Situation comedies (sitcoms) have their roots in the earliest days of television. These thirty-minute comedies are shot typically with three or more film or video cameras on a stage in front of a studio audience. Like most other television, sitcoms are edited digitally or on tape for later broadcast. A crew is hired for one rehearsal day and one shooting day each week.

Soap Operas (shot on tape)

Soap operas were one of the earliest narrative programming TV ventures. They are thirty- or sixty-minute narrative fiction programs that appear five days a week with running storylines. The production style is a mix of episodic and sitcom with multiple video cameras shooting on a closed stage. It is important to note that in most cases, technicians working on soap operas must belong to **NABET** as opposed to IATSE, which represents most non-videotape productions.

Music Video (shot on film)

A music video, made primarily to showcase and market music to increase record sales, is typically shot on film with a coherent storyline or is merely a juxtaposition of images. Budgets are generally small and schedules are tight. A typical shooting day can run upward of eighteen hours or more.

Commercials (film and tape)

Commercials are very short stories designed to market a product or service. They run the gamut from really low budget (such as for local car dealerships) to very high budgets (which run nationally to sell a company or specific brand). Physical production can be as short as an afternoon or as long as a week or more.

Game Shows (shot on tape)

Game shows, another one of the earliest forms of television, are generally shot with multiple video cameras on a soundstage in front of a studio audience. These are usually shot LIVE-TO-TAPE, meaning that a Director cuts the show live as it's happening so that a minimum of postproduction will be required. It is important to note that in most cases, technicians working on game shows must belong to NABET as opposed to IATSE, which represents most non-videotape productions.

Reality (shot on tape)

A reality TV program is a pseudo-documentary that tells a story or presents a day in the life of real-life participants. It is produced with event-coverage style (non-narrative) but with a touch of narrative drama created out of the footage that is shot.

Talk Show (shot on tape)

The talk show generally has a consistent celebrity host who discusses personal problems or other issues with invited guests. Relatively cheap to produce, it is typically shot with multiple video cameras, live-to-tape, in front of a studio audience.

News Shows (broadcast live and shot on tape)

News programming provides up-to-date reporting of important events that take place locally, nationally, or internationally. Produced mostly by TV networks at the local and national levels, news production takes place in the field as well as in the studio. Most employees are on staff, but freelancers are hired on occasion.

Sports (shot on tape)

Baseball, football, basketball, hockey, tennis, auto racing, etc. are produced by TV networks and independent production companies employing staff workers in the offices and freelancers for actual production work. A notable exception to traditional sports production is NFL Films, whose products are more documentary-like than traditional network sports coverage, which covers games as a live event.

Industrials and Miscellaneous (shot on film and tape)

There is an enormous amount of production work done mostly by freelance Producers, Cinematographers, Videographers, and Sound Mixers that is meant for broadcast TV or is produced for in-house or marketing use by various other industries around the world. An independent Producer, Cameraman, or Sound-man may be working on a Hollywood premiere one day and shooting footage for major corporations the next.

Film? Tape? What's the difference?

Film and tape are distinctly different ways of capturing an image for later viewing. Without being overly technical, film, which comes in a small canister, is the stuff you put into your (non-digital) still camera at home. It's generally a long, black, plastic-like strip that you wind every time you want to take another picture. A movie camera uses very long strips of film, usually 1,000-foot rolls, that move through the camera to capture movement instead of still action. Film undergoes a photochemical process that turns light into actual images you can see when you look at the strip itself.

Videotape uses an electronic process to store image information magnetically. Instead of converting light into an actual picture you can see, a video camera converts light into electronic information that is stored on the videotape, also a long strip of black material. If you hold a piece of shot videotape up to a light, you'll never see any pictures.

In both cases, an image is being saved, but there's a pretty big difference between the two. Traditional standard-definition video has a definitive sharpness and looks "real," like you'd see the action as if you were actually standing there. Film has a softer, almost more ethereal look. It does not capture reality per se but a more romantic and hyper-real version of what happened in front of the lens. Generally, fictional narrative and dramatic programs are shot using film stock with film cameras while nonfiction or live events are shot using video cameras.

The advent of high-definition video has allowed filmmakers to take advantage of the immediacy of electronic image acquisition while enjoying a near filmlike quality.

This is all very important to you because the working protocols can be very different when choosing a type of project that uses film versus one that is shot on tape. In other words, the way that feature films, one-hour episodics, commercials, and music videos are made is very similar. Someone who works regularly in one of those could transition very easily to another. On the other hand, news programs, talk shows, sitcoms, soap operas, reality shows, and documentaries have their own distinct ways of being made, so moving from one type of show to another isn't as easy a transition.

When you're just starting out in the business, it's important to learn the fundamental difference between film and video because it will have an impact on the types of work you choose to take and whether your career goes in the direction you desire.

This is all a lot more complicated than I thought. Where do I even start?

Finding the right job isn't as easy as just deciding what you want to do and applying for a staff position at a movie studio. The good news is that there are a lot of career paths, and every single one is open for you to pursue as long as you're willing and able to put in the requisite energy and commitment.

So step one is to sit down and think long and hard about what it is you specifically want to do in the movie business and where you'd like to eventually end up. Then step two: Find out what it *really* takes to get there and what your life will really be like as you make that journey toward success.

So how can this book help me?

The primary purpose of this book is to help you know what your life might be like if you choose an *on-set* job as a career. While it takes a great deal of effort and a lot of people to prepare all the elements necessary for a film to be shot (preproduction), shoot it (production), then finish it (postproduction), this book concentrates on those people *on set* who are involved in PHYSICAL PRODUCTION—that is, the work of actually turning the words from a script into moving images on film. The jobs you'll find described here are those that are most often found on the CALL SHEET every day. These are the people who typically wake up at five in the morning and work upward of fourteen hours a day. These are the people who call a movie set their "office." If that's the world you would like to live in, read on!

Chapter 2

What I Really Need to Know

Okay, I think I know what it is I want to do. Now what?

No matter which job you wish to have, first take some time to learn about the industry in general, its history, where it stands now, and where it's going. When searching for potential employees, established crewmembers look for enthusiasm and a willingness to learn, but they have little desire and even less time to teach someone from the ground up.

So how do I get a job?

Well, first, you need a realistic concept of how this industry really works. As mentioned previously, you don't just fill out an application at a movie studio and wait for an interview as you might in other professions. Unlike days past when studios had cast and crew under contract, today's entertainment industry is populated mostly by FREELANCERS, meaning that you will be hired for a project and then it is up to you to find another one after that, and another, and another, until you are earning enough money to make a viable career out of it.

With this in mind, when you first start out, you will most likely be doing a lot of DAYPLAYING. Instead of being hired for the full length of a project, you may be called in to work for a day or two at a time on various shows that already have a full-time crew. If you know enough people, you can make a decent living working like this, bouncing from show to show. These situations arise when a production adds extra cameras or SECOND UNITS, has a cast of a thousand EXTRAS coming in for a big party scene, or when someone on the crew gets sick. Take these day calls whenever possible. This is the best way to meet new people and show them just how great you are.

It is of the utmost importance that you do your very best on day calls, because you're the new face, and every mistake will be noticed and remembered. If you're good and the rest of your department likes you, you probably will be asked back for additional days. Make sure to keep in touch with other members of a crew after you've moved on to other projects. The best situation is when they need to hire for the next big movie and you've made a good impression on a day call. Suddenly you've got three months or more of steady paychecks instead of wondering when the next job will come up.

In an industry that runs on personal relationships, family and friends are the easiest ticket to breaking in and building a successful career. If you're reading this book, you probably won't have the benefit of having a relative pave your way into the business, and that's fine. True, NEPOTISM can become one of your obstacles. Anybody whose father or mother, for instance, is a Director of Photography, Director, or Producer will get access to opportunities before others. All this means is that you may have to work that much harder to get noticed. There are a lot of productions going on at any given time, and it is your job to figure out how to land one that will give you the chance to prove yourself.

If you've exhausted your personal contacts, volunteer to work on someone's student or low-budget project. You're not in this for the money, just the experience, so make sure you're still able to pay your bills as you commit your time to someone else. Visit a local university film department and look for postings asking for help. If you live in the Los Angeles area, there are a variety of publications available at newsstands in which filmmakers post ads asking for help with their projects. See Appendix C for more information.

What sort of pay can I really expect?

Good question. Let's ground your expectations in reality right away. If your motivation is to get filthy rich, you need to reevaluate your plan. The range and responsibilities of jobs in this industry are vast...and so are the pay scales. The media tend to focus on the extraordinarily high dollar amounts that movies GROSS and what a relatively few top Actors make. The reality is that the vast majority of people working in this business are lodged firmly in the middle-class tax bracket. Of course there are exceptions where certain established crewmembers will consistently earn $150,000 to $200,000 a year and up, but it wouldn't be wise to jump into this business expecting those kind of numbers, and definitely not for a few years. It might happen for you, and it might not.

The following chapters detail specifics concerning the pay for each particular job, but in general someone working in an entry-level position can reasonably expect to make $25,000 to $40,000 on a standard three-month feature film. However, when you are just starting out, don't expect to work on more than one full project a year. Similar productions pay at slightly different rates (such as sitcoms and movies of the week), but if you are fortunate enough to work on two feature films each year, you'll be doing all right financially. You should be making enough to pay your bills, anyway, as long as you are fiscally responsible. Remember to plan ahead, and don't count on consistent employment at first.

When it comes to low-budget, nonunion work, you need to figure out what you can and can't live with in terms of money. If your overhead is high, you won't have the freedom to take truly GREAT PROJECTS that pay very little. On the other hand, you don't want to get stuck in the low-budget world either, so setting limits as to how little you'll accept can be important.

You should love your job; otherwise, why do it? But as glamorous as Hollywood appears and no matter how much you appreciate the art of film, keep in mind that this is what you are doing for a living; you must make enough money to enable you to keep doing it *and* have a life outside the set.

Whether you're on the whole project or just taking a day call, you will have to fill out a DEAL MEMO and other tax-related forms on your first day there if you wish to be paid. This is the START PAPERWORK you'll complete every time you begin a new job. Be prepared by bringing along a copy of your passport or driver's license and Social Security card to show to someone in the Production Department. If you find yourself doing a lot of dayplaying, make multiple copies of these things and carry them with you. Be sure to check with the Production Department regarding your pay (what you will be paid per hour), because it can vary from the standard union contract, if you happen to be working on a union show.

I want to work on big movies. Do I really need to join a union?

Typically, yes. Most major studios and production companies have agreements with the various unions. These agreements allow only union members to work on their projects. There is a fair amount of nonunion work at any given moment and you will most likely find yourself working on those shows at first.

You may hear that more money can be made working nonunion. Sometimes this is true. But union membership offers health and pension plans while nonunion workers must find affordable coverage on their own. Ultimately it's up to you to decide what's best, but if you want to work on the big movies and have the benefits and protections of union membership, contact the IATSE, SAG, DGA, Teamster's union or the CONTRACT SERVICES office in Los Angeles to find out more.

What else do I really need to know?

It's crucial to know that a large movie set is designed around job specialization so that the day can move along at top efficiency. This may seem counterintuitive at first. What is so productive about having to ask for someone else to get a ladder, move a prop, or wrap up a cable when you could clearly just go do it yourself? For starters, you may not know where something is or where it is supposed to go. For instance, if you decided to be "helpful" and wrap up an extension cord that "was in the way," then you put it down somewhere, the next time the Electric Department goes looking for it and can't find it, how will they know where it is or who to ask about it? The same goes for a prop, or a chair, or a piece of camera equipment. The people who are in charge of specific items know what that stuff is, how it works, why it's on set in the first place, where it's supposed to go, and where to get it when they need it. If you didn't bring it to set, don't touch it until you get permission.

It's not only important for you to know what your job responsibilities are but also what everyone else is doing as well. Asking an Electrician for a sandbag is likely to result in a rude comment. Asking a Hair Stylist to take the shine off an Actress won't get you very far. A Grip won't help you plug in a light and a Camera

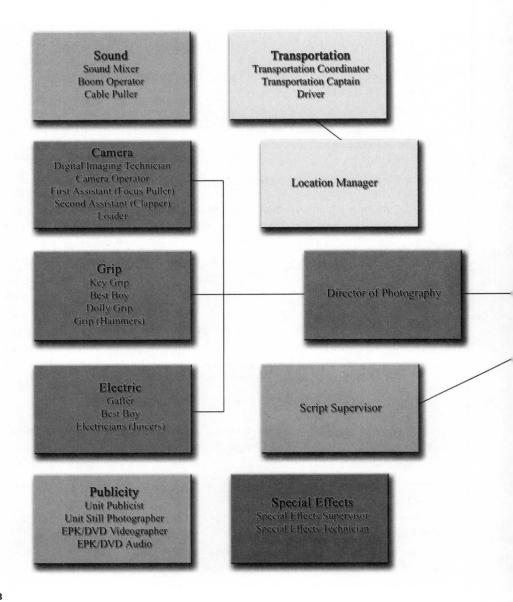

Assistant isn't going to lay dolly track. This isn't to say that they don't know how, but it isn't their specialty, which is why it's always best to leave it to those who have put in the hard work to train for their specific function.

You need to be aware of the hierarchy on a set as well. While it's indeed true that every job is vitally important (and if you don't think so, watch what happens when someone *doesn't* do his job), the reality is that some positions are more equal than others. The following chart gives you a basic map of how all the jobs on set interrelate:

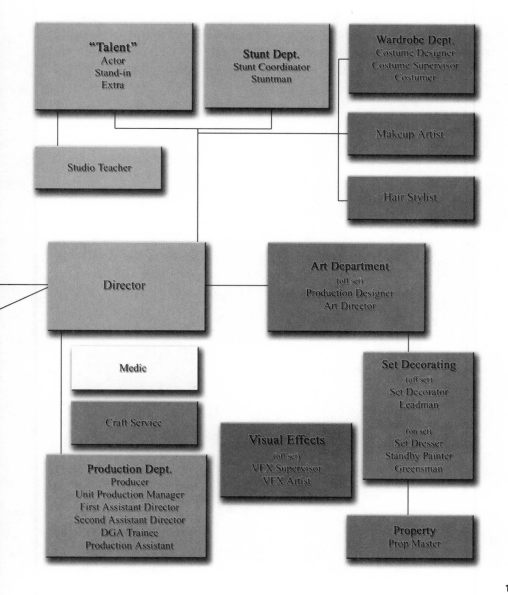

Finally, keep the following in mind with regard to freelancing in general: It's important to realize just how expendable you are at all times. Just because someone says she likes you or that you might be doing an awesome job does not mean that you automatically will be asked to return to work the next day. There are some things you have control over, like doing your job correctly to the best of your ability, and there are others that you have no control over, such as set politics. Whatever is going on, you need to remember that you could be off a show at any time for any number of reasons.

Because of this, you want to keep your personal life and your finances in such a state so that a decision by one employer cannot completely destroy your life. This means that no matter how "in" you are with the person who always hires you or the group of people you like to work with, it is vitally important that you take some time to establish other contacts who could hire you in the case of an emergency. To keep any of this from happening, do your best to meet as many potential contacts as possible as you work your way through the industry. And above all, live well within your means. No one can have power over you unless you let him.

Chapter 3

Where I Really Need to Go

Do I really need to go to film school?

The real answer is no; you don't have to go to film school to have a career in the movie industry. A USC graduate has the same chance of becoming a Director or anything else in the industry as the really weird but artistic kid down the street. In the end, it's about who you know and what you can do once given the opportunity.

That said, immersing yourself into a community of like-minded individuals who are all striving for the same goals can definitely have value. As you're studying the theory of filmmaking and gaining some practical experience while making short films of your own, you'll be learning from others around you as much as they are learning from you. While the specifics of what you can learn from a film school will vary depending on the school you attend, the general benefits of further education are invaluable in every aspect of life as well as to your career. By its very nature, filmmaking is a collaborative enterprise, so developing the skills to communicate effectively is a necessity. Higher education in general can help you learn how to do that, and your experience in a film school environment will require you to put it into practice.

If I go to film school, will a master's degree help?

Again, not really, unless you are looking for a career at the studio executive level, where your work experience and education mean more than your technical or creative skill at actually being on set and making a movie. However, for those actively working on set, a career in the motion picture industry can be lucrative, but quite often, it is not. There are some individuals who are able to work practically year round, but the vast majority of people may get only one feature film a year to work on full-time and must fill in the rest of the time with DAYPLAYING or with other non-industry-related temporary work. It's in your best interest to have an education and/or a second career to fall back on if times get tough.

So, if you have the means and desire, definitely take advantage of the benefits of obtaining a higher education. That said, nothing takes the place of real-world experience. Go to school *and* also find a production company, TV station, or equipment rental house in your area and ask for a part time **PA** position or an internship. Then work as hard as possible and learn as much as you can while constantly searching for new contacts elsewhere. On every level, the entertainment business runs almost entirely on networking.

Do I really need to move to Los Angeles?

Once you've learned the basics, found a way "in," and have collected the stuff required to do the job you want to do, you're going to need to pack up your things and move to where the action is.

Is there film work available outside of Los Angeles? Of course. New York City, San Francisco, Chicago, Detroit, Pittsburgh, Salt Lake City, Hawaii, North Carolina, Texas, and Florida as well as many foreign cities all have various types of production happening occasionally or throughout the year. The markets are smaller, but there are also fewer people trying to make a go of it in those areas, so your chances of working are probably fairly good if you break into the active circle.

Most larger Hollywood features and other high-profile projects are crewed out of and shot, at least in part, in the Los Angeles area. These productions do often venture out of Southern California and local hires (usually **KEYS**, or department heads) from those areas get the opportunity to travel and work on them, but your best bet to work a lot while in the United States is to move to Los Angeles.

The United States?

Over time, to cut costs Hollywood-based production companies and studios have sent a very large portion of production work over the borders to Canada and Mexico and overseas to less expensive locations like the Czech Republic, Australia, New Zealand, Russia, Hungary, and the United Kingdom.

What this means is that even if a story is set in Chicago, for instance, all of the interiors will be shot in a foreign country where locations and crew are less expensive. When the filmmakers need exterior shots to establish the location, only a small portion of the production work will take place in the city where the story is actually set. The Key personnel (principal Actors, Director, Producers, Director of Photography, Art Director, Costume Designer, etc.) will travel to each location while new local crews are hired.

If you are a citizen of the United States and are willing to make the move to establish a new life and citizenship abroad, then you could potentially build a film career far from home. If you want to stay in the United States, Los Angeles currently is the best option, at least to get started.

If you live elsewhere in the world, be aware that film/television production tends to migrate based on the economy of the moment. What that means is that when movie studios in Hollywood draw up a budget for a production, they will consider many different locations across the globe and will settle on the one that provides the most advantageous economic incentives within the parameters of the rest of production. So while a location such as Vancouver or Prague may be the hot spot one year, studios may move on to less expensive locales the next year purely for economic reasons. Moving to a country or city because you think that Hollywood is there to stay may get you work for a few years, but know that the run may not last a lifetime.

How much money do I really need to get by?

Wherever you choose to go, save some money before you move. You may have to work for nothing at first. The better prepared you are for zero income, the freer you'll be to pursue your goals. How much? It depends on how you like to live, but at the very bare-bones minimum, you should have $2,000 to $3,000 in cash and be prepared to get some kind of employment right away or else you'll go broke pretty fast. Don't count on making union scale money for at least a year or more.

I hear the freeways are clogged in Los Angeles. Would it be faster to walk?

Sometimes it feels like it. Because of the varying hours and remote locations, public transportation in Los Angeles and other cities is mostly useless to people working in the film business, so you'll need a reliable car. If you plan on having a job that requires carrying a lot of personal equipment, some kind of pickup, van, or SUV will serve you better. Be prepared for varying insurance rates as well as fuel costs.

Where should I live?

Have someplace lined up to stay before you move. Friends of friends, relatives, or college alumni are all good ideas. Don't overstay your welcome, though.

Assuming you're renting, you'll probably need a roommate in order to afford something decent and close to the action. You'll want to live in a place that is comfortable, but you should know where the typical shooting locations are so you don't move into a place that is too far away from any of them.

In Los Angeles, the studios and various soundstages are scattered through-out the area, and you're bound to work at all of them at one point or another.

Geez, I just want to make movies. Now what?

Anybody can pick up a camera, shoot something, and call it a movie. Making a true *career* out of it is an entirely different enterprise. Having a successful professional career goes beyond merely having "fun." It means taking on a tremendous amount of responsibility. What you're really getting yourself into, what your life will be like in the industry on a daily basis, and how to make the best career for yourself is what the next chapter and ultimately what the entire book is all about.

Chapter 4

What I Really Need to Have

Do I need to buy anything of my own?

For the most part, the equipment necessary to make a movie is rented from various places. Depending on your particular job, there will be items that you will be expected to bring with you. For the most part, these things will cost you between $10 and $1,000 or more each. The chapters that follow will explain more specifically the items you should have for each job and where to get them.

I don't know anybody. How do I meet the right people?

As you bravely step out into the world, you will be doing what is known as NETWORKING. Just as a spider's web has a single starting point, your contact list will begin with a single person and expand outward into an ever-growing network of people who know you, like you, and want to hire you.

If you do not live in Los Angeles and plan to make the move, you should start your journey by asking absolutely everyone you know if they know anyone who might be involved in the entertainment and/or movie industry. You might be surprised to find that an English teacher you had a class with in high school just happens to have a second cousin who works in Hollywood doing "something." Or maybe your best friend's mom is friends with somebody who works at the local TV station. At this point, you're just looking for anyone with real experience in media or entertainment. Even if that person isn't actually in the film industry, chances are he'll know somebody who is. You need to act much like a detective, tracking down leads until you end up talking with somebody who can actually help you get on a real movie set. Unless you have family in the business already, your biggest challenge is going to be breaking that bubble and getting inside the industry. You never know who will do that for you. Really.

And once you've made your move, you cannot be afraid to approach people or to talk to them. If you get a name and phone number, do not hesitate to call.

You might be nervous because your leads don't know you from a hole in the ground, but dial the number and explain who you are, how you got their name, and what it is you are looking to do. If they can help you (and they haven't had a bad day), most people in the industry will be more than willing to lend a hand by inviting you to observe for a day, to work with them directly, or by referring you to someone else that they know. People working in the entertainment industry are normal folks, just like you. Don't be afraid to talk to them. Chances are, you will not be the first person who has ever asked them for help.

Another option is to take a leap and call an established "name" directly. Watch the end credits of your favorite movies and make note of who is credited for doing the jobs that interest you. Then track them down via the Internet (www.imdb.com) or by calling their union (IATSE, SAG, DGA, Teamsters) local office. One way or another, you should be able to find a way to contact them. Sometimes they will help; sometimes not. It all depends on the individual, but all you really need is one "Yes!" to get going. Don't let the "No's" discourage you. Regardless of their responses, thank them for their time, because even if they don't want to help you now, later on down the road, once you are established, the chances are very good that your paths will cross again and they may want to bring you onboard. Burn no bridges.

Anyone who is already in the business is a potential source of work for you. However, depending on the job you want, there are limits as to how much others will be able to help. For instance, Producers and Directors are generally not the ones who will get you work as a Camera Assistant, but you'll need them later when you want to be a Director of Photography. You need to meet other people who work in your department of choice. Those contacts will be the key to sustaining a lasting career.

To complicate matters somewhat, crews move in different circles. Some crews only work on features, while others stick pretty much to commercials, music videos, or low-budget projects. This isn't to say that once you're hooked into one circle that you can't get out of it. Most crewmembers find themselves working on different types of productions at one time or another.

Depending on your luck and timing, your networking will lead you to one of two things: an unpaid trainee spot on a big-budget studio film or an unpaid "actual" position on a low-budget student film. Your career will progress from there.

I just got a call from somebody who wants me to work on her film! She says it's a "great project." Should I do it?

When an aspiring Producer/Director scrapes together the resources to finish her latest ultra-low-budget epic, she also needs to find a qualified crew. Because of severely limited resources (read: not enough money), the shooting schedules on these types of projects can range from a few consecutive days to being spread out over several weekends. And typically there is little to no money available to pay you or anyone else on the crew. This is where you, the young enthusiastic aspiring filmmaker, come in. Naturally, the Producer/Director wants the film to be as good as possible, so the first calls usually go out to people who are very qualified and well established in the industry. Generally because of the money issue, those people will politely turn the "great project" down and leave the Producer with other recommendations. If you have worked with any of these people in the past, either on other low-budget projects or perhaps as a PA, then this is how your name and number get spread around town. Because you are just starting out, the hope is that you are qualified enough to do the job and are willing to do it for very little money or for free. Their promise to you is that they'll "remember you on the next one."

Okay. So they get a warm body who they hope can do the job well enough. What do you get out of it? You're looking for two things on a project like this, and money isn't one of them. If nothing else, you'll walk away with more experience. Even the worst projects will teach you things that you will take with you throughout your career. Your other hope is for somebody else on the crew to notice and like you enough to call the next time he needs somebody. Of course you're also hoping that the next job pays better than the last.

So before you say yes or no to the strangers on the phone, you need to ask some questions of yourself and of them first. Number one is whether you can afford to take the job. If your bank account is low, a job that pays nothing or next to nothing may be out of the question. If you can afford to take it, then you need to figure out if it will be worth your time. Is there anything unique about this project that you haven't experienced before? Maybe there is new equipment to use or the locations are challenging. Or you may decide to take the job because of other people who are working on it. Maybe the person calling you is destined for great things (you hope), so by working for her, you're banking that you'll be invited along for the ride.

If you can't take the job or decide not to, politely decline ("I'm sorry, I'm just not available right now...") but don't close the door on the relationship ("...but please keep me in mind in the future!").

If you do decide to take the job, go in with a positive attitude and give the project 100 percent. Even if you are being paid nothing, you've made the choice to do the work under those conditions. This isn't to say that you're there to be abused, but complaining about the money or the hours won't help you impress anyone. You've decided that there is something to be gained by agreeing to work on this project, so go in and accomplish that as best as possible and leave the set every day with a smile on your face.

When you wind up on a studio project, you're in luck. While indeed your position may be less than flattering and your skills are underutilized, you're now on the "inside." That is to say, you're working with established crewmembers who can teach you the right way to do things and who can recommend you to their friends. You still need to put in the time and fulfill the union requirements, but at least you're now close to people who are truly making a living in the film industry.

The other (and more likely) project is a student film. The downside of this seems obvious: you're primarily working with other amateurs or wannabes. But this isn't always the case. Frequently, when students set out to make a small film, they manage to employ the help of skilled union members who are looking to advance their own careers. For example, a union Camera Operator wishing to move up to Director of Photography may practice on a student film.

However you get your start, keep showing up on as many sets as it takes until somebody actually puts you on the payroll of a real movie. You might get lucky and it will only take a month or two. For some people it takes significantly longer. As long as you have patience and maintain the means to survive, you will most likely reach your goals.

I'm not getting where I want to be in the business. What can I do?

If your entry into the paying world of movie production isn't happening as fast as your bank account is dwindling, you may have to find some temp work. If it comes to that, try to find work in the industry as close to the job you want as you can get. For instance, if you want to be in the Camera Department, a job as a Prep Tech (a staff employee who prepares a camera package) at a rental house will put you in contact with working professionals and give you access to all the equipment you need to learn about anyway.

Remember...the key is to meet the right people and be prepared when you sense a genuine and appropriate opportunity to sell yourself.

What kinds of contact information should I get or give out?

Keep in mind that people have to know how to contact you. If you haven't left your hometown yet, give them your home phone number and let them know when you're moving to Los Angeles or wherever it is you have to go to meet up.

Better yet, get a cellular phone and keep the number when you move. You want to be fiscally responsible, but you don't want to be changing services and numbers often. Have a consistent and reliable phone number to give out so that no matter where you are, people can call you and you'll be able to answer right away.

The other advantage to having a cell phone as opposed to passing out a home number is that frequently, when a crew needs additional people for day calls, they aren't going to call just one person. When you receive a call, the chances are that five to ten other people have also been called for the exact same job. Usually, the first one to pick up or respond to a message wins the day. Sometimes those simple one-day calls turn into full-time positions for the remainder of a project that can go for weeks or months. Missing that call can be costly. Bottom line: Get a cell phone and leave it on.

Having an e-mail account can also be a handy and relatively nonobtrusive way to keep in touch with those you've worked with or met. Get one e-mail address and keep it. You want to make the chore of contacting you as painless and streamlined as possible for others.

What do I do when somebody wants to meet me?

Okay, let's say that somebody wants to meet you. Do you just show up? Do you bring a résumé or a copy of the film you made in school? No, not unless someone specifically asks for those things, which is highly unlikely. It's nothing personal, but no one on the crew is terribly interested in your aspiration to become the next Spielberg. Perhaps you are a great Costume Designer, Cinematographer, or Director whose talents just haven't been discovered yet. That's really wonderful, and if you are genuinely talented, then you should strive to attain that goal.

But in the meantime, if you need to find other work on set to make connections or just to survive, show up with a smile on your face and concentrate on the job you're asking for instead of trying to convince those around you of everything else you think you're capable of.

Somebody wants to hire me! Now what do I do?

Well, go to work! If you have any questions about what you should bring with you, it's better to ask ahead of time instead of apologizing later. You should receive a call sheet from the Production Department that explains what will be shot on the day you arrive. If you don't, call the person who hired you and ask. Will you be shooting interiors or exteriors or both? Are you shooting all day, all night, or a SPLIT, which is half day and half night. Will it be rainy or cold or windy? Will the stage be super hot or super cold? The point is, you shouldn't be surprised by anything when you show up to work.

Should I dress up? I was always taught to make
a good first impression.

Do not dress up. The typical wardrobe is blue jeans or shorts with a T-shirt or a casual collared shirt. You're not trying to impress anyone with your clothes, and practically speaking, working on a set often involves being in dirty and potentially dangerous conditions. You don't want to come to work looking like a slob, but the set is no place for a coat and tie. Impress those around you by showing up slightly before you're supposed to, doing your job with a positive attitude, and helping to make them look good.

You'll also want to have a foul-weather bag packed and close by, either in your car or stashed on the production truck that you'll be calling home. A typical bag has rain/cold weather boots, extra socks, thermals, rain suit/coat, gloves, hats, a pair of shorts, extra shirts, hand warmers, towels, water/beach shoes, etc. You get the idea. A movie can take you to the beach one day and to the mountains the next. Best be ready for everything.

Maybe this is a silly question, but should I bring snacks or a bagged lunch or something?

Fortunately for you, no. Due to some foresight by our ancestors in the business, there is a Crafts Service Department that, amongst other duties, provides a supply of goodies for the cast and crew to graze on. This isn't just a perk but a very practical way of keeping the company energized throughout some very long days. As you'll notice as you read about the various jobs, quite often someone's call time is before the actual crew call time, so it may easily be seven or eight hours until that person sits down for a LUNCH break. The last thing a production needs is for its crew to become lethargic halfway through the morning or as it continues work late into the evening.

What sort of money do I need to get started?

You've probably heard the adage that it takes money to make money. Well, the same holds true for you, the aspiring moviemaker headed for Hollywood. For the majority of the jobs available on a movie set, you will find that you will have to purchase certain things on your own before you begin.

Depending on what it is you want to do, you might be able to get away with assembling your own "kit" piece by piece over time instead of buying everything at once.

And while you may need a hefty influx of cash to get started, remember that most or all of what you purchase is tax deductibleas a legitimate business expense. That consolation may not be very comforting if you just don't have the money to spend right now, but down the line on April 15, it will be worth it.

And more than that, you can often get a KIT RENTAL or "box fee" for everything that you bring to the job. This is an amount of money paid to you in addition to your regular set wage for the things you bring to help you do your work. Essentially the production is renting your personal gear. When you sign your deal memo, you negotiate this fee with the Unit Production Manager. Depending on what job you have and what you are bringing, you'll receive anywhere from $50 to $200 a week. Over the course of one full project, the cost of much of what you've purchased can often be recouped.

Is there anything else I should get that isn't obvious?

Be prepared to travel extensively and at a moment's notice. If you don't already have one, apply for a passport and then keep it up-to-date. Whether you're just a PA starting out or you've been doing this for a while, the call may come at anytime from almost anybody asking if you can hop on a plane "tonight!" to fly halfway across the globe. You're getting asked because somebody likes and trusts you enough to send you to an exotic locale. It would be a shame to not be able to go just because you don't have the proper paperwork in order. Put this book down (pick it up later) and go apply for your passport right now!

Chapter 5

What Am I Getting Myself Into?

Red carpets here I come...!

Whoa! If you've come for the glamour, you're in the wrong end of the biz. In fact, it's important to know that all of that premiere glitz is completely manufactured for marketing purposes. While, indeed, an award night is a great opportunity to dress up and party, none of that is for you. After all, you're just a member of the crew. Heck, you'll be lucky just to get a screen credit. The way it works is that you get the call to do the job, you do the job, get the check, then find another job.

So what can I look forward to?

The following is a description of what a typical location week might look like. Obviously, there will be differences based on your job, the project itself, and various call times that you will receive.

A typical workday is *at least* twelve hours (thirteen including lunch) and more likely fourteen to sixteen hours. This will be your schedule five days a week on a project that is in Los Angeles and six days a week on a distant location. Most often your CALL TIME on Monday morning will be 6:00 A.M. or 7:00 A.M. and by the time Friday rolls around, your "morning" call time will be sometime in the afternoon. The union contract specifies a minimum TURNAROUND, the amount of time required between wrap and the call time for the next day, for the cast and crew so that you will not be called back to work without adequate time off.

Monday
Pre-call—5:42 A.M.
General crew call—6:00 A.M.
Lunch—12:00 P.M. to 12:30 P.M.
Camera wrap—9:00 P.M.
Your department wrap—9:30 P.M.

Tuesday

Pre-call—6:12 A.M.

General crew call—6:30 A.M.

Lunch—12:30 P.M. to 1:00 P.M.

Camera wrap—9:30 P.M.

Your department wrap—10:00 P.M.

Wednesday

Pre-call—6:12 A.M.

General crew call—6:30 A.M.

Lunch—12:30 P.M. to 1:00 P.M.

Camera wrap—10:00 P.M.

Your department wrap—10:30 P.M.

Thursday

Pre-call—6:42 A.M.

General crew call—7:00 A.M.

Lunch—1:00 P.M. to 1:30 P.M.

Camera wrap—10:30 P.M.

Your department wrap—11:00 P.M.

Friday

Pre-call—7:00 A.M.

General crew call—7:18 A.M.

Lunch—1:30 P.M. to 2:00 P.M.

Camera wrap—10:30 P.M.

Your department wrap—11:00 P.M.

Saturday

Pre-call—10:12 A.M.

General crew call—10:30 A.M.

Lunch—4:30 P.M. to 5:00 P.M.

Camera wrap—2:00 A.M.

Your dept. wrap—2:30 A.M.

You'll notice a few interesting things in the above example. First, you don't go to work at the same time every day. The call times begin to get later in the morning even though the department's turnarounds could easily be met. What typically happens is that the SAG Actors have a much longer turnaround (twelve hours), and the next day's call is dependent on when they are released. This is extremely helpful because when you add in your commute time to and from work every day, that eight-hour turnaround that you have (per your union agreement) really only allows a few hours of sleep. Driving while fatigued can be potentially deadly, and it has been the tragic reality for some crewmembers.

Note too that while shooting all week, the call times will run progressively later each day until the Saturday call time could actually be in early to late afternoon. So while you came in around 6:00 A.M. on Monday and wrapped by 9:30 P.M. or 10:00 P.M. by Friday you might arrive around 1:00 P.M. or later (depending on how the week went) and wrap early Saturday morning! By the time you get home, the only thing you'll have on your mind is going to bed. This might not be a big deal if you're single and unattached, but if you're trying to date someone or are married/partnered and/or have children, that's time that you won't be spending with them.

There doesn't seem to be much time to hang out with my friends.

In this industry, balancing your work and personal life isn't always easy to do. The struggle it can take to get into the business in the first place and the time spent on set once you have a viable career makes maintaining relationships difficult both at home and socially. You'll find that most of your friends will be other people in the business who jump from one set to another just like you do. Your friends and family will have to be understanding and supportive of both your time at work and those periods when you are in between projects.

Sounds like I'll be at work most of the time. What's that like exactly?

When viewed from outside, the jobs in this business look pretty cool. The truth is that they are...or can be. So that you don't jump feet first into a career that isn't as glamorous as you thought it would be, the following section will describe a typical workday, and subsequent chapters will lay out in detail what a typical day might be like for you in your chosen field.

THE NIGHT BEFORE

At wrap you will receive a CALL SHEET, which lists the call times for everyone and the location to which you must report.

Union clocks run on six-minute intervals, which means that if you see 6.42 A.M as your call time on the call sheet, then you'd document that start time as 6.7 (because 42 = 6 x 7) on your time card. So 6:00 A.M. is written as 6.0, six minutes after 6:00 A.M. is written as 6.1, twelve minutes after 6:00 A.M. is written as 6.2, and so on. Lunch will be six hours after GENERAL CREW CALL at 13.0 (note the military time).

Director: Brian Dzyak	PAGE 1 of 2	**CALL SHEET**	PAGE 1 of 2	Production Office:
Producer: Daybright Films Writer: Brian Dzyak		**WHAT I REALLY WANT TO DO** Tuesday November 4th, 2008		What I Really Want to Do 14770 Broadway New York, NY 10000 contact@whatireallywanttodo.com
Sunrise: 5:10 AM				**NEAREST HOSPITAL**
Sunset: 8:11 PM	**CREW CALL: 7 AM**			
WEATHER REPORT			**Day 1 of 73**	
Bright & Sunny! Temp: Low 69 High 73	**SHOOTING CALL: 7:45 AM**			
		Travel time from hotels: 20 mins		

BREAKFAST AVAILABLE FROM: 06:00 AM

*** NO PRE-CALLS OR CHANGE OF CALL TIMES WITHOUT PRIOR APPROVAL FROM THE PRODUCTION MANAGER ***

ON WRAP - MUSEUM SET WALK THRU: BRIAN, LILLY, GARY, BJ, SUSIE,
@ STAGE #2

EPK ON SET TODAY!

SC.	SET/SYNOPSIS	CAST	D/N	PGS.	LOCATION
11	**INT. HOTEL** *Lovers reunite*	1, 2	D1	2	Stage #1 Santa Monica
38	**INT. BURGER JOINT** *Lovers talk about their future, she promises her love*	1, 2	N1	3	Stage #2 Santa Monica
66	**EXT. SCHOOL THEATER** (TIME PERMITTING) *Confrontation, Bad Guy gets what's coming to him*	1, 2, 3, X3	N1	1	Stage #4 Santa Monica

#	CAST MEMBER	CHARACTER	STATUS	PICK UP	MAKE-UP/WD	ON SET	REMARKS
01		The Good Guy	W	05:30	06:00	07:00	
02		The Beautiful Girl	W	04:30	05:00	07:00	
03		The Bad Guy	W/N	W/N	*****		
X3		Bad Guy Stunt Dbl.	W	per SC	*****		called to set @ 15:00

** 10:00 AM - VFX STILLS SHOOT FOR GOOD GUY/BEAUTIFUL GIRL COSTUMES - Loc: Rm #1138 Production
Office Dbls: Joshua D. & Jana Vetla

*** ADVANCE SCHEDULE ***
WEDNESDAY NOVEMBER 5th, 2008 - DAY 2

SCENE	SET/SYNOPSIS	CAST	D/N	PGS	LOCATION	NOTES
39	**EXT. HIKING TRAIL** *Hike to waterfall*	1, 2	D3	2	TOPANGA CANYON	Helicopter work today! Safety Mtg @ Call

If the general crew call is 7:00 A.M., however, your call is at 6:42, eighteen minutes earlier. Individual call times for each person on the crew are listed next to the position on the back of the call sheet.

4:30 A.M. —WAKING UP
What the...?! Why is my alarm going off at 4:30 A.M.?

You're getting up at this terrible hour because you live in the San Fernando Valley and the location today is in Downtown L.A. It's only a twenty-five mile drive or so, but you have to travel on the 405 freeway, reportedly the busiest freeway in the world. It doesn't start stacking up until around 6:00 A.M., but if you wait to get going, your chances of being late grow. Better to be way too early than to show up even a few minutes late.

Okay, I'm up. What should I wear?

Depending on the time of the year in Southern California, it is entirely conceivable that you will be in a heavy coat in the morning and be dying to change into shorts by lunch. Summers, especially in the valleys, can get brutally hot. The winter months mean forties in the morning with highs peaking anywhere from the sixties to the eighties. And while it doesn't rain often, it does happen on

WHAT I REALLY WANT TO DO — **DATE: NOVEMBER 4' 2008** — **FEATURE CALL SHEET**

#	PRODUCTION	TIME	#	MAKE UP / HAIR	TIME	#	CATERING	TIME
1	Director -	7A	1	Key Hairstylist -	4:42A		Motion Picture Catering Co.	
1	Unit Production Manager -	O/C	1	Hairstylist -	4:42A	1	Chef -	
1	First Assistant Director -	7A	1	Addtl Hair -	5A	2	Chef Asst. -	
1	Second Assistant Director -	4:30A				200	BREAKFAST RDY @ 6AM	
1	Key PA -	4:30A	1	Key Makeup -	4:42A	200	DRIVERS/CREW LUNCH @ 12:30PM/1:00PM	
1	DGA Trainee -	4:30A	1	Makeup -	4:42A			
1	PA -	5A	1	Makeup -	5A		EDITORIAL	
1	PA -	5A				1	Editor -	O/C
1	PA -	6A		PROPS		1	First Asst. Editor -	O/C
			1	Propmaster -	6:42A			
	PRODUCTION OFFICE		1	Prop Asst -	6:42A		PUBLICITY	
1	Production Coordinator -	O/C	1	Prop Asst -	6:42A	1	Publicist -	O/C
1	Production Secretary -	O/C				1	EPK Field Producer/Camera -	O/C
1	Office PA -	O/C		SPECIAL EFFECTS		1	EPK Audio -	O/C
1	Office PA -	O/C	1	Coordinator -	6:42A			
			1	Set Foreman -	6:42A		CASTING	
	CAMERA		1	Technician -	6:42A	1	Casting Director, LA -	O/C
1	Director of Photography -	7A	1	Technician -	6:42A	1	Casting Director, NY -	O/C
1	Camera Operator -	7A				1	Extras Casting -	O/C
1	DIT -	6:42A		RIGGING		1	Extras Asst. -	O/C
1	1st Assistant Camera -	6:42A	1	Rigging Gaffer -	O/C			
1	2nd Assistant Camera -	6:42A	1	Rigging Best Boy -	O/C		ASSISTANTS/SECURITY	
1	B Camera 1st Assistant Camera -	6:42A	3	Rigging Electrics -	O/C	1	#1 Personal Asst. -	O/C
1	B Camera 2nd Assistant Camera -	6:42A	1	Key Rigging Grip -	O/C	1	#2 Personal Asst. -	O/C
1	Loader -	6:42A	1	Rigging Best Boy Grip -	O/C			
1	Unit Still Photographer -	6:42A	2	Rigging Grips -	O/C		SET OPERATIONS	
						1	Set Medic -	6:00A
	SOUND DEPARTMENT			ART DEPARTMENT		1	Crafts Service -	6:30A
1	Sound Mixer -	7A	1	Production Designer -	O/C	1	Asst. Crafts Service -	6:30A
1	Boom Operator -	7A	1	Art Director -	O/C	1	Police -	per PC
1	Utility/Cable -	6:42A	1	Art Dept Coordinator -	O/C	2	Security -	per PC
			1	Art Dept. Prod. Asst .-	O/C			
	VIDEO						ACCOUNTING	
1	Video Assist -	6:42A		SET DECORATING		1	Production Acct. -	O/C
			1	Set Decorator -	O/C	1	1st Asst. Acct. -	O/C
	ELECTRIC		1	Asst. Set Decorator -	O/C	1	Key 2nd Asst. Acct. -	O/C
1	Gaffer -	7A	1	Leadman -	O/C	1	Payroll Acct. -	O/C
1	Best Boy Electric -	6:42A	1	Set Dresser -	O/C			
1	Electric -	6:42A	1	Set Dresser -	O/C		Transportation	
1	Electric -	6:42A	1	On Set Dresser -	6:42A	1	Transportation Coordinator -	O/C
						1	Transportation Captain -	per TC
	GRIP			CONSTRUCTION		1	Transportation Co-Captain -	per TC
1	Key Grip -	7A	1	Construction Coordinator -	O/C	1	Picture Car Coordinator -	per TC
1	Best Boy Grip -	6:42A	1	Construction Shop Manager -	O/C	5	Passenger Van Drivers -	per TC
1	Dolly Grip -	6:42A	1	On Set Painter -	7A	x	Drivers -	per TC
1	Grip -	6:42A						
1	Grip -	6:42A		LOCATIONS			COMPANY EQUIPMENT	
1	Grip -	6:42A	1	Location Manager -	O/C	3	Camera packages	
			1	Locations Asst. -	O/C	125	Walkies	
	COSTUMES			STUNTS			Visual Effects	
1	Costume Designer -	7A	1	Stunt Coordinator -	7A	1	VFX Supervisor -	O/C
1	Wardrobe Supervisor -	7A	1	#3 Stunt Dbl. -	7A	per S	VFX Technicians -	per VS
1	Key Costumer -	4:42A	2	Stunt Performer -	O/C			
1	#2's Costumer -	4:42A					ADDITIONAL CREW	
1	On Set Costumer -	5A				1	Studio Teacher -	O/C
						1	Technocrane Technician -	6:42A

occasion. Be ready for that from November to April or so. The point here is that the weather can be unpredictable. It is best to dress in layers and have clothes that represent all four seasons packed and available close by the set.

The choice of fashion is all yours, but as in the rest of life, making a favorable impression will make a difference in the way you are treated. If you come to work looking like a slob, you won't exactly command respect. You're never going to wear a jacket and tie on set, but having a neat and clean appearance instills confidence about you more than cutoff jeans and a dirty T-shirt will.

If you are going to be working around the camera all day long, it's a good idea to wear darker clothing. The Camera Operator will be looking for problems in his frame, including unwanted reflections, and you can help by not adding to any potential troubles. Unless you will be working outside in the sun all day long, avoid wearing white shirts or light-colored shorts or pants, especially on interior sets. Be aware of reflections from your watch face or other jewelry as well.

And wear comfortable shoes. Most of the crew are on their feet all day long. No kidding.

5:30 A.M.—THE COMMUTE

An hour to get ready?

Give yourself plenty of time to get to work. You never know what huge traffic calamity occurred while you were sleeping. Give yourself time to pack a lunch as well if you need to, though most of the time you won't have to. If you are working at a studio, the production may not provide the catered lunch you always get on location. Instead of the usual thirty minutes, you'll get an hour lunch break, presumably to give you time to walk to the studio commissary to purchase a meal. But brown-bagging it is a lot cheaper than buying from the commissary, and there really isn't enough time to go off the lot to find anything else.

By the time you get in your car and leave your home, it is an hour and a half until general crew call. Remember, though, that in our example, your call is for eighteen minutes earlier, at 6:42 A.M., so you really only have a little more than an hour.

After you've been in Los Angeles for a few weeks, you'll have a pretty good sense of traffic flow. At some point, you'll want to learn some alternate routes through the city in case of traffic tie-ups.

In other parts of the country, you worry about weather. In Los Angeles, it's all about the traffic. Local TV has regular traffic reports with attractive graphics and blinky lights. Tune in before you leave home to avoid any big accidents.

6:10 A.M.—FINDING THE LOCATION

Finally, I'm getting close...

Traffic wasn't so bad, but there was a stalled car on the way that slowed everybody down. It took you forty minutes to go twenty-five miles. Good thing you left early. The effects of that stall will grow exponentially throughout the morning.

As you get closer to the set, you will notice small cardboard signs that the production company has attached to signposts or telephone poles. The sign will have the company name on it, the movie (or TV and/or music video) name, or an abbreviation of either. Follow these signs to the parking area. Sometimes, multiple productions will be happening near each other. Make sure you head to the correct one!

The location isn't always the same place that you parked, so the Transportation Department will be running shuttles (maxi-vans that hold twelve or so people) to the set area. Bring everything you need out of your car, lock it, and get into the van.

6:20 A.M.—BREAKFAST

What!? Food?

The shuttle driver will drop you off as close to the catering truck as possible. Be sure to thank the driver when exiting, and grab all of your stuff. You now have twenty-two minutes until your call time. Just enough time to eat a quick breakfast. Don't expect anything like this on an independent or student project. Tight budgets can mean lots of day-old bagels in the mornings.

You may also want to hit the HONEYWAGON before work starts. If you're on location, you probably won't get the chance to go to the bathroom again until lunch.

6:40 A.M.—FIND YOUR TRUCK

If you don't see your production truck, find a Production Assistant (PA) or someone in Transportation and ask where it is. PAs generally are the younger members of the crew and are most easily identified by the headsets, walkie-talkies, and extra batteries clipped on their belts. If you see a blank stare on a PA's face, it probably means that she is listening to someone on the headset. Patiently wait until you are acknowledged.

6:42 A.M.—GET TO WORK

Your work day is now about to start, and you're on time. The rest of the chapters in this book will go into greater detail about what jobs are available, how to get them, and what your life will really be like once you get there.

Keep in mind that day one of production is not a "get to know you, ease into it" day. The assumption at nearly every level is that you are there because you already know your job and will do it with great efficiency. Naturally, the reality is different on ultra-low-budget films, where nearly everyone there is fairly new to the business, but when you get hired onto a large professional production, dive right in. Everyone else is there to perform his or her specific function as well. With 12- to 16-hour days and 80- to 100-hour work weeks, there will be plenty of time to get to know everyone around you.

The work that everyone does revolves around the SETUP (see sidebar below). This is the process of preparing everything needed to turn the words on a page into a 3-D reality on set, which is captured into a 2-D image on film. An individual setup may take anywhere from a few minutes to complete to an entire day. A feature film will manage to complete between ten and twenty setups on a typical day. A one-hour episodic television drama may complete fifty or more. Whatever the case may be, once the work day begins, completing a setup and moving on to the next one is the pattern that will fill your days.

A "Setup"

A script is broken into scenes. Each scene is made up of one or several individual shots. The process to get a single shot on film is called a "setup." The setup follows a predictable pattern that is repeated throughout the schedule for all shots. The typical setup begins with a rehearsal and ends when the First AD says, "Moving on!"

• **Rehearsal**—The Director runs a rehearsal with the Actors, usually to iron out dialogue and character issues. These are usually open rehearsals where everyone on the crew can watch. Sometimes, though, the Director asks that the crew step off the set so he can have a **CLOSED REHEARSAL**, which happens if the scene is particularly emotional or if the Director or Actors feel the need for privacy.

- **Marking rehearsal**—After the general rehearsal, the Director of Photography gets more involved as specific marks for the Actors are chosen with camera placement in mind.
- **Second Team**—Everyone is clear on where the Actors and cameras will be, so now it is time to actually set it all up. The cameras are built and the set is dressed and lit.
- **Through the works**—In the morning and after rehearsals, the Actors leave set and go back to BASE CAMP. While there, the Wardrobe Department gets them properly dressed before Hair and Makeup apply their touches.
- **Last looks**—When the set is ready, FIRST TEAM is called back and the First AD calls for "last looks" or "FINAL TOUCHES." This is the cue for everyone to get into place. Hair, Makeup, and Wardrobe do a final once-over on the Actors before cameras roll.
- **On a bell**—The First AD asks the Sound Mixer to "put us on a bell." A loud bell rings once, and this signals everyone to be quiet.
- **"Roll Sound"**—The First AD calls out for sound to roll. A few seconds later, the Boom Operator announces, "Sound speed." The cameras are turned on and the Second AC says, "Mark!" before clapping the SLATE. The Camera Operators say, "Set" when they are ready.
- **"Action!"**—The Director gets things going. While the Actors are working, it is important that no crewmember make noise, talk, or be in an EYE-LINE. And before anyone even steps near a set, all phones and pagers should be turned to silent mode or off.
- **"Cut!"**—The action has completed successfully or not. Either way, when the Director yells, "Cut," the sound and cameras stop and everyone waits to find out what will happen next.
- **"Going again"**—The Director has decided that he needs another take. Everyone goes BACK TO ONE (returning to the starting positions) to reset and do it all over again.
- **"Check the gate"**—The Director and the DP are satisfied that they have at least one good take. The First AD asks the First AC to "check the gate" before anyone undoes any of this setup.
- **"Movin' on"**—The gate was good, so the First AD announces that we're "Movin' on" or "New deal."
- **Off the bell**—The First AD asks the Sound Mixer to "Take us off the bell." The bell rings twice, and the entire process begins all over again.

1:00 P.M.—LUNCH

Union rules stipulate that there must be a meal break every six hours, with an entrée provided. Unfortunately, rules like this have to be written down because, even now, some Producers have no qualms about abusing their crews in the quest to get the movie finished on time and on budget. The first break is scheduled six hours from general crew call. Your call was at 6:42 A.M., so the meal break is eighteen minutes late. Much like a library fine for overdue books, the company must pay a MEAL PENALTY to any crew member who has not broken for lunch exactly six hours after his individual call time.

Meal penalties continue to accrue until you are broken for lunch or until you clock out at wrap. There may be days when the company chooses not to break for lunch at all due to time constraints. These days are rare, thank goodness, but at the same time they are very costly for production and lucrative for the crew.

If you are on a location, there will be a catering truck at base camp. Lunch in this case is thirty minutes long, counted from the last person to go through the line. An AD or PA will be standing next to the truck waiting for that to happen. Although the thirty minutes is timed from the last person through, the actual time broken may be forty-five minutes to an hour. When it comes to meals, this isn't a bad business to be in. One unfortunate aspect you get used to is that most of your meals will be eaten in parking lots where the tables get set up. Often, tents or awnings are there to provide shade, but sometimes you're eating in the hot sun. The décor might not be so glamorous, but the food is usually pretty good.

The ADs will call out over the radios when there are about five minutes left—but not always! Keep track of the time yourself, and work your way back to the set when necessary.

2:00 P.M.—BACK TO WORK

The second half of the day will be much like the first for you. In some instances, as the day progresses, the quantity of work completed increases exponentially while the demand for quality decreases. Another popular way of saying it on set is that you're making *Gone with the Wind* in the morning and *The Dukes of Hazzard* after lunch, meaning that a lot of time will be spent on shots that take place at the beginning of the day and a lot less time is taken on shots toward the end of the day. This typically happens on day exteriors or with less experienced Directors or ADs who haven't budgeted their time very well.

9:00 P.M.—WRAP

If you are in the entry-level position for your department, you may also be asked to keep track of and fill out weekly time cards for the rest of your crew. On a notepad or special form, keep track of in-times, meal breaks, meal penalties, out-times, and box rentals for each individual, as not all information will be the same for everyone. On a distant location, you will also receive a PER DIEM, which may be noted on the pay stub. It is important to keep copies of the times, if not the time cards themselves, in case the Accounting Department makes a mistake.

You can save yourself a lot of time in the mornings by quickly preparing a few things the night before. Keep an eye on the advanced schedule, and try to get a call sheet before wrap. You want to see what to expect for the next day and have the opportunity to ask your superiors any questions you might have.

Get as much prep completed prior to wrap as possible. Double-check your call time for the next day. Know where you are supposed to go. If you have any questions, now is the time to ask. This way your morning will go much smoother, and those above you will be impressed with your efficiency. You'll have more time to hang out on set, listen to war stories, and work the politics that get you hired again.

How hard is it to move up to the next level?

Assuming you've established a successful career at one level (meaning that you can pay your bills with the money you earn from your job), chances are that you're pretty good at what you do and you're a generally nice person. It's almost a foregone conclusion that most people in the business would like to move up the ladder in their specific department. Those above you did it, so they'll assume that you'd like to as well. Once you've expressed the desire and demonstrated that you're capable, it's merely a matter of being in the right place at the right time to take advantage of the opportunity.

Well, this still seems so cool...and I get to meet all those famous people!

When you are first starting out, being in the presence of famous people may be a bit overwhelming, if you're affected by stardom. For your own sake, it is helpful to keep things in perspective. Actors, Directors, Producers, celebrities, etc., are people, too. Unfortunately, a few of them tend to think that they are as important as the tabloids like to make them out to be. However, that doesn't change the fact that they are there to do a job just like you are. Be respectful, but don't put up with unnecessary abuse from anyone. Life is too short, and there will always be another job for a hard worker.

How do I use this book?

As you've just read, the first five chapters have described the business as a whole and given you an overview of some critical issues specific to the industry.

The rest of the book is divided into sections that describe each department on a Hollywood set and the individual jobs within those departments. Each section begins with the entry-level positions and progresses toward the Key, or Department Head.

Understandably, your first instinct will be to read all about the glory jobs, those at the top, like Director, Director of Photography, etc. By all means, read anything that interests you, but don't ignore the entry– and midlevel jobs. Not only will you be a much better Department Head when you know more about those people you are in charge of, but it is very likely that you will *have to do those jobs* for many years before you get to the top. This isn't to say that you can't just run right out and become a successful Director, DP, or Costume Designer. If you're that talented and you know people who can (and are willing to) put you right to work in your dream position, then absolutely take advantage of the opportunity. You'd be a fool not to...but only if you truly know what you're doing. But be aware that the vast majority of people who work above-the-line got their start in one of those other jobs that people in the theater seats scratch their heads wondering about ("What the heck is a Best Boy?"). Many successful Directors have come out of many different departments, like Camera, Production Design, Stunts, and Continuity.

And while learning as much as you can about your own career path is important, the more you educate yourself about what *everybody else* on set is doing all day, the better you can understand how the entire industry functions. It's that kind of wisdom that will help you successfully break into the business and embark upon a long-lasting career making movies.

Part II

TALENT SUPPORT

What I Really Want To Do Is...

Stunts

Stunt Coordinate

Teach

Costume

Costume Design

Makeup

Hair

Props

What I Really Want to Do Is Stunts!

WHAT THE HECK IS A STUNTMAN?

A Stuntman takes the place of a principal Actor when the required action is deemed too dangerous or carries a potential for significant injury.

That, and what else?

You need to perform your stunt well and also help other stunt performers with their work. You may find yourself moving landing mats or building boxes that you or someone else will fall into. You may also be asked to train principal Actors to perform some skills on camera themselves, such as sword fighting.

This is dangerous work. I must be making really good money, right?

As a member of the Screen Actors Guild (SAG), your rate is just over $600 a day plus overtime if you work over forty-four hours for the week. That's just slightly higher than what a "standard" Actor makes. Expect to earn around $36,000 if you're fortunate enough to be hired for twelve full weeks.

You'll also be paid an "adjustment," otherwise known as "difficulty pay," for each stunt you do. The amount varies based on what the stunt budget for the show/movie is and what the Stunt Coordinator thinks the risk value of the stunt was. You might get $200 for jumping ten feet off a balcony into a stack of boxes. On a project with a higher budget, you might get $400 for the same stunt. On a television episode, you might get $50. A big stunt, like crashing a car, will earn you more. A smaller stunt, like taking a fake punch, will earn you less.

As a member of SAG, you are also entitled to RESIDUALS according to the current contract.

While this all might sound like a lot of money for pretending to fight or jumping off things, the reality is that when you're starting in the business, you probably *won't* work 250 days out of the year.

WHAT DO I REALLY NEED TO KNOW?

It is the Stunt Coordinator's responsibility to hire people with the skills and experience necessary to create a safe working environment. Train yourself in a variety of physically challenging pursuits to become as versatile and marketable as possible.

Traditionally, the three most desirable skills are martial arts, gymnastics, and motorcycle driving.

Other stunt categories include any of the extreme sports, like snowboarding or skateboarding. Precision driving is one of the most used, but it's the hardest to train in. What can you make a car do without denting it? Can you slide it right next to a camera and stop without destroying a $250,000 piece of equipment... or worse? Can you drive on two wheels? There are various schools that will teach you how to be a precision stunt driver. If you like to be underwater, get your scuba certification. If jumping out of airplanes is your thing, you need to be a certified Jump Master to work in the film industry. There are **OSHA** rules in the United States to protect everyone involved, but overseas the rules are different or non-existent depending on where you are. Regulations or not, the most important thing is to feel confident enough in your own skills that you know that you won't hurt yourself or anyone else.

Do I need any acting skills?

Because you are usually filling in for an Actor, you should know how to act as well. Usually a stunt comes within an established film sequence; you'll continue the action that the principal Actor was just doing, execute your stunt, then continue acting until the Director yells cut.

You might also be cast as a Stuntman/Extra, such as a villain's henchman who is doomed to fall to his death or be blown into the sky. Knowing how to act throughout the movie prior to your stunt moment(s) will make you even more employable than if all you can do is stunt work. Take an acting class at some point. You won't be expected to recite Shakespeare onscreen, but knowing how to get into character is important.

Beyond that, all you need is a **SAG** card. See the glossary for more information.

WHAT DO I REALLY NEED TO HAVE?
What do I bring with me?

The Stunt Riggers (if any) will bring in any large stunt-specific equipment, like pulleys, air ramps, or mats, so you shouldn't worry about owning any of that.

What you do need is your own personalized safety gear. This will include shin pads, hard and soft kneepads, hard and soft elbow pads, a hip girdle, and small pads for your quads, hips, and tailbone. Also have black tennis shoes that can double as dress shoes. Expect to pay between $400 to $500 for your first set of basic pads.

What's the best way for someone to reach me?

One of the first things you need to do when you get to Los Angeles is to sign up with one of the three main answering services that specialize in the stunt industry: "Jonie's," "Teddie's," or "Bill's." You pay them about $50 a month and they take all of your messages and pass them on to you. The Stunt Coordinator who knows you will still call you directly to see if you're interested and/or available, but once you're hired, most of the calls from the production will go through the call service.

WHERE DO I REALLY NEED TO GO?
I just want to work.

Once you move to Los Angeles, call the STUNTMAN'S ASSOCIATION. Get HEADSHOTS done just like a traditional Actor does and attach your resume with special skills to the back.

You'll need a SAG card to work on most sets. It is also beneficial to get a good commercial agent who will represent you and sell your skills to projects in need. Contact the Stuntman's Association for more information on how to find a suitable agent.

So how do I get work?

Many Stuntpeople start their training in live shows like those seen at theme parks. It's still competitive, but it's slightly easier to break into than film and television work.

The most popular way to get your foot in the door is to get out and introduce yourself to Stunt Coordinators. Be willing to help out and work for free. If you have the proper technical skills, you might get hired to be a Stunt Rigger instead of an on-camera Stuntman (though you still need a SAG card to work on a union set). A Utility Stunt Rigger will set up anything from boxes to air ramps to rock-climbing apparatus. Aim to broaden your range of technical proficiency; this will guarantee the safety of your colleagues on set and give you a better chance at a profitable career.

No matter your age, working out, running, and doing gymnastics during your off time will keep you able to do the more difficult and lucrative work. Staying abreast of the technology that allows bigger and safer stunts will not only broaden your range of professional possibilities, but it will also help you avert injury. Most important, know your limitations and don't mislead others about what you can do. Your life and the lives of others may be at stake.

WHAT AM I GETTING MYSELF INTO?
So who actually calls and hires me?

Either directly or through the calling service, your first call will come from the Stunt Coordinator on the show. Often, you'll be hired to come in to perform or rig something very specific. He'll tell you what the stunt is and ask if you're comfortable doing it.

Okay, I got the job. What now?

Simple action like falls or basic fights will be worked out closer to the shoot day or on the set itself while the rest of the crew waits. Elaborate action may take weeks or even months to plan, rig, and practice. Because of this difference, you might get called anywhere from months prior to the shoot date to the night before.

What will my life really be like?

6:42 A.M.—GET TO WORK
As a Stuntperson, you most likely won't have your own trailer or room. You'll have to keep your personal belongings in your car or carry it on set along with your safety gear.

Grab some breakfast at the catering truck unless you have to get into Makeup or wardrobe right away for prosthetics or other major Makeup work.

7:00 A.M.—GETTING TO SET
Show up wearing casual and loose-fitting clothes in which to rehearse. Women often need to head straight to wardrobe before rehearsal. Their on-camera clothing can be skimpy, and the shoes may be difficult to walk in. There's no sense in showing a Director a rehearsal that you won't be able to duplicate once you get the real wardrobe on.

7:05 A.M.—REHEARSAL
If the stunt is elaborate, the stunt team has likely been rehearsing for days, or weeks, already. This rehearsal will be the first time they have actual cameras and the Director watching.

7:15 A.M.—CAMERA SETUP
The stunt team, which could be just two people or up to twenty or more, works to put padding or additional rigging into place.

Ensuring your own safety and the success of the stunt is your number one priority. You need to run through the choreography and timing both in your head and by practicing if possible. Some shots cost upward of $200,000 per take (e.g., pyrotechnics, car crashes, CANDY GLASS). Use every moment you have to make sure you are absolutely ready.

7:45 A.M.—ROLL CAMERA

Whatever the stunt, your timing is crucial because hosts of other people are also working based on the established choreography. Cameras move, helicopters may fly, explosions may go off, cars may weave around...there's a lot going on, and if just one person misses a mark or does his job too early or a little late, not only could the shot be a bust, but the safety of others on set could be in jeopardy.

Once you've done your stunt, your job isn't over yet. For this shot, you *are* the character whether the camera can see your face or not. Continue acting until you hear the Director yell "Cut!"

7:48 A.M.—CUT, LET'S GO AGAIN

After a stunt, the first thing everyone on set does is wait to make sure that no injuries have occurred. The Stunt Coordinator will rush out to make sure his team is safe. If there was a problem and the shot is repeatable, the Director will ask you to do it again. Work with the other Actors and/or your stunt team to reset everything BACK TO ONE: Get everything back to the starting positions to shoot another take.

8:10 A.M.—CUT, MOVIN' ON

Great! They got it. Everybody is happy...you hope. Some stunts are ONERS, meaning that they are either too elaborate or too expensive to do a second time.

If you are in a fight sequence or some other multipart stunt, the cameras will reset at different angles and you will perform the same action over again. This usually requires a re-blocking of the stunt so that the illusion of danger works from these new angles.

1:00 P.M.—LUNCH

2:00 P.M.—BACK TO WORK

You'll do more of the same if additional on-camera work is necessary. If not, you may go with the Stunt Coordinator and start choreographing the next big stunt on the schedule.

9:00 P.M.—WRAP

When stunts are completed and you are done for the day, the Stunt Department will have boxes to break down, mats to fold, and rigging to dismantle. If you have been in specific wardrobe or Makeup, head to those departments and give it all back so that those people can wrap up and go home. When you are done for the day, see the Second AD to sign your timecard.

WHAT I REALLY WANT TO DO IS MOVE UP!

Theoretically, you could work as a Stuntperson until you just can't move anymore. But realistically, most Stuntpeople are effectively done working full-time when they reach their forties. Taking punches and jumping from buildings will get difficult, but if you expand your skill set to include less physically demanding activities like precision driving or even just plain old acting, you could keep working for a long time.

The next logical step is to begin Stunt Coordinating. You'll be looked to as the voice of authority on how to accomplish any given action in a script deemed too dangerous or risky for the principal cast. Your extensive experience as a stunt player, Rigger, and even maybe as an Actor will help to inspire confidence in others (Producers) that you are capable of doing the job.

Chapter 7

What I Really Want to Do Is Stunt Coordinate!

WHAT THE HECK IS A STUNT COORDINATOR?

The Stunt Coordinator oversees and coordinates the personnel and the techniques that are required to execute the actions that hold potential danger for the Actors or stunt performers.

That, and what else?

Depending on the size and budget of the show, the Stunt Coordinator may also be the primary stunt double of the principal Actor. In a lot of cases, the Coordinator *and* one other Stuntperson will be hired for the duration of the project.

This is dangerous work I'm responsible for. How's the money?

On a large film with lots of stunts, you'll be working every day for a flat weekly fee in the neighborhood of $4,000.

WHAT DO I REALLY NEED TO KNOW?

While you're in preproduction, the Director and Producer will be asking you questions about what is possible to achieve on set. The Director will want to know if it can be done on camera. The Producer will want to know what it will cost. It's your responsibility to know the answers to those questions or how to get the answers quickly. Being able to break a stunt down into its pieces and know what it takes to accomplish each safely while staying within budget is what your job is all about.

WHAT DO I REALLY NEED TO HAVE?
I've been doing stunts for a while now. What else could I possibly need?

For the most part, you won't be the one who is actually doing the stunts anymore, but you might want to keep your basic pads with you just in case. Also keep a comprehensive contact list with you, so that if you need a question answered right away you can get on the phone and figure it out.

What's the best way for someone to reach me?

Remain signed up with one of the calling services that specialize in stunts (see page 47. Also, maintain consistent connections with everyone on your contact list.

WHERE DO I REALLY NEED TO GO?
I just want to work.

You most likely have to establish a name for yourself as a Stuntman before becoming a Stunt Coordinator. Once you've reached a level of experience that will allow you to land the Coordinator jobs, living close to the movie studios may make your life more convenient, but you will now have more freedom to live anywhere you wish.

So how do I get work?

As a Stuntman, you were making relationships with Stunt Coordinators, Directors, Unit Production Managers, and Producers. Now is the time to capitalize on that foundation. Keep in touch with all of these colleagues and let them know that you're interested in Coordinating.

WHAT AM I GETTING MYSELF INTO?
So who actually calls and hires me?

You'll likely get the call from a Unit Production Manager who either knows you from a previous job or has gotten your name from someone else. Before you take the job, find out what kind of stunts they have in mind. Hopefully by this point in your career you've experienced nearly everything at least once, but if the requirements seem to be more than you can handle, graciously bow out as soon as possible. For example, if the script calls for a large amount of precision driving and most of your experience is with martial arts, you may not be the right person for the job.

Okay, I got the job. What now?

The first thing to do is figure out exactly what kind of stunt work is needed. Go through the script and carefully look for anything that might even remotely call for the use of a Stunt Performer. You're looking for anything from a simple punch to a full-blown freeway chase.

Meet with the Director and Producer to discuss what they had in mind. The script could be highly detailed, so that you know exactly what is expected to take place, or the script could be fairly vague, which invites confusion and misunderstandings. Get everyone from the crew on the same page as soon as possible.

You won't just be showing up ON THE DAY (when the shot is ready to be filmed) and making stunts happen. You'll likely have several meetings throughout the course of preproduction. Once you get a very good idea of the schedule and what each stunt should look like, prepare a BREAKDOWN specifying everything and every person you will need and when you'll need them. Especially for bigger events, a significant amount of prep work and rehearsal may be required off set away from the shooting crew.

You may not be able to figure out on your own everything that is needed. This is where having a list of specialists in your back pocket will pay off. If you're not 100 percent sure how to safely accomplish a stunt, the very last thing you want to do is to fake it. Someone's life could be at stake. Gather the necessary resources required, whether it is hardware or people, and get them onboard.

As you gather your information, the Producer will be very interested in seeing a budget estimate, but don't ever let political or financial pressure get in the way of being safe. Accidents have occurred and people have died as a result of careless decision making on the part of overzealous Directors and inexperienced Stunt Coordinators and Stuntmen who were too eager to please somebody. Don't let it happen to you or anyone you hire. The movie business can be exciting, but no movie is worth dying for.

What will my life really be like?

THE NIGHT BEFORE

It's up to you as the Stunt Coordinator to make sure everything and everybody needed to pull off a stunt makes it to set on time. Coordinate with the AD Department to make it happen.

6:42 A.M.—GET TO WORK

You'll probably have a pre-call, especially if some rigging is required. The chances are slim that the first shot of the day will be your big stunt, so there should be plenty of time to get everything and everyone ready.

7:05 A.M.—REHEARSAL

The rehearsal that the shooting crew sees on set is likely just one of the many that the stunt team has already been doing since preproduction. Only now, you have the real environment to work in and several cameras to perform for. Some slight adjustments may need to be made, but for the most part, the camera placement will work around your requirements.

There may be a HALF-SPEED REHEARSAL if the elements allow for it so that everyone can watch exactly what should take place in slow-motion. This is the time when the Director of Photography will try to figure out his best angles and the Director may choose to make adjustments. Stay close to the stunt performers and work directly with them and the Director. Offer suggestions, solutions, and alternatives if something isn't working out as planned. Your goal is to get the idea from the page up on the screen in the most convincing manner possible while maintaining a safe working environment.

7:15 *A.M.*—CAMERA SETUP

Once the Director is reasonably happy with what you've told him to expect or with the rehearsal he's seen, the rest of the crew will begin setting up cameras and lights and decorating the set. If your Stuntpeople are not yet in the proper wardrobe, get them in to see the Costumer as soon as possible. Double-check the rigging yourself or confer with the Riggers to confirm everything is set.

In your head, run through the choreography of the stunt, piece by piece, moment by moment, to make sure you haven't left any stone unturned. Timing can be crucial in any stunt and can mean the difference between getting hurt and walking away unscathed. Some shots can cost upward of $200,000 per take! As long as you're confident that all precautions have been taken, the only thing to fear is in not making the Director happy. And if that's the worst outcome, take comfort that no one was hurt or died as a result.

7:25 *A.M.*—SAFETY MEETING

Once the lighting, cameras, and all else is in place, the First Assistant Director will stop *everything* on set and call a SAFETY MEETING. The First AD or you will run through the choreography of the stunt, step by step, so that everyone knows *exactly* what is supposed to happen.

7:45 *A.M.*—ROLL CAMERA

Your hard work is done. Now it's up to your team to make it happen for the cameras. Stay close to the First AD and keep an eye out at all times for anything that might be going wrong. If there is a concern for safety at any point in the take, tell the First AD *immediately* and he will stop everything. If the event warrants it, sometimes the First AD will hand control of the set over to the Stunt Coordinator for the duration of the shot just in case something unexpected happens.

7:48 *A.M.*—CUT, LET'S GO AGAIN

Some stunts are repeatable, such as fight scenes and driving sequences. Some are not so much, such as explosions and car crashes. In the event that the shot is a ONER, meaning that the first take had better be perfect (or close to it), you'll make sure everybody is okay and clean it all up. If the shot is repeatable, you'll initially make sure all came out of the first take unscathed and then begin resetting BACK TO ONE.

8:10 A.M.—CUT, MOVIN' ON

It is fairly rare to have back-to-back shots involving large stunts unless a fight sequence or a complicated vehicle chase is being filmed. Again, you've already rehearsed the stunts extensively in preproduction, but each time the cameras move, you may need to make adjustments to the original plans.

1:00 P.M.—LUNCH

If you had a major stunt the previous day, you might want to go see DAILIES with the Director to check it out.

2:00 P.M.—BACK TO WORK

Carry on as before. If the major stunt work is done for the day, you may be able to release some of your stunt performers and get them off the clock.

9:00 P.M.—WRAP

Whether a stunt is the last shot of the day or not, when your major work is done, have your Stuntmen and Riggers clean up everything that isn't going to be needed. Touch base with the Director to talk about tomorrow's work (if any). There may be some prep work that needs to be done right now, while the rest of the crew is wrapping, or early in the morning before call.

WHAT I REALLY WANT TO DO IS MOVE UP!

The next step up from being a Stunt Coordinator is becoming a Second Unit Director. In fact, in the interest of efficiency, quite often these positions are covered by just one individual anyway. If the Second Unit is shooting mostly heavy action sequences with little "acting" going on, it only makes sense to have one person in charge of "directing" the stunts and helping to place the cameras. Sometimes this dual position is taken by the Director of Photography, so just keep in mind that every project will be different.

If this is the direction you'd like your career to go, make and keep good relationships with the Producers, Directors, and Actors you meet. Those are the people who will help you to move from being a Stunt Coordinator to running the whole show.

Chapter 8

What I Really Want to Do Is Teach!

WHAT THE HECK IS A STUDIO TEACHER?

Whenever there are minors working on set, a Teacher is required to provide educational services in conjunction with the child's regular schooling. A Studio Teacher specializes in teaching multiple grade levels in this nontraditional school environment.

That, and what else?

The Studio Teacher is also responsible for overseeing the health and safety of all minors on set. In lieu of direct parental involvement, the Teacher becomes the children's guardian, responsible for their overall well-being while they are at work.

Do I ever get to work on set?

Your first responsibility is teaching, but when the children are required to be on set in rehearsal or during takes, you will be standing close by, ensuring that they are okay and that all the welfare and safety rules are observed.

I must be making really good money then, right?

You'll only be needed on days when minors are working, so your total time spent on set may vary widely depending on the project. Also, while the standard day for a film crew is upward of fourteen hours, children are limited to an eight-hour day. As a member of IATSE Local 884, Studio Teachers & Welfare Workers, expect to earn approximately $37 per hour or about $300 per day.

WHAT DO I REALLY NEED TO KNOW?

Because you are teaching multiple grade levels, you are required to maintain your elementary level to high school academic credentials and skills constantly. In particular, being well versed in advanced math and science as well as additional languages will make you a more valuable asset to the Producers.

WHAT DO I REALLY NEED TO HAVE?
All grade levels? Sounds like I'll need a lot of stuff!

You are essentially a mobile one-room schoolhouse, so you'll need everything that will enable you to teach all subjects to all grade levels at any time. In addition to normal office supplies like pens, pencils, paper, and rulers, you should also have dictionaries (English and foreign), maps, grammar and composition guides, colored pencils, markers, educational games, protractors, workbooks, and primary reading books. A laptop computer and portable printer will come in handy as well. Pack everything you need into easy-to-transport cases and take them to set. You could easily spend several hundred dollars stocking up on these basic items.

What's the best way for someone to reach me?

You're always moving between the schoolroom at BASE CAMP (where all of the cast and crew trailers are) and the set, so you need to keep your communications mobile as well. In addition to having a cell phone with you at all times, a laptop computer with Internet access will help you stay in touch with your student's base school teachers, who will e-mail you assignments as necessary.

WHERE DO I REALLY NEED TO GO?
I just want to work.

Because production schedules for minors may not be consecutive and you may be called for last minute day-calls, it will help to live close to where most production takes place, such as in Los Angeles. There is one Studio Teacher hired for every ten minors on set at any given time during "normal" school days. During vacations, holidays, and weekends, only one Teacher is required for every twenty minors on set.

To teach in California, you'll have to obtain an elementary and secondary California teaching credential (Dual Certification) just as you would if you were teaching in a normal school environment. Then you must pass the Studio Teacher Exam, which is a test on child labor laws in California. In addition, you must complete the twelve-hour Studio Teacher's Workshop, which is given only twice a year, after which you will receive your Studio Teacher Certificate.

So how do I get work?

As a beginning Studio Teacher, you can register with an agency that contracts jobs for motion-picture production. A list of agencies can be found at www.LA411.com. IATSE Local 884 also maintains a teacher referral service that is available for all union members.

WHAT AM I GETTING MYSELF INTO?
So who actually calls and hires me?

You'll be working closely with the Assistant Directors Department, so many of your referrals for work will come from ADs with whom you've worked previously. Expect to get a call from an AD, the Unit Production Manager (UPM) on the show, or the Production Coordinator in the production office.

Okay, I got the job. What now?

Find out the age ranges with which you'll be working. You'll have to have all age-appropriate materials for all the required subjects you'll be asked to teach. You may only have a single day's notice to confer with the student's base teachers and gather the necessary resources that the student won't be bringing on his own.

You also should be aware of what the working conditions will be, both for your own welfare as well as for the student's. Read the script and ask that you are given regular updates of the ONE-LINER, which outlines the schedule for the rest of the movie. The filming conditions (e.g., night exteriors, inclement weather, distant locations) may have an effect on how attentive the children may be, how miserable they become because of weather, and how well you do your own job.

What will my life really be like?

5:30 A.M.—GET TO WORK
The minor Actors for whom you are responsible will be arriving at 6:00 A.M. You'll want to be at base camp at least twenty to thirty minutes prior to give yourself time to organize the schoolwork for the day.

6:00 A.M.— "THROUGH THE WORKS"
While the Actors are going through the works, you will want to confirm with the parents or guardians that work permits and COOGAN ACCOUNTS are all in order. Students are required to bring their current entertainment work permit, all necessary school books, and assignments to work on for the three hours of required set schooling each day.

7:05 A.M.—REHEARSAL
The Actors will head to set for first rehearsal with the Director and crew. When you're not in the designated schoolroom teaching, it is your responsibility to

attend to the health, safety, and morals of all minors under the age of sixteen. This includes being aware of the working conditions on and off set and how the minor's mental state and level of fatigue are being affected. In other words, while those in Production concentrate on the myriad details that go into making a movie, the Studio Teacher is there specifically to advocate for the welfare of all minors on set in regard to their health, safety, morals, and education.

7:15 A.M.—CAMERA SETUP

There are very specific rules limiting the total number of hours a minor is permitted to work in a day and in a week and specifically when those hours are allowed. In general, a minor cannot work more than eight hours in any twenty-four hour period. In that time, minors are required by law to attend at least three hours of school per day. You'll work closely with the First Assistant Director to find blocks of time throughout the day when you can take the children to the schoolroom, which is at base camp. Major camera setups can take anywhere from twenty minutes to an hour or more so you'll never have the children for the entire three hours at a time. It will require diligence and cooperation from the Assistant Directors and Production Assistants to help you get the time you need.

7:45 A.M.—ROLL CAMERA

The First Assistant Director remains on set closely monitoring the progress of the camera setup. When preparation is near completion, he will call over his radio to the AD or Production Assistant who is running base camp to ask that the talent be invited back to set. There will be a knock on your door, and the students will stop what they are doing to head back to work. Keep track of how long your students have been "in school" and then follow them to set.

Be an extra set of eyes and look carefully for anything that might pose a hazard to any of the minors who are under your supervision. If anything looks suspicious or out of the ordinary, don't hesitate to ask the First AD. No one will blame you for keeping safety a top priority.

8:10 A.M.—CUT, MOVIN' ON

The Director is happy with the shot and the crew will move on to the next setup. Sometimes this is a simple lens change that takes just minutes, while a full-scale turnaround may take a half an hour or more. Good First ADs will be very aware of the schooling requirements, so you won't have to say a word when an opportunity to go back to base camp presents itself.

1:00 P.M.—LUNCH

The entire crew generally breaks for lunch at the same time, about six hours after the general crew call. Head to the caterer and enjoy your meal with other teachers, the parents, and talent or crew you've met during the day.

2:00 P.M.—BACK TO WORK

The kids were in at 6:00 A.M., so there isn't much time left for them to work today compared to the working crews, who typically have twelve to fourteen hour days. There are different limitations and requirements to follow for different age groups.

Work and School

- Babies six months to two years old can only work two hours a day with two hours of "recreation" as well as a half-hour lunch.
- Children aged two through five are allowed to work three hours a day with three hours of school and/or recreation plus a half-hour lunch break.
- Six- through eight-year-olds can work four hours per day and must have three hours of school, one hour of recreation, and a half-hour lunch.
- Minors who are nine through fifteen years old can work five hours a day with three hours of school, one hour of recreation, and a half-hour lunch.
- Sixteen- and seventeen-year-olds can work six hours a day with three hours of school, an hour of recreation, and a half hour of lunch, for a day totaling ten and a half hours.

So depending on the ages of the cast, you might be finished working before lunch or soon thereafter. Be cognizant of how long you'll have the minors each day so that you work hard to fit in the required hours of schooling. More specific details regarding the legal requirements you'll be asked to enforce and follow are available from SAG and at the Studio Teachers Local 884 official website. Consult Appendix A at the back of this book for more details.

9:00 P.M.—WRAP

It is entirely possible that the minors will have reached the limit of how long they can work for the day but have not spent enough time in school. If necessary, complete the time requirements as soon as the kids are wrapped from set, contact the base school teachers for assignments or feedback (usually via e-mail), then turn in any necessary paperwork to the Second AD for the Production Report.

WHAT I REALLY WANT TO DO IS MOVE UP!

Like few other jobs on set, you are a department unto yourself. Teaching in a traditional classroom has its rewards, but working in the entertainment industry opens up opportunities, like traveling and meeting new people, that you will be able to enjoy and remember for a lifetime.

Chapter 9

What I Really Want to Do Is Costume!

WHAT THE HECK IS A COSTUMER?

The Costumer works with the Costume Designer to obtain all the necessary articles of wardrobe and prepare them for photography. This includes shopping for clothes, renting them if necessary, and loading the wardrobe trailer. There are usually at least two Costumers per show. One works on set with the talent and the other works off the set as a SHOPPER. You will be one or the other for the length of a project.

That, and what else?

Your primary responsibility is to dress the Actors in the proper wardrobe to appear on screen, but you also may need to help keep them comfortable and happy with umbrellas or heavy coats in between takes. At times, an Actor might complain about not liking the clothes for one reason or another. Deal with the problem if you can, or take bigger issues to the Wardrobe Supervisor or the Costume Designer.

It doesn't sound that hard. What's the pay like?

Expect to make roughly $600 a week for nonunion low-budget work and upward of $1,500 a week once you're in the Costumers union, IATSE Local 705. You'll also receive $100 to $200 a week for KIT RENTAL. If you're hired for the entire show (prep, production, and a week or two of wrap) expect to earn around $30,000 for about fourteen weeks of work.

WHAT DO I REALLY NEED TO KNOW?

Presumably you're going to go into this with an established interest in working with clothes. When you first start out on low-budget projects, you'll most likely wind up doing everything yourself from limited designing to shopping to stitching.

As your career progresses, you won't be allowed to do all of those jobs because the union has clear divisions of responsibility. But this doesn't mean that those skills (cleaning, sewing) are wasted. Once you're on set, you'll be expected to solve problems quickly on your own. If an Actress has a major problem fitting into a costume, then an official Seamstress will probably be called in to deal with it. But as the on-set Costumer, you're allowed and expected to do the small things in the interest of efficiency, such as sew a button back on or quickly repair a tear.

Am I supposed to look fashionable because I'm in the wardrobe department?

Looking nice is always a good goal, but you're there to work, not to put on a fashion show. Working on a set, you need to wear **OSHA-**approved footwear, so no open-toed shoes. Dress comfortably in clothing that you can move quickly in.

WHAT DO I REALLY NEED TO HAVE?
We're just putting clothes on people. What could I possibly need?

Wardrobe that is being worn for days on end undergoes a considerable amount of wear-and-tear, so alterations and quick repairs may be needed from time to time. Your personal kit will include a blow dryer, safety pins, needle and thread, superglue, GAFFER'S TAPE, scissors, wardrobe tags, garment bags, towels, seam rippers, tape measures, Sharpie markers, TOP STICK, FEBREZE, an assortment of brushes, and a digital camera for continuity shots.

What's the best way for someone to reach me?

The union local maintains an availability list that you can put your name onto once a month. This doesn't guarantee you a job. It just lets others know that you are available.

DAYPLAYING happens a lot in this department, as movies will suddenly be shooting scenes with scores of Extras who all need to be dressed properly. Be ready to take those unexpected day calls. They could lead to more work down the line.

WHERE DO I REALLY NEED TO GO?
I just want to work.

There are some universities that provide courses and degrees in relevant fields, including costume design, footwear design, and textile design. Find internships on professional productions or volunteer to work on student-level films. You may be asked to run around town dropping off returns or dry-cleaning, but it's all part of the job.

So how do I get work?

To get into the union, you need to do one of two things. The first is to be working already on a nonunion show that turns union at some point. The second way is to work at a costume rental house and accumulate thirty paid days. Working at the rental house will give you unique one-on-one contact with Costume Designers, Costume Supervisors, and Costumers. As you pull wardrobe for them for a variety of projects, you'll get hands-on exposure to the clothing of various cultures and historical periods.

Another route is to be a Production Assistant for the Wardrobe Department. You'll most likely be working with the Supervisor helping with paperwork and petty cash, as well as running errands. If you are good at that and likeable, the Supervisor may try to help you get into a costume house to get your required days.

WHAT AM I GETTING MYSELF INTO?
So who actually calls and hires me?

Costumers or Costume Supervisors you've worked with before will refer you. In some cases, a Costume Designer may like the way you work enough to recommend you to a project.

Okay, I got the job. What now?

The Costume Designer has been working with the Director to establish the look of the costumes and then must have them manufactured or purchased. This is where you come in. The Designer or Supervisor will send you out for samples of clothing, which will either be approved or rejected. If rejected, you'll take it back to wherever you bought it.

As you amass the wardrobe, you'll organize it according to which Actor will wear each costume. A lower budget project will give you just a couple of weeks to set your truck up for production. Higher budgets with more involved costuming requirements will give you up to three months.

In addition to each Actor's rack, there will be a DAY RACK where you will eventually be pulling the wardrobe for the day and placing it on the rack for easy access. To keep all of this straight, you'll be labeling each and every article of clothing with a MASTER TAG that describes exactly who and what it is for. You'll also be keeping track of accessories, such as jewelry, hats, and watches.

You don't just get all of the clothes before production begins. Designing, fabrication, shopping, fittings, and returns all continue for the entire duration of the shoot. This occurs because not every Actor is hired during preproduction, and decisions may arise through the course of the shoot.

What will my life really be like?

THE NIGHT BEFORE

Using the call sheet as a guide, create tomorrow's day rack so that everything you should have prepared is ready. You may need to send some clothes out to be dry-cleaned, and you may have to clean clothes yourself using the washer and dryer that are in your trailer. And if need be, you'll also iron out wrinkles or steam clothing before putting the wardrobe on the day rack. Some Costumers like to place the first "change" of the day in the Actors' trailers so that they can get dressed upon arrival.

5:42 A.M.—GET TO WORK

The first Actors are coming in at 6:00 A.M. so you need to make sure everything is ready for them when they arrive. If you haven't prepared the clothes or the rack, now is the time to do it. If the day rack isn't ready, get it ready. If the first change isn't in the Actor's trailer, put it there. Push your set rack to the stage so it is standing by when you need it.

Once the first change is ready and out your door, prep the clothes for the entire day if you have time or ask your co-Costumer to do it.

The dry-cleaning from the night before should have been delivered by the Transportation Department. Check it all in and retag everything as necessary before replacing it on the racks.

While some Actors prefer the feeling that you're paying attention to them, try to avoid bothering them after they've put the clothes on unless necessary. Something as simple as lint should be taken care of before the clothes reach the Actor's trailer. Occasionally the costume may require that you help the Actor put it on. For example, a skimpy outfit on an Actress may necessitate using an adhesive so it doesn't fall off. Or you may need to sew in an extra button at the last second, take a hem in, or let it out. Some adjustments after the clothes are on just can't be avoided. At times you may have to work with naked or partially clothed Actors. Just go to it, doing your job as a professional.

Despite a Designer's best efforts, Actors may show up and decide that they simply don't want to wear what had originally been planned for them. Reasons range from the rational to the absurd. If the problem stems from something fixable, like a pair of pants needing to be taken in an inch, then do what you can. If the problem is out of your realm as the Set Costumer, notify the Key Costumer, who will talk to the Designer. It's now no longer your responsibility.

After the Actors arrive they will make their way to Hair and Makeup. Keep an ear on the radio and listen for the First AD to call First Team to set. You want to intercept the talent to see if they have everything on that they need. Before the camera rolls, look for missing jewelry, jackets, hats, etc., keeping an eye out for anything they might have removed while getting their hair and makeup done.

7:00 A.M.—GETTING TO SET

If an Actor is missing something, use your walkie-talkie and radio back to the truck for the other Costumer or the PA to bring it to set for you.

7:05 A.M.—REHEARSAL

You need to be paying attention to what the Actors will be doing and how it may affect the clothing. Generally you'll just be straightening out wrinkles between takes.

On occasion, something out of the ordinary will be planned, such as an Actor having to spill food or water on himself. If that is part of the shot, you should have known about it weeks in advance so you would have proper doubles of the clothing ready, as well as preparations to clean and/or dry soiled items on set quickly. You don't have time to take this stuff back to the truck, so you can dry off wet clothing with a hairdryer and just do your best with other stains. In any case, if you see this situation coming, get together with the First AD and give him an honest rundown of your parameters regarding numbers of changes available and how long it will take to clean used items. The last thing anyone wants is a very expensive crew waiting around for a shirt to be dried when you could have easily had doubles standing by on the day rack.

7:15 A.M.—CAMERA SETUP

After rehearsal is over, First Team will scatter back to base camp while the rest of the crew prepares the set. Take this time to double-check your continuity book, especially if this is a continuation from previously shot scenes or takes.

As the set preparation is nearing completion, the First AD will call for First Team to come back in. There may or may not be another rehearsal, depending on the complexity of the shot.

7:40 A.M.—FINAL TOUCHES

When everything appears to be ready to go, the First AD will call for "FINAL TOUCHES." That is your cue, along with Hair and Makeup, to approach the talent and check that everything is as it should be. You've been keeping an eye on them anyway from just off set, but it never hurts to get in closer just to be sure. Avoid any unnecessary primping throughout the day, though, as that may eventually wind up annoying the Actors.

7:45 A.M.—ROLL CAMERA

Back off and find a good vantage point from which to watch the take. You're paying attention to continuity of the clothing. For example, if an Actor rolls up his sleeves, make note of when and where he does it so that if additional shots come either before or after this one, you will know how to preset the wardrobe, ensuring the shots match up seamlessly.

7:48 A.M.—CUT, LET'S GO AGAIN

Right after the take, rush in as soon as possible and ask the Actors to hold still for a moment so that you can take continuity photos. They've been doing this awhile, so usually they'll cooperate without any trouble. Get in there, snap the shot, and then back off while thanking them.

You can use a Polaroid or a digital camera. Whichever you choose, you'll need to make notes regarding this scene, explaining what the talent is wearing and how they are wearing it. You won't need a photo after each take, just after each PRINT.

If there was a problem with the wardrobe during the take, let the Director know as soon as possible. Depending on how large a problem it was, she may or may not care to do another take. Just make sure you communicate the problem initially and then have the Script Supervisor make note of it in the official script notes in case there is flak down the line.

8:10 A.M.—CUT, MOVIN' ON

If the Actors need to change into new wardrobe, let the First AD know and he'll inform them that they need to head back to their trailers, where they'll find that the other Costumer has already placed the new change.

You can stay on set and finish writing continuity notes in your book unless you are needed back at base camp to help set rooms or tag new clothing.

1:00 P.M.—LUNCH

Keep your set kit and set rack tidy and head to the Caterer with everyone else.

2:00 P.M.—BACK TO WORK

For the most part, unless there is a scene with two hundred Extras, once the day and set racks are ready to go in the morning, your day should move along fairly smoothly. You should have time during lighting setups to relax for a few moments. Whatever it is you choose to do, it shouldn't be so engaging that you can't pay attention to what is happening around you.

9:00 P.M.—WRAP

What you gain during the day in downtime you make up for at wrap. You were in this morning before most of the rest of the crew, and you'll be heading out after most have left.

Take all of the clothes that were worn that day and prepare them to go to the dry cleaners overnight. You may have to wait until the Actors have gotten their makeup removed, or perhaps they'll have a meeting with the Director that will delay your wrap.

Set up the day rack with tomorrow's first items.

Keep track of your own timecard. Sometimes the Supervisor will keep photocopies for the department on file so that when the actual checks arrive, you can double-check that they are accurate.

After you've given the dry-cleaning order to the Transportation Driver, find an AD and give him your OUT-TIME, then go home.

What happens to all of those clothes at the end of the movie?

Good question. Over the course of twelve weeks or more you've had clothes constantly coming in and your truck is full. Now you have to empty it.

Once the entire film is wrapped, all the rentals need to go back to where they came from, and all the purchases and manufactured items need to be boxed up. There might be reshoots in a month or two, so a new crew will have to know exactly where to go to find the boxes and which boxes to look in for the proper wardrobe.

WHAT I REALLY WANT TO DO IS MOVE UP!

As a Costumer, your next step up is to become either a Costume Supervisor or the Key Costumer. If you've been at this awhile, you won't have too much trouble doing either. While some of the other departments have Best Boys, people to take care of equipment logistics and paperwork, the Costume Supervisor fills the same type of roll for the Wardrobe Department.

Working as a Costumer can be a good route to becoming a Designer. The Costumers are the day-to-day laborers, while the Designer is the creative force. Although it is vitally important that you gain set experience to learn what works on camera and what doesn't, designing is a vastly different exercise. Working as a Set Costumer or Supervisor in no way directly can prepare you or train you to become a great Costume Designer, so if this is something you really want to do, you need to take the time to develop those artistic skills and sensibilities during periods when you're not working. Meanwhile, the contacts you make while costuming will come in handy later on when you have a portfolio of ideas and/or a body of design work to show.

Chapter 10

What I Really Want to Do Is Costume Design!

WHAT THE HECK IS A COSTUME DESIGNER?

The Costume Designer works in coordination with the Director, Production Designer, and Director of Photography to design wardrobe for the Actors that is appropriate for the script and for the overall visual design of the project.

That, and what else?

While the overall "look" of the show will be determined far before cameras arrive on the set, you'll still be designing, shopping, fitting, and re-dressing Actors throughout the entire length of production. While film is rolling on set every day, you'll constantly be busy off-set designing new clothes, working with the manufacturers (Seamstresses, Cutters, etc.) and the Costumers and Shoppers, as well as fitting new talent.

While you're not doing any of that, you might find yourself on set helping the AD staff place Extras in the background. Seeing the wardrobe through, from concept to screen, is what your job is all about.

I must be making really good money then, right?

A nonunion low-budget deal will get you whatever the production can afford, which may be $100 a day or even nothing. Once you move up and can join IATSE Local 892, you may be able to command a salary of up to $180,000 for six months of fourteen hour days.

Local 892? But the costumers are local 705.

There is a fine line between designing clothes for use on a movie set and actually making it all happen. The Costumers Local includes all the personnel required to get the wardrobe off the concept page and onto an Actor. Not that a Designer doesn't have a hand in that, but the concentration of the Costume Designer is more conceptual while, at the same time, overseeing the execution of the design.

Currently, there are two separate union designations because the unions were formed at different times. While Designers were part of a studio's permanent staff in the earliest years of movie production (as were Writers, Actors, and some Directors), Costumers didn't have such job security and organized separately to form Local 705. In 1976, after studios stopped employing creative and technical personnel on a permanent basis, Costume Designers organized to form their own union.

WHAT DO I REALLY NEED TO KNOW?

If you do feel that you have the foundation to be a great Costume Designer, it isn't just as simple as designing whatever comes to mind. These aren't clothes that will be worn on the street or out on the town by ordinary people. Your designs are specifically made to be worn by Actors, multiple days in a row, and filmed under special lighting conditions. What looks good out in the real world may not be entirely practical on a movie set. Colors may not translate the way you think they should, certain fabrics may cause sound recording issues, and what constitutes normal wear and tear off the set is multiplied tenfold during production.

While you don't need to know how to build a set and light it, or how to apply makeup and style hair, it is in your best interest to have a basic understanding of how those factors will affect what you have in mind.

WHAT DO I REALLY NEED TO HAVE?

You'll want to save your ideas in a portfolio of TEAR SHEETS, so some kind of sketch-pad is necessary. You'll also be adding pictures to the portfolio that show how your designs looked when they were brought into reality.

And you'll find that you're constantly measuring things, be it Actors themselves or the clothes that they will wear. So always carry a tape measure and scissors with you just in case.

What's the best way for someone to reach me?

You'll want to enlist the services of an agent, who will aid you in your search for bigger and better projects and who also will help negotiate more lucrative deals.

Talk with your Designer peers about agent referrals, and also inquire at IATSE Local 892. Your own reputation will still be the primary source for getting calls, but the sooner you can get an agent, the quicker your career can potentially grow.

WHERE DO I REALLY NEED TO GO?
I just want to work.

Once you have a solid portfolio of work to show around, pick up the TRADES and look for upcoming projects that might suit your particular sense of style and your level of experience. For instance, if you've been working primarily with contemporary wardrobe, chances are that you won't want to jump right into a massive period piece that chronicles some event in the 1800s. This isn't to say that you can't, but don't bite off more than you can chew, especially at first. Concentrate on contacting those shows that are in the range of 1 million to 10 million dollar at first. You'll work up from there.

So how do I get work?

Nobody is going to hire you right away to design for an $80 million feature, so you'll have to set your sights a little lower. Experience and having work to show for it are essential for getting work in the industry. As early as possible, begin designing and costuming for free for local theater or small low-budget films. Build a portfolio of sketches that showcase your ideas. Then, as your concepts become reality on stage or on film, take high-quality photos of the wardrobe to include in your presentation so that potential employers will see how your ideas were executed.

WHAT AM I GETTING MYSELF INTO?
So who actually calls and hires me?

If you've made a name for yourself and your reputation precedes you, you or your agent may get a call from a Director who likes your style and wants to work with you. Otherwise, you'll be contacting Directors to express interest in working on their projects.

Okay, what now?

When you are being considered to design for a project, you may draw some initial sketches based on your discussions with the Director and your read of the script. While those initial sketches may be what got you the job, now you need to refine the ideas into workable concepts for the Director to approve. Your first designs will be based on the script and your conversations with the Director. Once casting begins, you'll undoubtedly be reworking those ideas, as the particular qualities of a specific Actor or Actress will influence what is to be worn. You'll also meet with the Production Designer and visit the sets under construction to get an idea of how your wardrobe will integrate with that world and make changes to the wardrobe designs when necessary to better complement the set designs and/or lighting.

Depending on the project, you may design new clothes that don't exist anywhere else and need to be manufactured. Or you may simply "create" looks of contemporary wardrobe that will just be off the rack. Or you may do a mixture of both. As soon as your designs are approved, you'll hire about six CUTTERS and their assistants.

As soon as possible, you'll either have the Actors come in for fittings or if the project (and talent) is sufficiently big and important enough, a body cast might be made so that you can test out clothes before the Actors arrive. This saves everyone time and energy. The most important thing you can offer an Actor is the confidence that you are out to make him look as good as possible.

As you break the script down to figure out who is wearing what and when, you and the Costume Supervisor will formulate a budget that invariably will be pared down by the studio to being just under what you truly need. You'll need to consider manufacturing, shopping, renting, and dry-cleaning costs. Big Extra days as well as the need for doubles and other specialty items (e.g., stunt modifications) can add up quickly. So, at times, product-placement deals will help smooth the budget woes as you get free clothes in exchange for screen credit. You and the Supervisor will work the phones to make this happen whenever possible.

What will my life really be like?

6:00 A.M.—GET TO WORK

Especially on the first day that Actors come to set, you should ideally be around during the time that they are getting dressed. Why? Even though you've already had multiple fittings and everyone has approved the designs, nothing is ever that certain when it comes to the wardrobe that an Actor should be wearing. Perhaps what looked fine a few weeks ago suddenly doesn't fit quite right. You should be available to help the Costumers fix the problem. Or another common occurrence is when an Actor suddenly just decides that he simply doesn't want to wear what was previously approved. This might happen for a variety of reasons, ranging from the logical to the irrational. Whatever the case, because you're the one who is placed in charge of the overall wardrobe design for the project, you need to be around to deal with all unexpected obstacles.

7:05 A.M.—REHEARSAL

Again, the first time an Actor goes to a new set wearing new wardrobe, you should try to be there. In most cases, there will be no problems. But there is a chance that once rehearsal begins, something might happen that requires your immediate attention.

7:15 A.M.—CAMERA SETUP

If there were any significant problems, now is the time to handle them...and fast! There is only so much you can do on the spot, so if the problem is a whole-sale change of wardrobe, you'll have to explain to the Actor or Director that you'll need more time if you don't have something else immediately available. Of course you'll try your hardest to make everyone happy by the time film is rolling through the cameras a few minutes from now, but your job is to communicate the situation and do the best you can within the given parameters. To delay shooting is the Director's call.

On occasion, there will be days when large groups of Extras will be called to work (e.g., a party scene). A cadre of additional Costumers will also be hired to help choose wardrobe for and dress these Extras. You should be around to help that process go smoothly. While cameras are being set up and the scene is being lit, the Second AD will begin placing the Extras in the background. While his placements might be fairly haphazard, you can help bring some design sense to it by considering the wardrobe and how it will appear on camera. For instance, you might notice that the AD randomly put several Extras together who are all wearing the same colors. Or perhaps an Extra has suddenly been pulled out of the crowd and is now a "featured" Extra who should be wearing something com-pletely different than what she has on. You'll want to intervene in these situations to make sure that placement and wardrobe are the best they can be.

7:45 A.M.—ROLL CAMERA

Once everything is perfect (or reasonably okay), you should watch at least a take or two just in case there is a real problem.

7:48 A.M.—CUT, LET'S GO AGAIN

There is no reason for you to sit idly on set once the "look" is established and all complaints have ceased. You may wind up back on set periodically throughout the day in case any problems crop up or if there are more Extras to place, but otherwise you are free to return to prepping. There is always a lot of work to be done as new Actors join the cast, requiring new wardrobe choices and fittings.

9:00 P.M.—WRAP

If you haven't had a chance to be on set all day, take some time to check in with your Costumers to make sure everything went okay. You might even glance over the continuity book just to keep up with any minor adjustments that had to be made.

WHAT I REALLY WANT TO DO IS MOVE UP!

You are already at the top of the Costuming and Wardrobe field for motion pic-ture and television work. Hopefully you enjoy your work and the environment enough to feel fulfilled. However if you're not entirely happy within this industry, you could consider a move toward fashion design outside the film business.

Chapter 11

What I Really Want to Do is Makeup!

WHAT THE HECK IS A MAKEUP ARTIST?

The Makeup Artist is responsible for applying makeup and/or special makeup effects to the on-camera talent so that they appear in the "look" approved by the Director. Most of the time, *beauty* makeup is applied, which *removes* imperfections so that the result makes the talent appear better than someone could in real life. Some of the time, however, *special effects* makeup techniques are used to *add* imperfections, to enhance the reality of life or to create something wholly *unnatural*. Most Effects Makeup Artists can do both, but not all Beauty Makeup Artists are qualified to do effects.

Most shows will have only two people for the duration, the Department Head and the Key. As far as IATSE Local 706 is concerned, you can move back and forth from Head to Key from show to show. There is no inherent seniority in those titles.

On very heavy days when, say, you've got a roomful of zombies played by scores of Extras, many more Makeup Artists will be hired as DAYPLAYERS to plow through the work so it is finished by crew call.

Hair is its own department in the union environment. On ultra-low-budget shows, you may be expected to do both Makeup and Hair, but once you start working on large union shows, you have to specialize in one or the other.

That, and what else?

You don't just apply the makeup at the beginning of the day and forget about it. Maintenance before every shot is just as crucial, so you'll be spending a lot of time on set as well as in your trailer. During the day, *you* are the Actors' mirror. They have enough to think about, such as remembering their lines and hitting their marks. You need to instill in them the confidence that they won't have to worry about how they look.

I've heard that I can make a lot of money doing this.

A Beauty Makeup Artist will make roughly $50,000 for twelve weeks of work on a union feature, including a BOX RENTAL of around $75 a day. You get this kind of money by working upward of fourteen to sixteen hours a day, usually starting at four or five in the morning and going home after eight or nine at night. A department head can make double that depending on the project and her level of experience.

WHAT DO I REALLY NEED TO KNOW?

Beauty makeup is fairly straightforward. Because women typically have been applying their own makeup for years, for a woman, learning how to remove someone else's imperfections shouldn't be such a big deal. An average male may have more trouble getting started.

Look in trade magazines for a makeup school near you. Most offer courses in straight beauty makeup. Some specialize in special effects makeup and mechanics. Some courses run just three weekends and are relatively inexpensive. Some go longer and cost significantly more. Some you can do from the comfort of your own home. You may come away from class with a diploma or certificate in your hand, but that's not what it's all about. The proof is in what you can achieve, not in a piece of paper that says you took a class. What does the art look like? You may have all the diplomas in the world, but if you can't "do it," then you won't be hired to work.

Once you're in the union, you are eligible to take special workshops that are offered in beauty and character to enhance your skills.

Eh, beauty. Whatever. That's for women. I want to make the cool stuff, like monsters! What do I need to know to do that?

Well, first of all, men who are reading this book and want to work in the movie business may think that beauty makeup is a "girl thing," but the truth is that practically everybody who goes on camera really needs some kind of makeup, even if it's just a little powder to take off the "shine." A steady supply of people need this service, and it can be extremely lucrative. But more important, even if you are interested in doing special effects makeup, you will need to know the basics of makeup application.

You may need to create an effects application someday that will then be covered by a "beauty" layer. If all you've ever done is create *imperfections* as a Special Effects Makeup Artist, then you'll be found out pretty quickly. Plus, once you're on a working set, you won't necessarily be looked at as just the "FX guy." Once you're in the Makeup union, you're telling the world that you know how to do makeup across the board. Get over any hang-ups you might have and learn to do it all.

Having said that, a lot of Beauty Makeup people are not 100 percent qualified to do special effects makeup. It should be obvious that there is much more to know if you're interested in that aspect of the department.

Material Safety

While making masks, creatures, and gory effects is fun, it can also be hazardous.

You will be using mostly silicon- or rubber-cement-based paints. You'll be spraying NAPTHA, which is a solvent for silicon and also happens to be carcinogenic. Just about every material you'll use in an effects environment is not biologically safe without taking the proper precautions.

Get MSDS (Material Safety Data Sheets) on all the materials you're going to use and read them before opening the lids. Find out exactly what the material can do to you and what you need to do to protect yourself from contact or particulates. Always work with adequate ventilation!

None of the stuff you use is good for you. Don't eat it, don't drink it, don't breathe it, don't touch it. Regular clay is fine, but the dust that comes from the clay after it is dry shouldn't be inhaled.

Because a special makeup or creature shop inherently contains many dangerous substances, those with respiratory problems may want to rethink this career path.

There are ways to protect yourself so that you will suffer no ill effects, but jumping into this process unawares could literally kill you.

The best way to embark upon a career in Effects Makeup is to start creating things on your own. Find books and magazines that feature the various products and processes for creating prosthetics and full-scale masks and costumes. *Take care to learn about the safety procedures to be followed when handling the various products.* Most of them are highly toxic. Once you feel confident in your base of knowledge, create some sculptures. Eventually, the sculptures will deteriorate, so you'll want to make molds to preserve your creation as a mask or resin material. Also, take pictures of *everything* you do. The pictures and the resin products will be the portfolio you will use to get a foot in the door.

Unless you are a child prodigy in art, sculpture, and creature design, your first step in the professional world of effects makeup will probably be as a Runner at a special effects shop. While this seems like a menial position, and can be at times, it is valuable in that you are learning how a real shop operates within a business environment. You learn firsthand where to get the various materials needed, what they cost, and how they are eventually used by the seasoned professionals.

Union?

When a studio or production company gears up to make a movie requiring special effects, a bidding process takes place in which several effects houses present their portfolios in hopes of getting the contract for that show. Unless there are personal relationships involved, the studio is likely to go with the effects house that looks like it knows what it's doing and has the lowest bid.

Creating "stuff" at your shop is not under the auspices of any union rules. However, much of what you make will wind up being applied to on-camera Actors on a set. If you're gluing or painting on somebody's skin on set, you have to be a member of IATSE Local 706. If you're just helping a Stuntperson put on a simple mask or a full suit, then you don't have to be part of the union. But if the mask requires that you have to blend it in to the eyes with makeup, then it is now a union job.

A Mechanic who helps construct the radio-controlled or internal mechanics of a mask or model does not have to be part of any union during preproduction. When that piece eventually does go to set to be shot, if that Mechanic is the best qualified person to operate it, then he is granted union status in the Screen Actors Guild.

You never have to join any union if you don't want to, but you won't be able to work on a union set, thus limiting your income potential in the long run.

Once you've shown that you're enthusiastic and reliable, you may be pulled from your running duties to become a full-time Lab Technician. Here, you are responsible for all sorts of things, like "running" foam, brushing latex, making armatures, casting silicone, assisting with life-casting, or even just assembling work tables.

Those two positions are sort of the support jobs for the artists in the shop. Of course, the glory jobs are in Sculpting and Painting. Your portfolio, coupled with the "who you know" factor, will land you work in those areas…maybe. But almost equally important to the process is the Mold Maker. The clay used to create a sculpture will eventually break down and fall apart. A mold must be constructed from which the final product can be produced. Using a variety of techniques and materials, the Mold Maker takes a sculpture and makes a negative of it so that it can be reproduced precisely as a latex or resin (or other finishing material) piece.

A very specialized position in the field is the Mechanic. This is a person who is well schooled in creating internalized armatures and motors for models, miniatures, or creature effects, such as eye movement and muscle control. If the film calls for such an elaborate creation, the Mechanic will be called in to collaborate with the Sculptor early on in the process to ensure that enough physical space is left for the necessary equipment to be added later. Eventually, when the product is completed, the Mechanic may also be asked to go to the set to work as the Puppeteer. Now the job takes on a whole new dimension as the technician must "act" via the mechanical device for camera.

The important thing for you to consider while pursuing this career is that while specializing in one area can be rewarding, it might not pay all the bills. Being a jack of all trades makes you far more valuable to a production, as they can count on you to do the jobs that might otherwise be assigned to several different people. For instance, a Sculptor may only need five days to finish a mask. Then what? If that's all you are capable of doing, then you are now out of work. But if you also know how to make molds, then you just picked up another few days of employment. If you are a highly skilled Painter as well, then you may get the privilege of seeing your creation from start to finish and get paid for it. Not only will you keep the checks keep coming in, but, as an added bonus, you will experience a sense of creative accomplishment.

WHAT DO I REALLY NEED TO HAVE?
Do the Actors have their own makeup?

No, you bring it all. To get started, you need a good set of beauty brushes, which will run you about $350. A quality case will be around $500. The makeup itself might very well cost $2,000 to $3,000 more by the time you're finished. You need a basic palette of neutral concealers, foundations, eye shadows, lipsticks, blushes, and face crèmes, which hopefully will work for most on-camera talent. The more you have, the better. For instance, if you walk onto a set and don't have the proper palette for a dark-skinned Actor, then you're going to have trouble doing your job.

If you're doing Special Effects Makeup, the goal, materials, and equipment you use are different. You'll need a variety of glues, skin protectors, palette knives, tweezers, scissors, and brushes (glue, air, paint), plus chemical removers to take it all off later. You'll also need a whole different palette of colors and materials that you wouldn't use in a beauty makeup application, such as rubber mask grease paints, aqua colors, and tattooing materials. Tools like palette knives (to spread glues and/or makeup) and air compressors (to spray paint) are necessary because you're usually trying to take a flat lifeless piece of foam or rubber and give it depth and dimension by adding imperfections that exist in real life.

Your complete set of supplies may run you upward of $25,000. But start out small by getting your brushes first; glue and air brushes for applying prosthetics, powder and beauty brushes for straight makeup. Expect to pay between $350 and $1,000.

What's the best way for someone to reach me?

Apart from handing your number out to people you meet, once you join the union, you can put your name on the AVAILABLE LIST. When a production has exhausted its own supply of people that it knows and likes, they'll turn to the Available List, which has names, numbers, and specifics of what people can do, such as effects and body makeup.

WHERE DO I REALLY NEED TO GO?
I just want to work.

Working on freebies, deferred payment jobs, or the "this is a GREAT PROJECT" call gives you more experience, a larger résumé and portfolio and more contacts to call in the future. But more than that, it gives you "days." To work on the big stuff where you can make better money, you almost always have to be part of IATSE Local 706. There are three main ways of gaining membership:

1. Do thirty days on a union show to get in the union. This is an obvious Catch-22 of course. How do you get on a union show in the first place if you're not already in? If you have created a special makeup in an effects shop and you

are the only one who knows how to apply it properly, and it (the effect and you) works for thirty days on a union set, then you get in.

2. 60/60/60: Do makeup application for sixty days every year for three years on any type of entertainment project or event. Take proof of your union or nonunion employment (checks stubs and call sheets) to the union office.

3. Star request: If you catch the fancy of a big movie star while you are both working on a nonunion project and that star specifically requests that you are on his/her next big show, the union isn't about to argue. You're in.

Everyone enters the union as a trainee. After you take the classes and workshops they offer, you advance to journeyman level. While this may seem like a positive step, the reality is that you still get hired based on who you know and what you are capable of, not because of any certification or special credit someone bestows upon you. If you've established yourself as qualified and good, it doesn't really matter what your union classification is.

Union membership doesn't guarantee work. You may get a slow start by just dayplaying for projects that have large Extra calls or if one of the regular crew members needs to take a day off. Be friendly and personable while you're there. No matter how big the crew is for that day, the Key Makeup Artist will notice if someone is a problem.

If you've been doing this awhile, the people who will hire you as a Key will be the Director, the Producer, or someone at the movie studio. Those ABOVE-THE-LINE will hear about you from other Keys whom they've used or have seen your work on other projects. Knowing how to apply great makeup isn't enough.

So how do I get work?

Starting at a makeup school is a good way to begin meeting people. Work on freebies and low-budget projects whenever the opportunities arise. There are schools and workshops that teach basic cosmetics available in almost every major city. Look for student films and other low-budget films or productions at local universities with film and theater programs.

Another way of breaking in is through a special effects shop. Learning how to create and apply prosthetics and other specialty makeup can be a ticket onto a working set and subsequently into the union. There are fewer people doing special effects makeup than straight beauty makeup, but nearly every project needs the latter, whereas only a few need the former. Take your growing portfolio around to any and all who have the time to meet with you.

WHAT AM I GETTING MYSELF INTO?
So who actually calls and hires me?

You may be referred by Actors who have liked you and your work in the past or by Producers and Directors who remember you. You may get a call from any one of them asking if you're available.

Okay, what now?

If you are the Key Makeup Artist or the head of an effects shop, you will meet with the Director and Producers during preproduction to agree on the "look" that the makeup or the makeup effects need to achieve. Straight beauty makeup may take just a few days of tests to solidify. If there are any makeup effects or full-scale creature/mask builds to complete, that process may begin two months or more prior to the first day of shooting.

What will my life really be like?

5:42 A.M.—GET TO WORK

General crew call is 7:00 A.M., but you arrive earlier than the majority of the crew because the lead Actress needs an hour to get THROUGH THE WORKS. If there is a special makeup application or there are a lot of Extras that day, your call may be as early as 3:00 or 4:00 A.M.

6:00 A.M.—"THROUGH THE WORKS"

The Actors have to go through Hair, Makeup, and Wardrobe, so depending on what kind of wardrobe the Actors will be wearing and what the hairstyles will be, you may or may not get the talent in your chair first. When you do get them, though, you need to work quickly and confidently. Actors have a lot on their minds, so don't engage in idle chitchat unless they initiate it.

7:00 A.M.—GETTING TO SET

About this time, the Second AD or DGA Trainee will knock on the Makeup trailer door. No matter what state of readiness the Actors are in, they will be asked to go to set for rehearsal. There will be time afterward for them to return to BASE CAMP to finish going through the works.

7:05 A.M.—REHEARSAL

Depending on just how much you had to finish on their faces, you could either wait in the trailer until they return or follow them to set so you can finish touching up right there. Either way, you'll want to see them eventually in the light to be used on set to make sure your application will look the way it's supposed to on camera.

7:15 A.M.—CAMERA SETUP

As soon as the Director and DP have seen all they need, the Actors step off set as the SETUP is built. This is your time to finish the makeup either in the trailer or on set. Once finished, you'll want to gather together your on-set kit, as you'll be staying close by for touchups all day long.

7:40 A.M.—FINAL TOUCHES

When everyone is happy with the setup, the First AD will call for FINAL TOUCHES. This is when you, the Hair Stylist, and the Costumer spring into action. Take your makeup over to the Actors and do a once-over on your previous makeup application. The Actors will probably be talking with others or rehearsing their lines to themselves, so this is not a time for idle chat. Get in, do your thing, and get back out. At this point, everybody else on set is waiting for you to finish and get out of the way.

7:45 A.M.—ROLL CAMERA

Keep an eye on the Actors during the take. Make mental notes if they do anything to their makeup that will require a touchup, such as if they wipe their brows or sneeze. Some on-camera talent tend to sweat a lot when under hot lights, so you're also watching to make sure they don't become too shiny, particularly during long takes.

7:48 A.M.—CUT, LET'S GO AGAIN

If you noticed anything that necessitates a touchup, head toward the Actor and wait for an opening. He may need to have a discussion with the Director, the DP, or the other Actors. Be patient and wait until he's done. Don't worry if it seems to take a while. The Actors know you are there and everyone else will wait until you've completed your task.

8:10 A.M.—CUT, MOVIN' ON

Usually this means the Director has at least two takes that she likes. The Actors will usually stay to do a quick blocking rehearsal and then step off while the next setup takes place. If it's a big change from one scene to another, you may have to completely redo someone's makeup. The Second AD will help guide the talent back to base camp so that you can work on them. Most of the time however, you'll find that the makeup application you do at the start of the day is the one that stays on until wrap. You're just there to do touchups whenever necessary.

1:00 P.M.—LUNCH

Head to lunch like everyone else. Know that when you get back to work, the Actors have been eating, too, so the makeup will need to be examined.

2:00 P.M.—BACK TO WORK

The second half of the day is much like the first, as everyone moves from one setup to the next. As the day wears on, the Actors may grow tired. The last thing they need is you constantly in their faces. Go in to do touchups only when you must.

9:00 P.M.—WRAP

Once wrap is called, the Actors will want to get out of there as fast as they can. They'll come to you in the makeup trailer so you can remove anything you've been putting on them all day. Straight beauty makeup shouldn't take too long to deal with, but any prosthetics or special applications obviously are more involved. Work swiftly, but carefully. Avoid injuring the talent or damaging their skin in any way.

WHAT I REALLY WANT TO DO IS MOVE UP!

Moving up from being a Makeup Artist to becoming a Key is all about having the skill, experience, and confidence to handle the logistics of heading up a department as well as letting others feel very comfortable with you and your abilities. Everyone who is working on set contributes to the project in one way or another, but it is your work that the audience will be looking at the most. If you've done a great job, they shouldn't even notice you were ever there.

But almost more important, it is how you interact with everyone on set that leaves a lasting impression. Building strong and sincere relationships is the key to longevity and a successful career.

Chapter 12

What I Really Want to Do Is Hair!

WHAT THE HECK IS A HAIR STYLIST?

The Hair Stylist is responsible for creating and maintaining the look and continuity of hairstyles for Actors. You need to know the basics of how to do various cuts and styles as well as how to apply extensions and wigs.

That, and what else?

Officially, your job along with the Makeup Artist is to make the TALENT look good, or at least appropriate to the requirements of the script. Because you are among the first people that the Actors and Actresses come into contact with each day, you also have some influence over their general mood. If an Actress comes in upset and you can put her at ease, then the day will be that much more pleasant for the other fifty-plus people on set. If an Actress leaves your trailer feeling grumpy or worse than she did when she arrived, the work environment may be negatively affected for everyone. To that end, you and the Makeup Artists actively do whatever is possible to create a calm and pleasant atmosphere inside the trailer and out.

Will I make more money than if I just stay in the salon?

In general, yes. In addition to your hourly rate, you'll also make between $50 and $100 per day for your kit. For a standard twelve-week feature, a Key Hair Stylist can expect to make about $30,000. The department head will make around $40,000 for the same twelve weeks. Often, those in the Makeup department make a little bit more per hour than you will, but sometimes the Key Hair Stylist can negotiate similar rates for everyone in the trailer.

WHAT DO I REALLY NEED TO KNOW?

Unlike working in a salon, where you see a new client every thirty minutes, you will be working intimately with just one or two Actors and Actresses over the course of twelve weeks or more.

As a Hair Stylist in California, you'll need to have a current cosmetologist license to work anywhere, including a movie set. You'll also be required to obtain this license for membership in the union. After you complete your schooling, application forms are available online at www.barbercosmo.ca.gov/formspubs/examapp.pdf. In addition, a union Key Hair Stylist is required to attend training classes covering basic hairstyling techniques, such as pin curling, lace fronts, finger waves, and wig placement. These are two six-week courses held over six Saturdays.

If there are extensive makeup effects to be applied to an Actor, hair often also gets special attention. Sometimes you might have to cover the real hair completely with a prosthetic (a latex application) and then apply a wig. If the requirements are very complicated and time-consuming, an effects specialist will be brought in so that you will still have time for the principal talent.

WHAT DO I REALLY NEED TO HAVE?
Do I have to bring all the stuff from the salon with me?

If you think of the trailer as a salon on wheels, you'll realize how portable you need to be. You're going to have an array of sprays, pins, irons, brushes, and combs that will stay in the trailer. You'll also have a smaller set bag with just the essentials that you'll take to set for minor touch-ups between takes.

What's the best way for someone to reach me?

If you are member of IATSE Local 706, the union that represents Hair and Makeup Artists in Hollywood, you are required to place your name on their AVAILABLE LIST when you aren't working. If a show is in need of someone and none of the regulars is available, the Key will call the Local office and request help from the list. Otherwise, keep in touch with everyone you've worked with before.

WHERE DO I REALLY NEED TO GO?
I just want to work.

If you are coming from a salon career, you already have experience in styling hair. To work regularly in the motion picture industry, you have to develop an understanding of how a movie set works and the proper way to work within it. Gain that experience by first getting jobs on low-budget independent projects and student films.

When you are ready to work on larger jobs with more pay, you'll want to join IATSE Local 706. There are two ways to join. The first is called 60/60/60 and means that you must complete sixty days of nonunion work per year for three years. You must complete that work within five years from the first day you were hired on that first job.

The second way to join 706 is called "off-roster hire." You can qualify for this method if you are hired on a union project for a minimum of thirty days. This generally only happens if all the union members are already working and the Producers have no other choice than to bring you in. You can also qualify if the nonunion show that you are working on turns union in the midst of production. Go to the local 706 website for more information.

So how do I get work?

If you are looking to join the union, call the local office consistently without being too annoying just to remind them that you are out there and available. Because of the licensing issue (hair needs a license and makeup doesn't), the hair department has about half as many members as makeup, so you might get lucky and call the day that the BOOKS ARE EMPTY. You'll be in the salon one day and finally on a Hollywood set the next.

When you are working in the industry as a member of Local 706, you are required to attend regular membership meetings. The meetings are a good place to network and meet new people who might be able to help you later on.

WHAT AM I GETTING MYSELF INTO?
What do I wear?

You're not the one in front of camera, so you shouldn't aim to be a fashion icon, but you do want to appear professional and confident. You're working behind the scenes for hours upon hours, so you have to be comfortable and casual with a sense of style that projects that you can do the same for someone else. However, you must also wear clothes and shoes that are safe and appropriate for working on a soundstage or rugged exterior location. Closed-toe shoes, denim jeans, and T-shirts are what most crew members wear to work.

Who calls me?

The Key Hair Stylist will get calls from Producers, Directors, Unit Production Managers, Makeup Artists, and even Actors who have special requests. As the Key, you'll still have to submit a résumé, but being on someone's wish list tends to give you priority over others who may be in line for the job.

If you are a Stylist, you will receive a call from a Key Hair Stylist who has either worked with you previously or has received your name from others who know you. You never know where your next job will come from.

Now what?

When you are the Key Hair Stylist, once you are hired, there will be a prep period of one week to several months, depending upon the complexity of the project. In that time, the Director will work with the Production Designer, Costume Designer, Key Makeup and Key Hair Stylist to design looks for the Actors. About a week prior to production, the Director of Photography will film camera tests so everyone can see how the choices actually appear on screen. The Key will also hire her crew of Hair Stylists and complete any additional shopping for supplies that are necessary.

What will my life really be like?

5:42 A.M.—GET TO WORK

Your first talent arrives at 6:00 A.M. so you need time to get to your trailer and settle in before he or she arrives. In general, women take longer than men to get THROUGH THE WORKS (women can take up to two hours to make it through Hair, Makeup, and Wardrobe, while men might require as little as thirty minutes). Your in-time will vary depending on who is coming and when. On a day with plenty of extras scheduled for work, additional Hair Stylists will be brought in to help.

6:00 A.M.—"THROUGH THE WORKS"

You'll be trading Actors and Actresses with Makeup and Wardrobe throughout the morning. While one Actor is sitting on one side of the trailer getting his make-up done, you'll have the Actress in your chair while you style her hair. Then you switch.

7:00 A.M.—GETTING TO SET

The major work is done, but you still need to stick close by for touchups. Follow the talent to set and take your set bag with you.

You'll also find that you have a lot of downtime as the Actors rehearse and everyone else gets the set ready to shoot. Bring along a lightweight portable chair in which to base yourself as you wait patiently. It's okay to read a book or magazine, but don't get too wrapped up in it, as you need to pay attention to what is going on with the Actors.

7:05 A.M.—REHEARSAL

For the most part, your work is finished, so you'll just be standing by for touch-ups. However, keep an eye on the rehearsal in case the action somehow affects the Actor's hair, such as in a fight scene. Don't just watch the Actor from one side of the set. Check the monitors at VIDEO VILLAGE to see how his hair looks from different camera angles.

7:15 A.M.—CAMERA SETUP

If the rehearsal took place before the Actors had finished going through the works, you may have to follow them back to base camp to finish getting them ready. Find out from the AD Department how long the SETUP will take and have the Actors ready to go within that amount of time.

7:40 A.M.—FINAL TOUCHES

When the set is ready to shoot, the First AD will call for FINAL TOUCHES or LAST LOOKS. The Actors will stand by for any final notes from the Director while you, Makeup, and Wardrobe move in to make sure everything on the Actors is the way it should be.

7:45 A.M.—ROLL CAMERA

Once things get moving, your work is mostly finished. Watch the monitors for a take or two just to know that the action isn't ruining the look that you established.

7:48 A.M.—CUT, LET'S GO AGAIN

Stay close to set and check in on the Actors between takes to make sure everything is still where it should be. If you have to go in for touchups, find an appropriate time. When you're reasonably certain that the look has been established one or two takes in, pull out your digital camera and take a photo for continuity.

8:10 A.M.—CUT, MOVIN' ON

If the camera is just TURNING AROUND to look the other way and your Actor is not on camera for the next shot, you can relax a bit. If you are moving on to a whole new scene, the Actors will head to base camp and you may have to redo their hair. At the very least, they will require touchups before the cameras roll again.

1:00 P.M.—LUNCH

You can eat with the crew or go back to your trailer for a quieter environment.

2:00 P.M.—BACK TO WORK

The second half of the day moves along similarly to what was happening before lunch.

9:00 P.M.—WRAP

Remove any special hair ornaments, barrettes, or wigs from the Actors or Extras as soon as you can. Removing a wig can take some time as you need to clean up the Actor and then remove makeup and glue from the hairpiece.

WHAT I REALLY WANT TO DO IS MOVE UP!

While there is no direct route to any other position apart from moving up to being the Key, if you find you'd like to expand your horizons, moving to the other side of the trailer to do makeup could be a viable option.

Another possibility for your career is to become a "personal" Stylist for a specific Actor or Actress. This situation arises when you and that person form a special relationship. Keep in mind that this can't be forced. If it happens, you could benefit from the talent's success.

Whatever you choose to do, just enjoy where you are and do the very best job you can every time someone sits in your chair.

Chapter 13

What I Really Want to Do Is Props!

WHAT THE HECK IS PROPS?

Anything an Actor uses or touches, or is an accessory to the wardrobe, is a prop. The Property Master BREAKS THE SCRIPT DOWN and derives a list of everything specifically mentioned that an Actor actually uses. In contrast, Set Decorators are responsible for everything else that is seen on set but not touched or used by an Actor.

That, and what else?

Sometimes items are merely alluded to in the script or just assumed to be on set, such as silverware at the dinner table or a pen on a desk. The Prop Master needs to anticipate everything that could potentially be used and have it standing by.

The lines of responsibility can get blurry between the Property Department, set dressing, and wardrobe. If an Actor handles, uses, removes, or adjusts an object it becomes a prop. If an Actor wears a watch as an identity piece, then it's wardrobe. Once he takes it off during a scene, it's a prop. If an Actress wears a string of pearls, it's wardrobe. If the string of pearls has to break, it's a prop. If flowers are handled, they are props. If they are in a vase on a table, they are set dressing. If the flowers are used in a hairpiece, they're either wardrobe or hair. In the case of an eating scene, the On-Set Dresser will redress the table, but the Property Department is responsible for the actual food and must employ a specific food handler. Got the idea?

The Prop Department is also responsible for all of the Directors' chairs that are used on set. Your department keeps them on your truck, pulls them out every day, moves them from setup to setup if necessary, and then puts them all away at night.

I'm just in charge of "stuff"? I get paid for that?

Of course! That "stuff" can be just as important as the dialogue a character speaks. You have to find all of it, maintain it, track continuity throughout a twelve-week shooting schedule, and then return it all to where it came from. For that, you'll make about roughly $40,000 for a typical movie.

WHAT DO I REALLY NEED TO KNOW?

You'll get a lot of guidance from the Production Designer and Costume Designer about how things should look overall, but it will be useful for you to have your own awareness of items that have been used in a variety of cultures, from various eras in history.

WHAT DO I REALLY NEED TO HAVE?
Every movie is different, so isn't everything just rented?

True, every story and character is unique. However there are some things that you will almost always need to have no matter what kind of movie you're working on.

For starters, you'll want some kind of electronic labeling machine. Once bought or rented props are obtained, you'll need to organize them into various "prop boxes" and properly label everything. You're also keeping track of continuity throughout the day and the entire project, so you'll be taking reference pictures of every setup that involves a prop. Polaroids were the camera of choice for a long time, but now a simple digital camera and a portable printer are preferred.

As your career builds, so will your personal kit of props. Some of the things that almost always get used from one film to the next include baby strollers, briefcases, eyeglasses, jewelry, bicycles, telephones... pretty much all of the mundane stuff that constitutes everyday life. You'll have to put these things into storage in between films, but you'll want them all close by when you do get on a movie, whether the script calls for them or not. You could easily spend upward of $100,000 over several years as you gather items. The good news is that you can earn $450 a week for the kit rental and another $500 a week for the trailer to carry it all.

Firearms are another very important set of items for which the Prop Department is responsible. A great many movies these days involve guns, so it is a requirement that the Prop Master be a licensed Armorer if he wants to handle firearms. You'll be fingerprinted and have a background check done on you before you get the official card from the federal government. It will cost you about $125 a year to maintain your license.

What's the best way for someone to reach me?

Keep your contact information current at the IATSE Local 44 office if you are a member of the union.

WHERE DO I REALLY NEED TO GO?
I just want to work.

You can certainly make a living in the low-budget nonunion world. If you want to work on larger projects and earn hours toward medical and pension benefits, you'll need to join IATSE Local 44. The downside is that there are well over six thousand members of Local 44 in a variety of departments, all of whom are allowed to move back and forth from one job to another. For example, if work in Props is slow, you could go work as a Set Decorator for one show and then back to Props again for your next job. The bottom line is that if you're a good person and pleasant to work with and also have a great eye for detail, you shouldn't have too much trouble maintaining a lucrative career.

So how do I get work?

Most of those who are actively working as Property Masters and Prop Assistants have had extensive experience as Set Decorators. You'll likely begin on low-budget nonunion projects helping to move furniture for the Art Department. If you find your interests point you specifically toward the Prop Department, working consistently with established Property Masters will give you the training, experience, and contacts you'll need to build a viable career and eventually join IATSE Local 44.

You might also consider getting work at a prop rental house. You won't be working on set, but you'll be learning how to track many different items as you pull props for shows and put things away. It's also a great way to meet Prop Masters.

WHAT AM I GETTING MYSELF INTO?
So who actually calls and hires me?

As a Property Master, you could receive a call from a Production Designer, Director, or Producer who has worked with you previously. That call could come as early as six months in advance of principal production or as late as the day before they need you on set.

Okay, I got the job. What now?

Go through the script and make note of absolutely every little thing that could be your responsibility as a prop. Then go through it again and make another list of the things that are not mentioned at all but most likely could or should be on screen.

Meet with the Director soon afterward to discuss any ideas she might have regarding anything special the characters might need. Go through the script line by line if necessary so that nothing is overlooked. You'll have a similar discussion with the Actors. You'll either call them up or go to their homes or offices or meet fittings to discuss what they have in mind. They may choose asses or a watch. Or an Actor may decide that he should be scene. The Director must approve of these decisions, but it will to obtain enough of the proper type of cigarettes or whatever that Actor will want to use on screen (and possibly off).

You then meet with all the relevant department heads with whom you're going to work. The Costume Designer and you will discuss jewelry, watches, and other clothing accessories to determine whether property will handle them or if some of the items should belong to wardrobe or even hair. You'll have similar conversations with the Set Decorator as you discuss every set and who will have which responsibilities on each. You'll be finished with wardrobe fairly early on, but you'll have constant contact with the Set Decorators throughout the show.

The Special Effects Department will also work closely with you in the event there is a specific "gag" or effect that needs to be achieved on set.

Now that you know what you need, sit down and create a budget, adding a little extra for unexpected contingencies. Some of the things may already be in your personal kit. You won't charge the company individually for those items as you are already being paid a KIT RENTAL for anything that is in there. For everything else, you'll have to find the items, buy them, rent them, or manufacture them. Get your budget approved by the Unit Production Manager (UPM).

The Prop Master will hire a Prop Assistant around the second week of prep. As you both gather what you need, you'll create individual containers for each scene. About two weeks before production begins, another assistant will be hired to help do final pickups, organize the containers, and load everything onto the truck.

Your prep time will vary greatly depending on the show. If there are some complicated items to manufacture, such as futuristic ray guns or other nonexistent gizmos, you might have up to five months to get everything approved and built. Or you might only get five weeks to pull it all together. Of course there are constant script changes, so you have to stay on top of that and adjust your own plan accordingly during prep and all throughout production. This will affect your budget, which is why you've built in a little cushion.

What will my life really be like?

6:42 A.M.—GET TO WORK

The assistants will arrive about eighteen minutes earlier than the general crew call to give time for pulling carts, props, and chairs off the truck. You'll have several containers for the day—one for each Actor and one for each scene to be shot.

7:00 A.M.—GETTING TO SET

The Property Master arrives and double-checks that everything that should be on set actually is out and ready to go.

7:05 A.M.—REHEARSAL

If the scene requires any props at all, you should already be aware of what is needed and have them out and ready to go. Work with the Director, the Actors, and the On-Set Decorator to determine where each prop should be placed.

7:15 A.M.—CAMERA SETUP

The master is usually shot first, so what was decided during the rehearsal probably won't change anything you were planning. Just keep an eye on walls and set dressing that might be moved to accommodate film equipment as this might affect your work.

7:45 A.M.—ROLL CAMERA

Watch each take carefully for continuity as Actors may be moving props from one part of the set to another.

7:48 A.M.—CUT, LET'S GO AGAIN

The Director decides to do the shot over, which means that everything and every person goes "BACK TO ONE." Retrieve the props from the Actors and place them back where they are supposed to begin.

8:10 A.M.—CUT, MOVIN' ON

When you are reasonably certain that the Director has a take that she likes, jump in and shoot a snapshot of the set and pieces of it that involve your props. Each scene is usually cut into a variety of pieces, and as the "coverage" is shot, you'll want to make sure that your props are where they are supposed to be. Paying attention to every minute detail is incredibly important; otherwise props or set dressing will appear to jump from one place to another as the angles are cut together to make the entire scene.

1:00 P.M.—LUNCH

You may want to attend the dailies session with other department heads, but typically you will just go to lunch.

2:00 P.M.—BACK TO WORK

Your entire day consists of having the necessary props available on set when they are needed as well as keeping track of their continuity. You'll also be working with food stylists (in the case of an eating scene) or cleaning up the set, if, for example, there is fake blood splattered around after a fight or gun battle.

During your prep time, you'll do your best to anticipate any props that might be called for, but sometimes surprises pop up out of nowhere because the Director or an Actor suddenly has a brilliant new idea. If you're in Los Angeles, dealing with the unexpected is a little easier because prop rental houses are usually nearby. You can probably have a new prop on set within twenty minutes or so. If the film is out on location, you have to take extra care to plan for the unexpected.

9:00 P.M.—WRAP

As wrap approaches for the night, the assistants can begin prepping the containers for the next day based on the preliminary CALL SHEET. If there are any concerns, you'll want enough time before wrap to ask questions and obtain anything that might not already be on the truck.

When the entire film has been shot, you'll have to wrap up your inventory of props. Photograph, box, and label everything that was ever used for the past few months. The Transportation Department will take all of those boxes to a studio warehouse, where they will sit until they are needed for potential reshoots. This wrap process could take up to four weeks or more. If any of the props used were specialized just for this project, the Producers may want some of them packed for marketing purposes at press events or theater screenings.

WHAT I REALLY WANT TO DO IS MOVE UP!

As an assistant, you'll be learning how to break a script down, anticipate those things that aren't specifically asked for by the script or the Director, obtain items in the most efficient and economical way, and work on a set. When you feel ready to take on all the responsibilities of being a Prop Master, you may get referred by Prop Masters with whom you've worked previously if they are unable to do a show. While you train for the technical demands of the job, you'll also meet others in the industry who may have the influence to hire you later. Work hard, pay attention, and be a genuinely nice colleague and opportunities to advance your career will present themselves sooner or later.

Part III

THE DIRECTOR'S UNIT

What I Really Want To Do Is…

PA

Train For The DGA

Second Assistant Direct

First Assistant Direct

Unit Production Manage

Direct

Script Supervise

Chapter 14

What I Really Want to Do Is PA!

WHAT THE HECK IS A PA?

PA is short for "Production Assistant." Generally seen as a catch-all entry-level position, the PA is one of the most vital, if arguably nonspecific, jobs necessary to keep the production machine running. Depending on the type of production, a Production Assistant could be doing anything from making copies in the office to carrying sandbags with the Grips. For the purposes of this book, the concentration will be on the Set and BASE CAMP Production Assistant as they pertain to on-set work in feature films.

The PA's primary duty is to assist the Assistant Directors with whatever they need. Again, the range of responsibilities can be wide, but for the most part, you'll either be helping to get talent to the set or helping to LOCK UP the location when the camera rolls. If you aren't doing one of those things, you may be distributing paperwork to various departments, handing out fresh walkie-talkie batteries to crew members, or getting coffee for the Director.

On a movie set, there are typically three PAs: a Key PA, a Base Camp PA, and a Background PA. The Key PA is in charge of the PAs. Additional PAs are hired as necessary, if, for example, there are a lot of Extras or a need for extra bodies to help lock up a location.

Usually the ADs go to the Key PA with requests that the Key then delegates to the other PAs. Otherwise, the Key PA will be on the set, standing near the First AD, ready to do whatever is needed.

The Base Camp PA deals with anything that happens in the AD trailer and in base camp. This PA helps to keep track of Actors who have gone to their trailers and may even be asked to invite them to set when the crew is ready. She also works with the Second AD on paperwork, such as call sheets for the cast and crew. The Base Camp PA can be the liaison between the main production office and the set.

The Background PA helps to shepherd any Extras who are hired for the day. She guides them from Makeup and Wardrobe to the set when they are needed. If there is no BACKGROUND for the day, she stands by to assist the other PAs.

The positions are interchangeable; you can be a Set PA on one show and a Base Camp PA on the next and a Background PA after that. You may really enjoy working on set, but it's in your best interest to learn how to do all the positions to make yourself more valuable to those who wish to work with you.

That, and what else?

The Production Assistant is one of the few jobs on set that doesn't require union membership (on a union studio production). As result, there are some things that the PA really isn't allowed to do (per DGA guidelines) when helping out the AD and Production departments, such as inviting talent to set or distributing some types of paperwork. However, you'll find that you wind up doing some of that anyway if for no other reason than to facilitate the greater needs of production. Technically, the DGA Trainee (if there is one), the Second Second AD (if there is one) or the Second AD should be handling a lot of the things that may get tossed into your lap. But "FEEDING THE CAMERA" is the AD department's number one priority, and helping to accomplish their job is yours.

While you don't really need particular skills to be a Production Assistant, what you do require is the willingness to do just about anything asked, even if it somehow seems beneath you. If you do have a special skill or talent, in time it will be recognized as long as you show up to be the best PA you can be. Going in with a bad attitude will only keep you from getting work and meeting the people who will help advance your career.

No skill necessary? Entry level? I'm afraid to ask what the pay is like.

As you've already guessed, it's not the greatest. On a decent-sized union movie, expect to earn between $130 and $150 for twelve hours. The upside is that you get overtime after twelve (based on the prorated ten-hour rate), and you almost always will be working a fourteen-hour day.

WHAT DO I REALLY NEED TO KNOW?

Unskilled doesn't mean uneducated. The more you know about film in general and set protocol specifically, the better you'll be at your job and the more valuable you'll be to those who depend on you.

Along with the ADs, you are there to take in information and disseminate it to those who need it. To do that, you have to know what information means. For instance, if you overhear the Prop Master or the Transportation Captain tell the First AD that he will be putting a vehicle on the stage after wrap for the next day, you should recognize how that may affect other departments and let each of them know. It might be as simple as sound or camera having to move their carts to the side, or as complicated as alerting construction for safety concerns. While you'll always want to check with the ADs first before solving a problem that might not really exist, in general, you'll need to stay aware of what is going on in the present while being mindful of the future in order to keep the production machine running at peak efficiency.

WHAT DO I REALLY NEED TO HAVE?
I do everything, but I don't really do anything specific.
What could I possibly need?

Not much, but a couple of things will help you out during the day.

Most productions either provide you with headsets that are bulky and uncomfortable or with no headsets at all. You'll want to purchase a surveillance headset to take with you from job to job. You'll have this on for sixteen hours a day, so comfort is a priority. This will cost you around $80 from a professional audio supply dealer. When you're only making $150 a day, this may seem like a lot, but remember that you can write it off on your taxes at the end of year, and it's something that you'll keep with you from one job to the next.

You'll want to carry one black and one red Sharpie marker with you at all times. These are needed primarily to make changes on the call sheet if there is a PUSHED CALL, which means that the call time printed on the call sheet has been changed to a later time in the day. Also carry at least two pens. Have one that you can hand out (there will always be someone turning to you for one), and keep one tucked away that you never hand out no matter what because you will always need a pen. Also keep a small notepad handy. You'll always be writing down a random request, a lunch order, in- or out-times, or passing on some pertinent information that has to be exactly right. The production itself should be able to supply you with all of these EXPENDABLES.

What's the best way for someone to reach me?

You could get a call to come in to work on a new job thirty minutes *after* they need you. Assuming you really do want to work as much as possible, get a cellular phone and keep it on at all times. Also have some business cards to hand out. They don't need to be fancy. You just need a way to hand out your name and number quickly and conveniently to those with whom you work. And by all means, if your number changes, let everyone know about it. They won't spend too much time trying to track you down.

WHERE DO I REALLY NEED TO GO?
I just want to work.

As with everyone else in this business, the people you know or who have heard of you will be the ones making your phone ring. The more people who like you and the way you work, the more opportunities you'll have. It sounds painfully simple, yet that is exactly the way it happens. Once you've gotten your first job on a movie set and have shown yourself to be a great person and a hard worker, it all branches out from there.

That's it. No secrets. No shortcuts. Just work hard and be a nice person who others will remember when it comes time for them to call someone to help them. Remember, they need someone, but not necessarily you. Developing your skills and making yourself invaluable almost guarantees success no matter what it is you really want to do.

So how do I get work?

Just about anywhere you find a film or video production happening, you'll find at least one PA working on it. When you are completely new to the business, your first task is to learn something about the logistics of a set. Reading this book from cover to cover is a very good start. Afterward, you need to find a production—any production—to go work on to get some practical real-world experience. Because you're fresh off the boat, you may need to work for free initially. Remember, nobody knows you and you really don't know much yet, so volunteering your services isn't unreasonable. But once you feel comfortable in a production environment and have some reliable contacts who can call you or refer you to others, you shouldn't be expected to work for nothing.

WHAT AM I GETTING MYSELF INTO?
So who actually calls and hires me?

Your call usually comes from the person who has worked with you before. This could be an Assistant Director, a Production Coordinator, a Producer, or even another PA. There is always a need for good PAs, so whomever you impressed in previous jobs will likely remember you and give you another opportunity.

Okay, I got the job. What now?

As mentioned, you might be called in at the very last minute. If this is the case and you're available, drop everything and get to set ready to work. Typically though, you'll be called with a little more lead-time than that. Office PAs will be hired to help the office staff during the months of preproduction.

About a week before actual production begins, all the department heads gather for a production meeting. One of the set PAs will help the ADs prepare for the meeting. This week is spent getting things ready for set, making copies for meetings, assembling and organizing walkie-talkies, and setting up the office equipment in the AD trailer. This prep period can be as short as a day or as long as three weeks or more depending on what they need.

What will my life really be like?

5:30 A.M.—GET TO WORK

The lead Actress comes in at 6:00 A.M., so the Hair and Makeup Artists will be arriving at 5:42 A.M. to get ready for her. The Base Camp PA shows up a few minutes before that with the Second AD to make sure everything goes smoothly.

6:00 A.M.—"THROUGH THE WORKS"

If you are at a new location, the PAs and ADs will get the trailer set up and paperwork distributed to the various departments as they all arrive during the next hour. If, however, you are returning to the same set or stage day after day (usually at the end of a schedule), your in-time can be a bit later, as everything pretty much remains ready from the days before.

7:05 A.M.—REHEARSAL

The Director is ready to run a rehearsal with the Actors on set. Regardless of anything else you have to do, once the First AD calls for quiet, the PAs spread out and "lock it up." This means that every PA on stage and outside the stage doors shouts out loudly "Quiet for rehearsal!" The goal here is for all personnel to be silent. When attacking this task, remember: This is no time to be meek.

7:15 A.M.—CAMERA SETUP

The First AD will call out "Cut on rehearsal," and you will repeat it loudly to everyone within earshot. This is important so that everyone knows that they can now get to work and make noise while setting up the shot or doing whatever else they need to do.

While setup goes on, you'll continue distributing paperwork, keeping track of talent, and doing whatever the ADs ask you to do.

A few minutes before the Director of Photography is ready, the First AD will call to base camp and ask that the talent be invited back to set. The Base Camp PA may be the one to do this if there isn't a DGA Trainee or Second AD available. This is as simple as going to each trailer, knocking on the door, and waiting for a response. It is imperative that the talent be aware of when they are needed. Again, this is no time to be shy. When the Actor comes to the door, be pleasant, confident, and direct by saying something like, "Mr. Cruise, they're ready for you." Actors are people with a job to do, just like you. If an Actor doesn't come to set, it shouldn't be because he wasn't aware that he was called for.

As the talent emerge from their trailers one by one, the Base Camp PA discretely radios updates to the PAs and the ADs about the Actors' whereabouts. This may sound something like, "Number one (on the call sheet) is on his way in."

Using call sheet numbers for announcements instead of names also serves to foil paparazzi or anyone else who may be listening in on your radio frequencies.

At this point, one of the Set PAs will be on the lookout for "number one" and report it on the radio when he's spotted with an, "I got him. He's heading to set." Think of it as a hand-off from one PA to the next to the next until the talent is where he is supposed to be. This has nothing to do with not trusting the talent and everything to do with helping the AD staff keep the day running at peak efficiency. If for some bizarre reason one of the Actors gets sidetracked between his trailer and his mark in front of the camera, it is the job of the AD Department, with the help of the PAs, to know what is happening, hopefully why, and how long it will hold things up. Every minute of a production day is enormously expensive, and every delay is costly. The ADs and the PAs working together as a team make everything converge in front of the camera at the same time.

7:45 A.M.—ROLL CAMERA

Very similar to the earlier rehearsal, but even more important, it is time to lock up the area again. The First AD will call out, "Put us on a bell," and the Sound Mixer will hit a button that rings a bell on stage. When this happens, all the PAs and ADs will call out loudly for "Quiet!" The First AD will say, "Roll sound!" to which the PAs call out loudly, "ROLLING!" At this point, anyone who is even close to the set should have no excuse for not knowing that they should keep quiet.

As the take is being filmed, the PAs keep a lookout for anyone who is making noise or anyone who wanders into the vicinity who might not be aware of what's going on. Your job during a take is to keep the filming area clear and quiet until the Director calls "Cut!"

7:48 A.M.—CUT, LET'S GO AGAIN

When you hear the Director or First AD yell, "Cut!" you need to repeat it loudly to everyone around you. Other work will always be taking place on the stage or around the set, and everyone has to know when it's okay to continue. If they decide to do the take again, lock down the area just like last time.

8:10 A.M.—CUT, MOVIN' ON

When the Director is finally happy with that setup, you'll hear something like, "Gate's good, movin' on!" from the First AD and on your walkie. Repeat that loudly as soon as you hear it.

1:00 P.M.—LUNCH

Something will always need to be done. On occasion, you'll be able to just sit and eat with the rest of the crew. Often, though, lunch is the time when the Director, the talent, and other important people catch up on work that they haven't been able to get to all morning. You may be asked to assist them in some way. You may also be asked to deliver box lunches to crew members who are going to view DAILIES.

Also, if there is no DGA Trainee assigned to do it, one of the Set PAs will stand by the lunch line and wait for the last person to go through. The reason for this is because while lunch is officially a half-hour, it is counted as thirty minutes after the last person goes through the line. So in reality, a typical lunch will run forty-five minutes or even an hour depending on the size of the crew. You make note of the time and report it to the Script Supervisor, who marks it in her own book. This time then makes it to the PRODUCTION REPORT, which is completed each day by the DGA Trainee or the Second AD. The First AD needs to be made aware of the proper in time so that he can announce over the walkies that "We are back!"

2:00 P.M.—BACK TO WORK

When you hear the First AD make the call over the radio, you repeat his words loudly so that everyone around you knows that it's time to get back to the set.

You'll continue the afternoon just as you did in the morning. And don't just wait around for somebody to tell you what to do. Be aware of what's going on around you and anticipate problems before they happen.

9:00 P.M.—WRAP

As wrap approaches, the First AD will approve the final call sheet for the next day and the Base Camp PA will make copies of it. If there is a company move to a location, a map will be stapled on every call sheet as well.

Sometimes, after the call sheet is already copied, the First AD changes the call time for the following day. When that happens, the PAs pull out their red Sharpies and correct every call sheet by hand before they are passed out to the crew.

Once the First AD calls out, "It's a wrap!" the PAs spread out and distribute call sheets to everyone on the crew. While you're doing that, you'll help the ADs by getting out-times for the production report from the departments. Again, you're there to help the ADs in whatever way you can, so be available and alert until you are told it is okay to go home.

When wrapping the entire show, your work will revolve around putting everything away. The walkies need to be accounted for, packed up, and given to the Transportation Department to be returned. The AD trailer needs to be wrapped out and all the office supplies sent back to their original source.

As a nonunion employee, one of the requirements to becoming a member of the DGA is to prove that you have industry experience. If you haven't been doing it during the course of the show, now is the time to make copies of every call sheet with your name on it, every production report, every pay stub, and every timecard from the entire show.

WHAT I REALLY WANT TO DO IS MOVE UP!

While being a PA puts you on a direct path to moving into the Assistant Directing Department, the job also gives you access and the opportunity to deal with everyone else on set and in the office environment as well. You do have your own job to accomplish, but it is expected that you won't be in this position forever and actually want to do something else. With that in mind, you are free to talk to others and observe what they do for a living. Many other crew members in every department began their careers as unskilled Production Assistants. Where and when you advance and how far you go is ultimately up to you. The more enthusiasm and devotion you illustrate as a PA, the more you'll impress those around you and the more likely you'll move up to bigger and better things.

Chapter 15

What I Really Want to Do Is Train for the DGA!

WHAT THE HECK IS A DGA TRAINEE?

For many years the only way a person could hope to be an Assistant Director in Hollywood was to either work his way up through the ranks after starting as a PA (Production Assistant) or by having relatives in the business.

Because of what was seen as a lack of diversity in the Production Department with respect to ability, race, and gender, the DIRECTOR'S GUILD OF AMERICA **(DGA)**, in conjunction with the ALLIANCE OF MOTION PICTURE AND TELEVISION PRODUCERS, created the DGA Trainee Program, specifically designed to give people from outside the Hollywood system the opportunity to join the industry.

Once accepted into the program, the DGA Trainee is placed onto a variety of actual working sets over the course of about two years as an assistant to the Assistant Directors (ADs) in the Production Department. You leave the program with a wealth of hands-on experience and a list of potential employers with whom you've now already worked.

Sounds great! Who do I have to know to get in?

Nobody. That's the point. No connections are required, no recommendations necessary, and there is no prerequisite for industry experience. However, admission into the program is highly competitive.

Applicants must be college graduates or have proof of professional film industry experience. And only around twenty to twenty-five people are chosen each year out of approximately one thousand who apply.

How do I compete against those odds? Why bother?

The alternative (and the reality for most applicants) is to make very little money while starting as a PA or by working as a Second AD on low-budget projects.

While the odds seem to be against you, there is very little to lose by applying and a lot to gain, as long as you're very sure that this is the department (and the industry) in which you'd like to work.

The goal of the program isn't just to train people how to be Assistant Directors but to train them to be *excellent* Assistant Directors. The incentive for the DGA is that they cultivate a better qualified group of people to do the job rather than only relying on chance that the nonunion environment will produce quality ADs. The strength that any guild trades on is that they can do things better than anyone else. Through training, a person can almost be guaranteed to come away with the breadth of experience that will prepare her to do the job well. This quality ultimately reflects back upon the DGA itself and encourages Producers to continue using its services.

What do I get to do?

In short, you'll be learning how to fulfill the duties of a Second Assistant Director. Or more to the point, you'll be doing the stuff that he'd have to do if you weren't around.

That, and what else?

You'll be spending *a lot* of time at work. The tradeoff is that in addition to learning more about your own department and what will be required of you, you'll get to interact with just about every other department and find out what they do as well. Ultimately, this knowledge will make you a more qualified *Producer* if you make it that far up the ladder.

Wait a sec. You just said "Producer." I want to be an Assistant Director because I want to direct eventually. Duh!

Right. The job titles are somewhat misleading. While it is true that Directors can come from anywhere inside the industry or out, the specifics of what you will learn in the AD Department are geared more toward logistics and management. If you happen to work your way through the department to become a Unit Production Manager (UPM), you will more likely find opportunities as a Producer after that. Anything is possible, but becoming an Assistant Director does not specifically train you to become a Director.

I've produced short films in school. Why can't I just move to Hollywood and get a job as a Producer there?

Unfortunately it doesn't work that way for the vast majority of aspiring filmmakers. There are a million things that a professional Producer should know before entering the major leagues of Hollywood big budgets. Unless you have significant family or industry contacts who can gift-wrap a producing career for you, learning the ropes through the Production Department is one way to go and being a DGA Trainee provides an excellent start.

Okay, okay. What do I need to do to get into the program?

Just like applying for college, you need to fill out an application form and pay a nominal registration fee. Paperwork (application, essays, payment) must be sent in by the November date as stated on the official website (www.dga.org) or by contacting the Guild office. Be sure to check the website for the latest information.

If your paperwork is in order, you're then invited to take an aptitude test the following January. If your test results put you into the top 120 (out of the approximately one thousand who apply and take the test in Los Angeles, New York, and Chicago), then you get to move to the next phase.

That May in Los Angeles, those 120 applicants meet for an "assessment." The essays that you wrote and included with your application now come into play, as well as any previous work, life, and/or military experience. Group activities take place, which measure your ability to work with others. Of those 120 applicants, only around fifty will move on to the next phase, which takes place the next week.

If you were one of the fifty chosen to advance, you'll get fifteen minutes in front of an industry panel that will bombard you with a variety of questions and scenarios to test your intelligence, ability to reason, and temperament. Based on those interviews, approximately twenty-five of those fifty people are chosen to become DGA Trainees. This number may vary slightly based on the amount of film and television production that is projected for the coming year.

After that, Trainees attend an orientation. Here, you will learn about the potential for ridiculously long hours and other pitfalls of the industry. For some, that reality doesn't sink in until they actually get on a real set and experience it for themselves. This occasionally results in applicants dropping out of the program, which is why several alternates are chosen as well. If you are not immediately chosen to be a Trainee, there is still a chance if you manage to become an alternate.

So, what? They just send me out on jobs?

Pretty much, yeah. You will be sent out for a total of four hundred days to work on a variety of different projects. It generally takes about two years to complete the program because the work is nonconsecutive. Random feature and television productions will put in requests to the Guild for DGA Trainees to be placed on their projects. When your number comes up, the program will send you to one of the shows for no more than a total of fifty days, after which time you will be sent to another show that desires the services of a Trainee. One variation is if you are working on a feature film. Often they prefer the consistency of having the same crew, so you will remain at that project for its entire run (which may be eighty days or so).

The point of all this moving around is to help you meet as many people and experience as many different kinds of production as possible. Some shows have a lot of stunts, others have a lot of child Actors, some are doctor shows, some have insanely high budgets, while some have budgets that are too small. As a career freelancer in this business, you mostly won't have the luxury of picking and choosing the specific shows you want to work on, so your longevity will depend on your ability to operate within every situation thrown at you.

Because of the nature of the business, there will be periods of days or weeks in which you will not be working on anything. As mentioned, it takes on average about two years to complete the four hundred days, which means that you will *not* be working for around 330 days in that time. Your mere survival is dependent on your ability to save the small amount of money that you do earn because you need to remain available at all times. A second job is out of the question. Unless you have some money saved before you enter the program, you'll likely have to share an inexpensive apartment to keep your overhead costs low and affordable.

In their first year of the program, Trainees are required to attend seminars the Guild presents every other weekend, whether you are working or not. Here, Trainees learn about the myriad rules and regulations that pertain to the various contracts for the unions (DGA, SAG, IATSE, Teamsters), as well as specifics regarding working with animals and children, stunts, and safety. If you are on a show that doesn't wrap until Saturday morning (after starting late on Friday), you still have to make it to the 10:00 A.M. meeting. Several seminars are held each Saturday so you may be there until 6:00 P.M. that evening. If your production works on Saturdays, they are required to release you for that time. After the seminar is completed, you usually are asked to return to work to finish out the day.

How much money will I make as a DGA trainee?

You will make a flat rate of $600 a week. The good news is that you receive overtime after ten hours, so on average, after taxes, expect to bring home about $650 a week ($2,600 a month).

You have to keep in mind that the program is four hundred days total, which are never consecutive. You won't be working on holidays like Christmas and New Year's Day. Plus, production usually slows down during the summer months, except for television pilots. If there are no shows or films requesting a Trainee then you will be unemployed for that time. However, you are expected to be "on-call." When a film comes up and the DGA wants you to go, you have to go. So save your money for the inevitable downtime.

WHAT DO I REALLY NEED TO KNOW?

To apply for the program, you have to have a college degree or some industry experience. But the idea behind the program is that you don't have to know anything about the film industry or know anyone in it before applying. However, your overall experience can be enhanced if you have some idea of what you're getting into beforehand. Aside from reading as much as you can about every aspect of the business, find some local production company around you and ask them, at the very least, if you could observe a shoot and perhaps even intern for a short time. Nothing beats hands-on experience, and you can find out right away if this is really the kind of work you want to be doing.

Long hours and low pay? Why would anyone want to do this?

That's a good question to ask, particularly *before* applying for the Trainee program. You must enjoy working with people and dealing with their problems all day. The AD Department spends hours upon hours creating schedules and call sheets knowing that things often do not turn out the way they planned. As things start to change, the appeal of the job is the ability to change with it...to move the puzzle pieces around and create the best fix so that the company does not have to stop shooting. You not only must embrace the chaos, but you also have to love it. The real challenge is when the plan falls apart and it is worthless. Now what do you do? People who hate that kind of scenario can't do the job. Those who love solving problems are perfect for this career.

WHAT DO I REALLY NEED TO HAVE?
I know nothing. What do I have to bring with me?

You'll need to buy a container-like tin, which the AD Department traditionally uses. It is essentially a lightweight yet durable metal folder where you will keep the daily paperwork. This will cost you around $20. Also bring along a pen and a couple of Sharpies. That's it.

What should I wear?

You are a walking office, so at the very least you'll need some kind of fanny pack to hold your supplies. A better idea is cargo pants or something with a lot of pockets. During the day you'll be hauling around receipts, petty cash, a cellular phone, walkie-talkie, pens, a stapler, paper clips, sunscreen, at least one call sheet, and SIDES (miniature version of the script pages to be shot that day). You don't want to dress like a slob, but you are also running around all day, so a certain casualness is expected. And invest in a pair of really comfortable shoes.

What's the best way for someone to reach me?

Because you're being "placed" on projects by the DGA, you won't be competing for jobs or DAY CALLS like other members of the crew. Regardless, there must be some way for you to be contacted at a moment's notice. You'll need at least one phone number that the Guild and each production can use to reach you, be it a home phone, cellular, pager, or an answering service. If you're relying on something other than a cell phone that you would have with you at all times, be sure to check for messages frequently, as production schedules can change without warning.

WHERE DO I REALLY NEED TO GO?
Production can happen anywhere. Do I really have to move?

Yes. While filming can and does occur all over the United States and the world, because of the nature of the program, you will have to move to Los Angeles. While some Trainees are placed onto feature films, the majority of the work will be on television shows, which film primarily on stages in Southern California. You must attend the seminars as well.

If you really have no desire to live in Los Angeles, an alternative is to move to New York City. The DGA does have an East Coast training program, but even fewer applicants are accepted than in L.A. Because of the unique nature of filming there, more PAs are required for traffic lockups and other tasks. For this reason, they don't rely as much on DGA Trainees to help with the work.

How do I start getting work?

Each fall, when television programs start filming again, production companies will put in requests to have a DGA Trainee join them. You will get a call with your assignment around that time.

WHAT AM I GETTING MYSELF INTO?
So who actually calls and hires me?

Someone with the training program will call you with your new assignment.

Okay, I got the job. What now?

Contact the Second AD as soon as you can and introduce yourself.

What will my life really be like?

5:30 A.M.—GET TO WORK

In most cases, you'll be working with the Second AD or the Second Second AD in the wee hours of the morning to greet people as they arrive. Because (in this example) an Actress needs one hour to get "THROUGH THE WORKS," her call time will be 6:00 A.M. Makeup, Hair, and Wardrobe departments will arrive eighteen minutes prior to setup. You want to beat them there to make sure Transportation or Security has unlocked all the trailer doors. As crew and cast arrive, you check them in on your PRODUCTION REPORT for that day, listing the exact times they showed up.

6:00 A.M.—"THROUGH THE WORKS"

All of the Actors have to get through Hair, Makeup, and Wardrobe before filming begins. It is your job to make sure they do all of this in the allotted amount of time. Accomplish this by establishing a friendly rapport and "inviting" them from place to place.

7:00 A.M.—GETTING TO SET

Actually, just prior to 7:00 A.M., the First AD on set will call you on the radio (walkie-talkie) and ask for "First Team." If you've done your job well and the Actors have been cooperative that morning, everyone should be ready to go. Knock on the appropriate trailer doors and invite them to go inside for a blocking rehearsal.

7:05 A.M.—REHEARSAL

As the DGA Trainee, your primary responsibilities will usually be at BASE CAMP. While rehearsal takes place inside on stage or outside on a set away from the trailers, your next duty is to finish off the production report from the previous day.

Production Report

During the course of every shooting day, someone in the Production Department has to fill out a production report. For a few reasons, this responsibility generally falls to the DGA Trainee. No one else has time to do it, and more to the point, no one else really wants to do it. The First AD is concentrating very heavily on *today*, making sure everything on set is running smoothly. The Second AD is concentrating on *tomorrow*, as he is drawing up the call sheet for the next day and helping you to feed the set with Actors. This leaves the business of *yesterday* to you.

The production report is a legal document that essentially gets the ball rolling on the financial aspects of the production. Cast, crew, equipment vendors, and anyone else providing goods or services to the production will be paid based on the information contained on each and every production report that gets filled out and submitted.

You have to find out and write down every in-, out-, and lunch time for each individual working on the project each day. You must also record any specific special equipment that may have been rented and used for a short period of time.

By looking at the production report, the executives back at the studio can quickly figure out how much each day of production costs and determine if the project is on budget.

7:15 A.M.—CAMERA SETUP

After rehearsal, the Actors will either go to their own trailers or return to finish up their hair and makeup. You need to keep track of their whereabouts at every turn.

7:35 A.M.—FIRST TEAM

A scant few minutes before the Director of Photography finishes lighting the set, the First AD will call on his radio for First Team. Just like before, it's your job to drop whatever paperwork you're doing and invite the principal Actors, Extras, and/or Stuntpeople to stage. Your number one priority of the day is to feed the set with whomever is needed.

7:45 A.M.—ROLL CAMERA

The First AD is on set next to the Director. The Second AD is most likely on or near set working on the call sheet for tomorrow. This leaves you and hopefully a small number of PAs to spread out in and around the set or soundstage to "lock up." This simply means that you are letting everyone in base camp and the vicinity of set know that sound and cameras are rolling.

7:48 A.M.—CUT, LET'S GO AGAIN

When the Director says, "Cut!" the First AD will repeat that on his radio. You then repeat it *loudly* to all who are near you. It's important that everyone outside is aware of when the camera rolls and cuts because a significant amount of work has to take place on other stages or nearby locations to prepare for later filming. Once everyone hears from you that the camera has cut, they will continue their work until the next time they hear you say "Rolling!"

8:10 A.M.—CUT, MOVIN' ON

A setup may require just one take or twenty. You never really know until it's done. But when the First AD hears from the Director that he has what he wants, the next thing you'll hear over the radio is "Movin' on." If the next setup is just a TURNAROUND on the previous action, the actors will probably exit the stage and head back to their trailers. If the next setup is a whole new scene, the Actors will most likely stay on set for the next rehearsal. If any additional Actors are needed who are still in base camp, the Second AD will have informed you earlier so that you can get them through the works. Again, the idea is that when the First AD calls for something or someone to come to the set, it or he/she will be ready. Invite them in and let the ADs inside know that the Actors are on their way.

8:15 A.M.—VISIT THE PRODUCTION OFFICE

By this time, you should have gathered any final out-times from the night before and recorded them on the production report. Hand the report to the Production Secretary or Production Coordinator at the office and then check for any paperwork that needs to be distributed back on set. While the Actors are on stage or in their trailers, you have to continue working on the report for the current day as well as tending to myriad other duties and a barrage of constant paperwork.

1:00 P.M.—LUNCH

If the company is on location or is providing lunch (via a caterer), then everyone working has to be back and ready to work thirty minutes after the last person passes through the line. The actual lunch break may in fact be closer to an hour long. But someone has to stand near the catering truck to watch for that last person through. The person watching is most likely going to be you. After writing down the time that the First AD called lunch, the next bit of info for your report is when this last person gets her lunch. Then you'll write down the time when the company was actually called back in.

2:00 P.M.—BACK TO WORK

Record the in-time and continue the second half of the day just like the first. Because you're representing the Production Department in base camp, anyone who isn't on set will be coming to you with his problems. When someone asks you for something or gives you some bit of information, your job is to be like a sponge. Gather all the information that you can and then squeeze it (disseminate it) out as quickly and efficiently as possible to everyone else who needs to know.

9:00 P.M.—WRAP

Actors, Extras, and Stuntpeople will pour from set and into base camp. The principal Actors will most likely know where to go and what to do in order to expedite their escape from work. Your bigger mission will be to shepherd the Extras to Wardrobe, where they will shed their costumes and then deal with their paperwork.

Finish as much of the production report as possible before the crew vanishes to their cars. The Script Supervisor will give you a sheet of paper, which tallies the progress that the company made that day through the script. The Second Camera Assistant or the loader will have paperwork, which breaks down the film totals for that day (how much stock was shot, what stocks were shot, current inventories, etc.)

In many cases, as the DGA Trainee, you'll get a lot more out of the experience by being around for as much of the shooting day as possible. For that reason, the Second AD will most likely want you to report for work no later than thirty minutes before crew call and then stay until the bitter end. Most shooting days aim for at least twelve hours (plus thirty minutes lunch), so you can expect to work at least a fourteen-hour day at minimum. On average, your day away from home will likely be around fifteen or sixteen hours because you'll be called in early (for makeup and hair) and leave late (because of location moves), plus drive time to and from work.

WHAT I REALLY WANT TO DO IS MOVE UP!

Well, you kind of have to. At the end of your four hundred days, the program says goodbye to you and you're on your own. Theoretically, you're now qualified to work as a Second AD. After all this time on all the different sets, the hope is that you've worked with enough people who will remember you as a hard worker who was easy to get along with. If not, then work can come from fellow Trainees who have gotten on shows that need additional help. Because there is just one DGA Trainee per project at a time, you are on your own during the process. The only time you'll see your fellow Trainees is after the seminars. Take that opportunity to socialize with them and build your network. You never know where your next job will come from.

Chapter 16

What I Really Want to Do Is Second Assistant Direct!

WHAT THE HECK IS A SECOND ASSISTANT DIRECTOR?

It is up to the Second Assistant Director (AD) to manage the day-to-day logistics of making the dizzying details all come together. The First AD created a best-case-scenario schedule in preproduction. Now, during production, the Second AD deals with the reality of limited time, unexpected weather, script rewrites, and every other element that is prone to change at a moment's notice.

While the First AD is on set, immersed in the minutia of each camera setup, the Second AD is off the set looking at the individual needs of each day, but a day in advance. In short, she is trying to make sure that whatever needs to be there *tomorrow* is coordinated *today*. She must ensure that whatever the First AD will need for each camera setup will actually be ready to go at the exact time it is needed. This includes everything from sets and special equipment to each person in the cast and on the crew.

That, and what else?

The entire production department is responsible for ensuring safety on the set by warning cast and crew when and how guns, smoke, fire, helicopters, or any other out-of-the-ordinary and/or dangerous elements will be used.

Geesh, it sounds like I won't even be working on the set at all.

Without the Second AD, nobody would be working on set. The Key Second is working all day long, every day during production, to create CALL SHEETS for the following days. The call sheet is the blueprint that everyone involved follows. It says who should show up to work, when and where they should go, and what they will be attempting to accomplish each day.

If that wasn't important enough, the Key Second AD is also building in contingencies in case what she plans doesn't, or can't, happen. This includes keeping in mind the scheduling of elements needed for shots that weren't achieved at the time they should have been. Not only is she concerned about the future, she also has an eye on the past so that nothing is missed.

And if she weren't doing enough yet, the Key Second AD must also keep an eye on the present. While the production may have a DGA Trainee, a cadre of Production Assistants, or even a Second Second AD on staff, ultimately the Key Second is responsible for making certain that Actors and other personnel are kept informed of the current needs of the day. In fact, while her work on the future scheduling is no doubt important, the highest priority is the present. The immediate needs of the set prevail over all. The whole point is to keep the company shooting, and concentrating too intently on the future at the expense of the present is counterproductive.

I must be making really good money then, right?

As the Second AD on a normal feature film you will work on average fourteen to sixteen hours every day for about thirteen weeks, sometimes longer. If you are working alone as a Key Second, there is no overtime until you reach thirteen hours. After the thirteenth hour, you'll get "half-check," which means that at four-hour intervals you'll get an additional day's pay. So at sixteen hours, you'll get an additional day's pay. At twenty hours you get another. At twenty-four hours, yet another, and so on (this does actually happen on occasion). In larger budget situations, when there are two Second ADs working, you won't get over-time until sixteen hours. Everything prior to the overtime hour (either thirteen or sixteen) is a flat rate. Whether you work one minute or thirteen hours, you'll get paid the same.

What all that boils down to is that for a five-day week, you'll make around $2,500. You can receive additional "bumps" for special circumstances.

WHAT DO I REALLY NEED TO KNOW?

If you're starting in a nonunion environment, the chances are still pretty good that you've had some previous set experience as a PA or in some other capacity. In the event you are given the opportunity to jump in with both feet as a Second AD, it will probably be on a very low-budget project where the paperwork requirements aren't as critical and the details you'll have to juggle won't be as numerous. Because entrance into the DGA training program is so competitive, the most traveled route to becoming an Assistant Director is through nonunion work. Just be prepared to work very little at first and for not a whole lot of money. The training program itself doesn't offer untold wealth, but a person who is fortunate enough to have that experience will likely have an easier time moving up the ladder quickly.

WHAT DO I REALLY NEED TO HAVE?
It sounds like I'm just talking to people.
What could I possibly need?

The Assistant Directors are the timekeepers for everything that happens during production, so if nothing else, you'll need a pen and a watch. Using the First AD's preliminary schedule as a guide, you will be creating a timetable of events *during* production and then doing everything in your power to ensure that it all comes together in front of the camera as planned.

In the past, schedules were created with a physical STRIP BOARD; however, a computer-scheduling program has proven to be far more efficient, particularly in television, where prior plans may change quickly. You'll need to have a reliable laptop computer and the necessary software.

What's the best way for someone to reach me?

Keep business cards handy with current phone numbers for those times you DAYPLAY as a Second Second AD. Because your job involves being in contact with just about everyone who needs to be on set and off, a cell phone may be a necessity for unexpected emergencies or schedule changes.

WHERE DO I REALLY NEED TO GO?
I just want to work.

The obvious answer is to go where the work is. The DGA has divided the United States into three areas: Los Angeles, New York City, and the Third Area, which is everywhere that isn't Los Angeles or New York. Los Angeles is the place to start, especially if you manage to get into the DGA training program. If you start out in New York, you'll most likely begin as a Production Assistant rather than as an AD or a Trainee because of the nature of production in the city. In Los Angeles, there are more sound stages and studio backlots as opposed to New York City, where the need for more location LOCKUPS requires more PAs.

To work on the really big shows, you'll have to become a member of the union, and there are four ways to do that. The first is to work four hundred nonunion days in a guild-type capacity (e.g., work as a nonunion AD or as a Production Assistant performing AD duties), where you do things like make call sheets and wrangle the cast to the set. Your name must appear on a call sheet and the production report. Although a small number of non-paid days can be used toward the four hundred days, you'll have a better chance to prove yourself by having pay stubs from a majority of that work.

The second way to get into the union is to be grandfathered in. This simply means that the nonunion show that you are working on suddenly becomes unionized. You're not entirely home free in that situation. You still must work the required four hundred days on that show to fulfill this requirement. Retroactive days on that grandfathered show only count if the pay is also retroactive. What this means is that if the production has already shot for sixty days and then suddenly becomes a union show, for those sixty days to count toward your credited hours, the production must give you back pay equal to the new higher union rate. If you don't get the total days from that project, you need to go work in the Third Area until you do. You can't work on a union show in the Los Angeles or New York area until you get the rest of your days.

The third and maybe most common way to become a Second AD is through the Production Assistant route. To do this you have to amass six hundred working days, of which 125 days can be in the production office. While you're doing this you have to save all the call sheets with your name on them, all of your pay stubs, and all of the production reports from those days. Assemble this paperwork neatly in a large binder and submit the book to the DGA. This proof makes you eligible to join the Director's Guild of America. Once you pay the initiation fee, you are on the Commercial/Third Area List. This means that you cannot work in Los Angeles or New York City as a Second AD on union features yet. However, you can work on low-budget features or commercials in Los Angeles or work as a Second AD in the Third Area.

Before you can work in L.A. on union shows you have to work a minimum of seventy-five days on commercials as a Second or Second Second AD in Los Angeles or the Third Area, as well as an additional seventy-five days on commercials or on anything in the Third Area for a total of 150 days. Point being, you have to get commercial experience in as well as feature and episodic television if you want to work in Los Angeles.

The downside to this is that commercials usually shoot for only two to three days total, so getting seventy-five days in might take quite a long time. While you're amassing these days slowly, you'll be taken away from any contacts that you previously made in the feature/episodic circles. The best scenario would be to manage your seventy-five commercial days and then hook up with a feature shooting in the Third Area, which would complete your 150 days much more quickly.

If that wasn't difficult enough, once you're eligible, there's a thirty-day waiting period before you can work. Meaning, you can't turn your book in with your initiation fee and then jump on a show the next day. Once you're "in," you have to wait thirty days before taking a union show.

Once you join the DGA and get your commercial days you can still work as PA to survive if necessary. But working two days on commercials at the DGA rate is more than you'll make doing a full week as a PA, so your incentive to "step down" to survive hopefully will be offset by your motivation to find AD work.

The fourth way is to go through the DGA trainee program. See the previous chapter for more details.

The union maintains an Available List that productions review to see who is available. However, for the most part, your jobs will come through networking connections.

So how do I get work?

If you've come up through the training program, hopefully you've made a good impression on all the union ADs you worked with so you might get the chance to Second for an established First AD right away. Another possibility is that projects sometimes need additional assistants to handle large numbers of Extras for a day or two. Or if you're really fortunate, the show may wish to have a full-time Second Second AD. Also, don't underestimate your fellow former Trainees who may be on a set in need of extra help.

WHAT AM I GETTING MYSELF INTO?
So who actually calls and hires me?

Typically, you'll be called by a First AD with whom you've worked previously, although there may be exceptions when a UPM or Line Producer may request you specifically.

Okay, I got the job. What now?

The amount of time between getting the job offer and actually beginning work will vary, but contractually, the Second AD will officially start about seven days before principal photography begins.

By this time, the Producer, UPM, and First AD have laid much of the groundwork for what needs to be done to get ready for production. It is up to the Second AD to come in and ensure that things are in process. This means a lot of meetings with people and a lot of phone calls. If a problem can be avoided by way of a little foresight, not only will your life be easier during production, but your value to that company will be recognized and you will continue to build a successful career. In other words, instead of running around putting out fires all day long, it's just better for everyone if they don't ignite in the first place.

What will my life really be like?

5:30 A.M.—GET TO WORK
You need to make sure that all of the trailers are open and ready to go by the time everyone arrives. If catering is ready to go that early, you might have time to grab a quick breakfast.

6:00 A.M.—"THROUGH THE WORKS"
The Second AD in base camp has to be confident and comfortable in approaching and talking to actors. If an Actor is on the phone, you have to make certain that he knows that you need him to be in Makeup or Wardrobe or on the set. If you communicate the relevant information and the Actor acknowledges you (and still doesn't do as asked), it's out of your hands. Then you can let the First AD

know that there will be a delay and why. But if you don't communicate it, then it's your problem. A quiet little knock on the door won't cut it.

7:00 A.M.—GETTING TO SET

Around 7:00 A.M., if everything is going all right on set, the First AD will call for First Team over the radio. Knock on the trailer doors and politely shepherd the Actors onto set.

7:05 A.M.—REHEARSAL

You should be nearby to help lock up the set.

7:15 A.M.—CAMERA SETUP

Once rehearsal is done, walk the actors out to the trailers so they can finish going "through the works" if necessary. Confer with the First AD regarding the day's schedule. He may have a shot-sheet, which will tell you which Actors need to be ready and when. Begin or continue work on the advanced call sheet.

7:45 A.M.—ROLL CAMERA

A few minutes before this, the First AD will call for First Team to come back to set. Help round the Actors up and get them in. Make sure your Trainee, Second Second, and/or Production Assistants are properly placed for an effective lockup.

Quietly continue working on the advance call sheet while paying attention to the walkie-talkie. If you are helping to lock up the area, shout out "Rolling" as soon as you hear the First AD call it out over the radio.

7:48 A.M.—CUT, LET'S GO AGAIN

Maintain the lockup and check-in with the PAs in case there were any problems.

8:05 A.M.—CUT, MOVIN' ON

Maintain the lockup as normal to ensure a calm environment in which everyone may rehearse the next setup. You may also need to bring in additional Actors and/or Extras.

Once rehearsal is done, have your people keep an eye on where the various Actors go and continue your work as normal. Look over the assembled production report for any errors. Hand it back to the Trainee or a PA for delivery to the production office.

1:00 P.M.—LUNCH

Assuming there are no major disasters to take care of, you get the opportunity to take a break.

2:00 P.M.—BACK TO WORK

Keep track of the Actors, get them to set when needed, lock up the area during takes, and repeat as necessary. With any luck, everything will go as planned. All day long it's a balancing act to accommodate various personalities, save money, and meet the needs of production. It can be very easy to allow that kind of stress to take a toll, but because you love this job, you actually revel in the chaos.

9:00 P.M.—WRAP

How the day ends depends a lot on how the day went. If all or most went successfully that day, the wrap out will probably just involve making a few phone calls. You need to let the Production Manager (if she isn't already on set), someone in the production office, and someone in studio administration know that everything went as planned and that nothing has changed for tomorrow. If you're on a studio lot, then security and the hospital need to know when the company is leaving for the night.

If there are some last-minute changes for the next day's work, you have to communicate that information to anyone who needs to know. For example, if the day goes long, call times will be pushed and anyone who isn't on set needs to know his new call time. At worst, you might have upward of one hundred phone calls to make as the rest of the crew wraps their equipment.

WHAT I REALLY WANT TO DO IS MOVE UP!

It's time to move up and become a First Assistant Director. All you have to do is work an additional 520 days as a Second AD to qualify as a First. That's the easy part. You also have to convince someone that you can do the job.

If the situation allows for it, you may get the occasional chance to run a set when a Second Unit gets called in. If the Key First is okay with it, an additional Second AD may be brought in to deal with First Unit while you go off to be the Key on the new, temporary unit. Given enough of this experience, the Producers of your show may recognize your ability and either hire you for a future project or recommend you to others.

You need to be at the place where skill, politics, and opportunity collide. The best way to achieve that is to work as much as possible, learn everything you can from every situation, and give it 100 percent all day long, happy that you are on your way up!

Chapter 17

What I Really Want to Do Is First Assistant Direct!

WHAT THE HECK IS A FIRST ASSISTANT DIRECTOR?

The First Assistant Director (AD) is the Director's right-hand man with respect to logistics. The entire AD team exists to facilitate the needs of the production and help realize the wishes of the creative elements of the company. To that end, the First AD works with the Producer, the Unit Production Manager, and the Director to create a schedule and manage the set in a way that will, hopefully, deliver the desired creative result in the most financially efficient manner possible.

That, and what else?

Your job isn't just to shuttle Actors around and say, "Rolling" and "Cut." Your job in preproduction and during production is about finding ways to complete the work in the time allotted. For example, there may be a situation in which a lot of time will be saved if you suggest that the Construction Department create a set with an additional WILD WALL. This will allow the Director to get the shot plus more because the camera and lighting crew will be able to work much more efficiently. You've helped solve a logistics problem without really affecting any creative decisions. Every second counts during the day. If you can save the company ten minutes per setup by thinking up some kind of time saver, then you can get everyone home that much sooner or the Director can get those extra bonus shots that will help the overall project look that much better.

I get a chair next to the Director?! I must be making really good money then, right?

Unlike most of the other crew, the First AD doesn't go into overtime until fourteen hours after his call, and that's roughly the length of the average shooting day.

Despite getting to leave at camera wrap and not going into overtime as often, an ordinary First AD working on union features or a television show will still make on average about $150,000 to $200,000 a year. Bigtime ADs may command more. Nonunion rates will typically be significantly lower than that.

Of course, what I really want to do is direct, so this is the perfect job to have...

While indeed, because of your close proximity to the Director throughout the shoot you probably can learn a great deal creatively, your primary skills are more in preparation for the *logistical* management positions of Unit Production Manager and/or Producer. Just because you are a member of the DGA and your title has the word *director* in it does not mean that you will automatically get a directing gig...ever. Remember, being an Assistant Director trains you to be a *Producer* who is adept at logistics. It does not necessarily teach you how to be a creative Director.

WHAT DO I REALLY NEED TO KNOW?

You need to know how to create a schedule using industry-specific scheduling software. Once you have a script to work with, you proceed to break it down word by word and create a shooting schedule that highlights every prop, location, and set, animals, background actors, and main actors, as well as wardrobe, hair, etc. that will be needed in front of or behind the camera. You are making note of possible special camera needs, like cranes, STEADICAM, high-speed, or extra units. Anything that will affect your schedule and budget needs to be noted. The shooting schedule gets updated throughout production as pages are revised. Every department refers to this shooting schedule so they can better anticipate their own needs and stay within budget.

WHAT DO I REALLY NEED TO HAVE?

The scheduling program will cost around $600. A reliable laptop computer to run the software and a printer will add on another $1,000 to $3,000. And wear a watch.

What's the best way for someone to reach me?

As a First AD, you won't be asked to DAYPLAY very often, so most work you do get will be for the length of the show. As a result, you should be able to form solid relationships with those above you as long as you stay in touch.

WHERE DO I REALLY NEED TO GO?
I just want to work.

About four months prior to actual filming, a production may hire a First AD at a lower weekly rate to break the script down. About three months before the start of production, you will be expected to be on hand to meet with the Producers, UPM, Director, and anyone else who is relevant to you as you create a schedule.

Once production begins, you won't see much of home, no matter where you live. So it is possible for you to live just about anywhere in the country, as long as you don't mind being away for months at a time.

So how do I get work?

Once you've moved up from Second AD to First AD, your employment is dependent on those who aren't usually on set during the day. The goal is to get your name out there to let everyone know that you are capable and available.

WHAT AM I GETTING MYSELF INTO?
Who calls me for work?

You'll likely get a call from a UPM or from a Producer with whom you've worked previously.

Okay, I got the job. What now?

Preproduction. The UPM will already have been working several months in advance of your first day in the office. Typically, the First AD will get anywhere from four to eight weeks to do all the prep work for the show.

Early in development, a Producer may make a de facto schedule to rough out the budget. The preliminary BOARDS are exceedingly optimistic by ignoring things like weather, locations, and Actor availability. Once officially hired, the First AD creates the first official schedule that takes into account contingencies and potential problems that could affect the daily page count and the true budget. After meeting with the Director (often), the First AD meets with any and all department heads as they are hired. Recognizing potential problems and dealing with them in prep will save countless dollars as well as help to avoid any unfortunate confrontations later on.

You also hire the Second AD, who comes in about one to two weeks prior to the first day of shooting. Turn your schedule over to her and continue to communicate any issues that may cause persistent problems. Once the show begins, the First AD stops worrying about the totality of the project and instead focuses on the day-to-day running of the set.

What will my life really be like?

7:00 A.M.—GETTING TO SET

Make your way to set, get any updates you need from the Second AD, find the Director, and then get the day moving by calling in First Team as soon as possible.

7:05 A.M.—REHEARSAL

You're like the ringmaster in the circus, and it is up to you to try to establish a pace and keep some momentum going throughout the day. Get pertinent people to the set and start the rehearsal.

Be mindful of where the Actors must go, if Extras are needed, where the camera(s) has to be, what lighting is required, and any other time-consuming details. If you need answers to any of those questions after rehearsal is completed, quickly approach the department heads and get their time estimates. Let the Director know how long it will be, and let First Team return to base camp to complete hair, makeup, and wardrobe. Call for Second Team.

7:15 A.M.—CAMERA SETUP

Stick close to set to keep an eye on the setup. In most cases, each department looks out for problems that they can solve on their own, but some challenges aren't immediately obvious. It's your job to facilitate the crew in getting the day's work in the can, so anything you can do to that end is expected and appreciated.

As the setup looks like it is close to being ready, ask the DP specifically for another estimate. When you are within five minutes, call to your Second AD and get First Team warmed up and on the move. Make sure the Director is also on his way, and then let the on-set crew know that First Team is coming in.

Once everyone is happy, call for "last looks," and let everyone know that the next one is for real and not a rehearsal.

7:45 A.M.—ROLL CAMERA

Make sure that camera and sound are ready, then call out to the Sound Mixer, "On a bell." Once you are reasonably sure that all unnecessary noise has ceased (trucks outside the stage door, airplanes overhead, conversations) call out to the stage and over the radio, "Roll sound!" The crew will take it from there. Once the Boom Operator says "Speed," the Focus Puller will turn the camera on, and the Second Assistant Cameraman will say, "Marker," and hit the sticks on the slate. A moment later the Director will say, "Action!"

At this point, you've accomplished your main job by getting all the necessary elements for that shot into this place at the proper time. With any luck, you're also on schedule.

7:48 A.M.—CUT, LET'S GO AGAIN

The shot is over and the Director calls, "Cut!" In most cases, you'll figure out without asking whether he wants to do another take. Sometimes, it isn't so clear; you'll have to get a clear answer either way.

Find out quickly what the problems were with that take, if any, and communicate that information to everyone. Do whatever you need so that shooting can resume as quickly as possible.

8:10 A.M.—CUT, MOVIN' ON

Great! The Director is happy and no one seems to have any problems that would necessitate another take. Get everyone quiet to run a rehearsal for the next piece. When that is done, release First Team and bring Second Team back in. Get the time estimate from the DP, communicate it to the Director, and do it all over again.

1:00 P.M.—LUNCH

With the busy work schedule, lunch can be the only time available for the crew (Director, DP, Focus Puller, plus other interested parties) to view DAILIES. In most cases, you will want to be present as well in case any notes come up regarding the need for reshoots or other concerns.

2:00 P.M.—BACK TO WORK

Hopefully, the day has gone according to plan. Once a show gets going, you'll get a pretty good idea of how fast the crew works, so estimating how many setups you can achieve each day will become easier.

The objective of the Assistant Directing team is to help bring the script, and the Director's vision of it, to life. The flip side of that is the need to balance the requests of the studio and Producers, who keep to a very strict budget that usually doesn't allow a great deal of leeway. Overall, the AD team must manage the set so that the Director can achieve what he wants, but within reasonable limits of safety and budget.

Sometime during the day, your Second AD will deliver an advanced CALL SHEET to you for approval. Run the schedule past the Director and the DP in case there are any major issues that need to be dealt with, then hand it back for correction and distribution.

When you get to the second shot from the end of the day, let everyone know that it is the ABBY SINGER. This will give the crew a chance to start cleaning up and put unneeded equipment away.

The last shot of the day is the MARTINI. Before calling this out, double-check with the Director and the Script Supervisor to make sure you have really filmed everything needed that day.

9:00 P.M.—WRAP

Either the company will finish all the work on the call sheet or the Producer will have mandated a hard OUT-TIME. Whatever the case, when that time comes, you wait for the First Assistant Cameraman to check the gate and say, **"GOOD GATE."** If he doesn't and there is a problem with the film, then you will do another take. If the gate is good, then loudly announce over the radio to the entire set, "That's a wrap." It's also not a bad idea to thank everyone for a good day. The little things go a long way.

Have a quick meeting with the Director if necessary and then check with the Second AD to make sure everything on his end is all right. Once you are reasonably sure that everyone is content, head home.

WHAT I REALLY WANT TO DO IS MOVE UP!

Why would anyone want a job like this in the first place? The creation of a movie could quickly become chaos if not for your careful orchestration of the various departments and people needed to make it all happen. But more than that, the job can lead you down the path to becoming a Producer. You've learned what it takes to put a project together, from scheduling logistics and budget to understanding how all the various departments really work together on a setup-by-setup basis. Before you jump to being a Producer, you'll first have to get out of the trenches and have a more direct involvement with studio Executives and other Producers.

So your next step up is into an office as the Unit Production Manager. As a First AD, let Producers know what your goals and capabilities are. In time, you'll be able to move up and be one step closer to your destination.

Chapter 18

What I Really Want to Do Is Unit Production Manage!

WHAT THE HECK IS A UPM?

The UPM, or Unit Production Manager, oversees, supervises, and coordinates anything that is purchased or rented during the course of physical production. He is involved in nearly all decisions regarding the below-the-line crew (including hiring and firing), equipment, expendables, film stock, locations, etc. In short, anything having to do with the day-to-day operations of the actual shooting company falls within the bounds of the Unit Production Manager's job.

He may also be involved in the shooting schedule along with the First and Second ADs and the Production Supervisor. For instance, if the company finds itself running behind, the UPM may help decide whether to work the company later that day or drop shots or scenes. However, unless the UPM has been given some amount of producing power, supervisors superior to him will make decisions that will directly affect the creative aspects of the project. The UPM is there mainly to advise regarding the budgetary concerns of any decisions.

The UPM looks at the big picture to make sure that the production stays within its budget. He keeps a careful watch over the day-to-day workings of the set to make certain that the things that are needed are actually showing up (including cast and crew) and that the money will be there to pay for it all.

That, and what else?

If you have been given a Co-Producer title on top of your regular responsibilities, you might have the authority to make creative decisions if no other senior Producers are available. But in general, the UPM job revolves around the implementation of the decisions of others. While there is no Unit Production Manager position in the realm of postproduction, the UPM may add extra camera days to the schedule to accommodate requests from the Editorial departments (e.g., reshoots or ADR or special effects, like green screen). Again, the UPM's responsibilities revolve around cast, crew, and equipment needed for actual physical production.

The job description is so all-encompassing that you don't have time for much else. If you are working on a television series, you'll be dealing with the previous episode, the one currently being shot, and with details for the next one in the schedule all at the same time. As an Assistant Director, you were intimately concerned with the minutia of schedules and of every shot. Even though your role on set is reduced, every day will be a challenge with rarely a dull moment.

This is more like a real office job. My paycheck must be getting bigger!

This much responsibility means that you will get paid accordingly. Suffice it to say that the standard DGA contract will net you in excess of $100,000 a year in most cases. Depending on your level of experience and how much you are in demand, you may be in the position to negotiate for a salary that is over scale.

Not that you'll have a lot of time to spend it. To earn those checks, you'll be facing some very long days encompassing a great deal of the year.

WHAT DO I REALLY NEED TO KNOW?

If you've gotten this far, the chances are pretty good that you have an excellent understanding of what it takes to make a film or television show. Beyond the logistical concerns of scheduling and finances, you'll be expected to deal with people in every level of the process. Being able to communicate well with studio executives will help secure your future career. Having the skills to deal with personality conflicts among the cast and/or crew will aid in keeping the process moving along efficiently. No matter how good you are with numbers and something as intangible as time, if you can't effectively communicate with people, your career will be short-lived.

So how do I get work?

If you are working with a particular production company, studio, or with a loyal group of people, an opportunity may crop up that allows you to make the move from First AD to UPM at their invitation. Essentially, again it all boils down to being in the right place at the right time and having the skills on hand to be successful. It's unlikely that anyone could ever jump into the industry at this level, so if you are ready to become a UPM, it is highly likely that you already have a few years of experience in the Production Department under your belt.

WHAT DO I REALLY NEED TO HAVE?
This is an important job. I must need something.

Bring an open mind and be ready for anything to happen.

Apart from that, no, you won't need a lot of stuff at this point in your career. A cellular phone, briefcase, laptop computer, and a watch. Your office and supplies should be there for you.

Your job now entails a lot less physical labor and necessitates much more mental clarity. You'll be in the office much more than on set during shooting. You won't be standing up all the time anymore. Your daily activities include a lot more meetings, phone calls, and paperwork than ever before.

What's the best way for someone to reach me?

If you're between jobs, make sure that the people you work with regularly have your home phone number at the very least.

If you're on a show, the last thing you want is for someone to call you on your time off. However, the office staff as well as the AD Department should be able to reach you at all times in case there is an emergency. Keep a cellular phone handy even when you'd prefer to leave it turned off.

WHAT AM I GETTING MYSELF INTO?
So who actually calls and hires me?

Your call to come to work could come from a variety of sources. But look to be hearing from Producers you've worked with before as well as Production Supervisors or other administrative personnel.

Okay, I got the job. What now?

The first person onboard most projects is a Producer. This is a person who has a vision, an idea, a property, or a deal with a studio and has the resources to begin developing a project. As the Producer develop the property into a script, he begins to attach different people to it (a Director and/or a movie star) and build a package. He'll put together a rough budget and take it to a studio. Based on the Producer's track record and the package he's created, the studio will toss out a budget range that they'd like to shoot for.

Then with that nebulous budget range in mind, he'll begin to hire a team, starting with the UPM. The two of them will start breaking down the budget with the script as it exists. By this time in the process, they'll have a pretty good idea of how expensive the key Actors will be so they can estimate the budget to within a few million dollars on a larger project and within a few hundred thousand on a smaller one. Once that is done, the Producer will take the numbers to the studio, and, as a matter of course, the executives will balk and ask for a lower estimate. That is, unless there is a particular relationship that is strong enough to bypass that step or if there is a need for a huge summer blockbuster.

Everyone involved negotiates the budget back and forth until an agreement is made. Based on that budget and a green light, the Producer and UPM will start hiring key personnel about six to eight months before shooting starts. Usually the Director has been approached before this point, so now they'll officially hire him. The Art Director and/or Production Designer will probably come on board fairly early in the process. The DP will be approached but won't be officially hired until actual production draws closer.

Soon after all of that, the Producers will start negotiating and contracting with the Actors. During this process, you will begin having meetings with all the department heads. They will each bring you their own script breakdowns specific to their department's needs. The UPM takes copies of each, and after discussions with the Art Director and other department heads, you'll get a good sense of where your budget really is. If necessary, you then go back to the studio if you need more money to make the whole thing really work.

Essentially, your job as the UPM boils down to this kind of scenario: You know you have $80 million to make the movie; $30 million comes off the top and goes to the Actors. That leaves about $50 million to actually make the film. Using that number plus actor availability and location requirements, as well as other considerations like a studio release date, you figure out how you will spend that money.

What will my life really be like?

6:42 A.M.—GET TO WORK

General crew call isn't until 7:00 A.M., but you can come in a few minutes early to clean up any lingering paperwork while it's still quiet and the phone isn't ringing off the hook.

You want to dress comfortably, but be presentable. There is no need to dress up in a suit and tie. Leave that for the executives at the studio. You'll be splitting your time between the office and the set, so you also need to dress for the environment (desert, cold, wet, etc.).

7:00 A.M.—GETTING TO SET

A few minutes before call, go down to the stage or to BASE CAMP. Check in with the AD department for an update. Make sure that the cast and crew are all showing up on time.

Sometimes problems crop up in Makeup or Wardrobe. At other times, somebody may be running late or has woken up sick. You'll want to be aware of any of these problems that may affect the schedule and/or budget.

7:05 A.M.—REHEARSAL

Again, you're just another set of eyes, taking it all in. Be there for the first rehearsal to make sure everything is running as planned.

7:15 A.M.—CAMERA SETUP

Periodically, you'll want to be around set just to watch the crew and look for problems. Everyone there has a function, and you need to make certain that no one is slacking off. Typically, a department head will already be aware of a tricky situation, but your presence can be more persuasive. Because of the long and monotonous schedules of production, particularly for a television series, complacency can be a big problem.

When you get the chance, have a quick meeting with the First and Second ADs to go over the schedule. While you might have a pretty decent estimate of how long the day will be, it will help to have a rough idea of when the company should complete each item on the call sheet. As the day progresses, it will be easier to gauge if they are running behind or right on schedule.

7:45 A.M.—ROLL CAMERA

Of course, everyone has a job to do, but as another pair of eyes, you should feel free to help out whenever you see an opportunity to keep the day moving along. This doesn't mean racing for an APPLEBOX or C-STAND, but if you notice something seemingly out of place on set during a take, take note of it and mention it to the First AD. A small problem gone unnoticed on set could turn into an expensive fix later on.

7:48 A.M.—CUT, LET'S GO AGAIN

Stick around as long as your schedule allows, but keep in mind that you have other office duties to deal with as well.

8:10 A.M.—CUT, MOVIN' ON

Go back to the office. You'll head back to set later on to check up on their progress, but for now, you've got some paperwork to do.

At some point in the morning, hopefully sooner than later, you'll receive a copy of the PRODUCTION REPORT from the day before that the AD Department has been creating. You'll also receive information concerning billing for vendors and other cast/crew. As most of this information directly affects money leaving the budget, it is up to you to review everything and either approve or reject it. For instance, if the company wrapped at 9:00 P.M. the previous night and one of the departments didn't clock out until 11:00 P.M., you'll want to get in touch with that department head to see what the problem was and see if the out-time is justified.

1:00 P.M.—LUNCH

This is your chance to sit at your desk and ignore phone calls or to escape the office altogether. You may also be interested in going to the dailies session along with the Director, AD, and DP, but if there are any pressing concerns, they'll let you know anyhow.

2:00 P.M.—BACK TO WORK

You have a lot to deal with throughout the day, be it paperwork, phone calls, meetings, or set observation. Hopefully the day will go smoothly and your stress level won't be very high. Unfortunately, sometimes problems do crop up. If there is an accident on set, you may want to get over there right away. If there are personality problems between crew members, you'll want to be aware of it. If an Actor is causing trouble, you need to help mediate. If the company is getting behind schedule, you should find out why. Sometimes you can use the phone to deal with certain problems, but it will make more of a statement if you face the issue in person.

The Second AD will deliver an advance call sheet for the following day. If it makes sense and there are no big surprises, you'll approve it and it will then be distributed to department heads.

9:00 P.M.—WRAP

As wrap approaches, check on the call time for the next day and make sure everyone is aware of it. The ADs know what to do, but it doesn't hurt to help out if you can, especially if there are any last-minute changes. The key to staying on budget is maintaining accurate and efficient communication.

After wrap, stay long enough to get any updates from the AD Department, and then go home.

Over the weekend, you might have to go over a call sheet or some late script changes. But, usually, try to do that the night before at work. Your time away from family and friends is long enough without dragging a full briefcase home with you. It's important to separate those work stresses from your life and leave them in the office. And vice versa. Your job is hard enough without having some personal problem plaguing your mind all day. The mental exhaustion can wear you down faster than being on your feet all day ever could.

WHAT I REALLY WANT TO DO IS MOVE UP!

Chances are, when you first had dreams of breaking into the movie business, a career as a UPM wasn't even a glimmer in your eye. The next step up the ladder is to become a Producer. Many Producers used to work as Unit Production Managers, so it is not just possible but an entirely viable choice to make.

Producers come in many varieties with a wide array of responsibilities. What those positions do not offer, though, is the job security associated with being a UPM. While the Producer has to rely on the whims of a studio or independent financing, a UPM's career hinges more on the relationships he has with people and the companies that have employed him. At some point, you may have to make the decision to "move up" to become a Producer, "move over" to be a UPM for a different company or show, or to remain loyal to those who you work with (and for) and stay put. You'll need to weigh the advantages of a steady position against your ambitions (producing, directing, writing).

Just like every other job, advancement boils down to being in the right place at the right time with the necessary skills. Once you have the experience of being on set and then working in the office and meeting powerful people (Studio Executives and Actors), you may get the opportunity to make that move by either partnering up with an established Producer or by acquiring and pushing a project of your own. Whatever you decide, you have to rely on the people you've gotten to know and impress while you've worked your way up through the ranks.

Chapter 19

What I Really Want to Do Is Direct!

WHAT THE HECK IS A DIRECTOR?

The Director coordinates and focuses the creative contributions of numerous cast and crew members in the production of a narrative or documentary motion picture project for theatrical, TV, or home entertainment release.

That, and what else?

While being the creative visionary is the attractive goal of the job, having the skill and willingness to communicate and collaborate with other creative individuals is not only key to producing a successful product but also is integral to having a pleasant working experience on a daily basis. To help secure gainful employment, you must also be willing and able to navigate the politics of the entertainment industry. Such diplomacy is also crucial in helping the Director maintain the creative freedom he desires.

And while the Director doesn't have to know how to perform the variety of technical crafts that are necessary to filmmaking, at the very least he should be aware of what everyone on set actually does.

I'm in charge! I must be making really good money then, right?

Depending on exactly what it is you're directing, you could make anywhere from nothing to millions of dollars per project. Typical pay differs greatly for the variety of television and film productions that are possible. However, if you are a member of the DIRECTOR'S GUILD OF AMERICA (DGA), you can expect to make a minimum of about $200,000 for a feature film. That amount can vary depending on your track record, the quality and skill of your agent, and the back-end deal you receive on the box-office profits.

Directing a one-hour episodic television program will earn you about $36,000 plus residuals for three weeks of work.

WHAT DO I REALLY NEED TO KNOW?

You are like the conductor of an orchestra, where the cast and crew are the musicians who express their own creativity by being adept at specific technical crafts. It is your job to bring together those individuals who can complement your own understanding of the project so that everyone is working toward the same goal.

Perhaps one of the most important character traits a Director can have is the ability to recognize what you *don't* know. You may feel you are the most creative person on set, but having the capacity to ask for help when you need it, both technically and creatively, will help everyone in bringing the project to its full potential.

Having some experience with all of the jobs on a set, whether through observation or by actually getting your hands dirty doing them, can help you be more efficient in communicating your ideas and wishes on a shot-by-shot basis when you do get to sit in the Director's chair. The tangible benefit of doing this is that what actually ends up on film more closely matches the ideas in your head. Each shot looks the way you envision, and, with communication with the cast and crew that is collaborative, efficient, and understanding, you can get more done each day and have a better daily experience doing it.

WHAT DO I REALLY NEED TO HAVE?

Your cast and crew are the "tools" you wield to create the illusion of characters in a world that doesn't really exist. With that in mind, you don't really "need" anything. However, if you are a Writer-Director, having a reliable laptop computer with screenwriting software is necessary all the way through preproduction and production as rewrites are going to happen nearly every day.

What's the best way for someone to reach me?

As a Director, your time is scarce and valuable, so your career will benefit greatly by securing the services of an agent. She can serve as a filter for those who try to get in contact with you, as well as help to land the most advantageous creative and financial deal possible.

WHERE DO I REALLY NEED TO GO?
I just want to work.

You may actually get your first directing opportunity via a relationship you have with an established Producer, Studio Executive, or Actor. Building those connections means living and working in places where those people are.

To that end, while you are writing and/or "selling" yourself with previous projects you've created (e.g., short films, screenplays), you should be willing to go to work in the industry no matter how menial your jobs might be. Working as a PA in the production office or as a member of the technical crew will give you some access to those with power who can help you become a Director. Nearly as important, working within the industry gives you opportunities to really learn the nuts-and-bolts process that gets a movie made. This experience will be invaluable if you ever get the chance to make a living as a Director. You've got your dream to pursue, but you also have to keep yourself clothed, fed, and sheltered in the meantime. The trick here is that while you are working in the industry as something other than a Director, you have to enjoy the journey toward your goal because that dream is elusive and may never be realized.

So how do I get work?

You have to prove to someone with money and/or power that you have the talent and skill required to guide a cast and crew in the creation of an entertaining and profitable product. Any previous experience you have, screenplays you've written, projects you've directed, and relationships you've developed all contribute toward getting you jobs that put money into your bank account.

There is no single way to do this and no guarantee that any of those elements will put you in the Director's chair. A certain amount of luck is involved, in that you must meet the right people at the right time. However, you can improve your chances by being prepared for these opportunities when they arrive. Don't just have an idea for a film. Take all the spare moments you have to sit down and write the screenplay so that when you meet a person who is interested in you and the idea, you'll have something tangible to give him. Instead of buying luxuries like big-screen TVs or a nice car, invest that money into producing a short film to highlight your skills.

And you're not just leaving it up to chance that you're going to meet the right people at the right time. When you have something real to present, like a screenplay or a short film, actively seek out those who can propel your career forward. Try to get your material seen by an agent by asking for referrals from others who are already represented. Submit your screenplays to writing contests. Enter your short films into festivals. You have to be enthusiastic and persistent, yet not to the point of annoyance. Your work might be great, but if people don't like *you*, there will always be that pleasant someone else around the corner with an idea that is just as good.

What I Really Want to Do Is Direct

You likely noticed that the title of this book was inspired by the well-known phrase "What I really want to do is direct." This train of thought is usually associated with people in and out of the film industry who would rather be in charge but are just doing mundane jobs in the meantime.

While undoubtedly funny, the perception is that everyone, particularly those already in the business, would rather direct than do anything else. This couldn't be further from the truth. The reality is that the majority of those who do have successful careers in the entertainment industry do NOT want to direct for a variety of reasons. They either never desired the job in the first place, saw the job and realized they didn't want it, or genuinely enjoy the job that they are doing and have no interest in changing.

What this means is that as an aspiring Director, your competition isn't as vast as you might have believed. You're not really competing with others for the job as much as you are working to prove that *you* are talented and skilled enough to create a project that is both creative and potentially profitable.

WHAT AM I GETTING MYSELF INTO?
So who actually calls and hires me?

There are a lot of factors that go into the decision regarding who will direct a project. Because of this, you may have meetings with a large variety of people, such as Studio Executives, Producers, and even Actors who all may have their own opinions regarding who is best for the project. After a decision is made, your agent will complete the deal.

Okay, I got the job. What now?

Up to this point, it's been just you working on your script alone or you've been brought into a project that someone else has been developing. Now it's your responsibility to focus your ideas and the creative input from others so that the technical and logistical requirements can be met. To this end, you'll hire department Keys with whom you will work closely all through preproduction and production.

You'll have meetings during which you approve locations, casting, production design, costume design, script revisions, and many other details that require an answer from you. You're dealing with a variety of very creative and ambitious people, just like you, who all have valuable ideas to contribute to the project. You're not obliged to implement every idea, but it is beneficial for you to at least listen to create a collaborative working environment. The more you know about the film you want to make, the easier it is to communicate very specific ideas and ward off any influence from others who might attempt to undermine your efforts.

On the other hand, it is important to keep in mind that while the average Director may work on just one film every couple of years or so, the average Key or member of the crew will have scores of movies on his resume and years of set experience under his belt. Don't be too quick to dismiss any valuable input that is put forth to help you and the project.

The amount of prep time you have varies depending on the complexity of the project, availability of locations and talent, and when the studio would like to release the final product.

Ultimately, everything you do is in service of what happens after you say, "Action!" The more specific you are in answering questions during preproduction, the better chance there is that everything will be right when you get to the set and roll camera.

What will my life really be like?

7:00 A.M.—GETTING TO SET

The First AD will be eager to begin the day as soon as possible. Come in prepared, knowing what scene is first and having some idea of how you might like to shoot it. If you have specific information that could be beneficial to any department in preparing the setup, pass it on as soon as possible so they can begin work right away.

7:05 A.M.—REHEARSAL

Some Directors like to have a shot list prepared. Others prefer to see how the performance guides the scene. Whatever your method, communicate your wishes clearly and succinctly to the Actors, the First AD, and the Director of Photography. Rarely can a scene be shot precisely the way a Director has envisioned it beforehand. Actors may play a character slightly differently, the camera may not be able to move in the exact way you wish, you might not have enough time to "find" the scene because you have so much more to do that day, or you might discover a better idea at the last moment. Whatever the case, being open to changing ideas that seemed so definitive in the script is crucial in creating a better movie than the one you imagined, not to mention just making it through the day.

Especially after you've been in production for a few weeks, one of the hardest tasks is to inspire your cast to wake up and play their characters in the wee hours of the morning the same way they would do in the middle of the afternoon. Eighty to one-hundred hour work weeks tend to exhaust people after a month or two, but you can't allow any of that to show up on screen, unless of course the story calls for it.

In addition to working with the Actors, the Director of Photography will be helping to choose the best way to shoot the action. Depending on your own level of competency with the technical requirements involved, you will collaborate in choosing angles and lenses that best capture the environment and the performances of the talent.

When the blocking is set and the DP feels as if he knows what you are looking for, the First AD will "cut on rehearsal" and call Second Team in while First Team retreats back to BASE CAMP.

7:15 A.M.—CAMERA SETUP

It will take anywhere from a few minutes to an hour or more for the crew to create the setup. You may have to consult with the Costume Designer about new wardrobe choices, or you could meet with the Casting Agent to help choose Actors for parts that haven't been cast yet, or you might just want to sit alone to work out a problem in the script or watch a rough cut of a scene from the Editor. There is an endless list of things to do, filled with people to see and decisions to be made. Attending to them during setups is the best way to keep the machine running.

When the DP is nearly ready, the First AD will put a call out on the walkie inviting First Team back in, and someone will notify you as well. Sometimes, slight adjustments have to be made from the initial blocking due to issues during setup, so it is usually advantageous for everyone to run another rehearsal now that the cameras are in place and the lighting is ready. Doing so allows the Actors a chance to get back into character and the technical crew the opportunity to discover problems before anything is committed to film. If there isn't a lot of time or everyone is fairly confident that all is in place, the First AD will announce that "We're SHOOTING THE REHEARSAL."

7:45 A.M.—ROLL CAMERA

After the Second AC clears frame, give the Actors a beat or two, then call out "Action!" From this point on, it is up to the talent, the Camera Operator, the Dolly Grip (in most cases), and the First AC (pulling focus) to work together to accomplish the requirements of the take. More complicated action may require Stuntpeople, Electricians to provide lighting effects, or Special Effects technicians operating "gags." You have to tune all of that activity out and concentrate solely on what is happening within the frame itself.

Typically, the Camera Department or a special Video Assist will set up VIDEO VILLAGE away from the camera where you can watch a video image coming from the cameras. The Sound Department will provide you with headphones so that you can clearly hear the dialogue.

7:48 A.M.—CUT, LET'S GO AGAIN

Everything may have gone perfectly, but unless there is absolutely no time at all, it is in everyone's best interest to do at least one additional take, if not more, for safety. This is important in case something is wrong with the film stock or sound recording that just captured that take. However, any number of things may have not gone well, from a missed line of dialogue or "wrong" performance to the First AC missing focus. You'll likely do COVERAGE, shots that you can use to edit around any mistakes, but ideally you are looking to get as close to a perfect take as possible so that you're not forced to cut around problems later on in editing.

Do your best to tune out everything that might distract you from paying attention to what you are trying to capture with this setup. Don't walk away from a setup or an entire scene until you know you have it on film. You likely won't get a second chance to return to a setup in the event you come up with a better idea later or have missed something.

However, you don't have an unlimited amount of time to spend trying to achieve perfection. Something that seems small on the page could require four more shots, which translates into at least another hour or two. If it's that important, then you could be losing time you wanted for some other shot or scene scheduled later that day. Being creative is what your job entails, but you are also limited by the budget, time, and allotted resources.

8:10 A.M.—CUT, MOVIN' ON

When you are absolutely sure you have at least one take that will work both technically and performance-wise, tell the First AD right away so that preparation for the next setup can begin without delay.

1:00 P.M.—LUNCH

Lunchtime is generally when you and some of the department Keys watch dailies. You might also need the time to work on rewrites or meet with anyone you couldn't break away from the set to see in the morning. There is almost always something to do every minute that you are at work.

2:00 P.M.—BACK TO WORK

Your main purpose is to concentrate on what ends up on screen. However it is important to realize that any difficulties that may be happening behind-the-scenes with the crew could affect what goes on in front of the cameras. Because you are seen as the commander of the troops, in a lot of ways, your own mood and attitude sets the tone for everyone else. A crew that dreads coming to work every day shows up exclusively for the paycheck. However, the more pleasant and cooperative you can be with your collaborators, the happier they will be to go above and beyond in helping to make a quality product.

Roughly 95 percent of your day is spent just answering questions. Actors will need to know how to play a scene or say a specific line of dialogue. You'll be working with the Director of Photography to find the best way to cover the scenes. The First AD will want to know how you plan to do work later that day or later in the schedule. The Production Designer will have questions about sets that are under construction. The Costume Designer will bring TEAR SHEETS for you to approve. Casting will need input regarding new hires and Extras. Studio Executives and Producers will approach you with their own questions and concerns. Keeping the totality of the project in focus amidst the chaos can be challenging.

9:00 P.M.—WRAP

The First AD and Script Supervisor will be looking to make sure that nothing gets missed throughout the day, like quick INSERT SHOTS or important coverage. Be sure to communicate as soon as possible any new ideas at all that should and can be shot before wrap if time permits. Otherwise, when all of the scenes on the call sheet have been shot or time has run out for the day, the First AD will call WRAP, and all of the equipment will be put away. Take a few moments to run through the expectations for tomorrow with the First AD and the DP so that everyone can get right back to work in the morning.

If you are also the Writer, you may have to do some rewrites before you can get to bed. Weekends "off" can be filled with revisions or meetings with department Keys or Executives. During production, don't expect to have much time for friends, family, or yourself.

Once the entire show wraps and officially moves into postproduction, the demands on your time lighten up. Assuming you're on schedule and not under a severe time crunch, there should be time to sleep and see family and friends again. You may still have long days, but you won't be trapped on a dark sound-stage until the wee hours of the morning.

Hopefully, you've been able to cut a version of the movie during production, so post will really be your time to revise and get a sense of the movie you have on film instead of the hypothetical idea you had in your mind during preproduction. What seemed like a great scene on the page may not work as intended once the footage is cut together. Whatever the cause, you are usually able to fix and remake the movie in the editing process and hopefully come out the other end with a better movie than the one you originally envisioned.

The DGA allows the Director ten weeks to deliver a cut of the film for review by the Producers. Undoubtedly, there will be pages of notes regarding elements that they'll ask you to change in some way. You'll recut and resubmit and repeat that over and over again until everyone is satisfied. There may be an audience reaction screening where "normal" people who are not in the movie business will watch your movie and give their own notes. Enough positive comments will signal the end of postproduction sooner. Enough negative comments could compel the studio to want to reshoot entire scenes that the audience didn't think worked.

The studio marketing team has been working hard to promote your movie even before you're finished. You'll be asked to sit for a few days of interviews at the press junket. An **EPK** interview that could end up in the promotions or on the DVD will also be scheduled sometime during production or post.

Once the movie is finished and you're done promoting it, the release comes and everything is out of your hands. Hopefully, you've created the best movie that you could under the circumstances, so your satisfaction should come from that accomplishment no matter how the audience and critics react.

WHAT I REALLY WANT TO DO IS MOVE UP!

Directing in the trenches can be a grueling experience no matter how rewarding it is creatively. The next step up is to become a Producer, who oversees an entire project, both creatively and logistically. You'll have the responsibility of meeting the creative objectives of the project while working within the parameters of the financing entity that is interested in making as much profit as possible. Business and art collide on your desk, and it's your job to find ways to make both interests happy.

To reach this level, you have to have amassed the political clout or financial resources that allow you to take an idea or existing screenplay and put it into production. Relationships you've formed with Studio Executives, A-list Actors, agents, Managers, other Directors, Writers, and financial entities are the key to attracting the talent and capital required to take an idea from script to screen.

Chapter 20

What I Really Want to Do Is Script Supervise!

WHAT THE HECK IS A SCRIPT SUPERVISOR?

The Script Supervisor keeps a detailed log of each take, notes dialogue changes, and tracks continuity.

That, and what else?

You will be watching every detail on every take and at the same time keeping in mind how it all works together. This encompasses everything from which hand an Actor picks a prop up with to making sure the set looks correct from one setup to the next. During each take you will also read the script and listen to the Actors speak the dialogue in case they change a line or miss one altogether. Your job can be mentally exhausting.

I get a chair next to the Director?! I must be making really good money then, right?

A lower-budget nonunion project will pay you around $225 a week. A nonunion Script Supervisor can expect $1,000 a week for mid-range budget projects. Larger television and film movies will pay around $400 a day. A commercial will pay about $550 for 10 hours, plus overtime.

You get additional compensation whenever more than one camera is rolling at the same time. Plus you get an additional half-hour to wrap out every day to finish up any necessary paperwork. A top Script Supervisor can negotiate a higher hourly rate that is over scale.

WHAT DO I REALLY NEED TO KNOW?

Because you are watching continuity primarily, it's important to know whom to talk to if something isn't right. For instance, if an Actor is wearing the wrong shoes or carrying the wrong purse, it's important to know if you should discuss it with Wardrobe or Props. If something has been moved on a desk, do you talk about it with Set Dressing, Property, or with the Camera Operator? You're not just noting problems in the margins. It's part of your job to help make corrections, and knowing what everyone does on the set is vital to that end.

While individual styles exist between Script Supervisors, there is a basic format for the paperwork. The books and classes available to teach you how to do it are essential; however nothing will take the place of actually being on a set and seeing how it is done.

WHAT DO I REALLY NEED TO HAVE?
I just have to read. What could I possibly need?

You'll need a three-ring binder/bag in which to keep the screenplay. This allows you to add pages easily as the script is rewritten and edited throughout the shooting schedule.

You're also going to need some pens, pencils, a pencil sharpener, a ruler, a stopwatch, small stapler, scissors, stick-on tabs, transparent tape, a calculator, and a Polaroid camera for continuity reference photos, with a hole-puncher to keep them all together for quick access.

You want to look professional, but it's more important to wear comfortable clothing. Most sets are quite casual, even for the Producers who visit.

What's the best way for someone to reach me?

The Script Supervisor Union (IATSE Local 871) has an Available List on which you can place your name once you've joined.

WHERE DO I REALLY NEED TO GO?
I just want to work.

Unlike other departments with entry-level positions, the Script Supervisor job is its own self-contained department. You don't work your way up to the job, and there is no direct job to move up to from it.

To get into IATSE Local 871, you need to show that you've worked one hundred nonunion days or thirty union days by presenting valid pay stubs to Contract Services.

Another way to get into the union is to gain employment on a nonunion show that turns union partway through the schedule. The union takes your $5,000 initiation fee and you are then eligible to work on any union project that you are offered. You will also pay quarterly dues of approximately $190 to remain in good standing.

Unless you get incredibly lucky or have relatives in the business, be prepared to struggle for six months to a year or more. There tend to be lulls in work during the summer and after the first of the year. To avoid this, try to hook up with Producers and Production Coordinators who can give you steady work. Attaching yourself to a big-time Director is only good for you when she's working, which can amount to just one feature every two years if you're lucky. Working at that level will look great on your resume, but that kind of schedule won't pay your bills. Television Directors don't take their favorites with them, as most shows have crews built in for the duration of production. You want to diversify your pool of people who call you. Unless you're at the top of everyone's list, you'll probably average about six to eight months of work a year.

So how do I get work?

Put together a résumé and send it out to smaller productions and student filmmakers who are willing to have you around. Working for free will give you some experience and build your résumé. Once you feel like you've got a good sense of how to do the job, look for larger budget productions and send your résumé to the Production Coordinator on them. Obviously you want the jobs that could actually lead you somewhere with decent pay, so keep an eye out for names in the listings that most likely have connections to bigger and bigger shows.

WHAT AM I GETTING MYSELF INTO?
So who calls me? The Director...Producer...who?

It depends on who knows you and where your name came from. If you've worked with the Director before and she asks for you specifically, you've got the job. Someone from the production office will call you in to fill out start paperwork and give you a script.

If no one above the line really knows you or your work, you'll most likely go in for a meeting with the Line Producer first. If he likes you and feels like you can do the job, you'll meet with the Director. If she likes you, then you get the job.

Okay, I got the job. What now?

You'll start your prep. Read the script and start to break it down into its various elements, like locations, characters, wardrobe, and props.

Before shooting begins, you might have a meeting with the Director to discuss how important elements of continuity are to her. Some Directors are militant about sticking to the written dialogue, while others couldn't care less. Those types of issues are important for you to be aware of before you get on set.

Your paid prep time varies per the type of project you're working on. A half-hour episodic will give you a day to prep each show. An hour-long episodic will allow two days prep before the season begins. You'll get two weeks for the really big movies.

What will my life really be like?

7:00 A.M.—GET TO WORK

Make sure your chair is next to the monitors at VIDEO VILLAGE and get your script prepared for the first setup. Number the lines and read through the scene again.

7:05 A.M.—REHEARSAL

As the Director, Director of Photography, and the Actors block the scene, you'll be paying more attention to the dialogue than to any of the action. If some of the blocking seems to be pretty well set, write that down in your notes, but be prepared for any of it to change ON THE DAY.

Some Actors come to the set knowing all of their lines, but most need some help at one point or another. When they get stuck, you may be expected to shout out the next couple of words to get them going again.

7:15 A.M.—CAMERA SETUP

The rehearsal is done and the Actors have gone back to their trailers. As the rest of the crew lights the set and prepares the cameras, you should be prepping your paperwork for that shot and for the rest of the day.

If it was a complete rehearsal and it appears to be a reasonably accurate rendition of what will take place on film, write down a description of the shot in pencil but be prepared to alter it after the first take.

Once the camera appears to be ready, ask the Second AC about the lens, T-stop, filter, and camera roll number. Ask the Sound Department which sound roll they're on. Give the scene number (and take, if applicable) to the Second AC and to the Boom Operator. Confer with other departments if necessary regarding continuity issues. If the Actors stick around set, they may ask you to run lines with them if they were having trouble in the rehearsal.

A typical setup will involve just one camera aiming at one Actor. The level of difficulty rises with additional cameras rolling at once, the use of a roving STEADICAM, and if you have no monitor to view the shot as it happens. Just do your best to understand what the cameras will be seeing, and feel free to ask the Camera Operators what the shots were after each take. Most Camera Operators will let you look through the lens, unless it is a handheld or Steadicam shot, in which case the frame lines are not certain.

When everything on the set appears to be ready, hop out of your chair, grab your Polaroid, and take some pictures. You don't need photos of everything; only the parts of the set that the camera will see on that specific take are important.

Take enough pictures to make following continuity easy, but not so many as to make it impossible to find anything later on. You're using a Polaroid instead of a digital camera because you have actual pictures to reference instantly and show to others if necessary. Wait to take any pictures until the last minute, as things change constantly right up to and throughout the setup.

The First AD will shout out for quiet then will say, "Roll sound." Sit right next to the Director. If there isn't a designated video playback person, it's in your best interest to push record on the VCR (if there is one) that is connected to the monitor. There's no better way to double-check continuity than by going back to the actual take on videotape.

Sit in your chair with the script in your lap and a pencil in your hand. Get ready to write. Give the shot 100 percent of your attention.

7:45 A.M.—ROLL CAMERA

When the AD says, "Roll camera," the Second AC will stick the slate in front of the lens. You should double-check the information on it in case he has written the wrong scene or take numbers. Depending on the mood of the set, you can either shout out a correction right then or just make a note of it and quietly bring it to his attention before the next take. It's possible that you "lost" a take somewhere, so it may be better for everyone to work it out later.

When the Director says, "Action!" start your stopwatch.

From this point on, you've got one eye on your script and the other on the monitor. You should go back and forth between them, watching for dialogue and all the action that takes place, including what the cameras are doing. If you look to the script too often, you're bound to miss some of the action. Using shorthand notes, you'll keep track of everything said and done and when and where they do it. If you happen to be looking down at the script when an Actor does something unexpected, you'll have to depend on him or the Camera Operator to help fill in the blanks for you. It's almost impossible to catch everything that is going on, especially in wide master shots that might have oodles of Extras, but just do your best to keep up.

As an added bonus to your task, if an Actor is absent, the First AD may ask you to read the off-screen lines. Obviously that takes you away from your primary job of paying attention to everything else that is going on. If possible, ask a dialogue coach or the AD himself to do it. The job is hard enough without having to be a surrogate Actor as well.

As soon as the take is done, the Director will yell, "Cut!" Stop your stopwatch and write down the time immediately. The Director will get up and start talking to Actors or the camera crew. Listen carefully to what everyone is saying. The Camera Operator may say that there was a problem with focus or framing. You need to hear that kind of comment and make a note of it. The Director may not have liked part of the Actor's performance. Write that down. Get out of your chair and go to the set if necessary to hear everything that is going on. The Editors will want to know which takes to use, and your notes will be their map around the problems.

7:48 A.M.—CUT! LET'S GO AGAIN

Unless you are under extreme time pressure or shooting an unrepeatable stunt, there will almost always be more than one take. The First AD will shout out, "Going again." You need to follow up with a shout of your own, "Take two!" loud enough that the Second AC and the Boom Operator can hear it. Hopefully, they will repeat it back to you so you know that the message got through.

Watch the set closely. The Set Decorator or the Camera Operator may suddenly shift things around on set for subsequent takes. If you're not paying attention, you may not notice until the setup is over. If a question of continuity comes up and your pictures don't reflect the new configuration (e.g., items on a desk), then you'll have to rely on someone else to tell you when things got moved around.

Also, the Actors may do things differently from take to take. Pay close attention to how they sit down, which direction they turn, and which hand they use to pick things up. Matching action is vitally important, particularly to the Editors who will have to make each cut look as seamless as possible.

8:10 A.M.—CUT, MOVIN' ON

When the Director is reasonably certain that she has at least one good take (but usually two), the First AD will shout out, "Movin' On!"

If you're moving on from the entire scene, run through your shot sheet and make certain that there isn't anything else needed, like inserts. In some cases, the Director may have just decided not to do a shot without telling you about it. Either way, it's your responsibility to double-check. Direct and edit the movie in your head to anticipate what the scene needs.

In most cases, only the best of the takes will get PRINTED, and it's your job to circle them in your notes so that the lab knows which ones to handle. As you've gone through the takes, you've noted what was good and what was bad in each. Now, as you prepare to move on to the next setup, the Director will ask you which of them were the best and why. Make her aware of any potential problems, like continuity or CROSSING THE LINE.

When you're ready, sit down to prep the next scene in your book. Number it and update the Editor's log as everyone moves into the next rehearsal.

1:00 P.M.—LUNCH

When the First AD calls "Lunch!" make a note of the time in your daily progress report. Don't run off right away. Hang out until the Director goes in case she needs to ask you about anything. Hand in your reports to the Second AD and head to the caterer.

2:00 P.M.—BACK TO WORK

The second half of the day will run pretty much like the first except that things tend to get a little more frantic as time runs out.

Get in the habit of reading through the next day's work while you're still on set. You want to know what's required for each of those scenes and prepare yourself mentally for any potential difficulties. By the time you reach home, looking at the script will be the last thing you really want to do so try to finish that work before you leave.

As you sense wrap approaching, finish off any notes that you can in the daily progress report and the Editor's log.

9:00 P.M.—WRAP

Finish up any last-minute notes and then make copies of all of your work and turn them in to an AD.

When the show wraps, you'll turn in the original completed script and the continuity Polaroids to the Production Coordinator. Although you have no official responsibilities during postproduction, you should keep a copy of the script and the Editor's log just in case there is an emergency (e.g., something got lost).

WHAT I REALLY WANT TO DO IS MOVE UP!

This is not a direct route to becoming a Director, or anything else for that matter. However, because of your proximity to the Director and Producers in video village, it could get you a job directing episodes of a television show. You're literally in a position on set where the creative decisions are made. You get to observe Directors interacting with Actors and the rest of the crew. It's kind of like getting the benefits of a film school without having to pay for it. Being a First AD also puts you into close proximity with the Director, but that is a job you have to work through the ranks to achieve. If you are a successful Script Supervisor, your chair is right next to the Director from the beginning.

So, particularly if you want to direct, it's really important to know what everyone else is doing on set. This will help you become a more efficient and understanding Director if your opportunity comes.

Part IV

THE CAMERA DEPARTMENT

What I Really Want To Do Is...

Load

Second AC

First AC

Operate

DIT

DP

Chapter 21

What I Really Want to Do Is Load!

WHAT THE HECK IS A LOADER?

As the entry-level member of the Camera Department, a Loader is responsible for putting raw film stock into the film MAGAZINES and taking it back out after it is shot. The Loader must keep an accurate inventory for every foot of film that is used during production. He is also expected to be of assistance on the set whenever possible.

That, and what else?

In addition to helping the Second AC's on set, you may also be asked to make phone calls for crew or equipment purposes. You will also most likely be the one at the camera truck for equipment pickups and returns. While equipment inventory and timecards are generally the responsibility of the Key Second AC, you may be asked to keep track of those things for everyone in the department.

But I shot film in college! I'm better than having to do this.

Working your way up through the ranks gives you an invaluable education. You'll learn about the tools large-budget projects use and the variety of situations that arise on set, all of which can only make you a better Director of Photography in the future. If you think that you are ready to enter the job market as a Director of Photography without working your way up from an entry-level position, then by all means go for it. Just be aware that there are a plethora of details that you probably aren't even aware of, and you'll have to rely on your experienced crew to support you until you get up to speed.

Still, it is safe to say that the Loader performs one of the most important jobs on set, even though it is considered an entry-level position. Almost every other person on the set has an opportunity to correct his or her mistakes as they happen. When the day begins, a roll of raw film stock is worth only what was paid for it, around $500 or so. After that roll has been exposed and taken off the camera, it is now worth thousands upon thousands of dollars. The efforts of all who are working on the movie are recorded on those rolls of film for which you are responsible. A single day of production may cost the company $100,000 and up, so your role is crucial.

How much can I make doing this?

If you are doing a nonunion low-budget production, your pay could be as low as nothing or up to $100 a day. Once you join the IATSE Local 600, expect to make between $35,000 and $40,000 on a typical twelve-week studio feature.

WHAT DO I REALLY NEED TO KNOW?

Learn everything you can about motion picture photography before setting out on the job hunt. While most of the specifics of photography do not apply to the Loader's job per se, being able to express some knowledge of the craft to those who are in the position to hire you can help immensely.

Take the time to practice loading film on your own and familiarize yourself with the various pieces of equipment that you are most likely to use. Your job and the job of the other Camera Assistants is less about photography and more about technical support.

On low-budget films you will be asked to be the Second AC in addition to loading film. With that in mind, learn everything you can about being a Second AC before looking for work on small projects.

WHAT DO I REALLY NEED TO HAVE?

There are just a few basic items that you should have as a Loader. You can (and will) add to your kit as you move up.

A changing tent is a portable darkroom, small enough to fold and use just about anywhere, yet large enough to fit a film magazine and film inside. You'll need this if you are working on a low-budget production that didn't rent a truck with a darkroom or if you are shooting on a location in which getting back to the truck to reload mags is too inconvenient. Expect to pay around $200.

Most ACs like to wear a waist pouch to carry things they need to keep close at all times. The specialized pouch itself will cost around $50. Fill it with lens tissue and fluid, chalk for marking Actors, a notepad and pen, a Sharpie marker, a flashlight, a "Leatherman" all-purpose tool, a small flathead screwdriver, and a dry-erase marker for the SLATE.

Besides the camera, the slate is probably one of the most iconic of all objects associated with movie making, and you should have one in your kit. Expect to pay about $50. On higher end shows, the Sound Department supplies "smart slates" or "time-code slates" so your old-fashioned model won't be needed.

There is a lot of stuff to move around during the day, so you'll want to have at least one cart as you begin your career. A collapsible MagLiner will cost about $400.

WHERE DO I REALLY NEED TO GO?
I just want to work.

In addition to Los Angeles, other major cities have camera rental houses that provide professional level equipment for projects of all types. Call a prep technician at one of them and explain that you would like to practice loading magazines. If they are not busy that day, most likely someone will help you for a few minutes and then let you work alone for a while. As you will see, it isn't particularly difficult to do; you just need to learn the basics.

Once you familiarize yourself with the different camera systems off the set, you'll be ready enough to ask for the Loader position on a small movie. Don't get ahead of yourself too quickly. Threading film through magazines is only part of the job. Dealing with film management, paperwork, and learning set etiquette are all vitally important, too.

So how do I get work?

Find a small student film or nonunion production in need of a Loader. Volunteer to work for free if necessary. Do your job competently with a pleasant demeanor and those you're working with will hopefully like you enough to call you for their next project or recommend you to others. Keep in touch with the Camera Assistants and the DP after the film wraps. In time, you'll either find yourself on a large project that turns union, or you'll amass enough days to qualify for IATSE Local 600. Call the union for specific membership requirements.

WHAT AM I GETTING MYSELF INTO?
So, who calls me for work?

Assistants with whom you've worked previously will call you or recommend you to others they know.

Okay, I got the job. Now what?

You and the other Assistants meet at the camera rental house to prep the camera package and load it into the truck. You'll be working with the First Assistant Cameraman (AC) to test every magazine for scratches. The Production Coordinator will have Transportation deliver boxes of film stock that you'll begin loading into the magazines in preparation for day one of filming.

What will my life really be like?

6:42 A.M.—GET TO WORK

Carefully get the carts out of the truck and to the ground. The First and Second ACs will prep the camera and other accessories before heading to set.

Find out from the DP what film stock he will be starting with and whether he might be using any other stocks during the course of the day. You may be able to figure this out by looking at the CALL SHEET.

Once everything is ready to go, you and the Second AC will roll the carts to the set. Once you get everything placed as per the Second AC's orders, ask if there is anything else that needs to be done and let him know what work you have yet to complete.

The Darkroom

The darkroom is your office. Every professional camera truck has one built in as part of the design. Some are better than others.

The bench is where you will be loading fresh raw stock into magazines and unloading exposed film into cans. Because of the size of the magazines and the film cans, a wide and deep workbench is better, but few darkrooms have the perfect working environment. You're stuck with what they give you.

The shelves are where you will keep your supplies: fresh film, empty cans, bags, cores, camera reports, labels, tape, pens, inventory forms, purchase orders, air, stapler, three-hole punch, scissors, and miscellaneous files.

The door always has a locking mechanism to prevent it from being opened while you are inside loading film. Most darkrooms have the lock accessible only from the inside. A few, though, are equipped with key locks on the outside so that the film can be secured while you are not around.

The light switch is usually easy enough to reach but not in a position where it might be turned on accidentally.

7:00 A.M.—LOADING FILM

While blocking and rehearsal is taking place on set, you get to do what your job title describes. In short, your primary responsibility is to make sure that there is film available to shoot on set at all times. The goal is to never have the company waiting for you.

Most of your mags should be up and ready from the night before. You always want to have at least one of each type of stock loaded (if there are just two stocks on the truck) so that the A-camera can be ready to go right away. Make sure that any ready mags are out on set as soon as possible.

7:15 A.M.—CAMERA SETUP

Once you're finished getting mags ready for the day, get to set as soon as you can to help out.

On some occasions, there will be a First AC and a Second AC for every camera that is working, so you will have less to do on set and can concentrate more on your actual job of loading film. Spend as much time on set as possible to help and to learn.

7:45 A.M.—ROLL CAMERA

You may be asked to help slate one of the cameras for the setup, so check with the Second AC prior to the take.

7:48 A.M.—CUT, LET'S GO AGAIN

If a single take is sufficiently long enough or when enough takes have been shot on a roll of film, the First AC will reload his camera with a new mag of fresh film that you've provided. If it's possible and necessary for you to reload that magazine right away, leave your slate with the Second AC and get to the darkroom.

8:10 A.M.—CUT, MOVIN' ON

The Second AC will hand over the completed camera reports to the Script Supervisor for verification. When she is finished, get the reports from her and keep your paperwork up-to-date throughout the day.

1:00 P.M.—LUNCH

On occasion, you'll be asked to do a FILM BREAK, which means getting everything to the lab that has already been shot up to this point in the day. You may have to finish off mags and paperwork while everyone else heads to lunch. In most cases though, you'll have a relaxing break like the rest of your colleagues.

2:00 P.M.—BACK TO WORK

Your day consists of constant diligence in making sure that shot film is CANNED OUT and the mags are reloaded with the proper film stock while simultaneously keeping an eye on set in case the rest of the crew needs your help during setups. Just because there is a magazine ready to go to the truck doesn't always mean that you drop everything else. After you've helped set the cameras up for the setups, head back to the truck to deal with any shot magazines.

9:00 P.M.—WRAP

As you sense wrap approaching, do whatever you can to get a jump on things. Make sure you have all the available camera reports back from the Script Supervisor. All the film (except what is in progress) should be canned out with the reports written up and taped on the cans. Put the cans in boxes or tape up what you have. All available numbers should be entered into the inventory, and you should have subtotals worked out. Have your P.O. (purchase order) completed as much as possible. The only thing you should have left to do when wrap is called is any remaining in-progress magazines.

Call "Transpo" on the radio and let them know the film is ready. When you are finished on the truck, find an AD and give him his copies of your paperwork.

You may also be asked to keep track of and fill out weekly time cards for the rest of the camera crew. Either you or the Second AC will be in charge of this.

You can save yourself a lot of time in the mornings by quickly preparing a few things the night before. Keep an eye on the advanced schedule, and try to get ahold of a call sheet before wrap. You want to see what to expect for the next day and have the opportunity to ask the DP some questions regarding equipment and film stock. If you know what stock will be shot the following day, you can have it ready beforehand.

Once you've finished with all of your work, see if the First or Second Assistants need help. Chances are, they'll be ready to go. Help strap the carts back in and close up the truck.

WHAT I REALLY WANT TO DO IS MOVE UP!

As a Loader, you will be given many opportunities to do the job of the Second AC and learn the next job up. Generally, after a few projects as a Loader, you will be hired on to be a Second AC and re-rate to that designation in the union. As the Second AC, you will be given opportunities to learn the job of the First AC. Most Loaders move up to be Seconds, and most Seconds move up to be Firsts. But not all Firsts make the jump to Operator, and not all Operators get to DP. And only a select few DPs are ever given the chance to direct. The influence of politics, rather than actual skill, over your rise up the ladder increases steadily as you get closer to DP status.

Chapter 22

What I Really Want to Do Is Second AC!

WHAT THE HECK IS A SECOND AC?

Second AC stands for Second Camera Assistant, or Second Assistant Cameraman. The Second AC is primarily responsible for keeping track of all the necessary camera equipment that is needed for the project. As an added bonus, the Second AC usually ends up in all the behind-the-scenes footage as well because he is also most visible as the person who "does the CLAPPER thingy" before each shot.

That, and what else?

The Second also assists the First AC when setting the camera up for new shots, getting focus marks, and reloading the camera with film. During rehearsals, the Second marks the Actor's positions on the floor with colored tape. The Second also keeps track of the footage used after each take.

At times, the Second may be asked to "BUMP UP" to pull focus on an additional camera.

Often a production will not hire a Loader for any number of reasons, so the Second must wear both hats during the day. The Second must also know enough about the Focus Puller's job so that he can anticipate what may be needed and why.

A move up means more money, right?

A union (IATSE Local 600) Second AC can expect to earn between $35,000 and $50,000 in three to four months' time. Be aware, though, that moving up potentially means losing some work initially as you establish yourself in a new position, so your overall yearly income may decrease at first.

WHAT DO I REALLY NEED TO KNOW?

Chances are that your first work in the Camera Department will be on a low-budget or student film as the Second *and* Loader. Despite the lack of money and often painfully long hours, these situations are excellent training ground for learning the basics of a movie set and the Camera Department in particular.

The most important assets a Second AC can have are good organizational skills and a great awareness of everything that is going on. It is vital that you know the various types of cameras and all the accessories that are available and what is necessary to make them work. You also need to know where to get them and when.

WHAT DO I REALLY NEED TO HAVE?
I gotta get more stuff!?

Not necessarily. If you started out on low-budget projects and came up through the ranks as a Loader, then the odds are that you have just about everything you'll need to be an adequate Second AC.

At some point, however, you'll want to start acquiring some of the tools of the First AC for those special moments when you are needed over on B- or C-camera to pull focus. See the next chapter for a list of those items.

What's the best way for someone to reach me?

As a union Assistant, your information will be listed in the membership directory and you will have the opportunity to place your name on the Available List.

WHERE DO I REALLY NEED TO GO?
I just want to work.

If you're Seconding, then you most likely have a decent foothold in the industry already. Keep in touch with everyone with whom you've worked, be they Operators or other Assistants. If you're not getting hired as much as you'd like or if you're stuck in the low-budget world, then be willing to go back to loading on bigger projects, if that's what it takes to get to work with more experienced people. The important thing is finding someone on the types of projects you're attracted to who is willing to take you on. Be persistent, but don't be a pest.

So how do I get work?

You may find yourself in the fortunate position of hooking up with a First Assistant who works consistently. If he likes you and your work, the chances are that you will travel from show to show with that one Assistant. The upside to this is a fairly steady income without having to pick up the phone. The downside is that if that

Assistant suddenly stops working or chooses to move up then you are on your own. The solution is to take day calls with other crews whenever you are available. This will spread your name around town. Be nice to *everybody*! You never know who will be your boss next week.

WHAT AM I GETTING MYSELF INTO?
So, who calls me for work?

One of the First Assistants with whom you've worked previously will call you or recommend you to others she knows.

Okay, I got the job. Now what?

You'll meet the Loader and the First AC at the camera rental house to prep the camera package and load it into the truck. You'll be working with the First AC and Loader testing every piece of equipment, big and small, to make sure that everything works before it goes on the truck.

What will my life really be like?

6:42 A.M.—GET TO WORK
Carefully get the carts out of the truck and to the ground. There may be upward of five to six carts of equipment to take to set every day.

Before you push them to the set, you'll load them with everything you'll need from the truck. Typically, most of what you need will already be on the carts, but some stuff comes off every night. Also, some of the gear from the night before may have to be cleaned up quickly, if it wasn't done at wrap.

While the Loader is responsible for film stock, double-check with him and the First AC about what stocks will be used that day.

Once everything is ready to go, you, the First AC, and the Loader will roll the carts to the set. Generally, the camera truck is the one parked closest, so you shouldn't have far to go.

7:00 A.M.—GETTING TO SET
Park the carts so that they won't be in the way or in danger of being seen by the cameras. The DP or the AD may already know where the safe areas are before the rehearsal.

If there is a DIRECTOR'S VIEWFINDER, have it out and ready. Also have your paper tape roll with you. Stand near the DP and wait for a rehearsal to begin. You should have looked at a CALL SHEET the night before so you know what to expect, but check it again for anything out of the ordinary.

7:05 A.M.—REHEARSAL
Typically the Director and Actors will rehearse a couple of times before calling for a marking rehearsal. As the rehearsal continues, you'll dash out to an Actor's

position and mark it on the floor with a **T**. Fall back and wait for the next position to be marked.

7:15 A.M.—CAMERA SETUP

Once rehearsal is finished, First Team will go away and Second Team will take the marks as lighting and camera setup begins. The First AC will need help getting the camera set up with the proper head, lens, and accessories. As the Operator lines the shot up, stay aware of what is going on. He may shift the Stand-ins around a bit for framing purposes, which means that you need to run in and adjust the T-mark that you laid down earlier.

If the show is big enough, a separate Video/Playback Department will be hired to handle VIDEO VILLAGE. Often, though, this task will fall on you and the Loader. Set up the monitors that came with your camera package.

If the Sound Department is supplying a SMART-SLATE, make sure it is prepared with the proper information from the Script Supervisor. All the information that you've written on the slate should show up on the camera report. Tape the report to the back of the slate.

Camera blocking and lighting will continue up to the very last second before the First Team comes back in, so you have to stay aware of changes to the T marks that may take place. Once the First AD has called for First Team again, get your slate ready and stand by the camera. Another rehearsal will probably take place to inform the Actors of any blocking changes that might have occurred since the first run-through. Sometimes, though, they decide to SHOOT THE REHEARSAL. Just be ready for that.

7:45 A.M.—ROLL CAMERA

When the time does come to actually roll film, grab your slate and step out onto the set. You need to place the slate directly in front of the camera so that the Operator will not have to move his frame to find the slate. It also must be at a distance at which the slate FILLS THE FRAME.

When the First AD calls, "Roll sound!" put the slate into the shot with the STICKS open. The Boom Operator says, "Sound speed!" Wait a beat, then say, "Mark." While holding the slate steady, clap the sticks together. Scurry off the set as quickly and quietly as possible. Find a place to go that will be out of the Actor's eye-lines and stay quiet as any movement or noise may distract them.

7:48 A.M.—CUT, LET'S GO AGAIN

Once the shot is over, the Director yells, "Cut!" and the Operator turns off the camera. If you can't see the footage counter, ask the First AC for the number and then write it down on the camera report. Write the next take number on the front of the slate in case they go again.

Keep up with the math on the report so that you know how long each take is. If it doesn't look like there will be enough film in the camera to complete another whole take, let the First know immediately. Take the spent mag, make sure that all the necessary numbers are written in on the camera report, and hand the report to the Script Supervisor. Put the new camera report on the back of the slate. Write the new roll number on both the report and the front of the slate. Double-check what take is next and write that on the slate, too. Let the Loader know about the reload.

8:10 A.M.—CUT, MOVIN' ON

Once the Director decides that he's got that shot, the whole process begins all over again for the next setup. On a typical shooting day, you may accomplish around ten setups or so requiring five to twenty takes per setup and anywhere from three thousand to thirty-thousand feet of film. This varies, of course, with the complexities of the shots or limitations of locations. But the gist of your job is to help set the camera up, hit the sticks, and move the carts around.

1:00 P.M.—LUNCH

Cover the cameras to keep dust away and also to ward off curious visitors. Head to lunch with everyone else.

2:00 P.M.—BACK TO WORK

If there is a FILM BREAK, help the Loader get all the magazines to the truck if it hasn't already been done. As with all the other setups throughout the day, stand by with the director's finder and your paper tape. As the day progresses, the pace will likely increase as pressure mounts to complete the work listed on the call sheet. This will happen especially on day exterior locations as the sun falls toward the horizon. Despite the frantic nature of everything around you, you need to stay calm and methodical. Be quick, but don't misplace equipment or get sloppy with film stock. That perceived sense of urgency will only go so far if you start making mistakes.

9:00 P.M.—WRAP

As wrap approaches, start tidying up your carts. Pick up all finished camera reports from the Script Supervisor and do the math on them for the Loader, if you've got the time.

Get a call sheet prior to wrap and check for any special requirements that will be expected from your department in the days ahead. You want to do this while the DP is still around...not when he's on his way home.

After the last shot has cut, the First will CHECK THE GATE one last time. If it is good, the First AD calls an official wrap. Get the film from the camera first and take it to the Loader as soon as possible along with any remaining camera reports. The First will start disassembling the camera and will hand you parts to put away. Pick up the tape marks from the floor before you go. Get the carts onto the truck when everyone is ready and tie them in securely. Before you leave, record the out-times of everyone in your department.

WHAT I REALLY WANT TO DO IS MOVE UP!

You've already experienced the trials of moving up from Loader to Second Assistant. In many cases, those two jobs are treated as one, so the transition isn't usually very traumatic. While the job of Second/Loader is primarily a support position, as a First AC you will begin to take an active part in what is actually seen on screen. While you are still playing a technical role, there is a certain art to pulling focus that can't be taught in a book. The best way to prepare to be a First is to practice being a First. Look through the lens as you turn the focus knob. Learn the relationship between what you're doing off to the side of the camera and what will happen on film. When you find yourself without work on large projects, sign on to small student films, where you can practice pulling focus without the big-budget pressure.

Chapter 23

What I Really Want to Do Is First AC!

WHAT THE HECK IS A FIRST AC?

The First Camera Assistant (AC) is responsible for managing the Camera Department, maintaining the cameras in working order, and keeping each shot in focus. This person is also referred to as the Focus Puller.

Wait a minute. Did you just say focus? He's not the one looking through the camera, is he?

It does seem strange, having someone in charge of making sure that the shot is in focus who isn't actually looking through the viewfinder. And unlike most home video cameras, there is no auto focus to rely on.

The reason that the Camera Operator doesn't actually focus the image is twofold. First, in many cases, the Operator is using a gear head that requires two hands. He isn't physically able to reach the lens to turn the focus knob, use the zoom gun, or anything else. Nor should he. Keeping the action framed up can be difficult enough at times and requires full concentration. That's also part of the reason the Director of Photography doesn't usually operate the camera himself. He has too many other things to think about.

Second, when the action is planned (blocked) by the Director, the Actors, and the Director of Photography, the choreography between the Actors and the camera is very precise. Actors usually have very specific marks to hit, and the Dolly Grip also moves the camera to very specific marks. By measuring the various distances between the action and the camera throughout the entire move, the Focus Puller can use the very precise distance markings on the lens to keep everything in focus.

That, and what else?

In most cases, the DP or the Operator will call the shots, but when it comes to the equipment, it is really up to the First AC to know the best way to set up the camera with the appropriate accessories. Equipment management and safety are the primary concerns the First will have on his mind.

With the help of the Second AC and, typically, the Dolly Grip, the First AC prepares the camera for each new setup. He gets focus marks, reloads the camera with film, and keeps tabs on his Second and Loader.

There may be instances where the First may get the chance to operate a camera, but this is not a normal circumstance unless the DP is ready to let the First move up.

This can be an incredibly difficult and thankless job. Ninety-nine percent of what you do during the day may be perfect, but one SOFT shot will get all the attention. In addition to learning to gauge distances to the inch or less, someone putting himself in the position to be hired as a First AC should achieve a very high level of technical proficiency. Each job may bring many different types of equipment into play, and it is the First AC's job to know about all of them. Adequate time spent as a Loader and as a Second AC should give you the opportunities to glean this knowledge. Rarely does one get the job of a Focus Puller without first coming up through the ranks.

Soft shot? You just said that the Actors have marks to hit. Why would any shot ever be out of focus?

Actors don't always hit their marks, and the camera isn't always where it was planned to be. The Dolly Grip will make adjustments throughout a take to help the Camera Operator keep the action framed up. Because of this, the Focus Puller has to adjust as well, using his experience and well-trained sense of distance. Numerous factors conspire to make the job difficult, such as longer focal lengths, wide-open apertures, and Actors who consistently miss their marks.

All that stress and money, too?

As with previous moves up, be prepared for less income overall as the number of jobs you do throughout the year may decline at first. A union (IATSE Local 600) First AC can expect to gross between $40,000 and $60,000 on a typical studio project. Some assistants augment their paychecks by purchasing and then renting out personal equipment.

When you move up from Second AC to First, there is no change in your union designation. First and Seconds are both listed as "Assistant," so you are allowed to float back and forth if need be.

WHAT DO I REALLY NEED TO KNOW?

You need to know everything there is to know about the Loader's job and that of the Second AC. There may be instances where you will have to do it all by yourself. Even when you have the help, it is important to remember that your Assistants probably haven't been working in the business as long as you have, though this is not always the case. You're in charge, but always be willing to listen to comments and suggestions from others. Instead of micromanaging your department, you're better off hiring competent Assistants who can help you.

If you didn't get adequate time to play with all the different types of cameras available when you were a Second AC, it might be a good idea to travel around to rental houses to familiarize yourself with them. Day calls will pop up and suddenly you might be facing a camera that you've only seen in magazines. Four in the morning on a strange set is not the best time to learn where the "on" button is.

WHAT DO I REALLY NEED TO HAVE?
More stuff? Don't I have enough already?

You've already collected a lot as a Loader and a Second. In addition, you'll need a cloth tape measure and a steel tape measure. Those will cost between $25 and $50 each.

A great deal of math can is involved with lens, focus, and T-stop settings, so you'll find the DEPTH-OF-FIELD calculators invaluable.

A frontbox should also be on your list. This goes on the front of the head under the camera and is used by you to store pens, Stabilos, and other small things, like a box of mints or the DP's light meters.

What's the best way for someone to reach me?

Keep in contact with other Assistants, Camera Operators, and DPs you've worked with before. When you're not working, leave your name on the AVAILABLE LIST at the union office.

WHERE DO I REALLY NEED TO GO?
I just want to work.

If you're ready to move up to being a Focus Puller, you're probably already in the right place!

WHAT AM I GETTING MYSELF INTO?
Who calls to hire me?

The Director of Photography relies greatly on the First AC and needs someone she can trust. Most of your calls will come from her. In between large projects, you'll be DAYPLAYING and will get calls from Second ACs who are looking for additional crew.

Camera Prep

After you get the job, your first duty will be camera prep. This happens at the camera rental house of the DP's choice. Take your carts and other things that will wind up on the camera truck. Contact the rental house prep techs to find out when your package will be ready.

When you show up, you will have a prep tech assigned to you. Learn his name. He should give you a list of everything that has been ordered. It is the job of the ACs to go through every piece on the list, make sure it is actually in the package, and determine that it works correctly. Depending on the size of the production, camera prep can last anywhere from an afternoon to several weeks.

The First AC is essentially in charge of making sure the camera functions and that all the accessories work to his liking. It may be tempting to skip a piece of gear, but Murphy's Law will take over for certain. Take the time to test out everything, down to the smallest cable, and make sure it all fits together and works the way it should.

If you have a moment or two during the day, network with other Assistants, Operators, and DPs who are also prepping gear. Don't neglect your own work, but take advantage of the opportunity to chat with other professionals who you don't usually get a chance to see.

Okay, I got the job. Now what?

With help from the Production Coordinator, you'll set up a time to begin the camera prep at the rental house. You'll also call and hire a Key Second Camera Assistant and a Loader.

What will my life really be like?

6:42 A.M.—GET TO WORK

Help get the carts off the truck. While the Second finishes loading the carts with batteries and accessories, begin prepping your camera for the day. Take a moment with the Loader and make sure he has the proper film stocks loaded up in the magazines. If you don't know what he should have, you should find out from the DP as soon as possible and then relay that information back to the Loader.

7:00 A.M.—GETTING TO SET

Get everything to set as soon as you can. Find the Dolly Grip and have the dolly standing by.

7:05 A.M.—REHEARSAL

Pay close attention so that when you need to pull focus on the scene, the blocking won't be a complete surprise. One rehearsal may be all you get to see.

7:15 A.M.—SETUP

For each shot, the DP will let you know the camera's placement and configuration, as well as the lens used. The Operator may have a preference as to which head (gear or fluid) he wants to use. The Second AC and the Dolly Grip will help you build the configuration (camera, dolly, crane, Steadicam, or tripod) as required with the proper lens as well as any additional accessories you might need.

Once the Operator is looking through the lens, you can start finding your focus marks. If the camera is moving on a dolly or crane or if a Steadicam or handheld is used, your job becomes more complicated. Sometimes the DP will sneak a zoom into the dolly move. Now you're trying to hit focus marks as well as lens positions. All this will be determined as the Operator works out the mechanics of the shot with you, the Dolly Grip, and the Stand-ins. Each setup becomes a carefully choreographed dance where everyone and everything has to work in unison.

If there is a B-camera (and C, D, etc.), the same procedure has been taking place wherever they have set up. If you are the Key First (A-camera), double-check with the other First Assistants concerning their lenses and filtration. As Key First, you should be on top of what everyone else is doing.

Before First Team arrives, check with the DP about filtration, camera running speeds, exposure settings, and any other special considerations for the scene. The time to realize that there is a problem is *not* after the take.

7:45 A.M.—ROLL CAMERA

Make sure that your lens is not being flared by any lights shining toward it. Double-check with the Camera Operator to make certain that none of the Actor's tape marks or any focus tape marks that you may have put down will be in frame during the shot. If an Actor's mark is being minimized or removed, make sure that you or the Second AC informs the Actor of the change.

First Team will come in and probably run at least one rehearsal. This is your chance to see what the Actors will really do despite the way it was set up with the Stand-ins. Run your tape out again if necessary. If ever in doubt, jump onto the set and take the measurements. The AD will be pushing everyone to roll and you'll hear tons of reasons why you don't have time to run the tape, but this is your job. Be efficient, but take the time to do it right.

When everyone is satisfied with the rehearsal, the AD will call for LAST LOOKS. Once everyone clears, the AD will say something like, "Let's go on a bell." The Sound Mixer presses the button that rings the stage bell once. Upon hearing this, all are supposed to stop what they are doing and stay quiet.

The AD says, "Roll sound." At this point, either you or the Camera Operator will have a hand on the "on" switch and the Second AC will have the slate out in front of the lens. Make sure you have focus set on the slate. Keep those slates in focus! The Editors need to be able to read what's written on them.

A few seconds later, the Boom Operator will say "Sound speed." You or the Operator flip the switch. You make sure the camera hits 24 fps then say, "Speed." Say this loud enough for the Second AC to hear. Once he does, he'll clap the sticks and clear out of the way. Roll your focus back to your starting mark and say, "Ready." The Operator may repeat that louder if he had to adjust for any reason.

The Director says, "And...action!" Off you go. Position yourself best to see the Actors and the lens at the same time. Some setups make this difficult, but do what you have to in order to get where you need to be.

7:48 A.M.—CUT, LET'S GO AGAIN

Once the shot is over, the Director will yell, "Cut." You turn off the camera. For a variety of reasons, the Second AC may need to do TAIL STICKS after the scene. In this instance DO NOT turn the camera off. Instantly shout out, "Tail sticks!" The Second AC will run in and put the slate in front of the lens, but upside down. You get focus on it while the Operator frames it up. The Operator will say something like, "Hit it," and the Second will hit the sticks together. Now you can turn the camera off.

If you are unsure of how well you kept things in focus, ask the Operator how you did. Not all Operators are created equal. Some see focus better than others. If you think that you blew it, don't be afraid to let the DP know so you can go again. Ask for retakes too often and you'll be looking for another job within the week, but it's ultimately better to do one more take while everything is in place rather than waiting to find out you were SOFT in dailies the next day.

8:10 A.M.—CUT, MOVIN' ON

Once everyone seems happy, the AD will ask you to CHECK THE GATE. You're looking for "debris," such as film shavings or other dustlike particles, that may have been in the frame during the shot. If you find something, show the Operator and/or the DP and they will make a judgment on whether the shot should be done over. More often than not, you'll have a "good gate."

Move on to the next setup and repeat the process from a different position or location in the same or different configuration.

1:00 P.M.—LUNCH

Cover your camera and unplug it. The Loader may want your magazine from the camera for his film break. Take a moment and do it.

Depending on where you are shooting, you may have access to dailies from the day before either in an office if you are on stage or in the camera truck if you are on location. Get your food and go see dailies. It is important for you to be there, both politically and for your own education. Not only will you see what you did right and wrong, but you can also pay attention to how the Operator carried out a shot and also how the DP's lighting actually looks on film.

2:00 P.M.—BACK TO WORK

Don't let a bad dailies experience ruin your afternoon. If you missed focus on a shot or two the previous day, learn from your mistakes and move on. Unless you're consistently off, your job is probably secure.

As the day progresses, the pressure will be on to finish the work that is listed on the call sheet. Help out your Second when you can, whether it be laying down tape marks, pushing carts, or slating. By all means, do your job, but keep your department running as efficiently as possible.

9:00 P.M.—WRAP

As you sense wrap approaching, make sure your Loader is caught up on mags and camera reports and have the Second start putting unused equipment away. If you are reasonably confident that you won't need anything else or the Second is pulling double-duty as the Loader, have the Second leave you with the slate, an extra mag, and an extra battery on the last setup. He will peel off to catch up on the mags and paperwork.

When wrap is called, the AD will ask everyone to wait until you have checked the gate. Once you have declared it to be okay, run a few feet of film, then pull the mag off the camera and put it in an empty case. Pull the lens off the camera and put it away also.

Get a call sheet and confirm your call time. Before the DP leaves, make sure that there isn't anything out of the ordinary happening tomorrow or during the coming week that you haven't already discussed with him.

Put your camera and carts away in the truck. You may have maintenance to do on the camera either now or in the morning if there is time. Lock the truck and go home.

WHAT I REALLY WANT TO DO IS MOVE UP!

A lot of people pull focus until they retire. They either have no interest in going any further or the money is just too good as an Assistant. However, perhaps you've been through the ranks and are just burnt out being an Assistant. If so, it's time for you to move up and start Operating. The first thing to do is to let the DPs with whom you work know that you are interested. The right moment may pop up and you'll get thrown onto the B-camera for a shot or for the day. If all the cosmic tumblers fall into place, you may get hired on as the full-time Operator.

Another option is to purchase a Steadicam and practice until you're very good at it. When you are reasonably confident of your abilities, take day jobs on student films or low-budget movies. They'll be happy to have you for free or a cut-rate price. You get to practice with Actors in a real setting. When you feel really good, make the calls to your DPs and let them know you'd like a chance to operate for them. Wait for those cosmic tumblers again.

A third way to move up is to skip the Operator level and start working as a Director of Photography. Attempting this probably means that you will be working on lower budget material and they won't have the money to hire an additional Operator anyway. You get the job by default. The downside is that you won't be working on high-profile projects as you had been, but given enough time and the right circumstances, somebody back in the big-budget world will appreciate your work enough to hire you as a full-fledged Director of Photography.

Chapter 24

What I Really Want to Do Is Operate!

WHAT THE HECK IS A CAMERA OPERATOR?

Using a variety of support tools, the Camera Operator points the camera at whatever the Director asks him to and composes it in an aesthetically pleasing frame.

That, and what else?

Once the basic parameters of the shot are defined by the Director and DP, the Operator works with the First AC and the Dolly Grip to choose which equipment is best for the setup. The Operator then adjusts the blocking marks of Actors, set pieces, and props if necessary to create the most aesthetically pleasing frames. It is also the Operator's responsibility to keep "movie stuff" out of the frame, like the boom pole, C-stands, lights, cables, tape, unwanted shadows, and even members of the crew.

While the First AC is really only guessing where to put focus, the Operator is the only one on set who can actually see if an Actor has proper focus on him. The Operator should try to watch for this and give the First AC feedback, both good and bad.

There may be instances when the Operator may be asked to split off from the main unit and shoot inserts or even entire scenes. In this case, he is considered a Second Unit DP and usually will be re-rated, meaning he will get a pay increase for the day as if he were the DP for the production.

While items like Steadicam and Wescam are considered specialty skills, an Operator should be proficient operating in all other circumstances. He should know how and when to use a fluid head, a gear head, a "low-mode" head, a remote head, and a Dutch head. Handheld operating can happen at any time, and the Operator should be comfortable with many different types (and weights!) of cameras on his shoulder.

The Steadicam Operator not only needs to be excellent at his specialty but can't overlook learning how to operate under "normal" circumstances. Many productions will hire a Steadicam Operator who is expected to also operate a regular camera when necessary.

Specialized Operators, like Wescam (aerial) and Hydroflex (underwater) are usually called on a day-to-day basis to perform their one task.

I don't have to push carts anymore, and my rate goes up!?

The union Camera Operator's rate is higher than the First Assistant, but because you end up working fewer hours overall, you actually make the same amount of money or sometimes less. Your call time is later than the Assistant's, and you leave as soon as wrap is called.

Also, it is harder for you to rent any personal equipment to the production as you had done in the past unless you own a specialized piece of gear, like the Steadicam. Expect to make between $40,000 and $50,000 on a three- or four-month studio project.

WHAT DO I REALLY NEED TO KNOW?

Knowing how to pull focus, how to maintain equipment, and how to load film aren't prerequisites for knowing how to operate a camera, but knowledge of the equipment is. You need to be aware of the various dollies, heads, cranes, cameras, and accessories that you will use and when to choose one over the other.

Of course, there is art involved. An Assistant's job is considered to be technical support, but the job of the Operator is directly involved with moving the camera and finding those frames that will help determine the overall look of the project. A basic understanding and appreciation of what makes an aesthetically pleasing picture is essential.

Because you might get asked to take on the role of Second Unit DP from time to time, you should also know how to use a light meter and at the very least have a working knowledge of how to light a scene. It also helps to know which lights are best for which circumstances and the nicknames that the Electrics have for them. The Gaffer will be able to help you with this, but eventually you should know these things on your own.

WHAT DO I REALLY NEED TO HAVE?
What things do I need?

Once your career as an Operator seems fairly secure, you may decide to clear some space in your garage and sell your assistant gear. As an Operator, you won't need a lot of that stuff anymore.

If you haven't acquired one yet, you should purchase an incident light meter and a spot meter for those times you are asked to shoot something on your own.

What's the best way for someone to reach me?

Stay in touch with the First ACs, DPs, and Directors with whom you've worked before. Also keep your contact information current with the union local and place your name on the Available List whenever you're not working.

WHAT AM I GETTING MYSELF INTO?
Who calls to hire me?

You may get the call from a Director who has enjoyed working with you, from a DP who trusts your work, or an AC who has been given the task of finding an additional Operator for extra camera days on a show already in progress.

Okay, I got the job. What now?

Prior to the start of production, attend the camera prep at the rental house to test the camera heads and the viewfinder. If you are a Steadicam Operator, you'll want to build the system completely.

What will my life really be like?

7:00 A.M.—GET TO WORK

Your call is later than the Assistants. Typically you'll come in at the same time as the DP. Assistants are usually grateful for whatever help you can give them, but ask them before you start moving carts and equipment around. Those are their responsibility, and if they don't know where something is, they get the heat, not you.

7:05 A.M.—REHEARSAL

Typically they'll rehearse once or twice before calling for a MARKING REHEARSAL. You should pay attention to this so that when you need to line up the shot with Stand-ins, you can make adjustments that are reasonably close to where First Team wants to be.

7:15 A.M.—CAMERA SETUP

Don't try to be too helpful while a shot is being worked out. The DP will take charge. Just follow his lead. Let the First AC know which head, eyepiece, etc., you'd like to use. The same goes for the Dolly Grip. Talk about how best to lay track or configure the dolly. Then step back and let everybody build the setup. Lend a hand when you can, but too much "help" can actually slow things down.

The Stand-ins will come in while this is happening so that the DP and Gaffer can light the set. Once the camera is built and ready, you can look through the eyepiece and make adjustments. It is tempting to rush right in, but wait for the First AC to finish what he's doing, including balancing the camera. Take the time to do it right the first time.

Be clear and be pleasant when communicating with the Assistants, Grips, Stand-ins, and all other personnel. Bad attitudes get remembered, and the cooperation you receive depends on how you choose to treat others.

As the set is being lit, keep checking through your eyepiece for unwanted items, like C-stands, lights, tape marks, cables, the boom pole, B-camera, flares, and shadows. Finding those kinds of things while the camera is rolling is too late and is easily avoidable.

7:45 A.M.—ROLL CAMERA

The First Team will come in and probably run at least one rehearsal. This is your chance to see what the Actors will really do despite the way it was set up with the Stand-ins. You may need the Dolly Grip to adjust slightly or have the Second AC move the tape marks.

The AD puts the set "on a bell," then says, "Roll sound." At this point, either you or the First AC will have a hand next to the "on" switch and the Second AC will have the slate out in front of the lens. A good Second will know how to find the right place to be, but you may need to adjust your frame slightly to get the slate properly framed up. If you can't move your frame, communicate clearly to the Second which way to move the slate.

A few seconds later, the Boom Operator will say "Sound speed," and you or the Focus Puller flip the switch. Once the First says, "Speed," the Second will clap the sticks and clear out of the way. Reframe to your starting mark if necessary and say, "Ready."

The Director says, "And...action!" and off you go. Your primary responsibility is to keep the Actors in a pleasing frame. You also can help the First AC by watching to make sure that focus is correct. Help the DP by staying alert for odd or distracting lighting. They may have the video monitor to look through, but you have the best seat in the house and are really the first person who gets to see the movie.

7:48 A.M.—CUT, LET'S GO AGAIN

Once the shot is over, the Director will yell, "Cut." Turn off the camera. The First will usually like feedback about focus from you. Remember, he's just guessing, but you were the one watching it. If there was a problem, let him know right away. If it was great, tell him.

8:10 A.M.—CUT, MOVIN' ON

Once everyone is happy, you'll all move on to the next setup and repeat the process from a different position or location. Step away from the camera so that the AC can check the gate.

If you are an Operator on an additional camera, A-camera will take priority over your position. Typically you adjust to stay out of the way of A-camera. Don't adjust Actors or set pieces without checking with the A-Operator first. If you are not being used on a setup, hang back out of the way. If your camera isn't going to be used for a long time, grab your newspaper and head to the camera truck. If you leave the set, though, stay close to a radio and listen up in case you're needed. Stay alert, but don't be in the way. They'll call you when they need you.

1:00 P.M.—LUNCH

Depending on where you are shooting, you may have access to dailies from the day before either in an office if you are on stage or in the camera truck if you are on location. Get your food and go see yesterday's work. Not only will you see what you did right and wrong, but you can also pay attention to how the DP's lighting actually looks on film.

2:00 P.M.—BACK TO WORK

The second half of the day will be much like the first as far as you are concerned. As an Operator, you have less to do than when you were an Assistant, so maintaining a state of alertness becomes crucial. Stay sharp, help out where possible, but don't get in the way.

9:00 P.M.—WRAP

When wrap is called, the AD will ask everyone to wait until the First AC has checked the gate. Once it is ok, grab a CALL SHEET from a roving PA and double-check your call time. Before the DP leaves, make sure that there isn't anything out of the ordinary happening tomorrow that you haven't already discussed.

WHAT I REALLY WANT TO DO IS MOVE UP!

Up to this point, moving up has most likely been a matter of waiting for the person above you to be promoted. Then you have been able simply to follow in his or her wake. The move from Operator to DP, however, may involve a bit more work than that.

An Operator looking to move up in the television world may get lucky. The DP may leave for a short time, or for good, which in turn opens up an opportunity for you. If the Producers are comfortable enough and trust that the regular Operator can light as well, they may decide to promote from within the company. Usually for this to happen the Operator will have previously demonstrated the skills needed by shooting Second Units for the show or by showcasing other DP work that he might have done elsewhere. The television replacement DP steps into an established lighting design and, for the most part, must simply emulate it on a daily basis. He also has a crew that is experienced with the show, so that they can back him up.

For the feature film Operator, moving up can be more difficult. A feature film is a brand new project every time. New look, new crew. A studio and/or Director will be looking to hire a Director of Photography who has a track record that they can trust, both in establishing a look for the story and in being efficient with the logistics of handling the budget, the resources, and the schedule. Between operating gigs, find smaller independent projects to shoot and start building a reel. Make it known to the DPs with whom you work that you'd like to shoot Second Unit footage whenever possible. Also begin to cultivate your relationships with Producers and Directors. Those are the folks who will hire you from now on.

Start developing those skills that you'll need before you burn out on Operating. Stuff you learned in the Camera Department is just one facet of it all. As a DP you'll be in charge of the Grip and Electric departments, as well as dealing more directly with almost every other department on the project. Once the technical aspects of the job become second nature, you'll be able to spend more time on the art of filmmaking, which is most likely what got you interested in this career in the first place.

Chapter 25

What I Really Want to Do Is DIT!

WHAT THE HECK IS A DIT?

For anyone coming out of the broadcast video world, a DIT, or Digital Imaging Technician, is a fancy way of describing the video engineer. While the job functions of a DIT and an Engineer are somewhat similar, the work of the DIT at present is highly specialized as it revolves specifically around the use of the newest high-definition cameras being utilized in a cine-style work environment (or, in layman's terms, when a video camera instead of a film camera is used to make a movie). You'll be working in tandem with the Director of Photography in adjusting the camera settings to create his desired look.

That, and what else?

While the primary responsibilities are inherently technical, a large part of what you do involves knowing how to navigate the protocol and the politics of a single-camera-style film set. The standard movie set has operated roughly the same way for the past hundred years. Quite suddenly, the basic camera technology is changing, and a new guy, the DIT, is appearing on set. The established Camera Department is being forced to change the way it has traditionally worked and must now share responsibilities with you. Being aware of the attitude and concerns of the Assistant Cameramen, the Operator, the Director of Photography, and the Sound Department is a vital part of your overall job.

Hmm? I'm helping the DP create the look of the show? Big money then!

Well, sort of. You'll be paid the Operator rate plus about 20 percent on a union show. Steady work on a large union feature will bring you around $45,000 to $60,000 for twelve weeks. The nonunion rate for a commercial could be as low as $500 for ten hours. When you are just starting out, you may be working on a very-low-budget project and may only be making $1,000 per week.

WHAT DO I REALLY NEED TO KNOW?

At present, most DITs aren't coming from a broadcast engineering background, so you don't have to either. It's almost more important that you know how a movie set functions, as the political aspects of the job will be a large factor in your getting work and keeping it.

Politics aside, your main function is to assist the Director of Photography and the Camera Assistants with the technical aspects of the high-definition system.

WHAT DO I REALLY NEED TO HAVE?
Don't they just rent all this stuff?

At present, the majority of cine-style projects will be renting the camera and support gear for use throughout the production. You won't need a whole lot of your own equipment, but some small items will help. You should own your own color calibration chart, a small set of screwdrivers, a tape measure for checking backfocus, a backfocus chart, a good flashlight for working in the dark, a head-cleaning tape, your own Magliner cart to wheel around the equipment and monitors, small BNC cables, protective covers for the cameras and other equipment, power strips, extensions cords, and a wide range of video connectors (BNC to RCA, etc). And a good pair of work gloves to wrap cables with. You will pay around $1,000 for these items.

If you are already a Camera Assistant you'll find that you have a lot of what you will need already, so the cost outlay won't be quite as high.

While the price of a new high-definition camera is prohibitively expensive for most people, you may find it advantageous to purchase your own if you begin to work as a Director of Photography. Expect to pay between $100,000 and $200,000 for everything you'll need.

Also, if you're coming from a Camera Assistant background, you'll want to dress "up" a couple of notches. Take your cue from the Director of Photography and mimic his clothing style if possible. You'll be dealing a lot more with the above-the-line people now than ever before, and your pay scale sits between Operator and DP. Dress comfortably, but appropriately.

WHERE DO I REALLY NEED TO GO?
I just want to work.

Go where the work is. As the technology advances, the number of independent owners of high-definition cameras grows, so no matter where you are, you may be close to someone who can give you access to learning the technology.

Smaller, independent projects may welcome the extra help as long as they are comfortable with you and know you won't screw things up.

The very best way to get a start is to attend a high-definition workshop, offered by camera manufacturers and equipment rental houses. A very good one will run you around $2,000 and the total immersion and introduction into the technology provides an excellent base of knowledge for you to build on with experience. Not only will it be worth your time and money, you can use the fee as a tax write-off.

Next, head to a rental house that tends to do a lot of high-definition business. There are several in the Los Angeles/Burbank area. Let them know that you've taken a workshop and would like to practice working with the camera. If the equipment is available, they'll probably be happy to help. Not only are they building a relationship with you, but they will also take comfort in knowing that you are qualified to use their equipment correctly and safely. You get to learn; they get a potential new customer. A win-win situation for everybody.

So how do I get work?

Once you've gained some facility with every function of the system, ask the rental house (and others) to put you on their list. What happens is that a production will decide to shoot high-definition and then choose a rental house. If the DP or Producer does not know of a DIT personally, they will ask the rental house for recommendations. Because of the goodwill and friendly rapport you've built with the rental agents, they may pass your name to the next big project that comes along.

If you've been working in the business already as a Camera Assistant, Operator, or perhaps even as a DP, call up everyone with whom you've worked in the past and, if necessary, reintroduce yourself. Let them know that you're qualified and available to work as a DIT. Getting your name out there with your credentials is the only way people will learn of your capabilities.

In time, you may have too many offers coming in and may be asked to recommend someone else. Get to know other DITs out there so that they can do the same for you. You're all in competition for the same jobs, but, at the same time, you can support each other. Networking is the key to a successful career.

WHAT AM I GETTING MYSELF INTO?
So who actually calls and hires me?

Most likely you'll be hearing from a Production Manager, the Director of Photography, or one of the Producers. Expect a lot of last-minute calls as those already onboard may not have even been aware that they need a DIT. Heck, for that matter they may not even really know what it is you do. But they know they need you.

Okay, I got the job. What now?

The next stop will be "prep" where you'll meet the Assistant Cameramen at the rental house. You might get as little as a single day of prep for a small project or a few days for a feature.

Hopefully you've already talked with the Director of Photography about any "looks" that he'd like to see preset in the camera so you can get to work setting those up. Much of the prep is fairly standard—the way any other film prep might go. If there is enough time, the DP may come in and want to shoot tests. It may be as simple as running through the "looks" that you've set up through the menus or you may take the cameras to the stage for full-on makeup tests with the Actors. This is your chance to test your stuff and get it set up physically for actual production.

What will my life really be like?

6:00 A.M.—GET TO WORK

On day one of production, you'll come in with the Camera Assistants about an hour before general crew call. It should take you roughly fifteen to twenty minutes to pull the carts off the truck. While the Assistants work to build and warm up the cameras, you can set up your monitoring carts and anything else you need to roll close to set.

6:30 A.M.—ROLL TO SET

By the time you're ready with the gear, the Grips and Electrics will be arriving. The Grip Department should be carrying a black EasyUp-type tent, which will be your HD monitoring station for the duration of the production. Be sure to work that arrangement out during prep. You also need to discuss your power needs with the Electric Department. You can have all your carts on set and the black tent ready to go, but without power, nothing will happen. Figure this out on or before day one if at all possible.

7:05 A.M.—REHEARSAL

You and the Assistants will just hold back until the Director and DP figure out where the cameras will go.

7:15 A.M.—CAMERA SETUP

Once the decisions are made, have the Grips help you move the black tent in as close as possible to the set. Sometimes where you want it to be and where the Director and DP want it are two different places. Be sure that you'll be "safe" before getting too far along.

The ACs will be setting the cameras up. Once you're ready, run your cables out and either hook them up or leave them on the ground and let the ACs know that you are ready for them. Once you've got an image, make sure that the back focus is set correctly. Watch the monitor for "lit pixels" or any other irregularities in the picture. And keep an eye on the waveform monitor to make sure that the exposure the DP has set for the shot is proper so he won't run into any problems later on.

Depending on his level of experience and his personality, a DP may be coming in and out of the tent to discuss issues with you while you refer to the monitor and vectorscope. At other times, he may just communicate with you via walkie as he adjusts lights or the iris from set. Some DPs won't ask you anything at all during the entire shoot. All you can do is make sure the cameras are set up properly and warn and/or recommend help if you see that there might be a potential problem. The last thing you want to be perceived as doing is "fixing" a DP's "mistake." You're better off showing a DP some options from which he can choose. Remember, you're not the DP, he is. So if he wants to blow out a part of the image by ten stops, that's his choice. But you'd be remiss in your duties if you at least didn't attempt to warn him of the technical ramifications of that decision.

7:45 A.M.—ROLL CAMERA

In a perfect world, your black HD tent will be specifically for you and the DP only so that you can properly adjust the paint and exposure settings. You'll be running a "down-converted" signal out so that the traditional VIDEO VILLAGE will have a signal for their standard-definition monitors. However, on a lower budget show or just in general, the Director, Actors and anyone else who has to be close for whatever reason may feel justified in invading your work station and turning it into the de facto video village. They "just have to" be able to see the full high-definition picture. Unfortunately, there isn't too much you can do about it.

Hopefully, though, you'll have a clear view of your monitors and the scopes. Before and during each take, you'll be scanning from one to the other and back again, looking for problems.

8:10 A.M.—CUT, MOVIN' ON

With a film camera, the First AC "checked the gate." With a high-def camera, you instead hit the lens return button, which rewinds the tape roughly three to ten seconds. This allows you to see if a picture and sound actually was recorded.

Once you know for sure that that setup is finished, disconnect the cables from the camera, wrap them back to your tent, and wait for the next setup, where you'll do it all over again.

1:00 P.M.—LUNCH

If you had any problems with the cameras during the morning, this may be your only chance to make adjustments until after wrap. Take a few minutes to set up a chart if necessary so that you can tweak the settings for color matching or back-focus checks. Otherwise, head to lunch with everyone else.

2:00 P.M.—BACK TO WORK

The second half of the day will be much like the first as far as you are concerned. Just carry on as usual and help out the DP as best as you can.

You'll want to get an advanced CALL SHEET, which describes the scenes to be shot for the coming days. Look for any special circumstances that might concern you, such as rain or underwater work, Steadicam, cranes, additional cameras, or high-speed requirements. Hopefully, you knew about these things in prep so you already have camera and cable protection or additional equipment lined up.

9:00 P.M.—WRAP

Unplug the cameras, wrap the cables back to your tent, and tidy up your cart. Once power is disconnected, roll everything back to the truck. Especially if the truck is moving that night, you'll want to put the very expensive monitors back in their cases and secure everything. The ACs will be taking care of the cameras themselves. You should be getting help with your carts and monitors from the Second AC, but sometimes you just won't. Be careful lifting the monitors, as they can be very heavy.

Grab a call sheet and double-check your call time. Before the DP leaves, make sure there isn't anything out of the ordinary happening tomorrow that you haven't already discussed.

WHAT I REALLY WANT TO DO IS MOVE UP!

A DIT career could lead a couple of different ways, depending on who you are and what your previous experience was. If you're just coming out of camera assisting, your exposure to and collaboration with DPs could land you some Operating jobs. If you've already got that experience under your belt, you could turn your DIT credits into Director of Photography work on future high-definition productions in which you can essentially be your own DIT. Of course, camera knowledge is only a part of what a Director of Photography needs to know, so it isn't an automatic move up. Regardless, the career advancement won't happen because the guy above you decided to move on. This move up will be dependent on both your (perceived) skill level and how well you play the game. Getting your name out there as a Cameraman, schmoozing, and consistently improving your work will all get you to your end goal that much faster.

Chapter 26

What I Really Want to Do Is DP!

WHAT THE HECK IS A DIRECTOR OF PHOTOGRAPHY?

Almost every department involved in the production of a movie is concerned with something visual, be it wardrobe, art direction, props, set dressing, or lighting. It is the Director of Photography's (DP) job to understand the desires of the Director and translate and record those written or spoken wishes into a visual reality.

To do this adequately the DP must have an acute understanding of all technical requirements of motion picture production, including, but not limited to, cameras, electrical, and lighting. While he doesn't necessarily push buttons and plug things in himself, he should know enough about all the various aspects so that he can be an effective manager of the Camera, Grip, and Electric departments on set while simultaneously being a creative partner with the Director in creating pleasing frames.

That, and what else?

It's not enough to know how a camera works or what the various lights can do. The job extends beyond the technical into the artistic and the political arenas. Limited schedules have to be considered when making choices as to how to accomplish each individual setup. Quite often, compromises must be made due to the limited resources that you are afforded. Politics come into play, not only in trying to negotiate for more time, equipment, or manpower, but also in integrating your own artistic ideas within the Director's greater vision.

Getting the job in the first place isn't as simple as filling out a job application. The previous work you've done will showcase your technical and artistic abilities, but personality and confidence will help instill the sense of trust that Producers and Directors require. They already have enough to worry about without having to fight the Cameraman.

Making movies isn't just about stringing together of hundreds of "cool shots." While interesting camerawork and dramatic lighting are commendable, you have to understand drama and story if any of that "cool" stuff stands a chance of being relevant and making sense. If you don't have a working knowledge of how the camera movement, lens choices, and lighting affect the story, then you'll most likely just shoot what's in front of you instead of actually creating something meaningful.

In close association with the Gaffer, Key Grip, Camera Operators, and Focus Pullers, the DP should do more than throw up enough light to give exposure or make the shot pretty. The challenge is in making the shot, the scene, and the entire movie more than it would be without your influence. The goal is to tell a story visually instead of simply showing Actors spouting out lines.

Those motivated by "art" are sometimes discouraged by this industry, as so much of the higher level work (studio financed) is viewed primarily as "product." Sometimes, however, art does manage to sneak through. A lot of the photography is not great, but it's good enough. Artistic integrity is difficult even for the top DPs to maintain. At times there may be arguments with Line Producers just so you can get the basic tools you need to shoot the project in the way the Director wishes. Of course nobody realistically expects a blank check for all the equipment and manpower necessary, but often the costs involved in getting the tools or time are relatively small in terms of what the overall expenditures and returns are. So part of your job involves looking at the project as a whole and picking your battles judiciously. If you can give up a little on one sequence, you may be able to bargain for more resources for a more important sequence later on in the schedule. Because of limited resources, all the people working on a film find that they have to compromise at some point, so the more you are able to stay within the parameters for each project, the more successful your work will be and, hopefully, the more fulfilled you will be creatively.

I have the word "Director" in my title! I must be making really good money then, right?

It depends. While you are managing three departments and have the responsibility for how all the work that others have done ends up being saved on film or tape, pay rates vary greatly.

A typical schedule for a low-budget film is from twenty-four to thirty-two days with six-day weeks. A standard Hollywood union job is roughly twelve weeks, where you are working five days a week.

A nonunion low-budget show could get you just about anything, from $200 a day to $500 or more. It all depends on what you're willing to work for. The low-low end might be $600 a week for a really low-budget movie.

Union salaries are negotiated beforehand by IATSE Local 600 and by your agent if you have one. The low end for a $3 million feature is about $3,000 to

$7,000 a week for four to six weeks of shooting plus two weeks of prep. Big-time feature DPs can negotiate for upward of $25,000 a week.

Commercials are an entirely different beast. You can easily make $5,000 to $10,000 a day for a project that will wind up being just thirty seconds long.

Many cameramen take the high-paying jobs as a way of filling their savings accounts. This financial cushion then affords them the ability to go shoot (or direct) smaller, less lucrative, yet more creative and meaningful projects.

Now, this all sounds fantastic, and it is...for a few. Not everyone gets the chance to DP anything substantial, much less the really big shows. Plus, while that money can certainly be great, you have to be prepared for the possibility that you might *not* be hired to do two or three big projects a year. It might turn out that you only get one per year or fewer. You'll hopefully be able to fill in your off-time by DAYPLAYING or operating on Second Units.

WHAT DO I REALLY NEED TO KNOW?

You need to learn all about the hardware involved, including the various cameras and lighting units, as well as all the Grip tools. You also need to be well versed in the various film stocks, what they do, and how the processing steps work. It is also becoming increasingly important for a DP to understand digital technology, how it can be used on set with the newest HIGH-DEFINITION cameras, how the DIGITAL INTERMEDIATE process can help you save time in production and in post, as well as how the images you shoot on set will be utilized to create special effects in postproduction. You need to learn how to be an effective manager of people and resources, as most films, television projects, commercials, and music videos have limited budgets and schedules. And of course you have to learn the art of being a good politician, both to get the job and to execute it, despite the many obstacles thrown in front of you.

Far too many Camerapeople of all varieties fail to gain enough understanding of the editing process. While it's nice to be able to frame up and light beautiful shots, you're not taking still photographs. That's a whole different discipline. Your "cool" shots will undoubtedly be cut together with a host of other "cool" shots that you may or may not have photographed yourself. Screen-direction and "look" are vitally important elements to consider, lest the Editor winds up with a roomful of disjointed "cool" shots that don't look right when placed next to one another. At some point in your budding career, get yourself into an edit bay or buy some editing software for your home computer and play around. You'll quickly learn what works and what doesn't, and as a consequence, you'll become a much better Cameraman in the process.

Wow, there's a lot to learn. Where do I start?

If you're reading this and are interested in the job, you probably already have started. The proliferation of affordable camcorders has made small-scale production possible for most people. While shooting with this consumer technology has its limitations, it still offers the experience of being able to frame up shots and observe how different lighting setups affect the visual mood and the story overall, even if you're just using normal everyday light bulbs or dealing with the sun.

At some point in your fledgling career you'll want the experience of exposing actual film. Super 8mm or 16mm is a relatively inexpensive way to do it. Your consumer camcorder probably won't allow you to change lenses or even set an exposure, but nearly all film cameras will. If nothing else, shooting film will force you to learn how to use a light meter and control the image in every way.

Some of the better film schools have classes geared specifically toward motion-picture photography, where you can learn theory and practical applications. There are also lighting workshops offered on occasion through schools and other film-oriented programs.

With so much practical stuff to learn, it is easy to overlook the most important skill of all: communication. You can be the biggest hotshot DP in town with the best-looking footage ever conceived, but if you don't possess the ability to communicate effectively with others, you'll go nowhere pretty fast. This extends beyond having just a charming personality. Much of your day-to-day experience will consist of interpersonal relationships with those you hire and those who hire you. The ability to speak beyond the techno-babble is what will separate you from the crowd.

WHAT DO I REALLY NEED TO HAVE?
Do I need to buy a camera? How does this work?

No, you don't have to buy a camera. In fact, all you really need to do the job is a basic light meter. Depending on your skill at using it and your knowledge of what the film stock or the HD camera can handle in terms of light, one simple light meter should be enough. A combination incident and spot meter will run you around $800.

A small director's viewfinder can come in handy, particularly in preproduction tech scouts when you won't have the full complement of lenses and a camera assistant at your side. This equipment will run you about $700.

What's the best way for someone to reach me?

Once you reach this level, it will be advantageous for you to get an agent. An agent will give you credibility that you don't necessarily have as just one of the thousands of random Cameramen out there in the industry. The agent also serves as your business manager; someone who can negotiate a better paycheck for you as your level of experience rises. It's in his best interest, too, as he will take 10 percent of your earnings as a fee.

But getting and having an agent isn't always as easy as it should be. For starters, agents in general are interested primarily in making money. They aren't really apt to help you build a fulfilling career unless, of course, it will make them lots of money. An agent or agency won't even take you on as a client if you don't have some pre-built level of marketability. You have to go into their office and sell yourself as a client who is worthy of their time and energy. In short, if they think that they can make money from you, then you are worth meeting.

WHERE DO I REALLY NEED TO GO?
I just want to work.

You really can live just about anywhere you'd like at this point in your career. Dayplaying as a DP doesn't come up all that often. But because you'll be working longer term, you have to be prepared to move to where the job is for that period of time. Most films are based out of Los Angeles, so everywhere else is a LOCATION, meaning the production will house and feed you while shooting takes place.

But when the project moves back to home base (i.e., Los Angeles), they may be reluctant to continue paying for your food and shelter.

So how do I get work?

There are really just three ways to go about having a career as a DP. The first involves starting at the bottom as a Camera PA. Soon after you'll be a Loader and hopefully join the union (see Appendix A). After a year or so you can move up to Second AC and then some time after that, perhaps in about two to five years, to Focus Puller. Then, several years down the line, if you play your political cards right, you may get the chance to Operate. Once you've done that for a couple of years, if you again know how to schmooze the right people and show that you can do the job effectively, then maybe...just maybe...somebody will offer you the chance to photograph his project.

The second popular way is to go through Electric or Grip and eventually work your way up to being a Gaffer or Key Grip. The upside to going through Camera is that you'll learn firsthand everything you should know about the vast variety of tools necessary to make a high-quality motion picture. The advantage of going through Grip or Electric is that you learn everything you should know about actually lighting an environment. The downside of both is that unless you're paying attention to what the other department is doing, you'll miss either the lighting or camera aspects of the job. Also this "from the bottom" approach will take a large portion of your life to accomplish, anywhere from ten to twenty-five years or more. Also, it is important to remember the pigeonholing aspect of this industry. You could very well invest all that time and effort into building a successful career and never, ever get the opportunity to shoot a sizable project. If you have even a little experience, film students might gladly allow you to shoot their own short subjects as you apply your knowledge to their own fledging career. But that may very well be as far as your DP career goes.

The other route to becoming a DP? Skip the entry-level positions and just go out and do it. What you risk is not having a foundation of experience to fall back on when presented with new and difficult challenges. This is where having an experienced crew to back you up comes in handy. The risk, of course, is that you'll be found out for the green go-getter that you are, but if you proceed carefully and give credit where credit is due, your crew won't sabotage your efforts and will likely be there to support you as you get better and better projects. This is where loyalty enters the picture. By entering the business in a position where you need the help of others, you in turn owe them the benefits of your career. Simply dumping your loyal crew when you hit the big time may backfire on you as word gets around of your poor ethics.

Still, if you manage to shoot some small movie that goes on to win an award or two and you can impress someone in Hollywood with it, then you'd be foolish if you didn't just jump in at the highest level. You can spend decades climbing the ladder and never make it. If you don't understand everything there is to know, that's okay. As long as you're comfortable stumbling your way through it knowing that you have a lot to learn as you go, then you can build a successful career.

WHAT AM I GETTING MYSELF INTO?
So who actually calls and hires me?

If you have an agent, you'll most likely hear from him as his should be your primary contact number. All scripts and inquiries coming in should go through the agency. All requests, reels, and résumés should go out through the agency.

At some point before you are ever officially hired, you will hear from either the Director or the Producer. Depending on your level of experience and whether they know you, they may request a resume, a reel, and/or a personal meeting with you. You'll be sent a copy of the script to read over, and they'll want to hear what you have to say about it. The Director will be interested in a couple of things. First, she'll want to know if you "get it." Are you on the same page as she is in terms of story and vision. If you have two completely different movies in mind, then the project could be in serious trouble. The second thing that the Director wants to know is if she can work with you on a personal level. Sure, you might put on a great game face during the meeting in the office, but how will your working relationship be while you're both standing under rain machines in the middle of the night after six fourteen-hour days in downtown L.A.? Will you be a pleasant person who remains efficient and helpful in times of perceived difficulty, or will you turn into an arrogant moody jerk?

The Producer wants to know if you'll do your part to make the page count every day or if you have more interest in being an "artist" on his dime. While there is indeed a vested interest in having the movie look as good as possible, no one's going to get a blank check and unlimited time to accomplish everything that needs to be done. So your ability to manage a set and crew and work well with the Director and everyone else may be more important in the end than if you have a couple of really cool shots on your reel.

Okay, I got the job. What now?

Now the work begins. When you read the screenplay, you'll be looking specifically for those moments that have specific photographic or environmental interest. For instance, an entire sequence in which the principal action takes place in a deluge of rain with heavy winds and lightning in the dark of night three hundred feet from shore on a floating platform should peak your curiosity for a variety of reasons. If it doesn't, you probably aren't ready to be a DP.

Break the script down, making note of absolutely everything that could affect you and your job in any way. Scribble down ideas that you get for possible shots, angles, camera moves, lighting, and mood. You'll share your ideas and any concerns during your preproduction meetings with the Director. Once decisions have been made, you'll disseminate these notes when you sit down with your Gaffer, Key Grip, and Camera Assistant to figure out exactly what equipment is needed and when.

And with that in mind, you'll want to start lining up your Keys (Gaffer, Key Grip, Operator, First AC) as soon as you can. Figure out with whom you'd like to work and find out if they will be available. Even if they won't be officially hired for a few weeks, it's good to get some people onboard as soon as possible so you're not scrambling at the last minute for whoever is available. You want the people whom you are comfortable with, not just the next guy on the list.

A "tech scout" means looking at the actual sites that will be used as shooting locations. Your Gaffer and Key Grip will be there as well as the Director, Producer, Production Designer, First Assistant Director, and Location Manager, among others. With any luck, the Director has a good idea of what she wants to shoot and exactly how she wishes to shoot it. This isn't always the case, so you have to be willing to go with the flow as much as possible. And really, unless she wants to do something completely out of the norm, such as a helicopter shot or a 200-foot dolly track move, your normal lighting, grip, and camera package should be sufficient to cover all contingencies. But this is what the tech scout is for. This is your time to talk with everyone involved to figure out what the plan is so that there are no surprises once there is an expensive crew standing around wondering what to do next.

You'll also want to shoot tests. Individual Actors need to be lit in various ways. Fabrics and colors take light differently as do set walls and specialty props, like shiny swords. And maybe this time the Producer wants you to shoot the movie with a high-definition camera instead of your traditional film camera and film stock. The very last thing you want to do is get to set on day one without a clue about how the technology is going to work or how you're going to have to light each location and each Actor. While you have to stay fluid and make it up as you go sometimes, anything you can do to avoid on-the-spot improvisation will be highly beneficial for everyone. Test, test, test!

What will my life really be like?

7:00 A.M.—GETTING TO SET

You get to show up at call time. Your Camera, Grip, and Electric crew have been unloading their gear and will be awaiting orders from you for the first setup.

7:05 A.M.—REHEARSAL

Depending on the complexity of the scene, this may be purely for performance or it may also include stops and starts as you work to figure out where the camera(s) will go.

Usually the Actors will get to run through the scene at least once without interruption. Then, when the Director is reasonably happy with what she is seeing from them, the official blocking rehearsal begins. The Second Assistant Cameraman will jump in to lay down tape T-marks on the floor so that the scene is fairly repeatable. All the while, you need to be figuring out whether the blocking will work for camera and thinking about the best way to light the set. You are usually free to make minor adjustments to the marks later on during setup, but you really need to stick close to what the final blocking winds up being before First Team walks away. Of course, during prep you already had a broad idea of what you would be doing, but this is the first time you've seen specifically where the Actors are and what they are doing in the actual dressed environment. There shouldn't be any huge surprises and most of your big decisions will already have been made. At this point, it's all just details on how to achieve your goals.

7:15 A.M.—CAMERA SETUP

Once the rehearsal is finished, First Team will exit the set and the First AD will call for Second Team. These Stand-ins will go to the T-marks on the floor and just wait there as the camera(s) are set and the lighting is done.

The Grip, Electric, and Camera departments will all be standing nearby awaiting instructions from you. There is no particular order to follow as to whom to address first, but generally speaking, try to get the ball rolling first on the job that will take the longest. On an interior set, the lighting may be quite complicated, so you'll want to have a quick discussion with the Gaffer and Key Grip regarding what it is you'd like to see. On a day exterior, the Camera Department seems to be the busiest. You can be as vague or as complicated as you'd like. This all depends on the experience and working relationship that you have with your crew. Sometimes giving out specific details will save you time if you know for sure that this is what is needed. But don't underestimate and underutilize the experience of your crew. They may have alternative solutions that could be quicker and achieve what you are asking for in a better way.

If you haven't already talked to the Camera Department, and they haven't figured out on their own what to do based on the blocking rehearsal, let them know what you need from them. Be very specific with your instructions, as there isn't always a lot of leeway for interpretation. You might say that you need a dolly move from "here" to "here" in low-mode on a 40mm lens and the camera needs to run at 96 fps. Then it's up to the Dolly Grip, the First AC, and the Camera Operator to get the equipment in place and make adjustments to make it work.

An experienced crew will be fairly self-sufficient and require little babysitting. Still, check on their progress, just in case something isn't working out the way you had hoped and needs to be rethought. Because every setup is unique, in a sense you are reinventing the wheel each time. And being familiar with the tools you have at your disposal will help the setup move along at peak efficiency and aid in getting the page count completed for the day in the time allotted.

At some point in the process, the First AD will start asking you how much longer you think it will be until everything is finished. While it can be very difficult to say to the minute, give him your very best honest estimate. He needs some idea so that he can get First Team on the move, THROUGH THE WORKS, and to the set as you are finishing up. Every second counts.

You've already seen the lighting setup and the camera move with the Stand-ins in place, so there should be no surprises once First Team has stepped in and taken their places at the marks. But Stand-ins are only close substitutes, so take a close look at the real Actors to make sure that you don't have any unexpected trouble. Little things like different hairstyles, makeup, and wardrobe can throw a wrench into your carefully constructed setup.

7:45 A.M.—ROLL CAMERA

You can either watch the takes from VIDEO VILLAGE next to the Director or from one of the camera positions, whichever is best for you to keep an eye on the scene. You need to know if the lighting and the camera move and configuration are working out from start to finish. You need to know if the Director is happy with what she is seeing. You need to know all of this because usually you'll get a chance to fix anything that is wrong before take two happens. Perhaps the Actors aren't hitting their marks and the light isn't right all of the sudden, or maybe the Dolly Grip needs to slow it down a bit, or maybe the sun is moving behind a cloud and all of your 18Ks need double scrims in them in a hurry. Any number of adjustments can be conceived, and you need to be on the watch for them and know how to adjust quickly once the take is over.

On a smaller project, you may not have or may not want to have an Operator working for you. In this case you'll most likely have your own eye looking through the eyepiece during the shot. The benefit of this scenario is that you have complete control and can perhaps more quickly gauge how well everything is working. The downside is that you are concentrating on the mechanics of operating the camera, which sometimes can be challenging, so you can't really pay as much attention to the big picture as perhaps you should.

On a larger production, where you might have anywhere from two to sixteen cameras rolling at once, you absolutely have to stay back and take on more of a managerial role. Getting into the thick of the action by operating a camera doesn't allow you to oversee properly everything that is going on. In the best of scenarios, you need to be paying attention to the lighting, framing, and focus on each camera, and you just can't do that if you are stuck looking through just one lens.

7:48 A.M.—CUT, LET'S GO AGAIN

If you saw anything at all that needed to be fixed, talk it over quickly with your Gaffer, Key Grip, Dolly Grip, Camera Operator, or First AC. If it will take more than a few seconds, you'll have to let the First AD know what's going on so he can decide whether to keep First Team on the set. If it's anything really big, the Director has to make the choice on whether it is worth her time. The decision to delay shooting could affect whether she MAKES THE DAY. While every shot is indeed important (or else you wouldn't be doing it), some are more so than others. Letting one shot be less than perfect is okay and actually is often necessary. The idea is that you can't obsess over one shot so much that it potentially compromises the quality of the rest of the day's work. Ultimately, that's a decision to be made by the Director, using your knowledge and experience as her guide.

8:10 A.M.—CUT, MOVIN' ON

Everything was good. The Director was happy with the performances, and the lighting and camera work was everything you had hoped for. It's time to tear that setup apart and do it all over again for the next one.

Sometimes the next setup is a fairly simple "punch in," meaning that you're just getting a tighter or closer shot of the Actor by moving the camera in closer or by putting a longer lens on. In this case, your lighting really shouldn't change much, if at all.

Eventually though, you'll have to TURN AROUND, meaning that once all the action has been filmed in one direction, the cameras will turn around 180° and shoot in the opposite direction. This isn't a small feat. Everything that was once behind the camera (lights, equipment, trucks, video village, chairs, people, craft service, etc.) now needs to move to the other side or someplace else so that it is not in the new shot. Because this is a major move, it is important to "shoot out" each side completely before committing to the turnaround. The Director and Script Supervisor will be keeping an eye on the shot list, if there is one, to avoid missing anything. It doesn't hurt for you to keep the story in your head and remind them of something in case they have forgotten.

1:00 P.M.—LUNCH

You'll be ushered off to see dailies, and a boxed lunch will be given to you there. This is when you get to see footage that has been shot in the previous days so that you can evaluate your choices and make adjustments if necessary.

2:00 P.M.—BACK TO WORK

It is vitally important that you stay alert and efficient throughout the entire day. The second half can be more difficult than before lunch. For starters, people in general are much more productive first thing in the morning. Energy is high and everyone is ready to get to work. As the afternoon goes on, the crew will get tired and productivity will naturally slow. Not to mention that the second half of the day is almost always longer than the first by at least two hours.

So it is really key that you stay as up as possible for you own sake, but that you also do what you can to keep your crew going strong as well. Everyone wants to do their jobs well, but they'd also like to get home at a reasonable hour.

9:00 P.M.—WRAP

The MARTINI shot is done and the gate was good. Another successful day IN THE CAN. If you haven't already, confer with the Director about what you'll be doing tomorrow, take time to thank your crew, grab a CALL SHEET, and go home.

After the entire show has wrapped, you still have work to do even though you may not be getting paid to do it. After the Director and the Editors have LOCKED the picture, you (should) have a vested interest in going back in to "time" the shots, which essentially means that you're going to sit down with a lab or computer technician and go through the entire movie, shot by shot, to adjust things like brightness, contrast, and color. While you do your very best to shoot the best NEGATIVE you can on set, there is still always some work to be done to make sure all the shots look like they belong together in the same movie. This timing stage of postproduction can happen as quickly as three months after physical production has wrapped or as much as a year or more. Keep in touch with the Producers and the Director periodically to see how things are progressing. Bigger shows won't leave you out of the loop, but smaller projects will try to just have a random lab technician "time" the shots without you in the interest of getting the thing done as quickly as possible. They're not always interested in losing days or money just because of your artistic integrity.

And when all is said and done, if the project is big enough, you'll likely get invited to attend the premiere! You get to rent a tuxedo or buy a gown and walk the red carpet answering questions shot at you by reporters from around the globe. And with any luck, you won't be able to make it because you're far too busy working that night on another bigger and better project.

WHAT I REALLY WANT TO DO IS MOVE UP!

Being an artist with lights and cameras is a complex job and not something that everyone can do well. But if you've achieved that and still want more, then the next jump up for you is to become the Director. Keep in mind that this is not a natural progression, nor is it one that every DP can make. Just because you know how to command the troops and complete a day efficiently on a film set does not make you automatically qualified to direct. Apart from dealing with the nuts and bolts of how to capture the action, you also have to know how to construct the action, work with Actors, and speak to them in their language. You also will be making tons of decisions regarding costumes, locations, set design, props, and makeup, all the while keeping artistic interpretation in mind as well as schedules and budgets.

But even if you can do all of that, it doesn't mean that you'll ever get the chance. Skill and experience count for little when politics intervene. The executives deciding who gets to direct one project or another may have preconceived notions about your qualifications based on your career as a Cameraperson and never take into account your potential as the overall creative artist. Or perhaps you are seen as qualified but there just isn't a project available for you at the time when you are ready to make the move up. Or maybe they just don't like you. There are countless obstacles that could get in your way as you try to become a Director, but that shouldn't stop you from trying.

If you've had a lucrative career as a DP, take some time off and dip into your savings while you direct a short film or a low-budget feature. Another avenue is to become a Second Unit Director. Often, larger projects will send out a Second Unit to shoot large action sequences or other pieces of the movie when the First Unit just doesn't have time. To be more efficient, the Second Unit is directed by either a Stunt Coordinator or by the Second Unit DP. Sometimes, those Second Unit directing opportunities can be enough to convince the powers that be that you are indeed capable and qualified enough to helm your own studio epic.

Part V

THE GRIP DEPARTMENT

What I Really Want To Do Is...

Grip

Dolly Grip

Key Grip

Chapter 27

What I Really Want to Do Is Grip!

WHAT THE HECK IS A GRIP?

The entire Grip Department works in coordination with the Electric and Camera departments to create each setup. While the Dolly Grip works closely with the Camera Operator, the other Grips work with the Electricians to light and prepare the set according to the instructions of the Director of Photography. Electricians are in charge of setting and powering the lighting units themselves, and Grips have the equipment to control the light.

That, and what else?

Production Grips set C-stands, flags, and provide safe rigging for set dressing, lighting, and camera equipment. In the meantime, Rigging Grips prepare sets for shooting ahead of the main unit.

How much can I make doing this?

A Grip in IATSE Local 80 can expect to make around $35,000 on a twelve-week feature film. Prior to that, you will make between $100 and $200 a day on low-budget nonunion projects.

WHAT DO I REALLY NEED TO KNOW?

Your job requires both the technical skills required to create a safe working environment and the creative sensibilities to help shape the light according to the DP's wishes. Using standard hand tools, like hammers, wrenches, screwdrivers, and rope, as well as specialized production equipment like C-stands, Mafer Clamps, and "flags," Grips safely set and rig lighting and camera equipment as well as help to move and secure set WILD WALLS. A solid knowledge of knot tying, heavy equipment rigging, and rock-climbing safety gear is invaluable.

WHAT DO I REALLY NEED TO HAVE?
You mentioned normal hand tools. Is that all I need?
Do I have to bring those things?

Yes, your own tool belt will hold your personal set of hand tools, like a hammer, crescent wrench, screwdrivers, Allen wrenches, razor blade, knife, and gloves. Specialized tools like C-stands and Mafer Clamps come as part of the rental package.

WHERE DO I REALLY NEED TO GO?
I just want to work.

Gain some basic set experience by working on student or low-budget films. As you move on to larger productions, you'll likely find yourself on the Rigging crew instead of working on set right away. Take these opportunities to learn from those who are more experienced. In time, you'll gain the trust of the Best Boy Grip, who may recommend you to the Key Grip. Through hard work and patience, you'll find yourself back working on set to help build each setup.

So how do I get work?

Volunteering to work on low-budget and student films is an excellent way to begin learning how to be a Grip and to meet people. Through those relationships, you'll move from job to job gaining a reputation that will help you land larger, paying projects.

In time, you'll have accumulated enough days to join IATSE Local 80. Becoming part of the union gives you access to working on large studio films with established pay scales and other protections. Check with the local office for all current membership requirements.

WHAT AM I GETTING MYSELF INTO?
So who actually calls and hires me?

You'll get a call from the Best Boy Grip or a Key Grip with whom you've worked before.

Okay, I got the job. What now?

You and the other Grips on the project will go to the rental house to prep the gear and load the truck. Most of the gear will come from the rental house, but some may be provided by the Key Grip. It will take from a day to up to two weeks depending on the amount of gear and the size of the show.

What will my life really be like?

5:30 A.M.—GET TO WORK

The first thing is to remove all of the carts off the truck and push them near the set.

7:00 A.M.—GETTING TO SET

Space may be tight, as you're sharing the set with the rest of the crew and their equipment. Do what you can to make everything accessible so that each setup during the day is built as quickly and efficiently as possible. The Key Grip may know of something that needs to be rigged for a shot later in the day. Get to work on it as soon as possible.

7:05 A.M.—REHEARSAL

Stay back, yet watch rehearsal so that you know what you'll be working to build later on. Keep an eye on the DP, Gaffer, and Key Grip as they work out the camera positions and the lighting.

7:15 A.M.—CAMERA SETUP

The Key Grip will let you know what he specifically needs you to do, but watch the Electricians and the Dolly Grip in case they need a hand with something they are working on. Double-check that all lights are secured safely with safety chains and sandbags.

7:45 A.M.—ROLL CAMERA

Once the camera and lights are set and the DP is happy, your work is essentially finished until the next setup. Stay alert, though, to any problems that crop up during the shot, like lens flares.

7:48 A.M.—CUT, LET'S GO AGAIN

Most of the time, nothing changes in between takes, so just keep an ear out for instructions. If you are working on a day exterior location, the DP may be using shiny boards or other types of sun reflectors to provide light. It is your job to SHAKE THEM UP as the sun moves and the position of the reflected light changes. Also stay aware of rigging in that situation, as gusts of wind can be hazardous if large silks or other equipment are prone to falling over.

8:10 A.M.—CUT, MOVIN' ON

Each setup is unique, so when the DP says so, pull any C-stands or lighting out of the way if the cameras will be looking at them.

1:00 P.M.—LUNCH

Make sure all of your equipment is safe or covered before heading to lunch. Check with the Key Grip to see if there is any pre-rigging he might need done immediately after the break.

2:00 P.M.—BACK TO WORK

The second half of the day is much like the first as you move from setup to setup. It is natural to get tired as the hours wear on, especially after a few weeks of hard work. As most of your job involves creating a safe environment for everyone else, keep focused on the tasks you complete and double-check the rest of the set's safety.

If you don't have anything specific to do on set, check with the Best Boy Grip in case there is any pre-rigging that can be done on another set or stage or if he has gear that needs to be repaired.

9:00 P.M.—WRAP

Most of your gear will be working right up to the very end of the day, so you won't have much chance to put some things away early.

When wrap is called, check with the Key Grip to find out exactly what should be left and what should be taken to the truck. Help the Dolly Grip pack up any track or disassemble the crane. Occasionally you may be asked to pre-rig something for the next day, so check with the Key Grip before going home.

WHAT I REALLY WANT TO DO IS MOVE UP!

Eventually you may want to move up in responsibility to becoming the Dolly Grip or the Key Grip. Take any extra time you have in between setups to learn about all of the gear that is on the Grip truck. Volunteer to push the B-camera dolly if such a situation presents itself. Learning how to complete the tasks of the Best Boy Grip in maintaining and organizing the extensive amounts of equipment is crucial in advancing to the level of Key. Above all, don't just mechanically complete your tasks. Pay attention to the DP, Key Grip, Gaffer, and Camera Operator to develop a comprehensive understanding of how all the elements come together when lighting and photographing a scene.

You may get the opportunities to move up on large union sets as others above you advance themselves or aren't available. Otherwise, find lower budget shows where you can practice the skills required. That way, when your chance on a large project arrives, you'll be ready to step in without hesitation from anyone.

Chapter 28

What I Really Want to Do Is Dolly Grip!

WHAT THE HECK IS A DOLLY GRIP?

The Camera Operator controls pan and tilt, but actual camera movement forward and back, up and down, and side to side through physical space is controlled by the Dolly Grip with a dolly or crane.

That, and what else?

The Dolly Grip is a part of the Grip Department, so he still helps set C-stands and flags and provides safe rigging when necessary. His primary responsibility, however, is in working with the Camera Department by laying dolly track and pushing the dolly, or setting up and operating a crane.

Many shots won't require movement, but you'll help the Camera Department anyway. Often, the DP will want the camera placed on the top of a twelve-step ladder. It's your job to get the ladder, place it in the correct spot, and secure it so it can't fall over. You'll also secure the high-hat to the top and assist the First Camera Assistant in getting the very heavy camera up and mounted on the head.

Or you might have to go the other way and dig a hole so that the lens will be even with the ground.

It's pretty much your job to assist in getting the camera mounted and moved in any configuration that is requested. Some setups will require a lot of assistance from you, like dolly and crane work, while some won't involve you very much at all, such as a simple high-hat on the ground. Either way, you'll stick close to the camera and listen for any changes, working with the Camera Department to get it all set up as efficiently and safely as possible.

When the camera is handheld or is operated with a STEADICAM, the Dolly Grip acts as the safety spotter for the Camera Operator.

Why move the camera? Can't they just use the zoom on the lens like I do at home?

It's not the same thing. By zooming in with a lens, the action is being "pulled" to the camera. By dollying or craning in, the camera itself is actually passing objects while moving toward the subject. The overall effect of using a dolly is far more dramatic than simply using a zoom. This isn't to suggest that a zoom is never used, but whenever time and circumstances permit, the Director and DP generally prefer moving the camera instead of just zooming with the lens.

Wouldn't using a Steadicam be faster than setting up dolly track?

Sometimes it is. But the Steadicam is just a tool like anything else on set, to be used in specific situations. The Steadicam is very heavy, which puts tremendous physical strain on the Camera Operator. Asking him to do that all day long is unreasonable. Also, mounting the camera on a dolly or crane typically offers a far more stable shot than the average Steadicam Operator can often deliver, especially when using longer lenses. And again, there are shots that a Steadicam Operator or an Operator on a tripod just can't deliver the way a dolly or crane can.

Sounds like I'll be busy. How much can I make doing this?

When you're just starting out on low-budget nonunion projects, expect to make about $150 flat for the entire day. Once you are able to join IATSE Local 80 as a Dolly Grip, you'll earn about $35,000 for a twelve-week feature.

Many Dolly Grips own track to rent to production. An average show will carry about one hundred feet of track for the course of the show. That and a set of good skateboard wheels may get you an additional $200 a week.

I don't know. Pushing the camera around all day. How hard can that be? It really doesn't sound all that challenging.

The Dolly Grip doesn't just casually push the camera around like a shopping cart. Anybody can push a dolly, but not everyone can truly operate it. You're working in tandem with the Camera Operator and the Actors who are moving around the set. The dolly itself with nothing on it is about five hundred pounds. Add 60 pounds of camera, a 200-pound Operator, a 170-pound Focus Puller, plus batteries and any other accessories, and things get interesting. You have to hit your marks with finesse while anticipating the action. You are keeping an eye out for the video and sound cables so that they don't wind up under your wheels. And even though you and the Camera Operator work out specific marks for you to move to, you have to make adjustments continually if and when the Actors don't hit their marks.

WHAT DO I REALLY NEED TO KNOW?

You're working as a Grip who specializes in camera support, which means that the more you know about the requirements of the Camera Department, the better you'll be able to do your own job. You don't really have to know how to use a fluid or gear head, but at the very least being aware of how they work and why a Camera Operator would prefer one over the other is valuable as you attempt to anticipate his needs for the shot. As you are, in effect, operating the camera along with the Camera Operator, it is also essential for you to know what the lenses see and how they react to your slightest touch. It isn't enough to just move the camera from point A to point B. You have to do that with an awareness of how your own actions affect the final image that ends up on screen.

WHAT DO I REALLY NEED TO HAVE?
Do I need all of my old regular Grip tools, since I'm just pushing the dolly all day?

Definitely. While you're primarily helping the Camera Department, you're still expected to be a "regular" Grip if necessary. But you're not just pushing a dolly around either. You have to build track for the dolly, which sometimes requires tools like Allen wrenches and a level. You might need to perform some minor maintenance on the dolly from time to time. You'll be building the crane arm and securing the remote head to it. You'll be helping to secure the camera to ladders, car mounts, boats, motorcycles, and just about anything else that a Director and DP dream up. Your normal assortment of hand tools should always remain close by.

As the Dolly Grip, you may want to purchase some of your own specialized mounting, rigging, and safety equipment to use. Mitchell mounts, leveling heads, car mounts, motorcycle mounts, dolly track, skateboard wheels, ropes, and body harnesses are items that you can consider adding to your personal kit. Besides the advantage of making a rental fee on them, working with equipment that you know well and maintain adds a level of comfort that will help you concentrate on doing your job well instead of worrying about the reliability of gear that isn't yours.

What's the best way for someone to reach me?

Even if you're not hired to be the A-camera Dolly Grip, productions frequently add cameras for larger scenes, which necessitates having a Dolly Grip for each. Calls can come at any time, so keep your contact information current with the union local. Also keep in touch with other Grips and Camera Operators you already know.

WHERE DO I REALLY NEED TO GO?
I just want to work.

As a beginner, you just want to get on any set at all. Union or not, finding work as a Production Assistant is a good way to situate yourself in a place where you can start meeting people. Low-budget independent projects and student films may provide you with Grip opportunities. Once you are comfortable working on a set, let the Key Grip know that you are interested in operating the dolly. Ideally you'll have had the opportunity to observe other Dolly Grips, so you won't be jumping in to this specialty completely blind.

So how do I get work?

When you feel that you have a firm grasp on how to do your job well, work toward joining IATSE Local 80. To join Local 80, you'll need thirty days of documented union work on independent features, music videos, or television shows, but check with the Local office for all current membership requirements.

Another way to get in is to be called on a Permit. What this means is that if the over three thousand Grips on the roster are working or unavailable, then the union turns to the Permit List, which is full of nonunion Grips who are working in the low-budget world. A movie set is an ever-changing environment, and Local 80 could get a call at the last minute as a crew is suddenly in need of a bunch of Grips to fix something or rig a set. If you call every day, you'll be on the top of the list and will likely get the chance you've been hoping for. However, don't just sit around waiting for this type of opportunity. Keep working on nonunion projects or find work as a PA in the meantime.

Once you're there on set with a bunch of people who don't know you, you'll have to earn their trust and respect. Make them look good with a smile on your face and you'll most likely get called back for another day or the entire next show.

WHAT AM I GETTING MYSELF INTO?
So who actually calls and hires me?

The Best Boy Grip will likely be giving you the call based on recommendations from Key Grips or Camera Operators with whom you've worked previously.

Okay, I got the job. What now?

You'll begin prepping the equipment along with the rest of the Grip crew. The standard grip equipment, like C-stands, flags, and ladders, will be provided by the Key Grip or come from a rental house. Your dolly and accessories will come from someplace else, like J. L. Fisher or Leonard Chapman. As the other Grips are going through the rest of the equipment, you head to the dolly rental house and examine every piece that you think you'll need.

If you're being called in as a replacement because someone was hurt, fired, or is on vacation, you might get the opportunity to remain on the rest of the show, depending on the reason that you're called there in the first place. In that case, you'll want to get familiar with the gear that is there as soon as possible.

What will my life really be like?

5:30 A.M.—GET TO WORK

On a normal day, you will arrive early with the other Grips to pull the carts off the truck. Often, your dolly will be the last on the truck at night and first off in the morning. Get that to the set, then help stage the rest of the equipment nearby. On low-budget shows, the dolly may be kept on the Camera truck.

Sometimes, the Director and DP already know that they'd like to begin the day with a crane shot, so you'll have an earlier call to build the arm and mount the camera before the first rehearsal.

7:00 A.M.—GETTING TO SET

Get your dolly to the set as soon as possible in case the First AC needs to mount the head and camera on it. Help the other Grips get the carts and other equipment staged close to the set, then get a set of sides from a PA or AD.

7:05 A.M.—REHEARSAL

While the Director and Actors are working out the blocking, the DP may begin lining up his idea for the shot. If it is a dolly move, he may give you tentative start and stop points, so you should mark those with chalk or tape in preparation for laying track.

After the Director is happy with how the Actors will play the scene, she and the DP will look through a director's viewfinder and line up the shot through an actual lens. Camera positions get more specific at this point so revise your old marks and lay new ones if necessary.

7:15 A.M.—CAMERA SETUP

You know where the camera needs to start and where it needs to stop. Work with the Camera Operator and the First AC to determine the configuration that is best for everyone. Ideally, track will be laid so the margin for focus errors is minimized. Sometimes, though, more complex moves that aren't in a straight line are required, so laying down dance floor is necessary.

After you've set up your equipment and the camera is built either on the dolly or crane, you, the Operator, and the Focus Puller will run blocking rehearsals with the Stand-ins to work out any problems. The idea is that once First Team comes back in, you'll all be ready to go, barring any last-minute changes by the Director or the Actors.

7:45 A.M.—ROLL CAMERA

You'll be given a cue to start your move, either on "Action!" or on a specific line of dialogue. Aim to hit your marks as was rehearsed so that the Operator and Focus Puller have one less variable to worry about in doing their own jobs. However, sometimes the Actors don't repeat their actions in precisely the same ways, so be prepared to make slight adjustments to the original plan if necessary. You may have a small monitor attached to your dolly to help you know exactly what the Camera Operator is seeing. Use that to make the shot look the best, no matter what was rehearsed.

7:48 A.M.—CUT, LET'S GO AGAIN

If you didn't hit your marks precisely, tell the First AC so that he can better gauge if he focused properly. Go back to one, and get ready to do the shot again.

8:10 A.M.—CUT, MOVIN' ON

Don't tear the setup apart yet. If possible, the DP may want to try to get the next shot from the same configuration to save time. A quick rehearsal for the next piece of the scene will help to answer that question. If you have to adjust the camera for a new angle or move, work with the Camera Assistants to get the dolly or crane out of the way while the On-Set Dresser makes room on set for the new setup. Move the track to the new position and do it all over again.

1:00 P.M.—LUNCH

Lock the wheels on the dolly or lock down the crane to make them safe while you walk away. Head to lunch with the rest of the crew.

2:00 P.M.—BACK TO WORK

Each setup is a unique creation, so being able to maintain mental focus and remain positive is important. You're working closely with two different departments (Grip and Camera), and getting along with everyone over the course of seemingly endless hours and weeks can become challenging. Do your best to roll with the punches even when others on set may be getting tense. You may find yourself laying down track only to have to dismantle it again right away because the Director or DP changes her or his mind. It's not always fun to run "fire drills," but you're all there to make the best movie possible, and better ideas can trump previous plans.

9:00 P.M.—WRAP

You typically won't be able to wrap the dolly or the crane and accessories until the final shot is finished. Once wrap is called, though, get all of your things consolidated on set (if you'll be back tomorrow) or repack everything and push it all to truck for loading. Help the other Grips get the rest of the gear on the truck before heading home.

WHAT I REALLY WANT TO DO IS MOVE UP!

Many Dolly Grips stay in that position and make very successful careers from it. However, you've been in the right place to learn a lot about the needs of the Camera Department as well as working with the Electricians and Set Dressing to create each setup. Because of this unique experience, moving up to Key Grip could be a relatively easy transition.

When you're not pushing the dolly or aiding the Camera Department, spend time helping the Key Grip with complicated rigging on set or with pre-rigging on nearby sets. You're not out to steal your Key Grip's job with the DP, but let your own boss and other DPs know that you are capable and interested in moving up. One day, the Key Grip you normally work with may not be able to take a job and will be looking for someone he trusts to fill in. Create the awareness that you are ready to fill that position and be prepared to take advantage of the opportunity when it happens.

Chapter 29

What I Really Want to Do Is Key Grip!

WHAT THE HECK IS A KEY GRIP?

In collaboration with the Director of Photography, the Key Grip works with his crew of Grips in coordinating with the Electric Department to control set lighting as well as with the Camera Department in camera setup.

That, and what else?

An excellent Key Grip brings with him years of experience in order to understand the unique tools that are available and necessary to provide safe setup and rigging of camera and lighting equipment. Controlling the light and setting up a camera isn't enough. Knowing the hardware that it takes to create the "art" that shows up on screen is the responsibility of the Key Grip.

There's more to being a Grip than I thought. I must be making really good money then, right?

When you first start out on low-budget projects, expect to make between $100 to $200 a day. It isn't likely that you'll make an instant jump from that level to becoming a Key Grip on large studio features in IATSE Local 80, but once you do get that far, you will earn roughly $40,000 for a twelve-week feature plus any rentals.

WHAT DO I REALLY NEED TO KNOW?

You're directing your crew of at least two Grips, also known as "Hammers," to work with the Electric Department in lighting the set as per to the DP's wishes.

The more you understand about lighting in general and the needs and limitations of the Electricians, the better your relationship will be with the Gaffer and his own crew as you can anticipate what has to be accomplished.

In the same way, the Dolly Grip works closely with the Camera Department in setup and operation of the dolly, as well as other special rigging and providing safety support on every setup. The Dolly Grip should be very experienced, and by this point in your own career, you should also know enough about the special requirements that it takes to place and move the camera in the variety of ways that Directors and DPs request.

The entire Grip Department is sometimes seen as a general catchall in providing hardware support and brute labor, but the services you provide and the tools you use are very specialized.

WHAT DO I REALLY NEED TO HAVE?

Everything the Grip Department needs is available from a variety of rental houses. However, at this point in your career, it could be advantageous to own some of your own gear for a couple of reasons. The first is that because the equipment is yours, you know that it works and have less to worry about when it comes to safety and reliability. The other reason is that you, instead of the rental house, can profit from the rental on your Grip package.

You could own just a few items or enough to fill a large truck. The list of required specialties is long, and as you move up through the ranks, you'll get a better idea of the kinds of things you'd like to invest in and have room to store in between shows.

WHERE DO I REALLY NEED TO GO?
I just want to work.

Getting the position of Key Grip will depend on your relationship with a DP. That comes as a result of years of experience on a variety of sets, where you've dealt with many different situations. Living in an area where a lot of production takes place is advantageous to maintaining those relationships.

So how do I get work?

As mentioned, your work will come about as a result of the relationships you've made with Cameramen as you've moved up through the ranks of the Grip department. The call from a DP is important, but be aware that the UPM and Producers will be interested in knowing that you can work within budget while helping the production run as efficiently as possible. Being able to illustrate past experience with copies of previous budgets and recommendations from other UPMs and DPs can help secure the job.

WHAT AM I GETTING MYSELF INTO?
So who actually calls and hires me?

The first call you'll get will be from a DP with whom you've worked previously or who has asked for a recommendation. Once you've agreed to do the job, you'll speak with the UPM regarding your deal and any rentals you might have to offer the production.

Okay, I got the job. What now?

You'll go through the script and have meetings and tech scouts with the DP in regard to any special items or setups that might be required. You'll place an order with a Grip supply rental house and arrive at a budget, to be approved by the UPM. Along with the crew you hire, you will prep the gear and the truck about a week or two prior to the first day of production.

What will my life really be like?

7:00 A.M.—GETTING TO SET
Check in with the DP right away in case anything needs to be rigged or set up immediately. Your crew has pulled the carts off the truck and moved the necessary equipment to set, so make sure that everything you think you'll need is close by.

7:05 A.M.—REHEARSAL
Stand near the DP as the Actors and Director go through the blocking. The DP may whisper instructions to you and the Gaffer as the rehearsal progresses.

7:15 A.M.—CAMERA SETUP
Consult with the Gaffer, Dolly Grip, and Camera Operator or First AC about any special rigging that might be needed for their own equipment. Otherwise, work closely with the Gaffer as his Electricians set lights that may require additional hardware, such as C-stands, flags, or silks.

7:45 A.M.—ROLL CAMERA
Any lighting or camera setup problems should have been worked out prior to First Team coming to set, but watch the take carefully in case changes are made that require some additional tweaking of flags or other hardware.

7:48 A.M.—CUT, LET'S GO AGAIN
The DP may have some adjustments that he'd like made to the lighting as everyone resets back to one. Stick close to him while instructing your own crew over the walkie.

8:10 A.M.—CUT, MOVIN' ON
The cameras will probably move to get different angles, but wait for instructions from the DP before having your crew pull any equipment out of the way. Once you know what the new setup will entail, proceed as before.

1:00 P.M.—LUNCH

Have your crew secure any equipment that may not be safe to walk away from. For instance, if you are shooting on an exterior set on a windy day, remove any large flags or silks from their stands and lay them flat on the ground so that they can't blow over and hurt anyone.

2:00 P.M.—BACK TO WORK

Continue to work safely and efficiently through the second half of the day. As the crew grows more fatigued, your attention to detail becomes even more important.

9:00 P.M.—WRAP

Consult with your Best Boy Grip regarding any pre-rigging that may need to happen now or first thing in the morning on the present set or future sets. Check with the DP for any additional instructions before heading home.

WHAT I REALLY WANT TO DO IS MOVE UP!

As you are working directly under the DP, the next logical move would be to that position. However, not as many DPs come from the ranks of the Grip Department as they do from Camera or Electric. This isn't to say that you can't make that transition. Moving up means learning more about the specific lighting units that are available to the Gaffer as well as everything there is to know about cameras, lenses, framing, and generally working with a Director in a collaborative creative effort. By the time you've achieved the rank of Key Grip, it's likely that you've spent many years on sets learning and observing anyway, so the move shouldn't be too difficult once you've decided to go for it. Be aware that you'll probably have to build a reel and gain experience on lower budget projects until you gain a reputation among the Producers and Directors with whom you've worked before as being capable of the DP job.

Part VI

THE ELECTRIC DEPARTMENT

What I Really Want To Do Is...

Electric

Gaffe

Chapter 30

What I Really Want to Do Is Electric!

WHAT THE HECK IS AN ELECTRIC?

Also known as a "Juicer" and frequently confused with being a Grip, an Electric is responsible for anything that has to be plugged in on a set. Generally, a crew of four Electrics run cable and set lights in coordination with the Grip Department.

So how much can I make doing this?

On a typical twelve-week feature, expect to take home between $30,000 to $40,000. As with all the other BELOW-THE-LINE jobs, your typical working scenario will be to do one or two twelve-week jobs per year, or one episodic television series, with the rest of the time spent dayplaying. A typical nine-month long episodic television series schedule can put approximately $80,000 in your bank account.

WHAT DO I REALLY NEED TO KNOW?
I just set lights and plug 'em in? What else is there to know?

It's not as easy as it sounds. The job can involve working extra long hours, dragging very heavy cable thousands of feet through filthy conditions, and being stranded a hundred feet in the air all night long.

One day the Gaffer may say to you, "I need a tweeny on a triple riser baby over there. Put some 216 and 1/4 O on it, and it's for a rim light kicking the Actor sitting where I am." If you know there's a lunchbox sitting right where it needs to be and you don't need a stinger, tell him, "I got that." You have to go to the carts at the staging area, get the correct stand out, put the correct type of light on it, making sure it has its barndoors and its scrim bag. Next get the cut diffusion and the cut color, have C-47s on your belt, bring some dirt if it's in danger of tipping over, and ask the Grips for help if there is anything else you might need to make it safe.

If you understood everything in the above paragraph, you're probably ready to be a Set Electrician.

If not, you have to learn about the equipment and how a set runs. Contact the large lighting supply companies in town, like Mole Richardson, ARRI, and LTM lighting, and get their catalogs. Look through them and familiarize yourself with all the various instruments (tungsten, open face, etc), including cable and power-distribution tools.

For the most part, you aren't required to have any special certification to do this job at any level. However, it's in your best interest to understand how power works. It's crucial for you to know how to prepare for and deal with any and all power-related problems that could arise.

One particular area that does require specific training is for operating a "condor." Both **OSHA** (Occupational Health and Safety Administration) and **IATSE** (International Alliance of Theater and Stage Employees) require that you have certification to operate this machine safely. A condor is used to either raise a camera or, more frequently, to mount lights. This requires someone who is not afraid of heights, who is comfortable with big machines, and who can handle really big lighting units (18,000–24,000 watt lights or Lighting Strikes units at 250,000, 500,000, or even a million watts). The standard household light bulb is a mere 100 watts.

Apart from the hardware, you have to understand phasing and power. IATSE Local 728 has a safety and training program available for that also; however, you have to be a member to take it. The program isn't required, but you need to know the things they teach in order to work. Chances are that you'll spend some time in the nonunion world first, so you'll get much of your education there. At the minimum, you have to know what "110 and 120" means and the difference between the two. You should know the purpose and function of the ground. Learn about rigging and using a dimmer board. If you have an electrical background in some other industry, the basics will be similar. However it's important to keep in mind that providing electrics for film isn't the same as for a house, for instance, because what you are creating on a set is temporary. A house is designed to last for decades, but each camera setup lasts just minutes. The equipment and the protocols are very different.

WHAT DO I REALLY NEED TO HAVE?
The lights are rented. What could I possibly need?

Practically anybody can figure out how to put a light on a stand and plug it in. But you're making good money because of your ability to a) create an environment where problems *won't* happen and b) quickly diagnose and solve problems if they do. For that, you'll need just a few tools and a tool belt to keep them close.

Start with a good pair of gloves. You're working with heavy equipment that gets very hot, very quickly. Leather or Kevlar-tip gloves are recommended. Expect to pay around $25 for a pair. Attach them to your belt with a battery clip, which is available from any auto parts store for just a few dollars. The belt itself will cost around $40, and a pouch to carry small things is another $30.

Aside from the gloves, you'll want to have an assortment of tools at the ready: a utility knife, a six-inch steel rubber-coated crescent wrench that opens extra wide, a 3/16 T-handle Allen wrench to tighten lug nuts, needle-nose pliers, an all-in-one screwdriver with a Phillips head on one side and a standard head on the other, and a pair of heavy wire cutters. You can buy most of these tools in a variety of handle colors. Keeping track of what's yours is easier if you pick one color that you can use for all your tools.

A stage can be very dark, particularly away from the set. A quality Xenon flashlight is about $150. A voltmeter that reads AC and DC voltage and continuity will cost you about $60.

Another handy tool to have is an inductive tester. Without exposing the copper inside the cable, the inductive tester tells you if a cable has electricity running through it by reading the magnetic field that is created if electricity is present. All you do is hold it close to the wire. It can be yours for around $30.

Everything is labeled very specifically when it comes to electrics. You need a red Sharpie to mark items that are "AC" and a black Sharpie to label items that are "DC." You'll also use phase tape, which is simply electrical tape used to label the legs of power from the generator with a color code system.

You'll also carry around an alcohol pad or two. There are some *very* expensive light bulbs that you will have to handle at some point. They are worth thousands of dollars each and can be damaged quite easily. Beyond just dropping a bulb like this, if you happen to touch it, the skin oil on your hand will cause that part of the glass to be a little bit darker. With that high-intensity light source mere inches away from the glass, that dark spot will heat up quicker than the rest of the bulb. The result is a violently loud explosion, which often destroys it and the unit that it's in. To avoid this unfortunate mishap, you will install the lamp into the lighting instrument with a cloth between your hands and the glass. Then you'll wipe it down with the alcohol pad, which will remove any skin oil transferred to the bulb. The alcohol evaporates quickly, so that by the time the unit is fired up, the bulb should be clean and safe to use.

What's the best way for someone to reach me?

Let everyone know when you're available and keep your name fresh in their minds. The Union Local's Available List (IATSE Local 728) might help you, but you're better off just leaving your cell phone and pager on all the time.

WHERE DO I REALLY NEED TO GO?
I just want to work.

Anywhere there is a stage, there will be a need to plug some lights in. You can learn a lot of the basics on small projects or in local theater productions. To break into the larger Hollywood arena, though, you'll need to be in a place where you can be available for very-short-notice calls. Let those who are working know that you are available. When work is slow (and it is periodically), most of the jobs will go to the established crew in the area first. Unless you have a specific "in," then you'll have to be patient until an opportunity arises.

So how do I get work?

The easiest way to learn the job is by working on a Rigging crew. As opposed to the pressure of working on a set with A-list actors waiting around for the lighting to be finished, on a Rigging crew nobody is watching the clock as impatiently. Simply put, the Rigging crew gets a set or location ready so the main unit can come to film there at some point in the near future and not have to waste time starting from scratch. If you're going to make a mistake by grabbing the wrong lighting instrument or dropping something, this is the time and place to do it.

On small independent projects, you'll start working on set right away. Once you've made the move to union work, the Rigging Crew will most likely be your first stop. Depending on the size of the project, the typical number of workers on a Rigging crew could equal or surpass the shooting crew. There is a Rigging Gaffer, a Rigging Best Boy, and anywhere from three to twenty or more Rigging Electrics. There may also be a Pusher, who acts essentially as a foreman. While there, learn the tools and equipment. See how the crew dresses. See what tools they carry. See how they interact with other departments. If you want to keep working, be quiet and aware. Don't show off to impress anyone. Just doing your job well and efficiently will go further than anything you can say in words. Once you've proven yourself as competent on a Rigging crew, you may be invited to work on an actual shooting set.

WHAT AM I GETTING MYSELF INTO?
So who actually calls and hires me?

Often, a production already in progress will suddenly need extra help. The Gaffer and Best Boy will probably have long lists of possible Electrics to call. If none of those attempts works out, the Best Boy will approach the other Electrics to see if they have any suggestions. If you have been networking well, with any luck, your name is on one of those lists and you might get a call.

Okay, I got the job. What now?

If you get called to dayplay on a project already in progress, make sure you know the call time, location, and environmental conditions you'll be working in. Grab your tool belt and get to set a little early to have time to introduce yourself and familiarize yourself with the equipment.

If you are fortunate enough to get hired for the length of a show, then your first stop will be to the rental house. The Gaffer and Best Boy most likely have already been there for a few days ordering all the minutia you'll need. You and the rest of the Electrics will come in to help the Best Boy test every piece of gear and then load it onto the truck. This may take up to a week or two, depending on the size of the equipment package. This process gives everyone the peace of mind that all the gear works the way it should.

What will my life really be like?

6:42 A.M.—GET TO WORK

With this call time and a general crew call just eighteen minutes later, you should be able to get the carts off the truck and staged on set. However, if you're ever given a longer pre-call, say two to three hours, most likely you'll be pre-rigging a set before the rest of the shooting crew arrives.

7:00 A.M.—GETTING TO SET

Find your truck, put your tool belt on, grab your walkie-talkie (with headset), get the carts off the truck, take what's needed to set, and stage it neatly. Make sure there is power everywhere and that the right equipment is placed where you'll need it.

You may walk into a pre-rigged set. The Rigging crew will have its own equipment and its own big truck. All of the Rigging crew's equipment should be labeled with a color specific to their unit. Your main unit equipment is marked with a different color. This helps to keep the gear separate and independent. When you leave that set, you'll take your stuff and leave theirs.

The Best Boy Electric and the GENNY Operator will be getting the lines energized, and one of the Set Electricians will be reading the voltages to make sure that everything was run properly.

7:05 A.M.—REHEARSAL

Although you will be getting specific orders from the Gaffer, it is always helpful for you to know as much as possible about the "action" that will take place on set. That includes what the Actors are doing as well as where the camera(s) will be. Find a place out of the way but within sight of the set. Watch and listen.

7:15 A.M.—CAMERA SETUP

Generally, you will work in teams of two. When the Gaffer asks you to set a specific light, you might be the one to get the instrument itself and your partner will run the power for it. A third Electric may set the stand or mount for you. However you choose to work it, the obvious goal is to work quickly and efficiently as a team.

7:45 A.M.—ROLL CAMERA

If you are the Gaffer's right-hand man on set, then you'll be watching every take, ready to jump in after the cut to fix any problems that arise.

Otherwise, you may be off to prep an upcoming set, strip a set that you left behind, or help the Best Boy Electric count inventory or repair something. Or, if there is really nothing else to do until the next setup, you can relax for a few minutes.

8:10 A.M.—CUT, MOVIN' ON

When you hear that the setup is finished, you should get back to set and await orders from the Gaffer. If the next setup is on the same set, but just from a different angle, the lighting may stay fundamentally the same, save for some minor adjustments.

You will continue the same routine throughout the day, setup to setup, until wrap is called at the end of the night.

1:00 P.M.—LUNCH

The Gaffer will probably ask that you or the Best Boy kill the lights. This can be done either at the unit itself or at a LUNCHBOX. Drop your belt at the carts or on the truck, then head to lunch.

2:00 P.M.—BACK TO WORK

In general, a day exterior will probably be the easiest part of the shooting schedule for Electrics. While the Grip Department runs around trying to control the natural sunlight, power may only be needed for monitors at VIDEO VILLAGE or for coffeemakers at Crafts Service. There may be special light "gags," such as emergency-type lights or one or two large units (like a 10K or 20K) used to fill in harsh shadows. More often than not, a day exterior scene will take longer than expected and the company will be racing to finish before night falls. As this MAGIC HOUR approaches, the Electric Department will spring into action and pull out enough equipment to give the illusion that the Actors are still speaking in daylight even though the sun is dipping below the horizon. This situation happens more often than it should, so be ready.

9:00 P.M.—WRAP

If you are shooting on a "hot set," the chances are that most of the lighting will remain in place overnight and the company will pick up where they left off in the morning.

If the set is wrapped, the Electrics will pull all the lights and power back to the carts and the truck. This can take anywhere from a few minutes to an hour or more after camera wrap. If there is Rigging crew equipment on set, leave that and they will come back later to pick it up after you've gone.

WHAT I REALLY WANT TO DO IS MOVE UP!

In a typical union progression, you have to be a Best Boy Electric before becoming a Gaffer. The Best Boy physically prepares and tracks all lighting equipment and manpower used by the Electric Department before, during, and after principal photography. He also works with the Rigging Best Boy and Rigging Gaffer to coordinate equipment and instructions from the DP. On set, the Best Boy coordinates with Transportation to park the generator in the correct position and energize the lines.

The best way to prepare for this is to help the Best Boy out whenever you have nothing else to do on set. Help him keep inventory, repair equipment, and organize the truck. Learn about the paperwork that needs to be done and kept track of.

You have to be organized to the point of being meticulous. Instead of goofing off while there is nothing to be lit on stage, you should be the one who is organizing things, cleaning up stingers that aren't being used, keeping the carts in good order, and preparing for future setups. Chances are that the Gaffer will notice your work ethic and know that he probably has a good candidate the next time his regular Best Boy isn't available. When you've got a reputation for being a good Best Boy, the Gaffer and other Electrics know they don't have to worry about your work and can comfortably go about doing their own jobs.

Chapter 31

What I Really Want to Do Is Gaffe!

WHAT THE HECK IS A GAFFER?

In tight coordination with the Director of Photography and the Key Grip, the Gaffer directs the actual nuts and bolts of lighting the set with his crew of Electricians.

That, and what else?

The Gaffer is also in charge of managing the resources that it takes to light the set, including manpower and equipment requirements.

Beyond having considerable technical skill, the Gaffer must wear the hat of a politician at times when dealing with budgetary concerns. As with all departments, your budget will be limited and you'll have to stay within it.

This is not just a technical or support job, as was the case with the previous positions. As the Camera Operator does for the Camera Department, the Gaffer in the Electric Department has the opportunity to infuse the project with his own creative input. Your choices are now directly influencing the image that will end up on the big screen, so possessing or developing an artistic sense becomes much more vital than ever.

Ultimately, you are the link in the Electric Department between the artistic demands of the script and the technical requirements to achieve the goals. As an Electric, you used a belt full of tools as well as your hands to move stands, cables, and lights around. Now, as the Gaffer, the people are your tools. It is your job to line up the manpower, actual lighting units, and various support gear that you'll need to accomplish the DP's wishes.

I'm at the top of the department. The money must be getting pretty good then. Right?

It can be. However, to rise to this position, you may need to take the occasional low-budget nonunion job where you will be happy to find work making between

$100 and $200 per day, if that. As a rough goal, though, aim to make between $300 and $350 a day if possible. Some nonunion commercials will get you $500 to $550 a day.

Once you're in the union as a Gaffer (Chief Lighting Technician, or CLT), the long-term feature contract will get you between $35,000 to $40,000 for twelve weeks of feature work. If the project is bigger, you very easily could see substantially more than that.

WHAT DO I REALLY NEED TO KNOW?

If you've gotten to this point, you should be completely proficient in the tasks that your crew has to accomplish. You should have a total understanding of what it takes to be a Rigging Electric, a Set Electric, a Best Boy Electric, and a Generator Operator. You also should be paying attention to what your boss, the DP, does in the event that you are asked to "cover him" for some reason.

WHAT DO I REALLY NEED TO HAVE?
My guys are climbing around now. So what do I need to have?

In a lot of cases, the DP will let you know what he wants the set to look like and then let you deal with the details of getting it there. For that you'll need a variety of light meters. As you direct your crew to place lights, it'll be up to you to control the light to a predetermined level of exposure. An incident meter, a spot meter, and possibly even a color temperature meter will all be on your belt during the day right next to the walkie-talkie.

You'll also need a neutral-density monocle, or contrast glass. This allows you to look directly into a bright light source so that it can be precisely aimed. For larger units (brighter lights), consider having a welder's glass around as well.

Depending on the situation, you may also be jumping in to adjust or fix a problem yourself, so at the very least, keeping a pair of gloves close by is a good idea as well.

What's the best way for someone to reach me?

If you've gotten to this step on the ladder, you're well aware by now that it is all about relationships. Having a reliable phone number available and having that number in the hands of everyone you know is the key to being remembered the next time an opportunity presents itself.

WHERE DO I REALLY NEED TO GO?
I just want to work.

If you're ready to begin Gaffing, you likely already have a foothold in the industry.

So how do I get work?

At this level, more now than ever, your work is having a direct impact on what ends up on film. You will get hired through personal relationships with DPs. Your experience and personality will most likely precede you, so having a résumé will be enough. What a DP wants to know from a Gaffer is whether he is easy to get along with and if he can do the job competently and efficiently.

The UPM will have final say, however. It isn't enough to know the tools and how to best use them. Your ability to work efficiently within a given budget is just as important and of direct interest to the UPM.

WHAT AM I GETTING MYSELF INTO?
So who actually calls and hires me?

Typically, when the phone rings, it will be a DP on the other end. After that, you'll have to apply to the Line Producer or UPM, who will want to see your résumé. You are now in a position of responsibility over a budget, and they want to know that you can handle that just as much as the technical requirements that the DP needs.

Okay, I got the job. What now?

You'll go into prep. Production will give you a copy of the script for you to read and break down. You'll be making notes in the margins regarding any and all issues related to the lighting and/or electric needs of the script.

At some point close to the start of production, or in many cases during production itself, you will go on a tech scout with your Best Boy, your Rigging Gaffer (if there is one), the Director, the Director of Photography, a Producer, Locations, and possibly a Transportation Chief, amongst others. During that time, you will take a look at the various locations that have been chosen and evaluate your needs regarding equipment, manpower, and expendables.

What will my life really be like?

7:00 A.M.—GETTING TO SET
Get your meters off the truck, grab a walkie-talkie with a fresh battery, and head to set. If you didn't do it the previous evening, you should review the script pages for the day as well as any notes that you might have made during prep.

In many cases, you will get to set and just wait for a rehearsal. If you already know the general details of how the scene will be shot, you will be coordinating your crew to begin running power from the generator to various areas of the set.

7:05 A.M.—REHEARSAL
When the First AD calls for a rehearsal, find a place to watch that will be out of the way of the Actors yet where you can clearly see what is going on.

7:15 A.M.—CAMERA SETUP

In most cases, after the rehearsal, you'll have a brief discussion with the DP concerning what he'd like to do with the scene.

There are two different types of instructions you might get at this point. At one end of the spectrum, some DPs will tell you exactly what to do, e.g., "take this specific light, put it on a stand this high, put this diffusion on it, plug it in, turn it on, walk away, and I'll tell the Grips what to do with it from there."

On other end of spectrum is the DP who wants "a warm light coming from this direction because that's the motivation for this scene. Pick the instrument you want, but give me this T-stop because this is the film I'm using. Give me that look and I'll come back in fifteen minutes." In this case, the DP is leaving the technical particulars up to you just so long as you can achieve the "art" that he's looking for.

After you have a plan, start directing the first lighting setup. Work with your Electricians and Grips to get the necessary instruments in place and power to them. Once everything is set, you'll confer with the DP for any additional instructions. When finished, you or the DP will let the First AD know and he will call in the principal Actors.

At this point, they may or may not run another rehearsal. If they do rehearse again, this will be your first chance to look at the lighting with the actual people who will be in the shot. After, or during, that rehearsal, you can tweak the lighting to suit the principal Actors better. If they do not rehearse before the camera rolls, you have little choice but to let it all go and hope for the best. There is usually a "take two," but not always.

7:45 A.M.—ROLL CAMERA

Find a place to watch the action itself or view the monitor during the shot. You should look for any problems that need to be fixed. On an interior set, that may involve an Actor who doesn't hit his marks correctly and thus consistently misses his light. On an exterior, a gel that is clipped to a lamp may get blown around and cause a noise that ruins the sound. Sometimes, you or an Electrician can fix this during the take, but most often, you'll just take note of it then work quickly after the cut.

7:48 A.M.—CUT, LET'S GO AGAIN

Now that everyone has seen the actual shot in motion, this is the time to make any adjustments necessary.

8:10 A.M.—CUT, MOVIN' ON

If the AD says, "Movin' on," then typically everyone in charge is happy with at least one of the takes. The process begins all over again with a new rehearsal and a brand new setup.

1:00 P.M.—LUNCH

Instruct your Electricians to shut down the set lights and go to lunch. As Gaffer, you may spend your lunchtime in consultation with the DP or watching dailies.

2:00 P.M.—BACK TO WORK

The process of going from setup to setup continues throughout the afternoon, either until you've finished the work scheduled for the day or until wrap is called.

You may need to get in contact with the Rigging Gaffer concerning upcoming scenes. If the Rigging crew is working nearby, you might actually head over to the new set to trade information. Otherwise cell phones, e-mail, or text messaging are good ways to communicate. You may show up on a set that has been pre-rigged and find a "map" of what was done taped up somewhere.

9:00 P.M.—WRAP

Put your meters back in their case, put your radio in the charger, and head home.

WHAT I REALLY WANT TO DO IS MOVE UP!

Facility with the electrical aspects of production isn't enough. To become a DP, you have to learn about camera movement, lenses, and the politics and manpower requirements of the Camera Department. You also must understand and respect the Key Grip and everything that department does. Once you grasp all that, plus the Director's artistic desires, as well as the *politics* of dealing with a Director, a Producer, a studio, and millions of dollars flying around, then you'll be completely ready to make the jump into becoming a DP.

However, it isn't necessary to know all of those things to become a successful DP. You may have shot a small independent film for some young film school Director who suddenly becomes Hollywood's next greatest hotshot. If that Director wants you to be at her side for her first $50 million epic (and the studio allows it...which is unlikely), then you will be. In this case, you'll most likely have to rely heavily on the knowledge and experience of a seasoned union crew. You may have the vision, but they'll have the know-how to make you look good.

Whatever the case, whenever you feel you are prepared and ready to take on the role of DP, you need to begin creating a reel. This is a collection of shots, scenes, or entire projects that best represent to others what you are capable of doing artistically. If you are Gaffing professionally on large studio projects, this may require you to take some time off to go shoot small student or low-budget films. Pick and choose these projects so that they give you the opportunity to create the kinds of images that you think will help sell yourself to others. For instance, if you need to show that you can handle shooting large night exteriors, find a lower budget project that has those types of shots in it. If you want to show that you can shoot green-screen elements, find a project that requires special effects. Rarely will you find just one project that will have it all, so you'll build your reel slowly over time.

Your practical on-set experience in the Electric Department coupled with a good reel will only be valuable if you have someone to show it to. As you work on projects both big and small, forge strong relationships with those who are, or will be, in the position to hire you later on. The world is full of very qualified cinematographers who just never get that lucky break to shoot big-budget projects. Luck is when preparation meets opportunity. Take the time to prepare yourself so that when the opportunities do pop up, you'll be ready to make that leap to the top.

Part VII

THE SOUND DEPARTMENT

What I Really Want To Do Is...

Pull Cable

Boom

Mix Sound

Chapter 32

What I Really Want to Do Is Pull Cable!

WHAT THE HECK IS A CABLE PULLER?
THAT'S REALLY A PAYING JOB?

The Production Sound Department usually consists of three people: the Sound Mixer, the Boom Operator, and the Utility Sound Person, otherwise known as the Cable Puller. While it doesn't necessarily sound like much, the presence of a third person on the Sound crew helps to ensure that a day of production will go smoothly.

Your primary job is to manage the equipment. This serves the dual purpose of giving you hands-on time with all the gear as well as allowing the Mixer and Boom Operator more time to concentrate on their own jobs.

On many lower budget projects, Production can get away with only having a two-man crew, so there will be no Cable or Utility person. In contrast, if a job requires a significant amount of "playback" (e.g., music), then a fourth person will be called in to manage that specifically.

That, and what else?

After getting equipment off the truck in the morning, the Cable Puller will spend the rest of the day keeping the Mixer happy as well as aiding the Boom Operator with the cables and his microphones. Also, if a second mic is required for a shot, he becomes the second Boom Operator.

Because you have more time off set than anyone else in the Production Sound Department, you also are in charge of keeping track of timecards and other paperwork. At the end of the day, you may also have the critical responsibility of getting the recordings into the proper hands.

Man, I'm startin' at the bottom and pulling cable and stuff. The money must be lousy.

One would think so. However, the Union Cable Puller makes only about $2 less per hour than the Boom Operator yet has around 80 percent less responsibility. But over the course of a twelve-week feature film, the Cable person will make roughly the same amount of money as the Boom Operator because of the overtime accrued by being the first to show up and the last to leave. Expect to bring in around $40,000 on an average union feature film.

WHAT DO I REALLY NEED TO KNOW?

Your primary responsibility is in taking care of the equipment by helping to keep it clean, well maintained, and safely stored when necessary. While you theoretically don't have to know anything before starting out, you'll be far more valuable to the Sound crew if you have some idea of how to repair cables and clean expensive recording equipment properly. Apart from that, just a general awareness of proper set etiquette and a likeable demeanor will be enough to get you going.

WHAT DO I REALLY NEED TO HAVE?
Cable Puller, hmm...I need some gloves! Right?

That's a good start. A movie set, whether outdoors or onstage, can be a pretty dirty place, so you want to wear clothes that you don't mind roughing up a bit. The stage floor is littered with cables and gear, and exterior locations are subject to any weather you can dream up, so you need adequate protection from the elements.

Because your job requires navigating through those hazards all day, good footgear is really important. One good pair of tennis shoes or work boots is better than two pairs of cheap ones.

Jeans and a T-shirt will help protect you from the heat and dirt as you climb in and out of trucks and pull equipment across stage floors, city streets, and maybe even wilderness areas. And, as you guessed, a good pair of work gloves to pick up and wrap cables will save your hands from unnecessary filth and potential damage.

You'll also want to have a small but bright flashlight, a voltmeter to test batteries, a small tool kit for small repairs, a pocketknife, and a tool belt to carry it all.

What's the best way for someone to reach me?

While the Sound Union (IATSE Local 695) maintains an Available List, your best bet is still through your own networking.

WHERE DO I REALLY NEED TO GO?
I just want to work.

When you're just starting out, it's important that you are available to show up on a moment's notice. With that in mind, you obviously have to move close to an area of production, whether it is Los Angeles, New York, or someplace else. But keep in mind that the smaller the market, the harder it may be to break in, as those who are already established may have little incentive to contribute to training their own competition. Also, larger production markets typically have more opportunities by nature of the volume of production going on. The tradeoff is that you will have more competition to contend with as well as a higher cost of living.

So how do I get work?

Ask anyone you know who works in the industry to connect you with a Sound Mixer or a Boom Operator. Call those people and tell them that you want to become a Sound Mixer someday and ask if you can come to set for a week just to observe and learn. Get there before call time and stay until wrap is done. Be there to learn and participate if allowed. Ask questions. Lend a hand in moving gear or cables. Then, if you've proven to be likeable and reliable, you'll have a first set of contacts who will remember you the next time they need help or are asked for a recommendation. That's how careers get started.

You'll first get hired on lower budget nonunion productions. When you are ready to work on larger projects (in the United States), you'll have to join IATSE Local 695. There are three ways to go about this. The first is to work thirty days on a union project. You'll have to put your name on the Available List and wait until everyone currently in the union is already working. You could be waiting a long time for that to happen.

The second way to join the union is to work at least one hundred days in your job classification (Cable Puller, Boom Operator, or Sound Mixer) on any production, union or nonunion, within a three-year period. You'll need pay stubs to verify those days.

The third way to join is when a nonunion project you are already working on becomes unionized and you have at least thirty days of experience.

WHAT AM I GETTING MYSELF INTO?
So who actually calls and hires me?

Most likely you will receive a call from the Sound Mixer. On occasion, the Boom Operator may be asked for recommendations, but it will still be the Mixer who picks up the phone to talk to you.

Okay, I got the job. What now?

At some point close to the start of production, you will have a prep day. Typically most Sound Mixers will own their equipment, so your prep may take place at the Sound Mixer's house. The goals of this time will be to familiarize yourself with the equipment, make sure it all works properly, and to load it all onto the truck. Prep can last a couple of days or up to a week or more if you have to deal with a special situation, like condensing a package for overseas shipment.

What will my life really be like?

6:42 A.M.—GET TO WORK
Depending on the size of the project, the Sound Department will either have to share room on the Camera truck or, in the case of sizable productions, you will get your own vehicle. As the Cable Puller/Utility Sound Person, you might have a pre-call to pull equipment off the truck. However, in most studio situations, if the company is starting at 7:00 A.M., they won't shoot anything until 8:30 or 9:00 A.M. because of Makeup, Hair, Wardrobe, Lighting, and Set Dressing, so there is plenty of time to set up the sound equipment and be ready with a normal call time.

7:00 A.M.—GETTING TO SET
Figure out where the first shot will be and find someplace close to park your carts. If the Sound Mixer trusts you with the task, turn everything on, connect all the cables, and determine that it's all working properly. Make sure the machines have tape or discs and that the Boom Operator has the correct microphones and support gear.

7:05 A.M.—REHEARSAL
As part of your training, you should be watching the rehearsal and how the Boom Operator and Mixer decide to set up as a result of the blocking choices made. As a practical matter, you should be paying attention anyway in case anything out of the ordinary comes up, like the need for a second mic.

7:15 A.M.—CAMERA SETUP
Put your gloves on and help the Boom Operator move his gear onto the set. Then string the necessary cables from the mixing board out to the mic. As camera and lights are set and rearranged, keep an eye out for your own cables to make sure that they do not cross power incorrectly.

7:45 A.M.—ROLL CAMERA
If you are not acting as a second Boom Operator, you can relax for a few minutes. Of course, if you have any interest in moving up, you should take the time to observe and learn how the Boom Operator and the Mixer do their jobs. If something doesn't make sense, don't be afraid to ask questions. This might also be a good time to clean gear or repair cables if need be.

7:48 A.M.—CUT, LET'S GO AGAIN

When the Director decides to do a take again, you should listen to see if there was a problem with sound. Check with the Boom Operator on occasion to make sure he doesn't need help with anything.

8:10 A.M.—CUT, MOVIN' ON

This setup is finished and the cameras will be moved elsewhere. Disconnect the cables from the boom and wrap them back to the mixer so that they won't be damaged. Pull the boom and stand off the set and wait to see where the next setup will be. Once you figure that out, ask the Boom Operator where he'd like his gear and reconnect everything as soon as it's safe to do so. Repeat as necessary.

1:00 P.M.—LUNCH

The Sound Mixer may or may not want his cart covered, depending on the location and conditions. If the cart does need to be protected from the elements or curious visitors, throw a space blanket over your gear and secure it with grip clips. Tidy up any cables that might be unraveling and then go to lunch.

2:00 P.M.—BACK TO WORK

The routine is pretty much the same from setup to setup throughout the day. A location environment will afford you more time to do everything. Typically, feature films will be easier because you're only shooting a page to a page and a half a day. The setups are longer as the crew will take more time with lighting and complicated camera moves. TV shows, on the other hand, cover six to eight pages a day, so you usually have something to do.

You really don't have a terribly complicated job and will serve the needs of the crew pretty well by running the cable out and back, distributing and monitoring the equipment, and just keeping a general eye out for their well-being.

9:00 P.M.—WRAP

As you sense wrap approaching, you can start to pull things back that aren't likely to be used. If you haven't done it already, get a jump on the timecards for the Sound Department so that all that needs to be filled in are out-times for the day.

Once wrap is officially called, the Boom Operator and the Sound Mixer are released. It's up to you to pull the boom back, put the microphone away, wrap all the cables, and get the carts back on the truck and secure them. If there are any batteries to charge, make sure that they get plugged in. If the Sound Department takes care of walkie-talkie distribution, you may have to deal with getting them all back from the various departments and making sure they get put on charge.

The most important thing to accomplish is turning in the tapes and logs. The recordings are worth hundreds of thousands of dollars. If misplaced, the day would be lost and would have to be redone. The Sound Mixer may have some log corrections to make or he may ask you to finish up the paperwork as part of your training. Whatever the case, make certain that everything is in order and see to it that the materials get handed in to the appropriate personnel, usually an Assistant Director, the Loader, or a Driver.

WHAT I REALLY WANT TO DO IS MOVE UP!

You'll have to work for at least a year as the Utility before being allowed to move up to Boom Operator. Not that that is a bad thing. A year might consist of a couple of features, if you're lucky, and a bunch of dayplaying wherein you'll meet more people. The key to a long-lasting career is in having your name be known by as many potential employers as possible. While hooking up with a successful Mixer who takes you from show to show would be a wonderful thing, what happens to you if he suddenly decides to use someone else, is forced to use someone else, or retires? Get the point? So take the opportunity you have to learn all you can and meet as many people as possible.

To move up, you have to find a Mixer who will take a chance on you. You'll get to show your stuff whenever a second mic is required. The day may come when the regular Boom guy has to take a day off or leaves a show early to do another project. Or maybe the Mixer has to leave so everybody moves up for a day. In some way, you'll get the opportunity to work as a Boom Operator and learn what he has to go through firsthand. In doing that, you'll demonstrate your ability directly to the Sound Mixer so that the next time he needs someone and his regular guy isn't available, or he gets the chance to recommend someone, your name will be at the top of his list.

Aside from the politics of it, there is the actual job to consider. After you move up, suddenly there you are on set holding the boom. You've got a whole new world of problems and responsibilities. Maybe you're not standing where you should be. Or maybe you've got three shadows from the mic that you didn't see before and two are on the Actor's face. Now what do you do? Moving up to Boom Operator takes practice and understanding, physical endurance, and knowledge of lighting and sound. Boom Operators get paid for their ability to deal with problems quickly and quietly.

As a member of IATSE 695, you're allowed to move back and forth between cabling and booming, so there is little risk to your income if your transition to Boom Operator isn't going as well as you'd hoped.

Chapter 33

What I Really Want to Do Is Boom!

WHAT THE HECK IS A BOOM OPERATOR?

The Boom Operator's primary job is to position the microphone, which is attached to a six- to twelve-foot telescoping pole, out over the heads of the Actors who are speaking. It sounds simple but can be a complex and physically demanding job. It requires paying attention to how a scene will be photographed, specifically the size of the shot and the framing so the microphone is as close as possible to the Actors but does not show up in the movie. It requires an understanding of lighting, because the mic and boom can create shadows. The Boom Operator needs to know the dialogue as well as or better than the Actors because the mic needs to be moved back and forth *before* lines are spoken.

The job also requires that the Boom Operator work well with other people. Not only will you have to deal with other crew members as you find a place to work, but you are swinging a large, heavy, and potentially distracting object over an Actor's head. Some shots may not be conducive to using a boom, so LAVALIERE mics have to be hidden someplace on an Actor. Good bedside manner is crucial when dealing with sensitive egos or modest sensibilities.

That, and what else?

Your primary goal is to place the microphone in the most optimal position for the best recording of the dialogue that is happening in the frame. However, to save the editorial staff a lot of trouble, you can cover off-camera dialogue as well. The potential danger is in missing the primary sound, so only do this if you feel there is enough time between lines to get the mic back where it should be.

Related to this, you also really need to memorize all of the dialogue. At the start of each working day, the ADs will hand out SIDES, which contain all the scenes for the day. Before each shot, you should learn all the dialogue to be spoken so that you don't miss any cues.

I move up and get a raise!

When you first start out making movies, you'll be on a two-man crew with no Cable Puller. A typical nonunion flat rate will net you around $100 a day.

Once you join Local 695 (see page 241 in Chapter 32 for membership requirements), your pay will go up substantially; you'll make about $40,000 for a twelve-week feature. But depending on your connections and experience, you may have to enter the world of union studio features at the Cable Puller level.

WHAT DO I REALLY NEED TO KNOW?

The classic B-movie problem is having a boom mic drop into the shot. So aside from just knowing how to position yourself and the mic to get the best recording without casting shadows, you also should know your lenses. This will come with experience, but in time you'll be able to call over to the First AC and ask him what lens is on the camera. He may tell you anything from a 10mm at the widest or "loosest" to a 200mm or more at the "longest" or "tightest." Using that information and looking at the distance between the camera and the Actor will tell you just how far you'll be able to drop the mic down without getting into the shot. If it's a particularly close call, you can ask the Camera Operator to give you a "line," which means that he'll look through his eyepiece and point down, down, down as you lower, lower, lower your boom. When you are just above his frame line, he'll stop you there. You need to make some kind of mental note or find some way of judging that distance so that a take isn't blown because you dip the mic into frame. Ask to look through the eyepiece so that you can learn. Most camera people will be very willing to help you.

You also need to know about lighting. Is the key light coming in soft or hard? Will a shadow you create fall on the Actor or the wall? Will it actually be in frame?

It helps for you to be flexible and in shape. Not only do you have to hold your arms up over your head for extended periods of time, but in the case of a tracking or Steadicam shot, you'll have to follow the Actors along without tripping or running into anything like seats, C-stands, other people, and walls. And keep in mind that you're holding a long stick over top of people's heads. At full extension, with a big windscreen on, it could snap in two with enough wind hitting it. You'll have to have substantial upper-body strength to hold it in place.

WHAT DO I REALLY NEED TO HAVE?
The Mixer owns all the gear. What could I possibly need?

Now that your job involves actually listening to the sound coming from the Actors, you might want to invest in a really good pair of headphones. Even though the Sound Mixer owns all the equipment needed, the better part of your day will be spent wearing CANS on your head. Not only do you get the benefit of a personalized comfortable fit, but it will be a tax write-off as well.

What's the best way for someone to reach me?

Aside from the union keeping an Available List, your best bet will be to just keep in touch with those Mixers and Boom Operators with whom you've worked before. Somebody might move up or get sick or just need another body for the day. Make sure everyone has your phone number so they can reach you at a moment's notice.

WHERE DO I REALLY NEED TO GO?
I just want to work.

When you're first getting started, you won't likely be called to be a Cable Puller on a union set. Your first foray into the Sound Department will probably be on nonunion low-budget feature films as a Boom Operator. If you don't already know someone in the business who can get you a job on a low-budget nonunion set, then another great way to meet people is to work at a rental house. There you'll learn what equipment is available and what gets used. In time you'll get to know the people who rent the stuff and if you're likeable enough, they might bring you out on a job for a day or two to help out.

So how do I get work?

Because the Sound Department is small, your best bet is to connect with at least a couple of Mixers to stay busy and make enough money throughout the year. Investing more time as a Cable Puller can translate into knowing more Sound Mixers you can call for work as you move up.

In feature films, the turnaround is about three months from one project to the next so, if you start out there, you'll potentially work on a number of different projects throughout the year. However, if you land on a TV show, the schedule goes for up to nine months, and this will take you out of the loop. Once the show goes on hiatus or ends entirely you'll have to remind everyone with whom you once worked that you're available again in hopes that they will find room for you.

WHAT AM I GETTING MYSELF INTO?
So who actually calls and hires me?

When the phone rings, the voice on the other end will most likely be the Sound Mixer. He may be checking your availability for a possible job or calling to hire you outright. In a lot of cases, the Mixer will also call the Cable Puller as well, but he may ask you for recommendations.

Okay, I got the job. What now?

Once you've got the job and have worked out the deal memo with the Production Department, your prep time simply involves helping the Mixer and the Utility person go through all the gear. You want to make sure that you have everything you'll need and that it all works. If there are any special requirements for the job, the Mixer most likely would have been informed and will have made arrangements for equipment that he does not own. This prep time usually will take only a day or two at most.

What will my life really be like?

7:00 A.M.—GET TO WORK

In the event that you have a Cable Puller/Utility person, he will have arrived eighteen minutes prior to you to pull the carts off the truck. If this is the case, you should go through the equipment you need and do a quick check to make sure that everything is connected and works. If you are on a smaller show, you may have to arrive a few minutes early to pull everything to set on your own. The Sound Mixer will typically arrive at the crew call time.

Request a set of sides from an AD and start going over the dialogue for that day. You will have to memorize the lines for each Actor so that you know where to place the microphone before they speak. The first shot of the day will probably be the MASTER so you'll have to know it all right away. After that, you'll move in for coverage and the dialogue will get broken up a bit, which will make your life a little easier.

7:05 A.M.—REHEARSAL

You should be paying attention to where the Actors are going (the blocking) and when they are saying their dialogue. Keep your sides handy and make notes if necessary. Once rehearsal is finished, you'll talk with the Boom Operator about the scene, where the mic should go, and what the problems might be.

In most cases, you'll be using the boom mic. However, some environments or shots will require you to wire the Actors with lav mics. If the decision is made to go with radio mics (or RF mics), the Cable Puller will pull the receivers from their cases and take them to the Sound Mixer. Meanwhile, the Boom Operator will take the transmitters and mics to the Actors. As these items must be hidden from view, you may need to get up close and personal with the Actors. Some Actresses, in particular, may have trouble with a male clipping things under their clothing, so this is where your charming and professional personality comes in. It's important for them to realize that this is just another part of your job and nothing else. You also need to put them at ease by letting them be aware that no one will be eavesdropping on them between shots while the RF is hooked up.

Also, you need to determine if you can adequately cover the scene by yourself. Depending on the number of Actors in the shot as well as camera placement and lens choice, it may be nearly impossible for you to move the boom around quickly enough from one Actor to another. In that case the Cable Puller will be pressed into service as a second Boom Operator. Of course, while this helps to solve your problems of getting all the dialogue recorded, the possibility of unwanted shadows for the lighting setup is doubled. If that second boom is to be used, be sure to get it set up quickly and make sure that the Gaffer is aware of your plans.

7:15 A.M.—CAMERA SETUP

Based on the blocking rehearsal you just saw, you'll have a pretty good idea where you're going to want to be to boom correctly. Not only do you need to stand where you'll be able to get the boom into proper position, but you have to steer clear of the cameras and any lights on the floor, avoid creating shadows with your boom or mic, and of course stay out of the shot.

You'll want to keep an eye on the set as the crew creates the next setup. As you gain experience, you'll be able to notice potential problems being created as lights are rigged and aimed. If you sense trouble brewing, it is beneficial to everyone for you to grab your boom right away and stick it out over the heads of the Stand-ins. That way, you can see for sure if there will be a problem and the Grip and Electric crew will know if they need to make any adjustments to avoid unwanted boom shadows on the set or the Actors.

7:45 A.M.—ROLL CAMERA

After the First AD calls out "Roll sound!" you stick the boom out to the first position and get ready. Through your headphones you'll hear the Mixer "slating" the shot. He'll then say, "Speed," which you need to repeat so that everyone on set knows, too. Your words cue the Camera Operator to roll the camera and the Second AC then hits the STICKS.

7:48 A.M.—CUT, LET'S GO AGAIN

If the Actor is making your job difficult, perhaps changing a bit of business or changing his mark, then you could go to him and say something like, "You did something different than the take before, and I wasn't prepared for it, so how are you going to do it this time?" Know that this is a potential political minefield, as some Actors aren't receptive to the concerns of the technical crew, and some Directors don't want crew people talking to "their" Actors.

In the best-case scenario, the Actor will cooperate with you and give you a heads up on how he might perform the scene in the next take. In the worst case, you'll get ignored or told to get lost. The best thing for you to do is to make sure that the Mixer and the Director are aware of what is going on. It may not make the sound any better, but no one can come gunning for you later on when there is a problem, such as a door slamming on a line of dialogue. The key is to prevent problems from continuing without at least letting someone know about them. You may not have the power to affect change, but someone else may. Your job is to capture the best sound possible within the given parameters, be it environmental or otherwise. Just do your best.

8:10 A.M.—CUT, MOVIN' ON

If you've just done the master then chances are that the cameras will move in closer for coverage. You'll want to move your boom and stand back while the Cable Puller wraps the cable back. You don't want your stuff to be in the way of the rest of the crew while you're not around.

If the next shot is an entirely new scene with new dialogue, you need to pull out the sides and start over again just like it was the first setup of the day.

1:00 P.M.—LUNCH

If you're returning to the same setup right after the break, just leave your boom in its stand and walk away. If a new setup is going to happen, pull your stuff back off the set.

2:00 P.M.—BACK TO WORK

More of the same. Take any downtime to learn upcoming dialogue. Continue to watch the lighting and camera setups to head off any problems before the Actors come onto set.

9:00 P.M.—WRAP

After the First AC calls out that the "gate is good" you can pull your mic off the boom pole and put it away. The Cable Puller will wrap out the cables and get everything back to the truck. Your day is done. Be sure to get a call sheet, know what's on it for tomorrow, and ask any questions before you leave.

WHAT I REALLY WANT TO DO IS MOVE UP!

At every opportunity you closely observe the Sound Mixer as he does his job. While your primary responsibility was to point the microphone in the right direction, the Sound Mixer has to handle problems like noisy environments, Actors delivering their lines in ways that aren't recordable, and political challenges with Actors and the Director. Once you're in the seat, you have to know what to do if you suddenly hear an airplane or other consistent noise while the take is in progress. Is it bad enough to stop everything? Can the sound be saved in post? Does the sound matter for this shot or angle anyway? What if you tell the Director that the sound was acceptable but then the Editors come back with a different opinion?

When you're ready for all of that, put your name out there to let others know you are interested. Sound Mixers you've worked with may be able to recommend you to shows that they aren't available for. It may also be advantageous to mix on lower budget projects to gain experience as well as more contacts.

Chapter 34

What I Really Want to Do Is Mix Sound!

WHAT THE HECK IS A SOUND MIXER?

When it comes to the sound for a film, there are really two phases: production and postproduction. Production is the period of weeks or months during which the photography occurs. The postproduction process can begin during the course of production and will continue for several months after the on-set production crew has wrapped.

The Production Sound Mixer's primary responsibility is to ensure a quality recording of the Actors' voices while they are being filmed on set. At the end of the day, he passes the recordings off to a member of the Production Department so that the Postproduction Sound Department can begin editing the dialogue and mixing it together with sound effects and music to create a finished soundtrack.

That, and what else?

The job does not just involve having a microphone stuck in front of an Actor and turning knobs. While 90 percent or more of the crew is concerned about some visual element of the project, only a few people are paying close attention to the sound. The Sound Mixer has a certain amount of authority when it comes to creating a quiet environment so that the sound will be as useful as possible. This goal often conflicts with the needs of other personnel on set.

After quiet is achieved, the next aspect of sound recording is to ensure the intelligibility of speech. Through speech, in part, the Actors convey the story. The words must be as natural sounding as possible so when the audience watches the movie, they'll get the sense that it is real. For instance, if a character is far away and yells across a canyon, the correct recording of that sound should match the viewer's visual perspective. If you put a LAV MIC on the Actor just because you couldn't get a boom in close enough, the sound would be too "close." If the character looks like he's in the distance, then chances are that the Director would like him to sound far away as well. It's the job of your department to mic the shot appropriately.

Your relationship with the Actors is also important. Sometimes you'll need to ask them to speak their dialogue a little more loudly or slightly delay a noise-producing action that overlaps their words. Keeping the relationship professional, quick, and to the point will render them confident that you are looking out for their best interests.

I finally get to sit down and work. And I'm in charge! This is the life.

If you start out on nonunion shows (and you probably will), you can probably expect to make around $100 a day. Also, since you're a novice, you probably won't own your own sound recording package, so you won't be making money on that. You could take the show and agree to provide gear and base a rate from there. Then you go sub-rent everything you need and mark up the price so you can eventually purchase your own equipment.

As you slowly build your own package, hopefully you'll be getting offers to work on bigger and better projects. At the high end, a union Mixer (IATSE Local 695-see page 241 in Chapter 32 for membership requirements) could negotiate a deal for over $100 an hour plus the equipment rental at between $2,000 and $3,000 per week. In general, the union scale is lower, and if you're working on a television project, you could wind up making only half of that. On a big show, you could eventually make around $100,000 in wages and rentals for a standard twelve-week project.

WHAT DO I REALLY NEED TO KNOW?

Fortunately you don't have to have a lot of technical background to start a career in sound. With the newest consumer gadgets, most people already have a basic understanding of what it involves. It is advantageous for the Production Sound Mixer to know what happens to his recordings after they leave the set. In purely practical terms, at the very least, the Mixer and the Postproduction Sound Department have to know and coordinate which recording formats they each plan to work with (Nagra tape, DVD, DAT, computer hard drive, etc.).

Having an engineering background is an advantage but not necessary. A single piece of equipment isn't that important because, on a major project, you've got a backup. You can't tell the Producer that you have to stop filming today because the recorder broke. You'd better have another one on the truck ready to go and another one on the way from the supplier coming to set. Technical repair capability helps, but is not essential.

WHAT DO I REALLY NEED TO HAVE?
It's just sound. Tape recorder and a mic. Good to go!

Uh, no. Not exactly, although you're on the right track. Whether you're renting the gear or own it outright, you still need the same basic things, no matter what project you're doing.

First you need microphones. The most typical way to capture sound is with a shotgun-type mic mounted on a telescoping boom pole. A good shotgun will run you about $1,200. The pole will cost around $700. You'll need to have, at the very least, two mics and two poles, one for use and one for backup. If you require two Boom Operators working simultaneously, you need those two setups as well as backups for each, so you're up to four mics and maybe even four poles, although you can probably get away with just two or three.

Radio mics have become an essential tool due to changing styles of filmmaking and acoustical environments. One system (transmitter and receiver) costs about $2,500. The tiny LAVALIERE mics to go with them are about $300 apiece.

To get the sound from the microphones into the Mixer requires cables. You'll need a variety of lengths of professional XLR cables, which will run you around $1,000 for the materials (cable and connectors) to build your own. Plus you'll need roughly another $1,000 for other types of cables and connectors.

Because you may have multiple sources of audio coming at you from set, you need a mixing panel or mixer to control the levels for quality recording. A standard quality mixer for feature production work starts at around $10,000.

After you've mixed the audio, it has to be recorded onto some kind of portable format. The industry standard for a long time was the Nagra tape recorder. Many Mixers still use them but only for a backup. Hard drive recorders and DVD recorders are taking over as the preferred method of capturing and delivering production sound to the postproduction team. You can expect to pay between $6,000 and $12,000, depending on the brand and type of recording device.

If the show is using traditional slates, they will be provided by the Camera Department. However if the decision is made to go with SMART SLATES, then you provide them. You'll need at least two of these, which run between $700 and $2,000 apiece.

That's it for electronic gear, but you also need a place to put it all. A standard sound cart will cost around $1,000.

You'll want a comfortable chair to sit in as well as some kind of umbrella for those day exteriors. You can find a decent tall director's chair for around $200.

A top-of-the-line production sound package will set you back $75,000 to $100,000. The good news is that if you work steadily on quality productions, it can pay for itself within a couple of years. After that, it's all profit for you until you have to upgrade again.

What's the best way for someone to reach me?

If you've got an agent behind you, just make sure that the people you like to work with have that contact number and/or your personal contact information.

WHERE DO I REALLY NEED TO GO?
I just want to work.

You have two choices. The first is to start off at the bottom as either a Cable Puller or Boom Operator on low-budget and/or nonunion projects and work your way up. This method involves a great deal of time, but the tradeoff is that you gain a wealth of experience and meet a lot of potential employers along the way.

Your second choice is to jump right in as a Sound Mixer. If you do that you won't be working on the top-budget films right away simply because no one is going to trust you. But you can start off doing your own and friends' projects and student films. There you can show off your skill and your own ideas and hopefully hook up with and impress people who can help you move on to higher-paying and more prestigious jobs.

Both methods have their pitfalls and advantages. Going the slow road in no way guarantees that you'll ever make it as a high-paid Sound Mixer. But neither does jumping into the pond with both feet for that matter. Your best bet is to just find projects that you can enjoy.

One can make a decent living as a sound recordist of some kind in almost any major city where production occurs. But if you want to get into the Hollywood feature loop, you have to meet the people who can hire you, and they live primarily in Southern California or New York. If you've come up through the ranks, you had to live in these places to be available for quick day calls. But it is rare for a Sound Mixer to be called in just for a day or two of work, so by the time you achieve this level in the department, you may find yourself with the freedom to move almost anywhere you wish.

So how do I get work?

Because it's a competitive environment, there are usually more people available to do the job than there are jobs open at any given time. All you can really do is work hard, be a great person and competent professional, and have your name out there.

After that, unfortunately, it's all kind of out of your hands. Based on one's experience and reputation, a Producer, a Director, a Production Manager, or possibly an agent will recommend a few Sound Mixers for a picture. Those candidates are asked to come in and meet with the Director for an interview.

Before the interview, ask for and read a copy of the script so you have an idea of the challenges it may present. If it's a musical, then you have playback to consider. If you are going to be shooting on a real train or at fifty thousand feet on an airplane, then you can count on a lot of background noise problems. If you are on top of a mountain, then you have to prepare yourself and the equipment for cold. Also ask about the cast and Director so you can get a sense of what the mood of the set will be.

When you sit down for the interview, the typical technical questions are asked, but more often than not, all the applicants will have roughly the same outlook on the problems and how to best deal with them. The deciding factor generally comes down to personality. It's a matter of evaluating whom the Director will be able to work best with for twelve weeks or more and who he thinks will mesh with the rest of the crew that is being hired.

WHAT AM I GETTING MYSELF INTO?
So who actually calls and hires me?

The first call you get will be from a UPM who knows or has heard of you. As soon as you think you might get the job, you'll want to put out calls to your favorite Boom Operators and Cable Pullers to see who is available.

Okay, I got the job. What now?

After you negotiate your deal and sign the deal memo, you'll want to prep the equipment you'll need for the project. If you have your own gear, your prep will just involve running through it all making sure everything works since the last time you used it.

If you are new and need to rent an entire package or even just need a few things, you'll have to go to the rental house. The Cable Puller and Boom Operator you hire will come in to help you. Depending upon the size and length of the project, prep should only take a day or two. If the gear is at your house, you will arrange for the Transportation Department to come by with a truck to pick it up. One of your crew will go to load it into the camera or sound truck.

What will my life really be like?

7:00 A.M.—GET TO WORK
Your first stop will be the Camera truck or Sound trailer, if for nothing else than to just drop off your personal gear. The Cable Puller and/or Boom Operator should have pushed the gear to the stage by this time.

7:05 A.M.—REHEARSAL
Take note of any unusual choices that are made in the blocking and camera setup that might adversely affect the sound, such as props being thrown around or excessive walking by either the cast or the crew.

You also have to decide on the most effective method of capturing the best and most accurate sound recording of that setup. The sound needs to relate to the image so if the shot is far away then the audio should sound far away as well. Work with the Boom Operator to get the optimal mic placement.

7:15 A.M.—CAMERA SETUP

While the other departments set up their gear for the visuals, it's up to you to control the environment and the variables that will have an impact on the sound. Put the headphones on and listen to where the noises are coming from. Kill the air-conditioning if possible, plug holes in the walls, cover windows with sound blankets, place mats on the floor (if they won't be seen), and grease any squeaky mechanical gizmos that will be used during the actual take.

If, during the First Team rehearsal, you notice that an Actor could hinder the sound recording, go now to the Director and express your concerns. Later in the show, the protocol and relationship may loosen up so that you can go directly to the Actor and ask if he would delay slamming a door on his line or speak up a bit. The Actor may not be entirely understanding for one reason or another, so then you'd take your concern back to the Director, who can either deal with it or not. It's important to know what's acceptable and what the proper channels are for fixing problems.

7:45 A.M.—ROLL CAMERA

About a minute to thirty seconds before the take, the First AD will shout out, "Put us on a bell." That's your cue to hit the button on your cart that sounds a loud buzzer. Hit it once for about five seconds. On a soundstage, this button will also turn off the air conditioning and activate some blinking red lights outside the doors.

When everything has quieted down, the First AD will then call out, "Roll Sound." Hit the switches on your recorders and do a quick scan to make sure everything is indeed rolling. Listen quickly for the output (the sound coming from the boom mic to the recorder then back to your headphones). Using the microphone you have mounted in front of you, identify the scene and take number (audio SLATING), such as, "This is scene 11, take 4." The Boom Operator is listening to the output as well so after he hears you slate the shot, he'll announce to the crew, "Sound speed," indicating that the equipment is up and running.

After that, the Camera Assistants will hit their slates in succession (A-camera first, then B, and so on). Soon after, the Director calls, "Action!"

If you've been doing this job for a while, you may have tricked out your sound cart with a monitor so you can see the shot as it is happening. Once you have a good sense of what the shot looks like, it sometimes helps to close your eyes so you can concentrate entirely on the sound.

7:48 A.M.—CUT, LET'S GO AGAIN

If there were any problems at all, take the time to try to fix them. If the shoes of an Actress make too much noise as she walks from one spot to the next, you can have the Wardrobe Department put tape on the soles. If the crew is making too much noise as they move around, you might be able to lay carpet down. Work with the Boom Operator to adjust the mic position if necessary. Your goal is to alleviate any potential problems that are within your control.

After each shot, you also want to fill out the Sound Log with the scene and take numbers. If there are any problems relating to specific takes, jot down some notes for the Editors to refer to later.

8:10 A.M.—CUT, MOVIN' ON

Once the Director has the performance he wants out of the Actors, he will want to go to the next shot. If Camera and Sound have no problems that necessitate having to go again, the AD will say, "Movin' on."

Just like the beginning of the day, pay attention to any rehearsals that take place or any significant changes that might affect your sound as the next setup is being built.

1:00 P.M.—LUNCH

If a show is big enough, a PA will bring you a boxed lunch as you head for dailies. In most cases, there won't be any major surprises for you. If there had been a major problem, the Editors would likely have contacted you earlier in the morning.

2:00 P.M.—BACK TO WORK

Just like the morning, you take it one setup at a time. While the day can potentially get boring and complacency can easily set in, it's best to keep in the proper frame of mind by not getting absorbed in some other activity, such as reading a novel. You usually won't need that kind of thing anyhow. The time manages to get filled in other ways. You can head to your truck and make new cables. Or maybe there is gear to be repaired or modified in some way. Often, other crew members have questions for you or just want to chat and trade stories.

9:00 P.M.—WRAP

As wrap approaches, if possible have your Cable Puller minimize the gear that needs to be put away. As soon as the First AD calls wrap, you are technically free to leave. Before you go, prepare the tapes and/or discs along with the written log. Either you or the Cable Puller must hand these materials in to the appropriate person. In the morning, the blank tape costs almost nothing. By wrap, those same tapes are worth hundreds of thousands of dollars.

Make sure your Utility Person is wrapping the gear correctly, say, "Thank you for a good day," and head home.

WHAT I REALLY WANT TO DO IS MOVE UP!

Well, there's nowhere to go from here really. While the basics of the job won't change much, you can have a lifetime of great (and sometimes not-so-great) experiences working around the world on wide variety of projects.

But if you ever get tired of mixing sound on movie sets, you could investigate opportunities in Postproduction Sound or switch departments altogether. If you've had aspirations to direct or produce, by this point in your career you will have met many higher-ups with whom you could start forming relationships and letting them know about other interests you might have. Other than that, sit back and enjoy your career.

Part VIII

SPECIAL EFFECTS

What I Really Want To Do Is...

Special Effects

Chapter 35

What I Really Want to Do Is Special Effects!

WHAT THE HECK IS SPECIAL EFFECTS?

The entire world of filmmaking revolves around creating many different illusions to make up one large fantasy world. In nearly every shot, the Production Designer creates brand new environments or enhances existing locations that are too difficult to shoot as is. The Director of Photography creates or enhances the light to create a mood or specific look. Actors pretend to be characters who only previously existed within the mind of a Writer and on the page. Except in documentary or news work, anything you see on a movie or television screen is really just an illusion.

But when it comes to creating real "magic," filmmakers call upon the Special Effects (SFX) Department. Just like illusionists on a stage, Special Effects technicians are there to create "tricks" that, when put on film, appear to be completely natural and real. You're there to make the audience believe in something that isn't really happening. The moment the audience becomes aware that a special effect was utilized is the moment that the work has failed.

Special Effects fundamentally covers the basic elements of wind, fire, rain, and snow, but they do much more than that. Really anything natural or unnatural that can be achieved "practically" on set via a mechanical or pyrotechnic process falls under the purview of Special Effects. Very often, you'll be fabricating parts and mechanisms from scratch. Even something as seemingly simple as a kitchen sink on a studio-backlot set requires someone to build the external hardware (Construction Department and Set Dressing) and then someone else to provide the water that comes out and a place for it to go to. Special Effects arrives with the water tank, the plumbing, and the pumps necessary to make it all work; then the department hooks it all up. Something that you'd otherwise take for granted, such as running water on a set, is just as "special" of an effect as the grandest of explosions.

I thought they just used computers for everything now.

It is important to note the difference between Special Effects and *Visual* Effects. Special Effects creates practical illusions that actually occur on set, such as wind (with fans), rain (with water trucks and rain bars), snow (with foam and blowers), and fire (with flame bars or explosives). Visual Effects takes the film that is shot on set and enhances it later on with computers or optical processes. For instance, anything that is shot against a green screen or anything that is created wholly within the computer, is considered a Visual Effect and requires a very different career path, one in which the work will be completed off-set.

This isn't to say that you don't need to or shouldn't know how to use computers in the Special Effects Department. Gimbals, large hydraulic platforms used to move vehicles or entire sets, require the use of computer controls. Rain bars, explosive charges, and squib hits may require a computer to make them work correctly. Your work still begins with steel, hydraulics, and hard physical labor to get it built and running in time for the shot.

In Special Effects, expect to get your hands dirty. There is a saying within the department that everything they have is heavy. There is a lot of physical labor in addition to the mental exercises you'll go through in trying to solve challenges that are handed to you.

That, and what else?

While you are there primarily to create illusions that will be filmed by the cameras, you also serve as support for the rest of the departments on the project. The Camera Department may need tripod hooks welded on a cart, Grips may need help to create special rigging, a Production Assistant's golf cart may need to be fixed, and the Producer may ask you to make it "snow" for the cast and crew Christmas party. Roughly 70 percent of the work you do winds up on screen. The other 30 percent is everything else. Your department is the most qualified electrically and mechanically, so you wind up dealing with almost everything that needs to be built and/or repaired over the course of the project.

Wow! Sounds like I'll be busy. How much will I make for this?

A Special Effects Coordinator can make around $60,000 per show. His assistants will make roughly half that over the same period.

WHAT DO I REALLY NEED TO KNOW?

Anything and everything you can. As the "MacGyvers" of the industry, you will be looked to by the Director to help her bring her script to life. Skills like digging ditches, welding, auto repair, hydraulics, engineering, computer programming, general mechanical aptitude, and pyrotechnic experience (with certification) combined with problem-solving creativity make a newcomer invaluable to the Special Effects Coordinator.

As a Coordinator, you aren't necessarily required to be an expert at any one thing. However, you will be asked to either overcome challenges yourself, or at the very least bring others on board who can. But the bottom line is that you have to have a knack for it. If you need someone else to fix your washing machine or car for you, you probably shouldn't be in Special Effects.

Aside from having mechanical aptitude, it also is important to understand the filmmaking process itself. Knowing how to blow things up is one thing, but understanding why you're asked to do things a specific way is important. You're creating effects that will be seen by at least one camera lens, if not more, and all in the proximity of a working crew. Safety, efficiency, practicality, and repeatability of the effect all play important roles in your work.

WHAT DO I REALLY NEED TO HAVE?
This job sounds huge. Sounds like I need everything!

It certainly seems that way. When you are asked to be ready to create or fix just about anything at all during the course of a normal day, what on earth shouldn't you have?

At the very least, you'll need a ditty bag or bucket of standard hand tools that you would normally use at home, such as screwdrivers, hammers, a knife, pliers, wrenches, and gloves. Nothing fancy is necessary when you're just starting out. The SFX Coordinator will provide the power tools and more expensive items.

When you reach that level of responsibility, you'll want to fill out your own "kit" eventually with an entire truck or trailer outfitted with all the basic tools you can think of as well as high ticket items like an air compressor, a welder, a lathe, and a mill. All of that can easily cost well over $100,000 by the time you're done. The standard kit for a Coordinator, though, is a basic assortment of tools (hand and power), a wide variety of nuts and bolts, and simple electronic components.

The general set of tools and machines set the stage for the specific work you need to accomplish. Once the method of creating an effect is determined, you'll obtain all of the necessary parts for that if you don't already have them, plus spares in case your creation breaks down.

You also need the proper licensing from the ATF (Department of Alcohol, Tobacco, Firearms and Explosives) and another from the state of California if you want to handle pyrotechnics on a movie set.

Do I get to be on set at all?

Remember, you're not just making things from scratch and fixing the stuff that breaks down; you have effects to create on set. A very specialized E-Fan was developed so that wind could be generated near the microphones without making any machine noise that would interfere with recording an Actor's dialogue. Atmospheric "haze" is created with various types of smokers and fog machines. And any practical effects that you fabricate specifically for a shot will have to be operated or supervised by someone in your department. Somebody has to be there to "flip the switch," as it were. So yes, you'll be on set whenever a special effect is needed.

What's the best way for someone to reach me?

The vast majority of your calls will come from people you've worked with before. Keep your contact information current with them as well as at the Local 44 office once you've become a member of the union. Hopefully you'll have plenty of advanced notice, but calls can come in at any time for work the very next day.

WHERE DO I REALLY NEED TO GO?
Local 44?

To get a serious career in Special Effects, you'll need to join IATSE Local 44, which covers many departments, such as Property, Set Decorators, and Special Effects.

When there is work to be done, an SFX Coordinator will first call the people he knows and with whom he likes to work. If they are busy, he will then call the local office. Members in Special Effects in need of work will have placed their names on an Available List. The Coordinator or someone from the office will choose people (sometimes randomly) from the list. If the list is empty because everyone in Special Effects is working, Local 44 will move to the Prop Makers list and send someone who is qualified from there. If no one is available from that list, the local office will check the Set Decorators. If no one is available from that list, they jump to Construction. If that fails, they will hire "permits." Permits are new people who have some experience but need to join IATSE to get better work.

Because of the system that is in place, it may be easier for you to join Local 44 in another department, such as Construction, Set Decorating, or Props. It's possible to move directly into Special Effects, but that depends on how long you're willing to wait or who you know.

So how do I get work?

First, of course, you're going to learn as much as you can on your own. Whether it is automotive repair, welding, computers, electronics, or pyrotechnics, you have to offer some established skill before you begin asking for work.

Located primarily in and around Los Angeles, there are several Special Effects companies that provide crew and services to the motion picture industry. Pick up the phone and call every one of them and ask if there is a current apprenticeship program available. If not, perhaps you might be useful as an "unskilled" laborer (e.g., digging ditches) or as an assistant in their rental department. You may have difficulty as most of the companies like this are unionized (IATSE), so without being a member yourself, they may not be able to let you work with them.

In the meantime, hone your skills on student films or low-budget independent projects. In addition to building a resume and gaining experience, you'll be meeting Producers and Directors along the way who may bring you along with them as their own careers flourish...or not. You just never know.

WHAT AM I GETTING MYSELF INTO?
So who actually calls and hires me?

As an SFX Coordinator, you will most likely be called for work directly by Producers, Directors, and Unit Production Managers. If you're getting the call in the first place, the chances are that somebody already is familiar with your work, so you won't have to "sell" yourself. Instead, they'll be more interested to know your approach in achieving the specific effects the script calls for and what they will cost. There may be ten different ways to do a specific effect, ranging from the ridiculously simple to the most elaborate RUBE GOLDBERGIAN mechanism ever conceived. If you demonstrate that you can safely get from point A to point B in fewer moves with less money than someone else, then you'll probably get the job.

Okay, I got the job. What now?

The first step is to read the script and do a breakdown, looking for any and all instances where Special Effects may come into play. Some are more obvious than others. Some effects may not be written specifically at all but are implied by the location or situation. As previously mentioned, a bathtub scene will likely be shot on a set where everything needs to be built as if it were in an actual home. This means that after Set Dressing has put in the exterior fixtures as chosen by the Production Designer, Special Effects needs to obtain and build the plumbing to make it work. This includes all the pipes, the water, a heater for the water, and a drainage system to catch the water in case of overflow or spills.

And it isn't enough to budget for just one effect. You need to plan repeatability into the mechanism for additional takes. In addition, it is also helpful to offer alternatives to the Director when appropriate in case you can give an effect that extra bit of specialness. Making a tree branch fall onto a wire can be dramatic, but adding really cool blue sparks to the event adds to the overall sequence. You don't want to spend a lot of money on cool ideas if they haven't been approved, but having them in your back pocket to offer to the Director makes you that much valuable.

What will my life really be like?

5:30 A.M.—GET TO WORK

When you actually arrive on set depends greatly on exactly what you need to do that day. At minimum, you may have nothing planned, so you arrive at crew call and wait around for someone to ask you to do something...and they will. A simple day may require that you just turn the water on for the sinks in the kitchen set. If there is a bathtub scene, you turn on the water heater so the Actress can be comfortable. If there is a big explosion on the schedule, you and the rest of the Special Effects crew will arrive hours earlier than everyone else to set the charges.

12:00 P.M.—REHEARSAL

Again, a lot depends on the kind of special effect or stunt that will take place, but in general, if there is a very large effect, the company will work to film all of the action that just precedes the stunt and/or effect throughout the morning.

The First AD will call for a safety meeting. All crew members stop what they are doing and listen for the few minutes it takes. The purpose is to inform the cast and crew of every detail of the upcoming effect and/or stunt so that there are no assumptions made by anyone. One misjudged move or one person being in the wrong place at the wrong time can result in serious consequences.

The Director will run a rehearsal in conjunction with the Special Effects Coordinator so that everyone knows what is about to take place. If there are explosives of any kind on the set, the Coordinator will physically point out each and every one of them to the cast and crew. He will explain how big the effect will be, how loud it will likely be, and how far away to stand to avoid any danger. The Prop Department will wander the set handing out earplugs to anyone who wishes to use them. If there are any questions or concerns regarding safety before, during, or after the effect, this is the time to address them so that everyone will operate with the same information.

12:10 P.M.—CAMERA SETUP

Once the parameters of the effect are established, the Director, DP, and SFX Coordinator work together to find camera positions that are appropriate and safe. Some cameras may have to be unmanned due to safety concerns. The SFX Coordinator is required to know what will happen and how to protect those who will be in close proximity. The First AD is the primary safety officer on set, but she will be relying on the SFX Coordinator for the best information with which to work.

12:45 P.M.—ROLL CAMERA

At this point, your job may be as simple as handing a "gag" you've built to an Actor. Otherwise, your job boils down to executing your carefully planned special effect, be it flipping the switch on a fan, having the water running, or activating the electronic match for detonation. You've tested and retested the effect so many times that there should be absolutely no concerns for the result or for safety.

12:50 P.M.—CUT, LET'S GO AGAIN

As you are considering the various ways to accomplish an effect, you generally want to plan repeatability into it with a relatively quick "reset" time. Be prepared for at least three takes if possible. For instance, if a Stuntman is crashing through a window, you should have one pane in place before shooting ever begins that morning plus an additional two standing by in case the Director wishes to go again.

1:00 P.M.—LUNCH

If an effect takes a long time to reset, you'll be asked to forgo your lunch break so that the rest of the company won't have to wait for you to reset after their lunch is over. It's less expensive to work your department during that hour than for the rest of the crew to stand around waiting.

2:00 P.M.—BACK TO WORK

You're really on standby most of the day unless you have a specific effect to accomplish. Typically you are either working as fast as you can or you are waiting. You might have had three weeks of prep before or during production for just one second of film time. Then it's over, and you start in on the next challenge.

9:00 P.M.—WRAP

With any luck, they haven't saved the biggest effect of the day for last. Not that you mind; it's just that once the effect is over, you may have a lot to clean up, which will delay the time you have at home. Take everything you've been using on set to the truck and put it away. You should consult the PRELIM and prep whatever you can for the next day's effects.

WHAT I REALLY WANT TO DO IS MOVE UP!

What for? You've got a great job. As a tinkerer, things couldn't be better. But if the appeal of working on a movie set begins to fade, you could pursue life in the private sector as an inventor with some of the gadgets you've concocted over the years.

Whatever you decide, it is likely that your drive to create new things and solve problems won't go away, so you'll be able to apply that same attitude to whatever it is you wish to achieve.

Part IX

SETS

What I Really Want To Do Is...

Location Manage

Greens

Paint

Dress Sets

Chapter 36

What I Really Want to Do Is Location Manage!

WHAT THE HECK IS A LOCATION MANAGER?

There are actually two aspects of "locations": scouting and managing. The Location Scout helps the production find and secure locations suitable for filming. The Location Manager works on set as the liaison between the production and anyone in the public who is affected. Often, the two jobs are done by just one person.

That, and what else?

The job doesn't just involve finding pretty sites and hanging around the set. The Location Manager is responsible for finding locations that serve the Director's creative needs and the production's logistical requirements. A beautiful mountaintop villa may seem perfect, but if getting a crew of one hundred plus the necessary equipment up there is too costly and inefficient, the place might as well not exist. You don't make decisions, but it helps to have a creative eye as you interpret a Director's requests. It's also beneficial to have some level of technical experience as you attempt to anticipate the practical requirements of production.

They didn't tell me about this job in film school. How much can I make?

There are approximately three hundred to four hundred people working in Locations, but only a small fraction are employed consistently in feature films, episodic television, and the commercial realm. On average, expect to earn between $9,000 and $15,000 a month, again, depending on your level of experience and the kinds of projects you work on.

WHAT DO I REALLY NEED TO KNOW?

Once a location is chosen by the production, the crew can't just show up to start filming. First they need permission. Whether the location is on public property or private, typically a filming permit has to be granted by the city that the property is in. First, the Location Manager has to get the okay from the property owner (homeowner, small business owner, or corporation). After that, the proper paperwork must be filled out and delivered to the appropriate city office within the specified amount of time.

So, the Location Manager first has to have the people skills and confidence to approach complete strangers and explain exactly who she is and what she'd like to do with the location. She must also have the experience to understand the needs of a film production so that all of the necessary permissions, paperwork, and fees are paid in time. And, of course, she has to know the ins and outs of city bureaucracy, what paperwork exists, and any limitations, such as vehicle restrictions and time constraints, that may be imposed for each requested location.

WHAT DO I REALLY NEED TO HAVE?
It sounds like I'm just talking to people. What could I possibly need?

For starters, a portable laptop computer with Internet access can help you research new locations and the city government offices that hold jurisdiction over them. Once you find a location, you'll have to take numerous photographs for the Director to evaluate. You'll want to have a quality digital camera, a tripod, and enough hard drive space to store the thousands of photos you'll amass over your career. And because sunlight is an important consideration for the filmmakers, have a compass so that you are able to note the time and direction from which each photo was taken. You should be able to charge about $50 a day for the kit rental.

A great deal of your work happens over the phone. Production may provide you with a cell phone, but it can be just as easy to use your own and write it off as a business expense at the end of the year.

And have a reliable car. You'll be doing a lot of driving around.

WHERE DO I REALLY NEED TO GO?
I just want to work.

When a project gets started, one of the very first people hired is the Location Scout/Manager. Ideally, over time, you'll have worked enough to gain name recognition among Producers, production companies, and UPMs, resulting in their calling you no matter where you are. Los Angeles is still the major center of most filming in the United States, so, with respect to building strong relationships, living there will give you the largest volume and variety of opportunities.

You can also get your start by working with local film commissions. As Los Angeles-based projects head out to shoot on distant locations, they'll sometimes get in contact with those who know the area best and use them as their Location Scout and Managers.

So how do I get work?

Some of your job is finding appropriate locations, but finding one is just the first step. Knowing how to get it is vital, but no school can teach you how to accomplish that. Most, if not all, Location Scouts and Managers began as someone else's assistant. With a mentor, you'll learn the best and most efficient ways to find locations, what paperwork to fill out, how to fill it out, where to send it, how much money locations should cost, and how to deal with the varied personalities you'll have to interact with both in the business and out.

You best avenue to finding a mentor is simply asking those who are already in the business if they know any Location Managers who need an assistant. See Appendix A for union and guild details and contact information.

WHAT AM I GETTING MYSELF INTO?
So who actually calls and hires me?

When your phone rings, it will probably be a Producer or UPM with whom you've worked before. If you have a relationship with a state film commission, you may also get referrals through that office.

Okay, I got the job. What now?

Your work begins long before most of the other crew is even aware that there is a project in preproduction. You may even be put onboard before a Director is hired. Some scripts are "location dependent," meaning that the action depends greatly on having just the right location. If an adequate location can't be found, the whole project may be cancelled.

The Location Scout/Manager will be one of the first people to get a copy of the shooting script. You'll typically sit down with the Producer and/or Director and go over each and every page as you discuss the types of locations that would be ideal. You need to listen not only to the basic requests (e.g., "we need a school") but also understand the overall mood or theme that the story demands (e.g., "we need a creepy school.")

For budgetary concerns, it is also helpful if you can find locations that are geographically close to one another. You might find the perfect house for Scene 41 on the coast of Maine and the perfect office building for Scene 121 in

Utah, but unless those locations are so unique that there is no option but to shoot in both places, that choice will be deemed impractical. Ultimately the Director and Producer make the actual decisions. However, by searching for locations that are reasonably close to each other, you can help everyone keep the company moves to a minimum.

After you get the script, you'll start looking for locations that seem to fit the descriptions. When you're just beginning your career, you can use a Location Service to help. Especially in large cities like Los Angeles where a lot of filming takes place, home owners and businesses will be on file with companies in much the same way that casting agencies represent Actors. You'll be sent a list of properties to choose from.

After the Director comes onboard, you'll be able to narrow your search down as the creative decisions become more specific. At this point, you will head out and actually go visit the best candidates. Take pictures of every angle and make note of the time you take them and the direction you are facing.

Show these photos to the Director. If he chooses one that you've found through a Location Service, you'll call the Service and they'll be the liaison between the homeowner and you. If the Director chooses a location that you've found on your own, it will be up to you to handle all of the paperwork, permits, and payments with the owner and the city government.

Once you have permission, you have to obtain a permit if the city requires it. If you are shooting in a relatively small city or town, it probably isn't a big deal to find the local government office and take care of the paperwork yourself within a short amount of time. However, on a large project with multiple locations and a Director who likes to change his mind, it can be helpful, if not necessary, to hire a Permit Service to do that work for you. Similar to a Location Service, you tell the Permit Service exactly what you want to do, where you want to do it, and when.

If the Director doesn't like any of the choices from the Location Service or your own files, you head out for a "cold scout." All the means is that you drive around until you find a new location that isn't on anyone's list. When you knock on someone's door, you'll politely tell them who you are, that you're working on a movie, and you'd like to know if they'd be interested in having some of the filming take place at their home or business. You'll get one of three responses. The person will say, "Sure, why not" and let you in. Or he might say "No thank you, I'm not interested." Or he'll say, "No, I hate you film people" then slam the door in your face.

Aside from having the experience with movie production and the skill to navigate the permitting process, it is vitally important that you have the right attitude and temperament before choosing Locations as a career. You may be shooting on a residential street and another homeowner may bolt out angry that you've parked a giant forty-foot trailer in front of her house. You've got the permit that allows the truck to be there, but that person comes out mad as hell that you're "ruining" her life that day. If you are a confrontational person, your first instinct may be to yell back until that person goes away. But that shouldn't be the way you handle problems. It is important for you to remain as calm and reasonable as possible. You're there representing the production company that hired you, and you always want to present yourself in the most professional manner possible.

So now they can come in to shoot?

Not yet. You're typically called in weeks or months ahead of everyone else who will be making the movie. All of that scouting and permitting work is happening as the script is being rewritten, the cast is being chosen, and other department heads are being hired. Ideally, a few weeks before the start of principal photography, there will be a tech scout for all who need to familiarize themselves with the locations. As the liaison between the filmmakers and the property owners, you must discern where Transportation wants to park the trucks, where the generator has to go, where the DP wants to put cameras, lights and condors, and what the Art Director plans to do with the location. It's your responsibility to be aware of anything that the production plans to bring to and do with the location.

As you gain experience, you'll be able to anticipate some of these needs/ requests when you first scout locations, but changes could happen at any time. You may be securing a permit for a part of a location, but if the Gaffer tells you at the tech scout that he needs to place lights in the building next door that you haven't even asked permission for yet, you've suddenly got more work to do.

This kind of scouting and permitting may continue throughout the course of production as the Writer revises the script and new ideas pop up. You may have secured a location only to have the owner pull out suddenly for any number of reasons. With that, you go back to your list and look for something else as quickly as possible.

As you nail down locations, you'll provide the Production Department with maps that they will later copy and attach to the daily call sheets for the cast and crew to follow. You'll also hire a Security company to provide personnel to guard the locations, BASE CAMP, and crew parking at each location. And if the location requires it, you'll hire a specific person who goes to set to spread protective layout board on the floors.

What will my life really be like?

5:30 A.M.—GET TO WORK

The crew call is at 7:00 A.M., so the Caterer will pull her truck in at 6:00 A.M. That means you need to be near location by 5:30 A.M. to hang directional signs to guide everyone in toward crew parking and base camp. Finish that in time so you can guide Transportation and the Caterer in to the designated parking spots.

Your Security Guards need to be placed and the layout board has to be put down before any crew or equipment is pushed on set.

7:00 A.M.—GETTING TO SET

Your work is more or less complete by the time the crew shows up to work. Step back, but stick close in case anyone has a problem or question.

7:05 A.M.—REHEARSAL

It doesn't hurt to watch the rehearsal just to know what will happen in general. You've been the person that the homeowner or business has been dealing with, so if there is a concern, they'll come to you, and it helps to know what production has in mind before you answer anything.

7:15 A.M.—CAMERA SETUP

Again, stick close by. As equipment is brought in and set up, different departments may have unanticipated questions or needs that they'll come to you about. For instance, the Art Department or Grips may need to pull a door off its hinges to get something through. It's up to you to know whether the property owner would allow that. Transportation may want to pull an extra truck in that wasn't discussed previously. They need to know if the city permit covers it.

You're in communication with anyone on set who has a question, but you'll have most of your contact with the First AD. He'll likely be the one coming to you with questions or concerns throughout the day.

7:45 A.M.—ROLL CAMERA

This is when it usually happens. Everything is set up, the Actors step into place, and the film starts to roll. Then you hear it: A lawnmower in the neighborhood starts up. The Sound Mixer says that the audio is unusable with that racket going on and filming stops. It's up to you to head over to the source of the problem and ask very nicely if it would be possible to stop for another twenty minutes or so. Sometimes the person will say, "Yes, no problem" and other times you might have to offer a little money for the trouble. Sometimes the person won't care at all what you and a hundred of your friends are doing down the block, and he'll keep on making noise. Unless someone becomes a nuisance for the sole purpose of disrupting the production, there isn't a lot you can do beyond asking very nicely for him to stop for a while.

1:00 P.M.—LUNCH

Go to lunch with everyone else. You may want to sit to talk with the property owner in a setting that lets her feel like she's a part of the production just as much as everyone else.

2:00 P.M.—BACK TO WORK

If everything seems to be going well and you have other work to do, let the First AD know that you'll be off the set for a while. Keep your cell phone close in case something does come up and you have to get back in a hurry.

9:00 P.M.—WRAP

You're the first in and the last out. As everyone else is wrapping their equipment and the trucks are pulling away, go through the property just to make sure that all the garbage is picked up and things have been put back where they belong.

Before you ever arrived at a location, all the paperwork and payments have been taken care of, so you should be able to walk away at the end of the night without anything else to do. Sometimes though, there is damage that you didn't see or items that weren't put back correctly, in which case the property owner will likely call you about it. Let the Production Department know and they'll contact the appropriate department to take care of the problem.

WHAT I REALLY WANT TO DO IS MOVE UP!

There is no natural progression from Locations to anything else on set. Because of your work in close proximity with so many other departments, you'll get to learn a lot about what they do from start to finish. Moving over to another department would mean starting over, but you are in the position to meet the people who can help you get right to work. It also isn't out of the question to move up to becoming a Producer for the same reasons. As one of the first people hired, you are getting a real-world education on what it takes to actually get a movie made logistically and politically. You can have a happy and successful career in Locations, but if you want a change, you're in the perfect place to make the leap.

Chapter 37

What I Really Want to Do Is Greens!

WHAT THE HECK IS A GREENSMAN?

The Greensman is the person on set specifically in charge of vegetation, real or artificial, who helps to dress the set in conjunction with the rest of the Art Department.

That, and what else?

Your primary job is to help decorate the set with vegetation, but you also help to create a safe work environment. Your most obvious work will happen on a soundstage in which an artificial outdoor environment has been created, such as a backyard or even something as elaborate as a jungle. Your work extends on location as well when the natural environment needs to be enhanced with more or less vegetation than what is in place when you first arrive.

I must be making pretty good "green" then, huh?

Depending on the needs of the schedule, you may or may not be working every day on the film. Expect to earn roughly $1,500 a week when you are there.

WHAT DO I REALLY NEED TO KNOW?

A lot of your job is just manual labor, moving plants from one place to another on stage. But you also are in charge of maintaining the vegetation and keeping it looking good. A movie may shoot for several weeks, so the plants under your care must maintain the proper continuity throughout a long schedule.

The best way to learn how to do your job correctly is to study horticulture and botany at the high school or university level. Learn everything you can about all different types of plants as well as landscaping and design. Something as seemingly simple as a backyard lawn isn't quite as easy when you're creating it on a dark soundstage on top of a plywood floor. Knowing how to keep all kinds of plants thriving out of their natural environment is key to your job on set.

WHAT DO I REALLY NEED TO HAVE?
Where do the plants come from? Do I bring them?

All the plants that are used are rented from specific companies in Los Angeles. All you need to bring along are any tools that you would use to maintain plant life. You should have pruners, loppers, handsaws, shovels, pliers, as well as a broom, hammer, a staple gun, wire, and rope. Expect to spend around $300 or so for the basics.

Larger jobs, like building a jungle on an interior stage, may require three or more Greensmen to be on set, so you should have additional tools for everyone to use.

What should I wear?

Expect to get very dirty, as you would if you were working in a garden or forest all day long. Steel-toed boots, quality work gloves, and even safety glasses are a good idea.

WHERE DO I REALLY NEED TO GO?
I just want to work.

Some Greensmen start out as Set Decorators and then specialize after that. Others begin by working at IATSE signatory greens supply companies in Los Angeles. These companies not only supply all types of plant life, but they also have crew who deliver the rental items to sets and can help put them in place. Starting at a company like that can give you fairly steady work as you build your own contact list in case you choose to work on your own as a freelancer later on.

If you're not in Local 44 and you want to be, contact the office and ask them to put your name down on the "permit list." What happens is that on occasion, if everyone in Local 44 is working and a production needs someone that day, the union will allow a new person to go in. You are known as a "permit" at that point. Once you've worked for thirty days within that year as a permit, you can pay the initiation fee and officially join Local 44.

So how do I get work?

Smaller budget productions typically won't hire a separate person to handle just the "greens." Your first work may very well be as the Set Decorator, who takes care of all aspects of set design, including the necessary vegetation.

After you join IATSE Local 44, you'll specifically only be responsible for vegetation while you work alongside other similar departments that handle the things seen on set, like the Set Decorator, Property, Drapers, Upholsterers, and Special Effects. Contacts you make in any of those related specialties may be able to recommend you for future work.

WHAT AM I GETTING MYSELF INTO?
So who actually calls and hires me?

The Production Designer or Art Director will call Greens Coordinators they've worked with before. If additional help is needed, the Greens Coordinator will call Greensmen whose work he respects, or he will call the Local if all of his regular guys are busy.

Or the Unit Production Manager may decide to hire one of the IATSE signatory rental companies to dress the set, in which case one of the union crew members from that rental house may stay on to be the on-set Greensman for the length of the show.

Okay, I got the job. What now?

The Production Designer will have created blueprints or sketches of the set that you have to bring to life. Sometimes the set will be totally fabricated from someone's imagination. Other times, you will be asked to replicate onstage a previously filmed exterior location.

Using the blueprints or reference photos, you'll order the required plants from one of the rental houses. When the set is ready to be dressed with your greens, the Transportation Department for the film will go to the rental house, where their workers will load the trucks. When Transpo returns to set, you and a small crew of Laborers or other Greensmen will dress the set according to the instructions provided by the Production Designer.

What will my life really be like?

6:42 A.M.—GET TO WORK

The Director will want to run a rehearsal on the set at 7:00 A.M., and once production begins for the day, you won't have easy access to take care of your plants. It's best for you to arrive a few minutes early in case you have anything to move, trim, exchange, or water.

If you are on an exterior location, such as a remote forest or hillside, it is your job to comb the landscape for hazards, such as poison oak, hidden rocks, or sharp sticks. Remove any potentially dangerous objects that could hurt the cast or crew.

Your primary responsibility lies with "exterior" plants, such as trees, shrubs, or grass. The On-Set Dresser takes care of smaller items like potted houseplants. Props or Wardrobe might ask you to find flowers for a clothing accessory, like a corsage, but they take responsibility for it after you've obtained it for them.

7:05 A.M.—REHEARSAL

Watch the rehearsal and keep an eye on where the DP wants to place his cameras. You may have to move some plants to make room for his equipment, or you may have to dress a part of the set that will be seen.

7:15 A.M.—CAMERA SETUP

Rehearsal is finished, so everyone goes into action. If you are on a small simple set, you'll be alone to do the work. If there are any large trees to move, you can borrow and use a palette jack from the Construction Department or call Transportation and they will operate a forklift for you. Work with the Camera Operators and other crew as they move their equipment into place and line up the shots.

7:45 A.M.—ROLL CAMERA

Stick close to the set, at least for the first take, to make sure there aren't going to be any major changes needed.

7:48 A.M.—CUT, LET'S GO AGAIN

Sometimes problems aren't evident until cameras have rolled and the Actors have done their thing. If any of your work needs to be adjusted, move in quickly and make the necessary changes as efficiently as possible.

8:10 A.M.—CUT, MOVIN' ON

The Director will generally shoot as much in one direction as possible, so you won't have much to do for a while. Once they decide to turn around though, you could have quite a bit of work as you'll have to dress the opposite side of the set. Interior forests or jungle sets usually require that you "shake up" the set dressing frequently so that the action doesn't appear to be happening in the same place all the time.

1:00 P.M.—LUNCH

Technically, you're broken for lunch with everyone else, but just like the morning, it is sometimes easier to do your work, like watering plants, when no one else is around.

2:00 P.M.—BACK TO WORK

Once the set is dressed in the morning, you typically won't have a lot more major work to do beyond some simple moving and maintenance throughout the day.

Every plant on the set is typically a rental, and the production is financially responsible for them just as they are responsible for any other piece of equipment on set. With that in mind, you have to spend a considerable amount of time taking care of every plant that arrives for as long as it is on your project. If a plant dies, the production will be charged for it and the Producer won't be too happy with you. A plant that costs $100 will cost the production $150 to replace due to vendor fees and insurance charges.

One of the hardest things you'll have to do is dressing exterior location sets. Digging holes and planting trees can be backbreaking work. Be prepared to work hard and get dirty no matter where the set is.

9:00 P.M.—WRAP

At the end of any production day, take a walk around the set again as everyone else is packing up to leave. Make sure that no trees are in danger of falling over and that all the tools are cleaned and put away properly.

The end-of-the-show wrap may take a few days, depending on the size of the set. Transportation will come back in with their trucks while you and a few dayplayers load every plant for return to the rental house.

WHAT I REALLY WANT TO DO IS MOVE UP!

Working in Greens is a rewarding job in and of itself for those who truly enjoy gardening and other aspects of horticulture. But Greens is just one part of the overall production design for a film project. If you feel as if you have what it takes to art direct or design other aspects of the set, take any opportunities to move through the various departments covered by Local 44 and prove yourself capable to Production Designers who enjoy working with you. And there's nothing to say that you couldn't be the Production Designer of an entire film on your own some day.

Chapter 38

What I Really Want to Do Is Paint!

WHAT THE HECK IS A STANDBY PAINTER?

The job title pretty much says it all. You are on set standing by in case something needs to be painted. Movie sets are like construction sites with WILD WALLS and heavy equipment moving around all the time. It is very easy for sets to be damaged during setup, so it is important to have people standing by to fix imperfections before they are committed to film.

That, and what else?

Standing by to do touchups is pretty much the extent of your work during a production day on set. However, many painters are also qualified Sign Writers and Scenic Artists.

The Sign Writer specializes in painting signs. It might sound a little simplistic, but the ability to create or recreate accurate quality signage using paint is an art of its own and not everyone can do it well. The Sign Writer has to know how to paint, and properly age if necessary, lettering and graphics on all kinds of surfaces in all sizes, anything from the large advertising on old barns and brick buildings to lettering on a glass door. Computers do some of this work, but the ability to work quickly by hand "the old-fashioned way" is a valuable and sought-after skill.

The Scenic Artist specializes in creating large backdrops that emulate exteriors. These are used on a soundstage so that it appears as if the constructed set is in a real environment. The Scenic Artist is also qualified and skilled at "artistic" painting, such as portraits and reproductions.

These two specialties go beyond the seemingly simpler tasks of being a Set Painter during construction or a Standby Painter on set, although these jobs aren't just about rolling paint onto a wall either. Knowing how to create different effects, such as aging and color matching, can take years to learn.

I must be making really good money then, right?

If you are a Set or Standby Painter, expect to earn roughly $35,000 for a twelve-week project. As a specialty Sign Writer or Scenic Artist, expect to make just a little more than that.

WHAT DO I REALLY NEED TO KNOW?

The basics of set painting are sanding, cutting, spackling, hanging wallpaper, and of course, painting. Many learn those skills in the real world first by working in commercial house painting.

Transferring these skills to a movie set will require some adjustment. First, if you're working during production as the Standby Painter, knowing proper set protocol (how a movie set works) is vitally important. You'll get a sense of that by reading through this book, but spending some time on an actual set will be most helpful.

The Set Decorator will tell you how something is to be painted and finished, but if you develop that sense of design and style on your own, you'll be more valuable to a production and more likely you'll find work. Learning skills like wood graining, roller coating, creating "cracked" walls and marbling, faux finishes, and knowing how to mix paint well will move you up the ladder quicker.

Scenic Artists need a solid background and a higher education in classical art. Schooling will teach you advanced drawing and painting skills in conjunction with form and layout design. Sign Writers benefit from a traditional apprenticeship from a commercial sign shop. It is also helpful to have an architectural degree. In both cases, when you start working in the film industry, you'll pick up a few trade secrets and shortcuts that will make your job go faster and a bit easier, but acquiring the fundamentals is always the best place to start.

WHAT DO I REALLY NEED TO HAVE?
Do I bring my own paint?

The production will give you a budget for supplies, like paint and crack fillers. You'll have your own kit to take from show to show. It will include a large selection of paintbrushes and rollers that you will use for basics, like painting walls, and more elaborate sign and scenic painting.

Sometimes the situation allows for the use of a projector to help paint layouts (specific patterns or logos) on walls. That "cheat" can speed up an otherwise difficult and time-consuming process. However, if you have to do a large painting on the ground, a projector isn't practical, which is why the skill of doing layout by hand is so important.

Wear clothes that you won't care too much about. You want to look as professional as possible, so avoid filthy pants and T-shirts, but know that whatever you have on will eventually be covered in paint and anything else you might wipe on yourself. Secondhand clothing stores are a great place to find items that look good but are inexpensive.

WHERE DO I REALLY NEED TO GO?
I just want to work.

As you work your way through the business, get to know as many people in the Art Department as possible. Production Designers will want to know that you are qualified and skilled at turning their concepts into reality within time and budget. Have a résumé of all your prior education and work experience as well as a portfolio illustrating any specialty skills you have to offer.

To work the bigger shows, you'll have to be a member of the Art Directors Guild & Scenic, Title and Graphic Artists, otherwise known as IATSE Local 800. However, Motion Picture Set Painters & Sign Writers are represented by IATSE Local 729. Ideally, you'll have the skills and connections to join both unions, giving you more opportunities for work.

To qualify for membership in Local 729, you will have to work thirty days on union shows over the course of one year. To get on those union shows, the department head or Lead Painter has to be authorized by the Union Local leadership, so it may take some patience on your part as you enter the process.

For Local 800 membership, you must first get employment on an IATSE show and then apply to the local within thirty days of that employment.

So how do I get work?

The first step is to develop the skills it takes to be a highly qualified Painter, Scenic Artist, and/or Sign Writer. Don't expect to show up on a professional set to learn the basics.

Every film or television production is in need of a Painter of one kind or another. On lower-budget nonunion shows, those duties will usually fall into the lap of the Production Designer, the Set Decorator, or someone in Construction. You may have to do those jobs at that lower level for a while until you find larger productions that can afford to hire a specialty Painter. If the production is sufficiently large enough, you could also find an opportunity to work under the Key Set Painter, but at that point you'll most likely have to be a member of one of the IATSE Locals (729 or 850).

WHAT AM I GETTING MYSELF INTO?
So who actually calls and hires me?

You'll receive a call from the Lead Set Painter, Production Designer, Art Director, Construction Coordinator, or Unit Production Manager. This person will contact you because you've worked with him directly before and he liked you, or because you were recommended by someone else who liked you.

Okay, I got the job. What now?

You'll meet with the Production Designer, Art Director, or Lead Painter and review the sets that are being built or the locations that will be used. Someone above you will tell you what each set should look like, usually with conceptual artwork and color swatches. From there, you'll submit a list of supplies you'll need to the production office and let them know when you need it all.

You typically won't have too much to carry around. You'll have your basic painting kit of brushes and generic supplies as well as a rack of tints, a bucket of white, bucket of black, cans of STREAKS AND TIPS, and any specialty tools you own for signs and scenics.

What will my life really be like?

7:00 A.M.—GET TO WORK

You'll usually arrive at the general crew call just prior to rehearsal. If your supplies are still on the Art Department truck, move everything to set and stand by to see if there is anything you'll have to do.

7:05 A.M.—REHEARSAL

While you're waiting, take another look at the set that is being shot on and set up the basic palette of colors that you'll need. Using something as simple as a large plastic bucket lid, lay out your colors so that all you have to do is add tints to adjust the values and hues to match any of the walls that are on set.

7:15 A.M.—CAMERA SETUP

Often, wild walls will be pulled or replaced. You'll have to jump in to do touchups so that it looks as if nothing had ever moved. You may need to use crack filler like Plastylene before you are able to apply any paint.

You might also be asked to "age" set dressing items, like lamps or furniture, using removable paint or Streaks and Tips. On occasion, you might also be called to work with Greens in case foliage is dying or isn't quite the right color. Real grass often gets painted green to simulate a lush lawn. You'll be applying paint to things they'll never think of in art school.

Once all the obvious touchups have been done, ask the Camera Operators to look through the lens in case they see anything that stands out. They may spot a problem before you do and will call you over to take a look. So don't disappear off set just because you think you've fixed everything. Stick close and pay attention to what everyone else is doing too in case you missed anything or new damage is created during the setup.

7:45 A.M.—ROLL CAMERA

Once camera rolls, your work is done until the next setup threatens to scar some of your work. You can move out of everyone else's way at that point, but keep an ear out in case something unexpected comes up as they are filming.

8:10 A.M.—CUT, MOVIN' ON

Head back to set and stand by. You most likely won't be needed again until the TURNAROUND or until they move to a new set. Stay close though, because as camera angles change, new parts of the set will be seen that may need some TLC.

1:00 P.M.—LUNCH

Cover your paints to keep them moist and clean up your brushes before heading off to lunch with everyone else.

2:00 P.M.—BACK TO WORK

Stay on top of things on set. As the day wears on, the crew gets tired and someone may inadvertently scrape or take a chunk from one of your walls. Jump in to do your work and get back out again as quickly as possible.

In the event that you are also hired to do some scenic art, use your time to work on wall hangings, reproductions, signs, or anything else that will be needed in the coming days, if those items haven't been finished in preproduction. The Art Director will keep in touch with you regarding any changes that might come up.

9:00 P.M.—WRAP

Generally, once the last setup is ready to be shot, you're probably done for the day. But you'll stay until the final shot is finished and the First AD calls "Wrap!" Cover your paint so that it stays wet for the next day, clean your brushes, keep your work area organized, and then go home.

WHAT I REALLY WANT TO DO IS MOVE UP!

As mentioned earlier, if you begin as a Set Painter, you can expand your skill and marketability greatly by becoming a Scenic Artist and/or a Sign Writer. You can gain mastery over the basics of paint on your own, but to learn the fundamentals of creating real art, you need to consider continuing your education in a fine arts program on the university level.

It's also possible to move up through the Art Department to become an Art Director or even the Production Designer, who is supervising and guiding the Set Decorators, Set Designers, Model Makers, Illustrators, Prop Master, Construction, Painters, Graphic Designers, and Matte Painters (in Visual Effects). A lot more than paint goes into creating a believable set, and you can head in any direction that your desire and enthusiasm take you.

Chapter 39

What I Really Want to Do Is Dress Sets!

WHAT THE HECK IS AN ON-SET DRESSER?

After the Production Designer has drawn up the plans, Construction has built the sets, the Painters have painted, the Art Director has chosen the items for the set, and the Leadman (see sidebar, page 291) has dressed the set with those items, the On-Set Dresser arrives on day one of principal photography to be in charge of all set items that are not props. In other words, a bunch of other people get the set ready and the On-Set Dresser takes over and works with the film crew when things like furniture or hanging pictures need to be moved and/ or changed during actual production.

That, and what else?

In a perfect world, the set would be built and dressed and nothing would have to be moved or changed as the Actors perform in front of the cameras. However, because film equipment takes up a lot of space and scenes are filmed in multiple takes from different angles, all the hard work from the Set Decorator and the Leadman has to be "undone" and then "redone" constantly. Your job is to keep careful track of where everything is supposed to be and make sure that it gets back where it belongs so that continuity is consistent from take to take.

You have to watch absolutely everything on set, from table lamps to bookcases, dinner dishes to curtains. If paint is damaged on a wall, you'll call the Standby Painter to come in and fix it. If shrubs or trees need to be moved or trimmed, you'll call the Greensman. If the dining room table or anything else that is heavy needs to be moved, you'll ask a Grip or PA to help you. You're watching to make sure that everything that creates a set for the camera is where it is supposed to be at the time it is needed. Having the finest eye for detail prevents the smallest of errors from ever being filmed.

In addition, you'll also be working a bit with the Actors. After all, they are playing characters and you are helping to create the environments in which those characters are supposed to be living. In a sense, you need to understand the characters just as much as the Actors do. If the character is messy, the room you are dressing has to reflect that. If the character is meticulous, then you have to dress the set accordingly. Whatever you can do to anticipate the requests of the Director and Actors as well as the requirements of the story will go a long way toward making everyone happy.

Sounds like I'm really busy all day. How much money can I make doing this?

Unless there is a major reset to finish either before call or after wrap for the next day, you'll usually arrive on set at crew call and be heading home fairly soon after wrap. Expect to work about fourteen hours a day for the length of the project. A typical twelve-week feature will earn you about $30,000.

WHAT DO I REALLY NEED TO KNOW?

Ideally, the set is decorated and the look approved before any film rolls through the camera. But sometimes last-minute changes are asked for, and it is up to you to fix them. Because of that, you need a wide range of skills from basic construction to minor electrical wiring. The only thing you aren't allowed to do by yourself (on an IATSE union set) is paint.

WHAT DO I REALLY NEED TO HAVE?
I'm moving furniture around. What could I possibly need?

You'll need a modest amount of hand tools and other small items. A battery-powered screw gun, saw, hammer, nails, screws, different kinds of adhesive tapes and glues, pushpins, and rubber bands will be a part of your kit. It's also a good idea to wear a tool belt equipped with pliers, a knife, a Leatherman tool, small gauge wire, wire cutters, a small level (for hanging pictures), a tape measure, and quality work gloves. You should receive somewhere between $10 and $50 a day for the kit rental, depending on what you have and the size of the production.

WHERE DO I REALLY NEED TO GO?
I just want to work.

Wherever there is a movie, TV, or music video being shot, somebody is there dressing the set. When you want to work on larger productions, you'll want to join IATSE Local 44. Production happens anywhere in the world, but for sheer volume and variety in the United States, Los Angeles is still the city to live in. See Appendix A and contact the Local 44 office for more information.

So how do I get work?

Find the nearest low-budget project and look for the head of the Art Department. You may have to start as a Production Assistant, moving heavy furniture around and performing other so-called menial duties. Work as closely as possible with anyone in the department, including Property, the Painter, the Decorators, and the Production Designer. Smaller productions may not have enough money to staff the department fully, so you may get the opportunity to learn everything.

WHAT AM I GETTING MYSELF INTO?
So who actually calls and hires me?

The On-Set Dresser is continuing the work of the Leadman, Set Decorator, the Art Director, and ultimately the Production Designer. For that reason, any or all of them will be interested in hiring someone they can trust. Expect a call or recommendation to come from any of them.

Okay, I got the job. What now?

You might get one or two prep days, but mostly you're being hired to take charge of the set from the Set Decorator and Leadman once the shooting crew arrives. When you get to set, everything should already be in place, and it's your job to know where everything is supposed to be. Everything from floor to ceiling is now your responsibility.

Art Department — Off Set

Production Designer
Before a movie can be shot, somebody has to figure out what everything will look like. Collaborating with the Director, the Production Designer envisions the overall look of a movie and shepherds that vision from conception to the filming process.

Art Director
It's the responsibility of the Art Director to assemble the set-decorating team (Illustrators, Set Decorators, Painters, Storyboard Artists, Leadman, On-Set Dresser) and guide the department toward turning the concepts into reality. The Art Director works closely with the Construction Department, which actually builds the sets, as well as the Property Department as they find and/ or manufacture necessary props.

Set Decorator
The Set Decorator does the research as to what furnishings and other decorations a set will need per the request of the Production Designer and Art Director. She will go to a prop rental house or find an item and then ask for it to be acquired or reproduced by the Property Department or the Art Department. Once the items are brought to set, she decorates the set according to the instructions of the Production Designer and Art Director.

Leadman

The Leadman is the person who handles the logistics dictated by the requests from the Set Decorator. With a team of laborers and assistants, the Leadman will do the actual physical work to acquire the items and put them on the set, coordinating manpower, schedules, and budgets. Essentially, it is the responsibility of the Leadman and the Set Decorator to get the set ready before handing it off to the On-Set Dresser when the filming unit arrives.

What will my life really be like?

7:00 A.M.—GET TO WORK

You won't have a lot of extra things to move to set, as the Set Decorator and Leadman have already done most of the heavy work. There may be some "spares," or extra pieces of set dressing, available, such as framed pictures or table lamps, just in case the Director asks for something to be added quickly at the last minute. Those things may be kept on stage somewhere close, in a garage on a practical set, or on the Prop truck if there is room.

Because everything is usually ready to go, you'll show up at crew call with other department heads and get ready for the first rehearsal.

7:05 A.M.—REHEARSAL

You need to watch the rehearsal very carefully. Remember, the set is put together at this point as if it were a real place, but very soon, a lot of camera and lighting equipment will be brought in to film Actors who will possibly be moving your stuff around. Make sure that you have reference pictures of everything on set so that if it has to be moved, you can put it back exactly where it belongs later in the day.

7:15 A.M.—CAMERA SETUP

Any number of things could happen that could affect you, or you may be required to do nothing at all. Each setup is different. At worst, WILD WALLS will be pulled by the Grips and you'll be asked to move all of the living room furniture to accommodate dolly track, lights, and all the people who will be working on the next setup.

Or, the next might only involve your paying close attention and snapping any reference photos you might need for later.

Either way, at this point, you'll work closely with the Camera Operators as they line up the shots and tweak the set so that it looks as good as possible. Other departments like Grip and Electric may also ask you to move items to make room for their own equipment.

When the Set Designer or Set Decorator creates a look, they ideally want it to stay that way. But the saying goes that camera is king. The set may appear amazing on its own, but oftentimes things have to be changed. The Director may review a shot and decide that he wants a different picture on the wall or doesn't like the color of a throw pillow on the sofa. Hopefully you've got enough extra stuff in your truck or on stage that you can come up with some options quickly.

Some changes are easy to handle while others may require the help of other departments, such as Greens, Paint, or Construction. Sometimes the changes asked for are so significant that you'll have to call the Set Decorator, who will help obtain whatever is needed.

For the most part, though, the set will remain pretty much as planned. You can help enhance a scene by understanding what is going to take place in the story. For instance, the cast and crew may walk into a kitchen set and block the action of two Actors talking with one another. Nothing odd about that, but should the kitchen be clean as if they were talking long after dinner or should it be a mess as if they were in the midst of still cooking? The script may not spell out that kind of detail, but it is your responsibility to read between the lines if possible. If you don't know, simply ask the Director how the environment should look.

While everyone else is finishing up their own work, you're the last person to touch everything on set before it ends up on film.

7:45 A.M.—ROLL CAMERA

Watch each take carefully, either at the monitor in VIDEO VILLAGE or on set itself. You need to know if anything on set changes or moves during the take, either intentionally or by accident.

7:48 A.M.—CUT, LET'S GO AGAIN

Especially if things have moved during the take, you should jump in and take some quick snapshots for continuity reference.

8:10 A.M.—CUT, MOVIN' ON

The Director is happy and you're on to the next shot, which is either a continuation of that scene or something new altogether. A single two-minute scene could be shot from ten different angles or more. Take as many reference photos as you think you'll need so that you can maintain continuity of the set throughout the day.

1:00 P.M.—LUNCH

Often, lunch is called but the work on a particular set hasn't been completed yet. It's in your interest to keep others off the set so that nothing is moved while everyone is away. Something as simple as stringing yellow "HOT SET" tape around the doorways to the set is usually enough to prevent unnecessary problems.

2:00 P.M.—BACK TO WORK

The day can get monotonous as you move from one setup to the next. Moving furniture and hanging pictures doesn't seem like a very exciting time, but it is vital that you remain mentally alert throughout the day.

Unless the job is sufficiently large enough to warrant additional help, you'll be on your own. That's not too big of a deal until you have a large couch to move. Typically, other members of the crew, like Grips or PAs, are willing to assist you when you need it most. Try to return the favor by helping with sandbags on occasion or other "small" duties. You don't want to go overboard, but the little things here and there can make a difference.

9:00 P.M.—WRAP

Usually, you get to just walk away. Make sure everything is back where it belongs or locked up if it is valuable. If there was a dinner scene and your dishes were used, the Property Department will wash them and return them to you. When the set is wrapped for good, the Leadman and a Swing Gang will arrive to wrap it all out. Your responsibility for the set is while it is being shot and it ends when the cameras are wrapped.

WHAT I REALLY WANT TO DO IS MOVE UP!

The next step after working as an On-Set Dresser is to become a Leadman. Your life will be filled with countless phone calls, paperwork, driving, heavy lifting, scheduling, and anything else that it takes to get the set ready for the On-set Dresser to take over.

To move up, you'll want to have a solid relationship with an established Art Director or Production Designer who trusts you and your abilities to handle the particulars of putting a set together. You might also have the chance to move up as a Leadman makes his way up to becoming an Art Director. Either way, observe and learn about everything that is on the set as you work with the filming unit. Take the time to understand the logistics that a Leadman must know to put items on the set in the first place. Once you learn that, you should be ready to make the jump when the opportunity presents itself.

Part X

PUBLICITY

What I Really Want To Do Is...

Unit Publicity

Unit Still Photography

Behind-The-Scenes Camerawork

Chapter 40

What I Really Want to Do Is Unit Publicity!

WHAT THE HECK IS A UNIT PUBLICIST?

The cast and crew who actually create the movie are called the "unit." As the Unit Publicist, you act as the liaison between the unit and the studio or production company marketing department. It is your job to facilitate any and all publicity and marketing requirements on set during physical production.

That, and what else?

The majority of your time will be spent in collaboration with the Unit Still Photographer. As she is snapping upward of 250 shots per day, the studio will be sending proof sheets back to you and you will distribute them to the talent for approvals or KILLS.

You're coordinating set visits by a variety of media outlets and the **EPK** crew. It is also your responsibility to act as the point of contact for local media when out on location.

During the course of preproduction, production, and postproduction, you are writing and assembling production notes, which are used as the primary copy for the studio marketing team as they work to promote the film.

Essentially, your purpose is to deal with anything having to do with scheduled and planned publicity and handle any surprises that might occur along the way, such as uninvited paparazzi or curious bystanders.

So, I'm not actually helping to make the movie then?

No, not really, but making the movie is only a part of the overall process. The finished product is no good if audiences don't show up to see it, so your work to help put together the elements for a publicity campaign is crucial if the entire project is to be considered a success.

I'm a department head of one? How's the money?

When you are beginning, you'll be on a flat rate of about $1,800 per week. As you gain experience and are in demand, you could ask for upward of $3,500 a week. Additionally, you'll usually get another $100 week in box rental for your computer and related supplies. Overall, expect to make around $35,000 for a twelve-week feature film.

WHAT DO I REALLY NEED TO KNOW?

A large part of your job involves writing. Whether you're captioning the Still Photographer's photos or creating the production notes for the studio, having some type of journalistic and literary background is imperative. In everything you do, you're telling a story about the movie itself, the characters, or what is going on behind the scenes, all in service of promoting the project in the best possible light.

WHAT DO I REALLY NEED TO HAVE?
What could I possibly need?

Not much really. Have a reliable cellular phone, which, in some cases, the production will provide for you. Either that or they will pay your bill for the duration of the show.

You'll also need a laptop computer and access to some kind of printer, either portable to use wherever you are or one at home to use after being on set all day. You'll have to have Microsoft Word as well as some kind of reliable e-mail service so that you can send and receive information from virtually anywhere.

One other thing that comes in handy is a loupe, or viewing glass. You'll give the Actors the proof sheets for their approvals and they can use the loupe to help make their choices.

What's the best way for someone to reach me?

Keep in regular contact with your studio and agency contacts. Opportunities happen all the time; staying on top of upcoming projects and making the calls to get yourself into the mix can keep you working throughout the year.

WHERE DO I REALLY NEED TO GO?
I just want to work.

Once you've established the contacts necessary to get work as a Unit Publicist in Los Angeles, you should be able to relocate just about anywhere you'd like, so long as you're willing to travel and be away from home for weeks on end. Otherwise, living in or around L.A. will keep you close to the business so that those who will hire you won't forget that you're around.

So how do I get work?

The chance of becoming a Unit Publicist as your very first job in the entertainment business is unlikely. The executives at the studio need someone whom they know and can trust to be their point person out on the set.

With that in mind, to get a job as a Unit Publicist, you need to know the people who are in charge of hiring for that position. To do that, you'll first have to work at a studio or a private publicity firm for at least four years, if for no other reason than to gain experience in how to manage the various media requirements surrounding the industry.

You'll start at an entry-level position at a studio as an intern or as an assistant in the Publicity Department. In due time, you'll work your way up to Junior Publicist, then to Senior Publicist, and even perhaps a Director of Publicity or a Vice President of the department. Somewhere in that career path, you may grow tired of that structure and decide to join the exciting freelance life on set with the rest of the crew, and that can become your chance to become a Unit Publicist.

Another avenue to take is to work as a Personal Publicist, perhaps for an Actor, and then become an assistant or intern for a large and respected personal agency that handles a cadre of "important" Actors and other talent. It is through the course of this kind of work that you will learn a lot about publicity—what is required, what you need to avoid, etc.—and from there you can potentially move onto a film set represented by your agency. A lower budget film is likely to hire a smaller agency to handle its publicity, and that agency will put one of its own people on the film as the Unit Publicist.

In the end, you're going to learn by doing. Hopefully by the time you make it this far, you've seen enough examples of all of the Publicist's work, from photo captioning to copies of production notes, so that you'll be familiar with the technicalities of how to do everything before you actually start.

WHAT AM I GETTING MYSELF INTO?
So who actually calls and hires me?

Either the VP or a Director of Publicity at a studio will call you, based on your previous working relationship. The call might even come from a Producer, a Unit Production Manager, or even an Actor.

There aren't that many Unit Publicists, and only the top 10 percent or so of those get most of the work. And among those, there aren't a lot of new people simply because it takes so long to get through the system to become a Publicist.

If the calls aren't coming in, take a look in the TRADES and talk to other Publicists to find out what projects are in development. And don't be afraid to call up the studio or production company. Their first pick might not be available or they might not have anyone lined up yet. It never hurts to ask.

Okay, I got the job. What now?

You'll have a prep week in which you'll read the screenplay thoroughly, put together information on the talent and ABOVE-THE-LINE personnel if applicable, visit the filmmakers so they know who you are, and get to know everyone in the production office.

If you're flying off to a distant location, it's likely that the local press is already aware that the circus is coming to town as the Production Designer and Construction personnel have probably been working for several weeks in advance of the main unit. When you arrive, you'll want to contact them to establish the rules regarding set visitation and what their access to the talent will be.

It is also time to begin writing. Jump in with a Start of Production Press Release. This is roughly three pages that describe the who, what, why, when, and where of the project.

The trades also will need to be updated. Early on, as the project is just coming together, either a Producer or the UPM will submit very sparse information about the project to the *Hollywood Reporter* and *Daily Variety*.

Also, begin writing and assembling early production notes. These are just a smaller version of the final production notes, which include biographies of the principal cast, Producers, Director, Writers, Director of Photography, Production Designer, Editor, and Costume Designer, as well as a synopsis of the story and the locations that will be used.

Getting as much of this research and writing done early on makes assembling the final production notes much easier. Plus, you'll have something to hand to visiting media when they come to the set.

What will my life really be like?

7:45 A.M.—ROLL CAMERA

Ideally, arrive on set in time to see the master being shot. Later on, you'll have to know what each scene is and what happened so that you can more easily caption the Still Photographer's photos and create more complete production notes. It's not enough to write based on the script pages. You need to know how the production is moving along, what the mood is, what the relationships between the principal cast and crew are like, and how the acting is.

It's also helpful to be around in case something out of the ordinary occurs, such as an accident. Especially on location, the local press will find out very quickly if an ambulance is called to your set. Studio Executives and Producers will learn about unusual incidents from the Assistant Directors, but you also should inform the studio marketing department, as the inevitable inquiries will be phoned in from the media.

Your day will be fairly unstructured, but you usually have enough to keep you busy. The Unit Still Photographer is on set every day, so your primary activity will revolve around him and the photos he generates. You'll be responsible for overseeing the approvals of every single photograph (approvals from the studio and the talent) as well as labeling each with a descriptive caption.

On occasion, outside press (e.g., *Entertainment Tonight*, local press, foreign press) will want to make a set visit to shoot B-roll and possibly even do an interview or two with the principal cast. You'll work with the studio marketing team as well as the First Assistant Director to find the most interesting and appropriate days to schedule these. As those chosen days approach, you'll remind all affected via memos and verbally so that no one can be surprised on the day that the press arrives. They'll be allowed on set to shoot **B-ROLL** or just to observe, and the Actors will graciously sit down for their interviews.

When a broadcast crew comes to the production with a video camera and a correspondent, their time on set will be fairly limited, so you'll be escorting and guiding them every step of the way every minute that they are there.

The same goes for non-camera journalists (writers), who usually will be scheduled to be in a large group on the same day. You'll help arrange their transportation to set if necessary, greet them when they arrive, take them on a tour of the stages and sets, introduce them to the filmmakers (e.g., Producers, Director), arrange time for them to observe a few takes being shot, and finally sit them down with the Actors for a thirty-minute group interview before sending them on their way. You've delivered news of your movie to the world in a single day, and everybody is happy.

The other area that you'll be overseeing to some extent is the EPK/DVD crew (see Chapter 42) that has been hired by the studio. For the most part, this is a camera crew of two or three (Videographer, Sound Mixer, Producer) who show up periodically throughout the course of production. In some cases, an EPK Field Producer/Cameraman is hired to be on set every day for very thorough behind-the-scenes coverage.

1:00 P.M.—LUNCH

Because you are a department of one, autonomous and setting your own schedule, where you go depends on what you need to do. While it's essential to establish a presence on set so that everyone there knows who you are, it is equally important to spend some time at the production office for the same reason. If nothing groundbreaking is or will be happening on set for the rest of the afternoon, head back to the office to work on any photo captioning or other writing that needs to be done.

9:00 P.M.—WRAP

Again, because of the nature of what you contribute to the overall project, it isn't necessary for you to be around for every single shot. Unless you have an EPK crew or other visiting media on set, you are free to head home whenever the essentials of your day have been completed.

When the show wraps for good, you still get paid for a "wrap week" so that you can finish up any loose ends, turn in the last of the Still Photographer's proof sheets, and write your final production notes. You won't be able to finish everything in that week though, particularly the production notes. In reality, it will take another month or two to get that far because you're waiting for transcripts from the EPK interviews to get back to you. What this means in practical terms is that (hopefully) you'll already be working on another project while you're still finishing up the last one. So for the first few weeks of prepping and shooting your new film, you'll still be in contact with the old production as you receive and deliver material. Life can get busy for a while as you write production notes on your weekends and other in between time that's left over after working all day on the new project.

WHAT I REALLY WANT TO DO IS MOVE UP!

Since there's a good chance you left a studio job to do this, "moving up" doesn't mean going back to the studio, unless it is in a Production VP position. More likely, you'll become a Producer for a film itself as the contacts you've made can put you in a position to build a package of script, talent, and financial resources. Naturally, there is no guarantee that this will happen, and your success on that path depends entirely on your own initiative (with some luck thrown in for good measure).

If that doesn't appeal to you (or work out) and being a Unit Publicist isn't where you'd like to be, another option is to become a Personal Publicist either with an agency or just attached to a specific talent. This doesn't happen all too often, but one of the upsides is that you are on a retainer for the entire year, meaning that you're not scrambling to find new projects to work on every few months.

By now, you've developed relationships with a variety of major media organizations. So another option is to expand the writing skills you've developed and segue into becoming an entertainment reporter for print or television.

Whatever you decide, your experience promoting for other people will come in handy when you are ready to promote your own skills and move forward in your career.

Chapter 41

What I Really Want to Do Is Unit Still Photography!

WHAT THE HECK IS A UNIT STILL PHOTOGRAPHER?

The entire group of people who gather together on set to make a movie is known as the "company" or "unit." The Unit Still Photographer is simply the Photographer who is assigned to stay with the unit to take still pictures, primarily for a movie studio's marketing purposes.

What you will find yourself doing a majority of the time is standing close to the A-camera to take still photographs of the Actors during rehearsals and takes. Those photos are then sent to the studio marketing department, where they go through an approval process before being launched out into the world to promote the project.

That, and what else?

Getting those shots isn't always as easy as it looks...or as easy as it should be. Besides the physical limitations that sometimes keep you from getting in a decent position to take useful pictures, often there will be one or two Actors who would rather you didn't take pictures of them while they are working, even though it is publicity for them and their careers. The reasons range from the logical to the irrational, but the end result is the same: Sometimes you're not able to do your job as effectively as you should be able to, if at all. Mostly, you'll have no problem getting what you need, but it is up to you to establish a good working rapport with every Actor and an understanding of what will be permissible throughout the length of production. It is imperative that you also know how a movie set operates and have an awareness of when it is appropriate to shoot and when it isn't. Developing a keen sense of when to move in and when to back off will keep you employed for a lot longer.

How's the money?

Union scale is about $45 an hour for a ten-hour day. You'll make some overtime on top of that as well as about $200 a day for equipment rental. You can expect to earn between $35,000 and $40,000 for a typical twelve-week project.

WHAT DO I REALLY NEED TO KNOW?

You need to know everything you can about photography, including the available technology and lighting. Because your photos are to be used primarily for marketing purposes, in particular, you need to learn how to shoot people well. Using a combination of portrait photography and photojournalism, you have to know how to tell a complete story in a single frame.

WHAT DO I REALLY NEED TO HAVE?
A camera probably, huh?

It's a start. Actually, you should have at least two. If you're shooting film, you'll need one camera for each different film stock you're using—up to six or more—so that you can just grab the camera you need instead of having to reload a roll that may be in progress.

But as of late, most studios are now asking the Still Photographer to shoot digitally. You'll want at least two bodies and possibly a third as a backup. While there are a lot of choices, you specifically need something with sufficient "continuous firing" that is quiet! Expect to pay around $4,500 on the camera body alone.

You'll also need a variety of lenses, most likely zooms, although some Photographers prefer to use fixed focal lengths on occasion. A good zoom that can handle low light levels will run between $1,200 and $1,500.

And whether you're using a traditional film camera or a new digital camera, both make noise, so you'll need a BLIMP plus tubes for the lenses. They are custom made for your camera, and configuration and will cost you at least $850 for each.

Because you're shooting digitally, you'll need a laptop computer with Adobe Photoshop with you on set. In between setups, you'll take your memory cards and download the photos onto a hard drive or burn the files to a compact disc.

The Still Photographer used to handle all the still photography needs of a production; however, that isn't always the case anymore as prop photos are often created by the Art Department. Because your duties revolve around the set and covering the scenes that are shot, you aren't left with much time to do special setup photo sessions, such as for the movie poster. But sometimes you are asked to do so. For those situations when you are asked to handle these tasks, you'll need some kind of large-format camera with the lenses and accessories. You'll also need your own lighting package plus a light meter to do it right. A basic lighting setup will cost you around $4,000 and a light meter is about $500, although if you aren't shooting setup shots that often, you could easily rent everything necessary as well.

What's the best way for someone to reach me?

Apart from the contacts that you've already made and maintain, introduce yourself to the heads of the Stills Departments at each studio. No one can call you for work if they don't know you exist!

WHERE DO I REALLY NEED TO GO?
I just want to work.

As long as you're on somebody's list to call, you could live just about anywhere. Your work will typically be for the run of a project instead of being merely a day or two at a time. But Producers will want you to work as a "local" if shooting in Los Angeles, so be prepared to put yourself up if called to work "in town."

So how do I get work?

Normally, you won't apply and go in for an interview. People for and with whom you've worked previously will remember you or make a referral. If they are not directly familiar with your work, at the very least they'll want to see a portfolio.

If you've made it far enough through your career that you're being asked for a portfolio, chances are that there is less concern over whether you can take adequate pictures and more interest in how you will get along with the Director and Actors on set. Personality is just as important, if not more so, than technical skill.

When you're just starting out, look in the TRADES for non-studio movies. These are typically nonunion with lower budgets. You won't get the big-time rate, but it's a way to gain set experience and build a body of work. Drop by the production office and talk to the Production Manager or the Producer. Take the portfolio you do have and a résumé to leave with them. Calling will just result in a brush-off. If you don't have a portfolio yet, work for free on really-low-budget or student films. Eventually you'll have amassed enough examples of your work plus enough paid days to join the union. Contact IATSE Local 600 in Los Angeles for current requirements.

WHAT AM I GETTING MYSELF INTO?
So who actually calls and hires me?

It depends on who knows you and how your name got in the mix, but usually you'll hear from the head of the Stills Department at a studio. You might also get a call from the UPM or even the Production Coordinator if you have an established relationship with the company.

Okay, I got the job. What now?

Talk with the Producer or Stills Department head at the studio about how they'd prefer you deliver your pictures. While almost every company is now asking that you shoot digitally, there may still be exceptions that ask for actual film.

Prep your own equipment. Make sure that everything works the way it should and buy or rent anything extra that you might need.

What will my life really be like?

6:42 A.M.—GET TO WORK

The first rehearsal is scheduled to begin in eighteen minutes, and ideally you want to be on set to see what is going to happen. Sometimes the UPM may ask that your call time be adjusted so that you'll arrive a little bit later, just prior to the actual take being filmed. But usually, you'll be around to prep with the rest of the crew and get into the swing of things for the day.

7:00 A.M.—GETTING TO SET

Roll the cart with your laptop computer, cameras, and other accessories on it to set and leave it someplace close but out of the way.

7:05 A.M.—REHEARSAL

In most cases, you'll just want to watch the rehearsal to figure out exactly what the Actors will be doing, as well as which camera/lens you'll need and where you'll be able to stand during the take. However, some Actors will request that you don't shoot any pictures at all during the actual take, so that leaves only rehearsals for you to shoot. This can pose problems, as Actors sometimes aren't completely THROUGH THE WORKS at this point. An Actress might have rollers in her hair or an Actor might still have on his street clothes. The Marketing Department needs photos of the Actors in character. During rehearsal, an Actor might not have the wrong clothes or look, but he also might be focused on mundane issues like hitting his mark or perfecting some bit of business. Do your best to get what you can.

7:15 A.M.—CAMERA SETUP

Now that you've seen what the Actors are going to do and how the camera(s) will be moving, choose your camera and lens and put them into your blimp. On occasion, you might need to stand up higher to see over someone else's head, so ask the Grip Department for an APPLE BOX or a ladder. You want your pictures to look as much like what the A-camera is seeing as possible, so position yourself as close to that lens as you can.

7:45 A.M.—ROLL CAMERA

While you are definitely standing in the front row watching the scene, you have to be as inconspicuous as possible. Fortunately, because the Still Photographer has been a traditional part of each setup, experienced Actors are used to you being around and generally won't take special notice of you anyway. But you want to keep your movements to a minimum and make no noise at all.

You're looking for those shots that tell the story of the scene. You won't want all singles or all two-shots but a good variety of everything. Also you want to take a lot of pictures if possible. On average, you'll find yourself taking upward of 250 shots each day. That adds up to nearly fifteen thousand stills over the course of a twelve-week production.

Actors have "kill rights" written into their contracts in which they are allowed to KILL a certain percentage of the shots you take. Naturally, they prefer that only the very best stills of themselves make it out into the world, so they might disallow a photo that bothers them for any reason at all. Sometimes the reasons are understandable. At other times, a picture that you are proud of taking will be killed for seemingly no reason at all. Because of this, it's in everyone's best interest to have the largest pool of photos to choose from as possible. This ensures that the Actors are happy with the images being sent out and that Marketing will have plenty to work with.

The other thing to keep in mind is that most of the time you're not really shooting "behind the scenes." To that end, you need to keep all of the "movie stuff" out of your frame and try to emulate what the motion picture camera is seeing as best as possible.

7:48 A.M.—CUT, LET'S GO AGAIN

Unless it is a major stunt in which there is only one chance to do it, you'll likely have several opportunities to get the shots you're looking for. However, if the Actors seem somewhat annoyed by your presence at times, it's best to go in for two or three takes to get what you need and then back off. A feature film is a long process over many days, so you don't want the talent to be tired of you too soon, or ever. Get what you need, but budget your "in their good graces" time as best as possible.

8:10 A.M.—CUT, MOVIN' ON

Move back out of the way and wait to see if there will be a rehearsal for the next setup. If not, listen in to find out what the next shot will be and then retreat to your own cart to download the photos that you just took.

1:00 P.M.—LUNCH

Put your camera back on the cart and cover everything with a space blanket if necessary, then head to the caterer with everyone else.

2:00 P.M.—BACK TO WORK

Just continue to get the best photos possible while being sensitive to the requests and moods of the Actors. During the day, the Publicist may drop by and talk to you about the pictures you've taken or to deliver requests from the studio (e.g., they want more close-ups). Keep up with your downloading and prepare the hard drives or CDs that will be delivered at the end of the night.

Some Photographers like to touch up their own work before it is sent in to the studio. Unlike the old days when all you had to show for your work during the day was a pile of film canisters, with digital technology you can immediately see what you've just shot and pull out what you're not happy with. You can also fix small problems, by dodging unwanted glares or erasing errant C-stands that might be cause for someone to kill an otherwise wonderful shot. Providing this service isn't necessarily part of your job description, so some Photographers choose to do it while others would rather not.

9:00 P.M.—WRAP

After the last shot, get your last pictures ready to be delivered and hand the material over to an Assistant Director. Push your cart back to the truck and secure it in case the truck has to move that evening.

WHAT I REALLY WANT TO DO IS MOVE UP!

There isn't really any direct route to anything "up" from being a Unit Still Photographer, but that shouldn't stop you from trying to move into other disciplines or areas of the business. Some Still Photographers have made the move to becoming Directors of Photography, although such a transition isn't common.

Generally speaking, being a Unit Still Photographer can be an enjoyable and sufficiently lucrative career. As a department of one, your work speaks for itself; so as long as you're doing your job and turning in great photos, you may not ever have the desire to do anything else.

Chapter 42

What I Really Want to Do Is Behind-the-Scenes Camerawork!

WHAT THE HECK IS A BEHIND-THE-SCENES CAMERAMAN?

As part of the marketing for a new film, a studio will give media outlets a package of promotional materials (an Electronic Press Kit, or **EPK**), including a videotape with behind-the-scenes footage and interviews with cast and crew. Additional **B-ROLL** and interviews may be shot for bonus features found on most DVDs. The Behind-the-Scenes Cameraman (or Videographer) shoots all of that material.

That, and what else?

Getting that material isn't as easy as it should be. One of the biggest obstacles you'll face is Actors who don't want you around. They may feel entirely comfortable having two or more film cameras recording their work, but the presence of your video camera isn't acceptable to them. Even though you are on their team and working with the studio to sell the product, some Actors (and even Directors) don't want a behind-the-scenes video camera on set. In this situation, unless a Producer steps in, you will be asked to leave. When that happens, you exit immediately and leave any discussions about it to the Unit Publicist and the EPK Producer, if there is one.

So a large part of your job involves politicking and making friends on set if for no other reason than to let them get used to you. See, unlike the Still Photographer, who is hired to be on set every single day of production, the behind-the-scenes crew might pop in days or weeks after the rest of crew has already been working. You might shoot for just one day or several in a row, disappear for a few days or weeks, then show up again. Because of this, you never really become part of that crew and tend to remain an outsider. So any headway you can make to ingratiate yourself to everyone on set can help you get the shots you need to make good behind-the-scenes footage. Not to mention that you should just be nice anyway...it's good to make new friends!

I must be making really good money then, right?

Because Behind-the-Scenes falls under the marketing aspect of a film and not production, a non-studio production company that has the contract to do the EPK/DVD content for a film will typically hire you as a freelancer. If you also happen to hold a union card as a Cameraman (IATSE Local 600), unlike almost everyone else working on set, you typically won't earn hours toward your benefits or be paid on any contracted scale.

Because you are technically being subcontracted out, you invoice the company that hires you for the agreed-upon day rate plus any overtime and/or equipment you rent. In general, expect to invoice between $500 and $800 a day plus the rental fee for the camera equipment if the company is renting from you. A typical camera package will rent for anywhere from $500 a day for an older BetaSP to upward of $1,000 a day or more for high-definition. And while a typical movie production schedule is roughly twelve weeks, you can expect to shoot only between seven to fifteen days total in that time, nonconsecutively. So you'll be filling the in-between days with other behind-the-scenes work, the usual assortment of industrial and corporate shoots, or other random stints on network or cable programming.

WHAT DO I REALLY NEED TO KNOW?

There are really just three things to know how to do before jumping into this line of work. First and foremost, you must be able to shoot video well. You have to know the best way to capture what's happening in front of you and how to anticipate what's going to happen *before* it happens. It doesn't do you any good to see something interesting going on next to VIDEO VILLAGE or on the set and then decide to shoot. By then, it's too late.

Which leads to the second thing you should know: how a movie set works. Nearly every set follows the same protocol. Each movie, TV show, and music video follows the same basic pattern to get from setup to shooting. Knowing that is half the battle. Getting a feel for the mood of the set, the way the Director works, how friendly a crew is, how the Actors react to everyone else including you and your camera...all of those things are vitally important. Knowing what to shoot is of course important. But perhaps even more so is knowing when to *stop*. When things aren't going well, if the Director or the Actors aren't happy, if somebody makes a mistake or an accident occurs...all of that sounds like juicy "reality" stuff, but you're not there for dirt. You are there to help promote the project positively.

While you are looking out for good material to shoot, always keep an observant eye on all of the principal Actors in case one of them decides to suddenly wave you off. If that happens, you immediately turn your lens away and leave the set so that he doesn't think that you'll try to steal shots when he isn't looking.

The "event coverage" is only part of the job. Usually out of sight from the rest of the crew, the EPK crew (EPK Producer/Interviewer, Cameraman, Audio Mixer) will set up and shoot interviews with principal cast and crew. It is usually these interviews that provide the soundtrack over which the footage you've been shooting will be laid. So in addition to bringing a video camera along, you will fill your personal vehicle with all of the lights and other equipment you could possibly need to shoot a "talking head" interview. You may be shooting on a working set so that the busy crew appears in the background, or you may get a small corner of a stage or set away from everyone else.

WHAT DO I REALLY NEED TO HAVE?
Do I need to buy my own camera package?
Isn't that expensive?

Yep. It's expensive. The good news is that you don't have to buy anything at all. Not really.

Many companies now own their own equipment packages and only hire cameramen willing to use them. It saves those companies the compounding cost of renting from freelancers or rental houses.

What's the best way for someone to reach me?

The world of freelance video moves pretty fast. Rare are the times when you get more than a few days' notice on an upcoming job. More frequently you'll be called for something that's happening tomorrow or a couple of days from now. Keep a cellular phone with you at all times and return calls as soon as possible. Unless the company really likes you or needs you, the Production Coordinator won't just sit around waiting for you to call back. Even a thirty-minute delay can mean that the job went to someone else.

WHERE DO I REALLY NEED TO GO?
I just want to work.

You can get videography work in just about any decent-sized city, but steady EPK work will go to people living in the Los Angeles area. Currently, there is no nationwide or international contractual requirement that you be a member of IATSE Local 600 to shoot EPK on a union project, but more often than not, the EPK Producer and/or the production itself will ask and/or require that you be.

So how do I get work?

You most likely aren't going to start your freelance videography career as a Behind-the-Scenes Cameraman. Most people in this niche of the business have and continue to shoot an array of other types of projects ranging from industrial and corporate needs to high end TV network programming. Through your contacts in those other areas you will be recommended to EPK/DVD Producers. Once you have sufficient experience as a Videographer, you can approach EPK companies directly with a résumé, recommendations, and/or a reel that highlights your best work.

WHAT AM I GETTING MYSELF INTO?
So who actually calls and hires me?

In most cases, you'll get the call from either the EPK Producer who will be out on set with you or from the Production Coordinator from the company that has the behind-the-scenes (EPK and/or DVD) contract with the studio. Those Producers and companies may shoot a variety of other types of programming in between set visits, so to build and keep a relationship with them, it never hurts to take as many days with them as possible, no matter what the job is.

A few individuals have developed personal relationships with Directors, Producers, or Actors and are requested to handle all of the behind-the-scenes work. If this is the case for a particular project, the studio might hire one person as the EPK/DVD Producer who shoots all of the material on set, interviews all of the relevant cast and crew, and edits the footage for EPK use and features for the DVD.

Okay, I got the job. What now?

As with every other job you do, double-check the tape format (BetaSP, DigiBeta, high-definition, HDV, etc.) and the aspect ratio (4 x 3, 16 x 9), and the frame rate (59.94I, 23.98P, etc.). Find out if you're shooting interior or exterior, day or night, and whether there are any specific circumstances you should know about, like rain or other special effects that might affect you.

What will my life really be like?

6:45 A.M.—GETTING TO SET

Your primary mission is to shoot the principal Actors as they rehearse with the Director and do the actual takes. Therefore, you won't have to arrive on set until just before the first rehearsal. Your Producer should find the Unit Publicist and all four of you (Publicist, Producer, Videographer, and Audio) go onto stage together. Assuming this is your first time on the set, nobody will know who you are. There should be an announcement on the call sheet that states "EPK ON

SET TODAY" in bold letters, so everyone should be expecting to see a video crew, but don't just rush in on your own. If there are any questions as to your purpose, you'll want the Unit Publicist with you to head off any trouble.

7:05 A.M.—REHEARSAL

Before you barge onto set and start shooting, make doubly certain that the First AD, the Director, and the Actors all are aware that you are there. Get the First AD's attention—introduce yourself to the Second AD if necessary to do this—then ask him to talk to the Actors about you. Remember, in a lot of cases, the Actors aren't too thrilled to have a video camera shooting them, so anything you can do to establish a respectful relationship with them will go a long way.

If everyone is cool with you shooting the rehearsal, find a spot or two that doesn't get in the way of the Director and the DP. You'll sometimes be including them in your footage anyway, so it shouldn't be a problem. Hopefully they'll do enough rehearsals that you can get the standard assortment of establishing shots and cutaways. Don't be too much of a nuisance as you record the blocking process. If at any point you sense that things are getting tense between the Actors and the Director or anyone else, back off and stop shooting. The more they recognize that you are just there for the good stuff, the more you'll be allowed to shoot without too many limits.

7:15 A.M.—CAMERA SETUP

Unless there is something extra special going on that your Producer wants to cover, this is your time to step away while the crew lights and sets cameras. On occasion, you may be there to cover a stunt or some other out-of-the-ordinary setup, in which case you'd jump in there and shoot anything and everything pertinent. But in general, just stay out of the way as much as possible.

Figure out where you'd like to be during the shot. Often there is just one good position, and the Unit Still Photographer already has it. She enjoys a certain unstated priority over you, mostly because she's there every day and you're not. If you establish a good relationship with the Unit Photographer, you'll find that you can work in tandem, trading off good shooting spots and trading important information.

7:45 A.M.—ROLL CAMERA

Be in your predetermined spot and start shooting the second you hear the First AD call for quiet and/or "last looks." Your shots will range from including the behind-the-scenes stuff, like cameras and crew, to tighter shots featuring only the Actors. Shoot what you need, being as quiet and unobtrusive as possible.

7:48 A.M.—CUT, LET'S GO AGAIN

Shoot wider or tighter or find another position to cover the action. If the Actors and/or Director are prone to goofing off in between takes, keep rolling. Just because the film cameras are told to cut doesn't mean you take the same cue. You're there to capture the process, which means that, if allowed, you could be rolling several hours of tape per day.

8:10 A.M.—CUT, MOVIN' ON

Again, if anything remotely interesting happens after the cameras cut, keep rolling on it as permitted. They'll continue in the routine of rehearsal, blocking, setup, and shooting until lunch. Make an effort to get the ground rules established before you begin shooting anything at all. Some Actors will let you shoot anything and everything, while others prefer that you don't shoot rehearsals. A few don't want you rolling on actual takes, which makes your job quite difficult. Some Directors want you to shoot everything they are doing, from them working with the Actors to catching reactions at video village. Other Directors, though, will shy away from the camera and would rather you concentrate on everybody else. Find these parameters out as soon as possible and then follow the rules.

1:00 P.M.—LUNCH

There is nothing happening on set, so in most cases you will go to lunch with the rest of the crew. On rare occasion, if there is an interview to do and there will be absolutely no time to do it during the course of the shooting day, the Unit Publicist may ask you to shoot during this period. In that case, you will have gotten some warning and a place to preset and light your shot.

2:00 P.M.—BACK TO WORK

More of the same, unless you have interviews to do. As you integrate yourself with the rest of the crew, take time to seek out and establish a relationship with the Electric Department. Along with the Assistant Directors, you will probably need the services of the Electrics more than anyone else on set as you set up for interviews and charge your batteries.

4:45 P.M.—WRAP

What's this? Wrapping early? The rest of the crew is still shooting and will probably go at least until 9 P.M. You come in late and leave early because you're on a ten-hour day. EPK budgets are relatively small compared to what is spent on the movies themselves, so studios are reluctant to pay overtime for this three-person crew unless absolutely necessary. Your Producer should arrange an appropriate call time for the next day (if you are returning the next day) and send you off. You might stay longer if the scenes being filmed justify the footage you'd shoot, such as an impressive stunt or if you absolutely have to get an interview done.

Behind-the-Scenes Audio

Getting great behind-the-scenes footage isn't just about shooting interesting visuals. It is important to hear what is going on as well. Whether it is getting an audio feed from the Production Sound Mixer, capturing conversations on set, or recording sound during interviews, it is the responsibility of the EPK Soundman to help deliver the best audio possible, often in less than ideal conditions.

Because the EPK crew (and standard video crew) consists of just you, the Videographer, and a Producer, you'll be asked to help the Videographer in whatever ways you can, from transporting equipment, helping to set up lights (for interviews), and being a sit-in while he lights. Some Cameramen may even expect a high level of aid from you, as they feel you are their "assistant." Some EPK/EFP Audio Mixers enjoy the chance to help lighting and contributing to the overall setup. However, your primary responsibility is to record audio, and anything else you choose to contribute will depend on whom you work for and whom you want to work with.

You are also usually asked to label the shot tapes as they come out of the camera if the Producer doesn't want to do it herself.

Like the Cameraman, you're hired as a freelancer, either directly by the studio or through an EPK/DVD production company. You may be a member of Local 695, but your position on the behind-the-scenes crew isn't currently recognized under any union contract.

Expect to be paid similarly to what you've made doing standard EFP (Electronic Field Production) and industrial projects. You can usually invoice $500 for ten hours plus an additional $50 a day for your audio gear. An EPK crew will typically be hired for ten to fifteen nonconsecutive days during the course of a normal twelve-week movie, so you should be able to take home almost $7,000 per project.

While you obviously need to know the ins and outs of your own gear, you'll also be connecting to a variety of camera and audio equipment. In addition to understanding the various field video cameras, from the inexpensive DV to the latest in high-definition, you also have to be ready with connections to plug into Production Audio on set.

Field audio equipment is relatively inexpensive compared with camera and lighting gear. An EPK sound package includes a portable field mixer, boom pole with shotgun-style microphone, lavaliere microphones, a pair of high-quality headphones, and two radio microphones. You also need the support gear to carry all of that plus batteries and cables, such as a PORT-A-BRACE style bag and harness. Expect to invest around $10,000 to get started.

After helping the Cameraman push the camera and lighting gear toward set, you'll need to find the Production Sound Mixer and get a FEED as quickly as possible. The feed is necessary so that the audio recorded for the movie is also going to the video camera that the behind-the-scenes footage is being shot on.

Getting behind-the-scenes footage is only a part of EPK. You'll set up and shoot interviews with the principal cast members as well as important off-camera crew.

All too often, there won't be a choice as to where the interviews will take place. In the best of circumstances, you'll be set up near the set, but in a quiet space where you can't hear any activity outside your door. Usually you won't have that luxury, so it is up to you to advise the EPK Producer if you feel that the extraneous noise will be excessive. Again, there may be absolutely no choice, but it is your responsibility to at least warn your boss if you suspect that there might be a problem.

While the Videographer is lighting, you will bar and tone a new tape in anticipation of a long interview.

When the talent arrives, mic them up quickly, as the time allotted for EPK interviews is usually squeezed in between setups on set. Adjust your boom mic over the talent so that it is close enough to pick up usable audio but not so much as to dip into the frame.

Sometimes the Producer may want a separate audiotape to use for transcription purposes. Coordinate those needs at least the day before in case any additional equipment has to be obtained.

After the last interview, help the Videographer wrap the gear and get it back to his vehicle. Make sure the tapes are all labeled, and give them to the Producer before going home.

WHAT I REALLY WANT TO DO IS MOVE UP!

Working as a freelance Videographer is a career unto itself. You are several film-style departments all in one. A natural path to travel is to become a freelance entertainment Producer/Director or EPK/DVD Producer (non-narrative production). You've likely spent many years working with Producer/Directors or you've been sent out on your own. It shouldn't be too big of a leap to segue into an ABOVE-THE-LINE job. This isn't to imply that you'll be producing or directing large narrative studio features. Your experience and clout will still be in the video realm of EPK, industrials, reality, and anything else that requires the protocol of video work.

If this is the way you wish to go, you'll need to augment your experience with knowledge about legal contracts and postproduction requirements. You need to learn how to contact and deal with clients, talent, and crews and familiarize yourself with all aspects of production and logistics. You'll find that you probably are aware of most of it in an indirect way, so use your list of contacts and let them know what it is you want to do. Chances are, if they've trusted and liked you enough to shoot for them, they'll be more than happy to help you move up.

Part XI

CAST AND CREW SUPPORT

What I Really Want To Do Is...

Crafts Service

On-Set Medic

Transportation

Chapter 43

What I Really Want to Do Is Crafts Service!

WHAT THE HECK IS CRAFTS SERVICE?

Crafts Service is the department on the movie set that provides refreshments, such as water, coffee, and snacks, for the cast and crew. On a union set, the department exists within the larger umbrella of IATSE Local 80 as specialized "Laborers."

That, and what else?

At minimum, the job requires that water and coffee be provided to the cast and crew during a production day, and for a long time, that's essentially all it was in addition to a few doughnuts. Today, however, Crafts Service has gone beyond a lonely table to a bountiful spread and also, in most cases, a truck stocked with fresh lunchmeats, fruits, other snacks, hot and cold beverages, microwaves, and cappuccino machines.

The point of providing anything at all is to give the cast and crew a nearby respite from the demands of being on set all day long. Filmmaking is a time-consuming and often tedious enterprise. Workdays typically run at least thirteen hours and sometimes upward of sixteen or more. With that in mind, many in Crafts Service take the time to create an inviting presentation and set a pleasant emotional tone. The job goes far beyond providing food and has more to do with offering a pleasing environment to keep the cast and crew happy as they work long hours.

Crafts Service is also responsible for the general housekeeping by picking up random garbage, sweeping floors, and cleaning up after inadvertent spills or other accidental messes on set and off.

So I'm not really helping to make the actual movie?

Not in the direct sense, no, but without the benefits of Crafts Service, those working on set would have a more difficult time completing the day's work. Particularly on a sound stage, filmmaking can be monotonous. Simple things like fresh coffee and healthy snacks help to keep a crew happy. The result is a more efficient crew producing higher quality work. Crafts Service is not an insignificant job.

How's the pay?

Expect to make around $35,000 on a twelve-week project. Most successful Crafts Service people now own their own customized trucks and receive about $1,000 a week in rental fees on top of their hourly wage.

WHAT DO I REALLY NEED TO KNOW?

You're not really cooking so much as setting out prepackaged snacks, fruit, and providing beverages ranging from canned sodas to hot coffee. On occasion, you might prepare some hot soup or small sandwiches, but generally speaking, it isn't necessary to be a qualified chef. An entirely different catering crew prepares hot breakfast and lunch sit-down meals for the cast and crew.

You will need a food handler's license, however, which you get after taking a class and passing the test given by the health department. It only costs about $50 and is good for five years.

WHAT DO I REALLY NEED TO HAVE?
Food?

Well, yes, but that you'll buy with the budgeted money you're given from the production. Before that, you need someplace to put it all. At the very least, you'll need a van for hauling all of your materials. Ultimately when you've decided to commit to this as a career, you'll want to invest in a truck customized for food preparation and storage. A truck outfitted with cupboards, sinks, refrigerators, a dishwasher, deli counters, coffee makers, microwaves, running water, electricity, etc. will run you approximately $100,000. Plus you'll need a small assortment of folding tables and serving dishes to create your spread.

What's the best way for someone to reach me?

The best thing for you to do is to maintain periodic contact with various production personnel you've worked for to keep your name fresh in their minds. Also, keep your contact information at the union local current in case anyone tries to reach you through that office.

WHERE DO I REALLY NEED TO GO?
I just want to work.

Anywhere there is a sizable production, there will be a need for someone to handle Crafts Service. While production does take place in various areas around the United States, currently Los Angeles provides the greatest volume of opportunities, both on large- and small-budget projects.

So how do I get work?

When you are just starting out, you can get some experience on low-budget nonunion projects.

At some point though, you'll want to work on larger movies so you can make a better living. Jobs will come as a result of recommendations from Production Managers, Production Supervisors, Producers, Actors, and anyone else who thinks that you're great at what you do. There are only a handful of top Crafts Service people who work consistently on the biggest movies, so the competition for the best work is tight. Most will have a few months off between projects or will work on a ten-month episodic and take the two-month hiatus off.

To get to that level, you'll need to join IATSE Local 80. To do that, you should call them up and ask to be put on the permit list. Essentially, this means that once all the Crafts Service people already in the union are working, the union can pull names from the permit list to fill a vacancy. It isn't impossible, but it can take a long time, so if this is really what you'd like to do, be prepared to wait it out for a while until you get your chance.

WHAT AM I GETTING MYSELF INTO?
So who actually calls and hires me?

You may be recommended by just about anyone, but the actual call will likely come from the Production Coordinator. She will provide all the details you'll need regarding the project.

Okay, I got the job. What now?

The budget you're given by the Producer will dictate the level of service you can provide. Once that is determined, you'll want to start prepping your truck by purchasing everything you'll need to be ready for day one of production. You won't buy everything for the entire project, just enough to get started.

What will my life really be like?

5:30 A.M.—GET TO WORK
Crew call may not be until 7:00 A.M., but that doesn't mean that no one shows up until then. The Second Assistant Director and Makeup, Hair, and Wardrobe

personnel are arriving an hour and a half before call so that they can get the talent THROUGH THE WORKS. You'll want to show up around the same time if not a little earlier to have coffee ready when people start to arrive in BASE CAMP.

Whenever you're at a new location, you'll want to make sure that Transportation has arranged to provide power to your truck (if your truck doesn't have its own) or to your area.

After that, you (and your assistant if you have one) set up for the day. You'll unload any tables you'll need, plug in extra coffee machines, line trashcans and distribute them around the set, fill coolers with ice and beverages, and create your spread of healthy snacks.

When you're just starting out, you'll probably be doing all of the shopping yourself, either at night after wrap or in the hours prior to call time. Once you're working with a larger budget, you'll be able to utilize various delivery services that specialize in dealing with Crafts Service companies. You can have all of your ice delivered daily as well as all of your groceries, hot food requests, and deli platters. This benefits you in two ways. The first is that all of the food that you put out for the crew is guaranteed to be fresh. No day-old bagels like you used to serve on student film sets. The second is that you aren't working eighteen-hour days. When wrap is called, you get to clean up and go home like everyone else instead of having to leave set and go spend an hour or two shopping for the following day.

8:10 A.M.—CUT, MOVIN' ON

Cast and crew will be wandering in and out of your area and truck all day long. During setups, you'll likely see cast members stop by for a cup of coffee and something to eat on the way to their trailers. After setups are finished, other crew members who have been working hard and now are waiting for the next change in camera position have time to kill and will come on over.

Not everyone gets the opportunity to get away from the set, though, so every few hours you can perk up their lives a little by taking some snacks to them. You don't want anything terribly fancy or messy. Small sandwiches, fruit, or cheese and crackers can be enough to tide them over and break up a potentially monotonous morning until lunch is called.

1:00 P.M.—LUNCH

Crafts Service is for snacks. Catering is for meals. You break and go to lunch like everyone else. Some people will have work to do during lunch and will help themselves to your deli service on the truck if need be. That's what it is there for. Crew members who have been in the business for a while are very self-sufficient, so you won't have to be around constantly to help or clean up after them.

2:00 P.M.—BACK TO WORK

The afternoon will move along much like the morning did. Some people may not have liked the Caterer's lunch, so they'll stop by "Crafty" on their way to set.

During this time, you continue to keep everything tidy in your area and around set by emptying trashcans, filling coolers, and rotating new snacks onto your tables. A few hours after lunch, you might put out a pot of fresh hot soup and a platter of deli sandwiches that you ordered from one of the convenient delivery services.

You may need to come to set with a broom or mop to help clean up an inadvertent mess. Most of the time, the On-Set Dresser will take care of something like that, but he may be too busy and you'll get the urgent call. Drop what you're doing and go help out in any way that you can. Keeping the cameras rolling is second only to safety.

In between your maintenance duties, find time to work up your delivery orders for the following day.

You'll get a feel for how the day is going, but talk to the First AD about how late he thinks everyone will be working. If it looks like a late night, it is up to you to order a SECOND MEAL and have it ready. This doesn't mean that the company will have an actual meal break like they did at lunch. Instead, there will be a WALKING MEAL, meaning that the food is there, but everyone keeps working as if it weren't. Again, not everyone can just leave set to visit the Crafts Service table, so you'll make a lot of people very happy by taking food to them.

9:00 P.M.—WRAP

Like everyone else, you want to head home as soon as possible. As you sense wrap approaching, you can start to clear some of the food off the tables, empty trashcans, and move some things back to the truck. People are still working up to and beyond the final shot and may still want water or something else, so don't start putting everything away until everyone else is cleaning up, too.

WHAT I REALLY WANT TO DO IS MOVE UP!

Crafts Service is its own specialty within the film industry. There is no way to "move up" to it and nothing to move up to. If you enjoy working with food and are looking for an alternative, you could transition into Catering, which provides hot breakfasts and lunches for film and television production. Otherwise, take pride and comfort in knowing that the service you provide helps to make the lives of so many people a little better while they are away from home.

Chapter 44

What I Really Want to Do Is
Be an On-Set Medic!

WHAT THE HECK IS AN ON-SET MEDIC?

Your primary purpose is to provide medical care to injured or sick crew, cast, or other production personnel. The Medic holds the distinction of being the only member of the crew who the Producers would rather see not working.

A Medic is required anywhere work is taking place, not just on the shooting set. There needs to be at least one Medic during actual production, one for the construction crew, one for any rigging crew (Lighting, Grip, Stunts, Camera), and one when the sets are struck (taken apart).

That, and what else?

The Medic is also the unofficial safety advisor as the eyes and ears of the Occupational Health and Safety Association (**OSHA**). Whenever an incident occurs, you are asked to fill out forms for the Production Department as well as Worker's Compensation and OSHA. You make note of everything in your own log that is used later on by Production for legal and financial purposes.

Mostly, you tend to be the unofficial drugstore. Headaches are more common than any kind of trauma, so you'll wind up dispensing more over-the-counter remedies than doing anything else.

I must be making really good money then, right?

Just about everyone who works as a Medic in the motion picture industry has come from the real world. So why choose to work in this environment where you're just waiting for trouble that rarely happens? There are several reasons, but the pay can definitely be a draw. Out in the field, a typical EMT may make little more than minimum wage, somewhere between $8 and $10 an hour. In contrast, a union film project will bring you $30 to $35 an hour. You're certainly not the highest paid on set, but because of the vast amount of overtime you accrue (eighteen hour days at times), expect to make $30,000 to $40,000 for twelve weeks of hopefully uneventful work.

In addition to your own wage, your medical kit is on rental as well. Expect kit rental deals as low as $15 per day to the standard of $25 or $30 per day.

WHAT DO I REALLY NEED TO KNOW?

A film set always has the potential to provide you with medical emergency experience, but mostly it's just a lot of sitting around. Unless you have some kind of deep interest in the filmmaking process, the primary draws will be the higher wage and better benefits than you can get in the field.

You'll still need to know pretty much everything any other medic would know about dealing with emergencies and trauma. At the very least, you have to be an EMT (Emergency Medical Technician), be CPR certified, AED certified (Automatic Defibrillator), know the basic ABCs (airway, breathing, circulation), how to treat minor injuries (breaks, lacerations, burns), and how to stabilize more serious injuries before transporting the victim to the hospital.

To further specialize and increase marketability, you may want to become a certified lifeguard, and/or a Beginner or Advanced Rescue Diver. Big movies involving a lot of water will bring in a number of extra-qualified crew.

Any time there are babies on set, a Nurse must be available along with the normal Medic. Each Nurse can take care of up to three babies from three to eight months old. There is more work available if you are also a certified Nurse (not just an EMT) because you can work pediatric. The more certifications you get, the more you can do and the more you could potentially work.

Currently, there are approximately three hundred Medics in the union. Most of them are EMTs and the rest of the roster is made up of those classified as First Aid, RN, LVN, and LPN. A few doctors have given up lucrative private practice careers to work in the film industry just for the change of pace.

It's important that you get used to dealing with amputated limbs, electrocutions, heart attacks, and other terrible occurrences so you won't freak out. On the whole, Hollywood is a pretty safe environment, but accidents do happen from time to time, and the Medic has to be ready for anything.

WHAT DO I REALLY NEED TO HAVE?
So how much stuff do I take to set?

As the designated medical representative, it is your primary purpose to provide the first response care that stabilizes the victim until he can get somewhere for more advanced treatment if necessary. The union provides a very specific list of items that you are required to have with you to serve that end. You might not have an ambulance or the convenience of a vehicle close by (unless a major stunt or dangerous special effect is being shot) so you must organize and pack everything in easily transportable bags and cases.

The items you need are pretty basic, and all you'll really be carrying will be a soft pack or bag, a hard box or toolbox for medicines, and a canister of oxygen.

Medic Kit

Here are some of the items you will need to purchase and carry with you:

Airways (plus pediatric)
Antiseptic towelettes
Band-Aids
Burn kit
C-collars (plus pediatric)
CC syringe
Dramamine
Dust-Off
Earplugs
Electrolytes
Eye drops
Eyewash
Floss
Gauzes
Gloves
Goggles
Hydrocortisone
Lidocaine
Lip therapy
Needle dispenser
OTC meds (cold, cough, diarrhea, pain)
Otoscope
Oxygen level box
Oxygen tank
Saline
Salt pills
Scissors
Splints
Sunscreen
Tampons
Tapes
Thermometer
Tongue depressors
Trauma gear

Unfortunately, you can't get by with just the basic list of required items. A lot of your time won't be spent treating blood and guts trauma (thankfully!). Instead, you'll be doling out pills for headaches, backaches, cramps, and other assorted mundane problems. Expect to spend around $700 to get started with the basic required list, but you'll find that it just isn't enough. You're going to need every-thing, especially as you find work on bigger and bigger projects. You'll spend roughly $4,000 for the little gadgets to check the eyes, ears, throat, and blood pressure. You may end up needing four different oxygen tanks in addition to the backboards, stretchers, floating stretchers, collars, C-collars, splints, trac-tion splints, etc. To go above and beyond, you might have an EKG to the tune of $8,000, but you don't really need it on set. Very quickly you can have upward of $10,000 invested in equipment before you even get to the over-the-counter medications.

There is really no cutoff for what you need. If there is a biological process, you should have the medical and/or emergency supplies to deal with it. You also don't have a truck or trailer on set to call your own, so you will be transporting all of this back and forth everyday.

The one thing you cannot do is have or dispense any prescriptions at all.

The production company, studio, and OSHA all want to know what is hap-pening on set. Whenever someone is injured, you must fill out the Workman's Compensation forms in addition to reporting the incident on a daily log, which gets turned in to the Assistant Directors. If nothing happens, you fill out a form stating that and turn it in the same way. So you'll also need a portable filing sys-tem as well as a clipboard and other office materials to take care of all of this.

Filling out the OSHA paperwork is not specifically in your contracted duties, but it doesn't hurt you to do it if you are asked by the Production Department. If anyone is injured, hospitalized, or gets significantly ill (e.g., a virus), OSHA wants to know about it. Generic forms are available from the state, the insurance agency covering the film, and the payroll company.

What's the best way for someone to reach me?

Your union keeps an Available List in case a production is in need of additional medics. Make sure you get your name on that list when you are not working and keep the information current.

Also, have a cell phone and keep it turned on. Not only will it help you get work, but it may come in handy while you are on a job but away from an emergency.

WHERE DO I REALLY NEED TO GO?
I just want to work.

To really make a living, you need to become part of the union, IATSE Studio First Aid Local 767. The bad news is that with about 330 Medics already on the list, it is extremely difficult for someone new to join. All the established members must be working or unavailable for a new "non-roster" Medic to get a chance. But if you have all the certifications plus a minimum of two years emergency room experience, begin your search for anyone who is in the union. Talk to friends and co-workers and try to visit a set and meet with the Medic. Do anything you can to get your name on the list of interested Medics for that rare time when they might need you.

So how do I get work?

While you're waiting to do that, seek out nonunion productions that are in need of an on-set Medic. While you could possibly get the thirty days on a union set needed to join the local, a more likely scenario is that the nonunion show you get on will turn union. If that happens, you are grandfathered in, provided you meet the requirements. But choose your nonunion projects carefully. Not all of them will necessarily be beneficial for you to spend time on. It's important to get some real set experience, but once you've got that figured out, there isn't much point in sitting around on a "deferred payment" or other low-budget show unless there is a distinct possibility of it turning union.

IATSE Local 767 requires all of its members to check in each week. You will call their answering machine and leave your name, the show you're on, the production company, and whether you're working with construction, rigging, or production. Or put yourself on the Available List.

Also, keep in touch with other Medics and crew members with whom you've worked. Let them know when you're available so that your name is fresh in their minds.

WHAT AM I GETTING MYSELF INTO?
So who actually calls and hires me?

No matter who remembers or recommends you, the Production Department will be calling and hiring you.

With a minimum of two Medics per show (one on Construction and one on Production), around 160 major productions have to be happening before anyone new gets a chance to work. Some shows are big enough that they need more Medics—up to eleven or more. If something like that happens, a Supervisor is needed just to keep track of what is going on. The Medic who is on set with the A-unit becomes the Supervisor and gets compensated a bit more for the added responsibility.

Okay, I got the job. What now?

When you get your deal memo, you should also get a script. Read it and look for any scenes that are potentially hazardous or special in other ways. Children on set may require having a pediatric nurse around. Or major stunt sequences may necessitate having additional Medics or a paramedic unit standing by. The Stunt

Department is specifically required to provide their own rescue and extraction people while you are there to administer to the victims once they are pulled free of whatever situation they are in. Of course, if you are the only person standing there when someone is ailing, you're going to help him. In the case of serious trouble, such as a helicopter crash, you will be able to help more people by letting others bring the victims to you. If you go in and get hurt, then there is no one left to treat the injured. As odd as it might sound, your first priority is your own safety. Work with the Stunts and AD Departments so that everyone knows who is responsible for what before anything happens.

What will my life really be like?

6:42 A.M.—GET TO WORK

General crew call is 7:00 A.M., but much of the crew comes in eighteen minutes earlier to unload the trucks and get the gear to the set. Setup is when most accidents will occur, so the Medic is brought in at this time just in case. The Medic may get an earlier call with Makeup, Hair, and Wardrobe if there are a lot of Extras, if the shoot is in a rugged location, or if there is a large lighting or stunt pre-rig.

Get your equipment to set and find out what's going on and where. Get a walkie-talkie and make a base for yourself somewhere out of the way but close enough that you are within earshot of any problems. Make sure that the ADs know where to find you, and get ready for a long day of hopefully nothing serious happening.

You're just basically hanging out and waiting. Observe everyone. Scan the area consistently. Watch everyone working and keep an eye out for the "regulars," those guys who tend to put themselves into precarious situations and need help more often.

7:15 A.M.—CAMERA SETUP

After the rehearsal, there is a sudden outbreak of work by everyone. While the Actors, Hair, and Makeup disappear back to BASE CAMP, the Camera, Grip, Electric, Set, Prop, and Stunt departments spring into action doing what they do. There is a lot going on in many different areas of set with lots of potential for medical attention. Especially on the bigger productions, the crews are well seasoned and know how to avoid problems. But accidents do happen from time to time anyway. Look out for people tripping or dropping things. Electrics, Grips, and Camera people are up on ladders or in the rafters. Watch out for burns from Electrics or Special Effects. Exterior work invites sunburns or dehydration.

Most injuries that happen on set will be relatively minor. The occasional laceration, major burn, head injury, or electrocution will unfortunately keep things interesting for you.

7:45 A.M.—ROLL CAMERA

The time of greatest potential for injuries has passed for the moment. You can settle in at this point. You're not required to stare at the set all day long either.

As long as you're in close proximity to the set and accessible by radio, feel free to read a book, solve crossword puzzles, study...whatever. The key is to have patience and remain alert while you wait for the inevitable trauma, headache, or upset stomach to occur.

8:10 A.M.—CUT, MOVIN' ON

Once again, the activity level will rise while everybody scurries around doing their jobs.

1:00 P.M.—LUNCH

Technically, you're off the clock while you go to lunch with everyone else. Some Medics bring their trauma bags with them just in case something happens. Most of the time, lunch is served near the set by a caterer, but if you have to leave the area, just let the AD know where you're going and when you'll be back. They won't call you if somebody needs an aspirin, but if an emergency happens, they'll be looking for you first.

2:00 P.M.—BACK TO WORK

As the day progresses, the drudgery of watching everyone else work may set in. Now is a great time to concentrate on the office work required of you. Keep your daily log up-to-date. Fill out any Workman's Comp paperwork that is necessary. Keep your own work records up-to-date and organized.

As the end of the day approaches and the creative team (Director, Producers) realize that they might not finish the scheduled work for the day, they tend to want to rush the crew to squeeze in those last shots they need. Rushing around invites accidents, so keep a wary eye out for those individuals and departments that seem to be getting a lot of pressure. If you're on an exterior location, the Camera and Grip departments will be encouraged to move quickly all day long. As evening approaches, the Electric Department will join the fray. On interior sets, just about anyone can get hurt all day long. Except for the shooting set itself, the rest of the stage is really dark, and it is very easy to trip on equipment or cables.

9:00 P.M.—WRAP

When the First AD calls "Wrap!" there is still another thirty minutes to an hour of work left to be done by the crew as they put their equipment back on the trucks. You can start to put your own things away, but stay available by radio until everyone else is finished. Once the Second AD tells you "Last out," you're done. Make sure you have the call time for tomorrow and go home.

WHAT I REALLY WANT TO DO IS MOVE UP!

Being a Medic on a movie set isn't a stepping stone to anything else. Medically speaking anyhow. If you're an EMT, you could take the hours of idle time to study and advance your own medical career. In terms of filmmaking itself, there is an ever-so-slight chance that you could wind up as a consultant on a medical show and then parlay that experience into some kind of creative position one day, such as directing or producing. But that kind of hopeful scenario isn't one to build a career on. If it happens it happens, but in the meantime, take the Medic position because you want to do it and nothing else.

Chapter 45

What I Really Want to Do Is Transportation!

WHAT THE HECK IS TRANSPORTATION?

There are a lot of people and there is a lot of equipment to move around constantly to and from the office, the sets that are being built, and the shooting set. The Transportation Coordinator supervises any transportation needs of production. The Transportation Captain works directly with the Drivers, who are assigned to specific vehicles. Anything that has to be moved, from crew and their equipment to Actors' vehicles and their accommodations (trailers), plus rental cars, picture cars and boats (cars and boats appearing in movies), motorcycles, and snowmobiles are all the responsibility of the Transportation Department.

That, and what else?

Transportation's primary responsibility is to provide and operate safe and reliable vehicles so that the needs of the production are met. In practical terms, that means that Transportation must coordinate getting the trucks parked on set and drive the crew vans back and forth wherever and whenever personnel or supplies and equipment are needed.

While a Driver isn't required to help, the crew always appreciates an extra hand when packing or unpacking their trucks. You don't have to push the carts around, but simply helping to raise and lower the lift gate is extremely useful and serves to make the entire day more efficient for everyone.

We just move trucks back and forth? Geesh, it sounds like I won't even be working on the set at all.

Not necessarily. Transportation Drivers also drive picture cars and camera platform vehicles (e.g., Shotmaker). Pretty much anything with wheels is driven by someone in Transportation. The exceptions are stunt precision driving, a picture car with a recognizable talent, and background vehicles driven by Extras. Also, the Camera Department arranges helicopters used as camera platforms (e.g., Wescam), and the Production Office deals with airplanes for crew transportation.

Transportation falls under the Teamsters, right? So I must be making pretty decent money then.

Technically, yes, Studio Transportation Drivers IATSE Local 399 are a part of the larger Teamster organization. However, motion picture work is considered a specialty field, so not just any member of the national Teamster union is eligible to join 399. There are nonunion productions that don't require the Drivers to be members of the Teamsters or IATSE Local 399, but you still have to be properly licensed by the state to operate different types of vehicles.

The Transportation Coordinator is not required to belong to IATSE but typically is a member by virtue of having moved up through the ranks. What this means is that while Drivers and Captains are represented under an IATSE contract with a set wage scale, Coordinators are not.

With that in mind, a Transportation Coordinator will be paid a flat rate of $2,500 to $3,500 per week no matter how many hours he works. Typically the Coordinator will be hired in time for the tech scout so that all transportation and parking needs are addressed. On a feature-length project, the tech scout could happen as early as three to six weeks prior to the first day of production.

The Transportation Captain will be brought on a week or two prior to production to help the Coordinator with the logistics of obtaining vehicles for department preps and rental house pickups. He can expect to make roughly $40,000 to $50,000 for a typical feature film.

Truck Drivers, those who are in charge of the large tractor-trailers for departments like Camera, Grip, Electric, and Wardrobe, make roughly $25 an hour. Passenger Van Drivers make slightly less.

Another opportunity for working in Transportation is in maintenance. A Mechanic will make around $25 an hour and his boss, the Chief Mechanic, will make nearly $30 an hour.

For the most part, everyone who is hired will be working on a show every day, especially when production is out on location. When the work winds up back onstage to shoot interior sets, some of the Drivers may be laid off because the trucks are just parked for the duration and the crew gets to set on their own. Because of that, while the Coordinator and the Captain may have work for twelve weeks or more, the rest of the Drivers may only be employed for a fraction of the time.

WHAT DO I REALLY NEED TO KNOW?

It's not enough to just know how to drive various types of vehicles. A Transportation Coordinator is responsible for understanding how a film set operates and should be able to anticipate the needs of all the departments, on set and off. Working in conjunction with the Location Manager, you'll coordinate parking all of the production trucks for maximum efficiency while being mindful of the concerns of the surrounding community. For example, while it's in the company's interest to have BASE CAMP set up as soon as possible, it's not always a good idea to roll ten or more tractor-trailers into a neighborhood at 3:00 A.M.

The Transportation Department is the largest department on set and deals with every other department there is. The Coordinator and the Captain must know how to manage a large crew properly and have budgeting skills on par with the Unit Production Manager.

WHAT DO I REALLY NEED TO HAVE?
I'm driving trucks around. What could I possibly need?

Even in nonunion work, you must be properly licensed by the Department of Transportation for the type of vehicle you will be driving. In most cases, you must have a Class A license, which enables you to drive anything. If nothing else, having that class makes you more versatile and useful, so you may work more. A truck-driving school will cost about $2,000 for a month of training, and the license itself is around $50.

To drive a tractor (truck) with a generator attached and operate it, you must hold a Teamsters Local 399 card *and* a Local 40 IBEW card. (This is different than IATSE Local 728, which represents Set Electricians.)

As you move up the chain and become a Transportation Captain or Coordinator, you might consider buying and renting vehicles, like camera trucks and stakebed trucks. Studios own fleets of vehicles, but often they don't have enough to cover all the projects in production at any given time, so it is necessary to rent from an outside vendor. A quality tractor-trailer can cost $300,000 and up, plus insurance and maintenance.

A Coordinator is responsible for maintaining a separate budget for the department. A simple-to-use computer program made specifically for the movie industry costs around $1,500, plus your own computer.

What's the best way for someone to reach me?

Local 399 maintains an Available List that Captains and Coordinators can refer to when they need Drivers. Keep your contact information current and let those you've worked with before know that you are available.

WHERE DO I REALLY NEED TO GO?
I just want to work.

Technically, any Teamster in the nation is eligible to drive a vehicle for a film production. However, the industry is so specialized that it is in the best interest of Coordinators to hire only those who have experience in the business. Getting that kind of exposure to production driving means living near a major city where a lot of production takes place, such as Los Angeles, New York, or Chicago. You also need to be available to take day calls on short notice.

So how do I get work?

There are essentially two ways to go about it. The first is to put your name on a list and wait. When all the Drivers in the union are being used, the union is allowed to go to the permit list and put new Drivers on a production. With upward of 3,500 Drivers in Local 399, breaking in isn't necessarily an easy thing to do. Once you've made your way to a production, you'll need to work thirty days within a twelve-month period to become a Group 3 on a union payroll. This is the bottom level of the seniority system. A production cannot hire a Group 3 member unless the union is down to 2 percent of Group 2 members who are available. And Group 2s cannot be hired unless they are down to 2 percent of Group 1s. So the reality is that a Group 3 person will have a hard time finding steady work unless he or she drives special equipment. Group 2s work about eight months out of the year. Group 1s work pretty much as often as they'd like because they are first on the list.

Once you've gotten your thirty days as a Group 3, you have to work for two years before becoming a Group 2. Then it takes about eight to ten years to become a Group 1.

The second way to break in is to drive specialty equipment, such as a **HONEYWAGON**, a water truck, a Chapman crane, or a generator truck. You gain that position by working through an equipment vendor who supplies those kinds of unique vehicles.

WHAT AM I GETTING MYSELF INTO?
So who actually calls and hires me?

Soon after a project gets going, the Unit Production Manager hires the Transportation Coordinator. The Coordinator will hire a Transportation Captain, who then hires Drivers, beginning first with Van Drivers for small production runs and tech scouts.

Okay, I got the job. What now?

The need for transportation begins early in preproduction. Relatively minor runs, like script delivery to Actors, can be done by office Production Assistants. But more involved runs, like wardrobe or construction material pickups, are done by the Transportation Department. The Coordinator will work with the Unit Production Manager to create a budget. The Captain hires Drivers as preproduction moves closer to day one of shooting.

What will my life really be like?

5:30 A.M.—GET TO WORK

Drivers arrive at location and begin parking the vehicles according to the prearranged plan put together by the Coordinator, Captain, and Location Manager. Power is run and turned on to provide light, heat and/or air-conditioning, and hot coffee at Crafts Service.

The Generator Operator/Driver will park his truck near the cables that the Rigging Gaffer left from the setup the day before. He plugs them in and energizes the lines as soon as the Best Boy Electric arrives.

Drivers may be dedicated to specific Actors or other ABOVE-THE-LINE personnel and will be picking them up and delivering them to set according to the times on the call sheet, which are laid out by the Second AD.

6:42 A.M.—CREW ARRIVES

Crew-van Drivers line up their vehicles and wait for crew to arrive at crew parking when on location. Crew members get in the vans and the Drivers transport them to base camp.

The various department crews begin pulling equipment out of their respective trucks and trailers. Truck Drivers help by operating the lift gates and keeping a watch on the equipment, particularly when on somewhat less-than-secure locations.

7:15 A.M.—CAMERA SETUP

To adhere to Department of Transportation rules, every Driver is required to keep a log detailing every minute of driving time as well as rest time. Most of your work happens at the beginning of the day and at the very end as vehicles will be moved upward of three hours or more prior to crew call and late at night after everyone else has gone home. For that reason, Truck Drivers are required to rest (sleep) during the "working day" while shooting takes place on set.

Van Drivers will remain on standby throughout the day for run requests from the crew or from the production office.

Picture-car Drivers remain close to set and will take direction from the Transportation Captain and the Second Unit AD.

12:30 P.M.—LUNCH

Drivers eat about a half-hour before the rest of the crew breaks for lunch. There may be runs to make during the official break. Also, your entire department began the day far earlier than everyone else.

9:00 P.M.—WRAP

Clean and lock up any vehicles that won't be needed as wrap approaches. Help the crews by operating their lift gates just as you did in the morning. One Driver will be assigned to gather the shot film from the Loader in the Camera Department and the audio recordings from the Sound Mixer. Another Driver will work with the Wardrobe Department to deliver laundry that will be dry-cleaned overnight.

Crew-van Drivers will shuttle the crew back to their cars as they finish wrapping for the night.

If there is a move to a new location, the Captain will have the Truck Drivers either move the vehicles there or a secure lot for the night. Power must be supplied to the Camera truck at all times for battery charging.

WHAT I REALLY WANT TO DO IS MOVE UP!

The first step to moving up is to get from being a Group 3 to a Group 2 Driver. After eight to ten years, you can advance to Group 1. Your personality and dependability will go a long way in proving to the Transportation Captain that you are worthy to have on the crew. In time, the Captain may see you as having more value as his Co-Captain. A Captain may get to coordinate his own show based on his experience and contacts or the Coordinator he has worked with before may move on from the business altogether. When a space opens at the top, everyone gets the opportunity to move up, so the Captain may become a Coordinator and his Co-Captain will become the Captain.

Patience and dedication is key, as you will be working upward of eighty hours a week and will be away from home and family for most of that time while on a job. The pay is very good and can afford you more time off in between projects to help make up for spending so much time at work.

Afterword

If you are seriously interested in making movies, you're not alone. So many of us got our start goofing off in the backyard with Dad's old Super 8 camera. Nowadays, kids can grab the home video camera and edit a slick production in the time it used to take to get the film back from the corner drugstore.

There's no doubt that filmmaking can be a really fun hobby whether you're young or old. Maybe that's why the possibility of earning a living at it sometimes seems hard to believe. Seriously, making movies is a real job? Those working on a set often vocalize that question when we realize that the Actors are just playing make-believe and the rest of us are creating a world that doesn't exist and capturing it on film for everyone else to see. The thought of sitting in a cubicle somewhere under fluorescent lights day after day is enough to make most of us contemplate sinister thoughts. Add the significant money that can be made in a short amount of time and it just doesn't seem fair when you compare what we are doing with more important professions in society, like teaching little kids.

As fun and improbable as the whole situation can be, it is important for you, the aspiring filmmaker, to remember that if you choose to take on this "hobby" as a real career, this will no longer *just* be an enjoyable thing to do in your spare time—it will also become your livelihood. Agreeing to help someone else out on a "great project" where you'll earn little to no money is admirable. It can give you experience and, hopefully, useful contacts to call later. But at some point, you'll have to begin treating your work as a serious career.

The obvious concerns are financial, as your choices will directly affect how much money you can and do earn, which in turn contributes to the lifestyle you wind up leading. Almost more important is the issue of that life in and of itself and what you want to accomplish in the short time we each have here on Earth. Some of you out there may be perfectly fine living the nomadic life that takes you far from home for countless hours, shooting on dark and cold soundstages, working for nights on end, and eating your lunch in parking lots. For others, you may find that you desire more from life than just working from film to film when you realize that you haven't seen your home, family, or friends in any meaningful way for days, weeks, or months on end.

On a film set, you'll never be lonely and seldom bored, as there is always something going on and plenty of people around to do it. That may be enough for a lot of you. However, for others, working fourteen-hour days, six days a week only to come home long after the kids have gone to bed and your spouse has fallen asleep on the couch (again) waiting for you can become too frustrating. Or you may find that you just *can't* get enough work so the stress that a lack of meaningful income places on you and/or your family, not to mention the time spent at home that you never counted on, can have the same affect.

This isn't meant to talk you out of or into pursuing a career in this business. The point is to help you think about everything that is likely to happen on your journey into a real career and what could occur while you're there. This book is meant to help you think past the excitement and glamour that drives so many of us to try so hard and sacrifice so much in the name of earning a living making movies. There's no substitute for knowledge, and having a better idea of what you're getting yourself into can only help you to make wiser and more informed choices along the way. That, tossed in with your own perseverance, charm, enthusiasm, and a bit of luck, will undoubtedly give you a happy lifetime doing what *you* really want to do.

Appendix A

Union, Guild, and Organization Contact Information

The following is a list of filmmaking unions, guilds, and organizations throughout the U.S., Canada, the United Kingdom, Australia, New Zealand, and in several other countries.

Part I:
The Business...Really!

Contract Services Administration Trust Fund
15503 Ventura Boulevard
Encino, CA 91436
(818) 995-0900
www.csatf.org

IATSE (The International Alliance of Theatrical Stage Employees, Moving Picture Technicians, Artists and Allied Crafts of the United States, Its Territories and Canada, AFL-CIO, CLC)
1430 Broadway, 20th Floor
New York, NY 10018
(212) 730-1770
www.iatse-intl.org
Employment Development Department/ Unemployment Insurance
(800) 300-5616
www.edd.ca.gov/eddhome.htm

Part II:
Talent Support

Stuntmen's Association of Motion Pictures
10660 Riverside Drive, 2nd Floor, Suite E
Toluca Lake, CA 91602
(818) 766 4334
www.stuntmen.com

SAG (Screen Actors Guild)
Los Angeles Office
5757 Wilshire Boulevard
Los Angeles, CA 90036
(323) 954-1600
www.sag.org

New York Office
360 Madison Avenue, 12th Floor
New York, NY 10017
(212) 944-1030
www.sag.org

AFTRA (American Federation of Radio and Television Artists)
Los Angeles National Office
5757 Wilshire Boulevard, 9th Floor
Los Angeles, CA 90036-3689
(323) 634-8100
www.aftra.com
New York National Office
260 Madison Avenue
New York, NY 10016-2401
(212) 532-0800
www.aftra.com

Studio Teachers & Welfare Workers—IATSE Local 884
PO Box 461467
Los Angeles, CA 90046
(818) 559-9797
www.studioteachers.com

Motion Picture Costumers—IATSE Local 705
4731 Laurel Canyon Boulevard, Suite 201
Valley Village, CA 91605
(818) 487-5655
www.motionpicturecostumers.org

Costume Designers Guild—IATSE Local 892
11969 Ventura Boulevard, 1st Floor
Studio City, CA 91604
(818) 752-2400
www.costumedesignersguild.com

Make-Up Artists and Hairstylists Guild—IATSE Local 706
828 North Hollywood Way
Burbank, CA 91505
(818) 295-3933
www.local706.org

Affiliated Property Craftspersons (Props)—IATSE Local 44
12021 Riverside Drive
North Hollywood, CA 91607
(818) 769-2500
www.local44.org

Part III:
The Director's Unit

Directors Guild of America
Los Angeles Headquarters
7920 Sunset Boulevard
Los Angeles, CA 90046
(310) 289-2000
www.dga.org
New York Headquarters
110 West 57th Street
New York, NY 10019
(212) 581-0370
www.dga.org
Chicago Headquarters
400 N. Michigan Avenue, Suite 307
Chicago, IL 60611
(312) 644-5050
www.dga.org

*Assistant Directors Training Program
(West Coast program)*
14724 Ventura Boulevard, Suite #775
Sherman Oaks, CA 91403
(818) 386-2545
www.trainingplan.org

*Assistant Directors Training Program
(East Coast program)*
1697 Broadway, Suite #600
New York, NY 10019
(212) 397-0930
www.dgatrainingprogram.org

*Script Supervisors/Continuity and Allied Production
Specialists Guild—IATSE Local 871*
11519 Chandler Boulevard
North Hollywood, CA 91601-2618
(818) 509-7871
www.ialocal871.org

Part IV:
The Camera Department

*International Cinematographers
Guild/Publicists—IATSE Local 600*
7755 Sunset Boulevard
Los Angeles, CA 90046
(323) 876-0160
www.cameraguild.com

NABET Local 59053
1918 W. Burbank Boulevard
Burbank, CA, 91506
(818) 846-0490
www.nabet53.org

Part V:
The Grip Department

Motion Picture Studio Grips—IATSE Local 80
2520 West Olive Avenue
Burbank, CA 91505
(818) 526-0700
www.iatselocal80.org

Part VI:
The Electric Department

*Studio Electrical Lighting Technicians—IATSE
Local 728*
14629 Nordhoff Street
Panorama City, CA 91402
(818) 891-0728
www.iatse728.org

*IBEW (International Brotherhood of Electrical
Workers)—IATSE Local 40*
5643 Vineland Avenue
North Hollywood, CA 91601
(818) 762-4239
www.ibewlocal40.com

Part VII:
The Sound Department

*Production Sound Technicians, Television Engineers,
Video Assist Technicians, and Studio
Projectionists—IATSE Local 695*
5439 Cahuenga Boulevard
North Hollywood, CA 91601
(818) 985-9204
www.695.com

Part VIII:
Special Effects

Affiliated Property Craftspersons—IATSE Local 44
12021 Riverside Drive
North Hollywood, CA 91607
(818) 769-2500
www.local44.org

Alliance of Special Effects & Pyrotechnic Operators
12522 Moorpark Street Suite 111
Studio City, CA 91604
(818) 506-8173
www.asepo.org

Part IX:
Sets

Studio Transportation Drivers/Location
Managers—Teamsters Local 399
4747 Vineland Avenue
North Hollywood, CA 91602
(818) 985-7374
www.hollywoodteamsters.org

Location Managers Guild of America
8033 Sunset Blvd. Suite 1017
Hollywood, CA 90046
(310) 967-2007
www.locationmanagers.org

Association of Location Scouts and Managers
(New York)
(917) 439-5588
www.alsam.net

Affiliated Property Craftspersons
(Greens; Set Dressers)—IATSE Local 44
12021 Riverside Drive
North Hollywood, CA 91607
(818) 769-2500
www.local44.org

Motion Picture Set Painters and Sign
Writers—IATSE Local 729
1811 West Burbank Boulevard
Burbank, CA 91506-1314
(818) 842-7729
www.ialocal729.com

Art Directors Guild & Scenic, Title and Graphic
Artists—IATSE Local 800
11969 Ventura Boulevard, Second Floor
Studio City, CA 91604
(818) 762-9995
www.artdirectors.org

Part X:
The Publicity Department

International Cinematographers
Guild/Publicists—IATSE Local 600

7755 Sunset Boulevard
Los Angeles, CA 90046
(323) 876-0160
www.cameraguild.com

Part XI:
Cast & Crew Support

Motion Picture Studio Grips/Crafts
Service—IATSE Local 80
2520 West Olive Avenue
Burbank, CA 91505
(818) 526-0700
www.iatselocal80.org

Motion Picture Studio First Aid
Employees—IATSE Local 767
14530 Denker Avenue
Gardena, CA 90247
(818) 655-5341
www.iatse767.org

Studio Transportation Drivers—Teamsters Local 399
4747 Vineland Avenue
North Hollywood, CA 91602
(818) 985-7374
www.hollywoodteamsters.org

NON-U.S. CONTACTS
CANADA

Directors Guild of Canada
111 Peter Street, Suite 402
Toronto, ON M5V 2H1
(416) 482-6640
www.dgc.ca

Canadian Society of Cinematographers
3007 Kingston Road, Suite 131
Toronto, ON M1M 1P1
(416) 266-0591
www.csc.ca

NABET 700
(represents the following departments in Toronto:
Script Supervisor, Construction, Grip, Hair, Lighting,
Makeup, Paint, Props, Set Dressing, Sound, Special
Effects, Videotape, Transportation, Wardrobe)
100 Lombard Street
Suite 203
Toronto, ON M5C 1M3
(416) 536-4827
www.nabet700.com

IATSE Local 210
(represents the following departments in the
Province of Alberta and in Calgary: Accounting,
Production Design, Construction, Costume, Editing,
First Aid, Crafts Service, Greens, Grips, Hair,
Electrics, Makeup, Painting, Paramedics, Props,
Script Supervisors, Set Decorating, Sound, Special
Effects, Visual Effects)
10428-123 Street
Edmonton, AB T5N 1N7
(780) 423-1863
www.iatse210.com

IATSE Local 212
(represents the following departments in Southern
Alberta: Accounting, Art/Production Design,
Construction, Costume, First Aid, Crafts Service,
Greens, Grip, Hair, Lighting/Electrics, Makeup,
Painters, Props, Script Supervision, Security, Set
Decorating, Sound, Special Effects)
57th Avenue S.W.
Calgary, AB T2H 2K8
(403) 250-2199
www.iatse212.com

IATSE Local 411
(represents the following personnel in the Province
of Ontario: Production Coordinators, Assistant
Coordinators, Production Secretaries, Craft Service
Providers, Honeywagon Operators)
629 Eastern Avenue
Building C, Suite 300
Toronto, ON M4M 1E4
(416) 645-8025
www.iatse411.ca

IATSE Local 461
(represents the following departments in the
Niagara Peninsula: Carpenters, Crafts Service,
Electrics, Grips, Hair, Makeup, Special Effects,
Transportation, Wardrobe)
P.O. Box 1594
Niagara-on-the-Lake, ON L0S 1J0
(905) 468-0513
www.niagara.com/iatse461

IATSE (AIEST) Local 514
(represents the following departments in Quebec:
Construction, Special Effects, Hairstyling, Logistics,
Wardrobe)
705 Bourget Street, Suite 201

Montreal, QC H4C 2M6
(514) 937-7668
www.iatse514.com

**IATSE Local 849—Atlantic Canadian Motion Picture
Studio Production Technicians**
(represents the following departments in
Newfoundland and Labrador, New Brunswick,
Nova Scotia and Prince Edward Island in Atlantic
Canada: Animal Wranglers, Costumes, Craft
Service, Diving, Greens, Grip, Hair, Lighting,
Makeup, Marine, Props, Scenic Paint, Script
Supervision, Set Construction, Set Decoration,
Sound, Special Effects, Transportation)
15 McQuade Lake Crescent, 2nd Floor
Halifax, NS B3S 1C4
(902) 425-2739
www.iatse849.com

IATSE Local 856
(represents the following departments in the
Province of Manitoba: Animal Wrangling, Art,
Catering, Construction, Continuity (Script), Costume,
Extras Casting, First Aid, Craft Services, Greens,
Grips, Hairstylists, Lighting & Electrics, Makeup
Artists, Paint, Props, Security, Set Decorating,
Sound, Special Effects, Transportation)
454 Edmonton Street
Winnipeg, MB R3B 2M3
(204) 953-1100
www.iatse856.com

IATSE Local 873—Motion Picture Technicians
(represents the following departments in Toronto:
Construction, Crafts Service, Electric, Greens, Grip,
Hair, Makeup, Paint, Props, Script, Set Decoration,
Sound, Special Effects, Transportation, Wardrobe)
104-1315 Lawrence Avenue East
Toronto, ON M3A 3R3
(416) 368-1873
www.iatse873.com

IATSE Local 891
(represents the following departments in British
Columbia: Accounting, Art, Construction, Costume
Department, Editors, First Aid, Craft Services,
Grip, Greens, Hair Department, Lighting/Electrics,
Makeup, Painting, Production Office, Props, Script
Supervisors, Set Decorating, Sound, Special Effects)
1640 Boundary Road
Burnaby, BC V5K 4V4

(604) 664-8910
www.iatse.com

ACTRA—Alliance of Canadian Cinema, Television and Radio Artists (National Office)
625 Church Street, 3rd Floor
Toronto, ON M4Y 2G1
(416) 489-1311
www.actra.ca

UNITED KINGDOM

Directors Guild of Great Britain
4 Windmill Street
London W1T 2HZ
(20) 7580 9131
www.dggb.co.uk

BECTU (Broadcasting Entertainment Cinematograph and Theatre Union)
(representing Arts & Entertainment workers in the areas of Scotland, Yorkshire/Humberside/Northern, North West and Cumbria, Midlands, Wales, Western, Ireland, and London and South East)
373-377 Clapham Road
London SW9 9BT
(20) 7346 0900
www.bectu.org

British Society of Cinematographers (BSC)
PO Box 2587
Gerrards Cross, SL9 7WZ
1753 888052
www.bscine.com

The Guild of Location Managers
PO Box 58010
London W10 6UZ
www.golm.org.uk

AUSTRALIA

Media, Entertainment and Arts Alliance (The Alliance)
245 Chalmers Street
Redfern NSW 2016
1300 656 512
www.alliance.org.au

Stunts Unlimited
PO Box 133 Kalorama
Victoria 3766
(613) 9761 9723
www.stuntsunlimited.com.au

Australian Cinematographers Society (ACS)
PO Box 207
Cammeray, NSW 2062
www.cinematographer.org.au

NEW ZEALAND

New Zealand Film and Video Technicians' Guild (NZF&VTG)
PO Box 68 294
Newton, Auckland
(+64 9) 3022 022; National Freephone: 0800 832 467
www.nztecho.com

Stunt Guild of New Zealand
PO Box 90301
Auckland Mail Centre, Auckland
www.stuntguildnz.com

HUNGARY

Hungarian Society of Cinematographers (HSC)
H-1145 Budapest
Rona u. 174
(+36 1) 251-07-68
www.hscmot.hu

GERMANY

German Society of Cinematographers (BVK)
Brienner Strasse 52
D-80333 Munich
+49 (0) 89 340 19 190
www.bvkamera.org

PEOPLE'S REPUBLIC OF CHINA

Hong Kong Society of Cinematographers
Flat B, 19/F, Block A,
Wylie Court 23 Wylie Path,
Ho Man Tin, Kowloon
(+852) 9021 5449

INDIA

Federation of Western India Cine Employees (FWICE)
113, 1st Floor
Kartik Complex
New Link Road
Andheri (W) 400053
Mumbai
(91) 22 26302552

Indian Society of Cinematographers (ISC)
'Aditya', 1, Akshara Veedhi
Pettah, Thiruvananthapuram
Kerala
PIN – 695024
www.iscindia.org

TURKEY

SINESEN - Cinema Workers' Union
Gazeteci Erogl Dernek Sokak No:10 /8
Beyoğlu/Istanbul
(0212) 244 16 07
www.sinesen.org

SED—Cinema Workers' Association
Hasnun Galip Sokak Içel Ishanı Katip
Mustafa Çelik Mah.
Taksim/Istanbul
(212) 252 81 31

BULGARIA

The Union of Bulgarian Film Makers
(represents the following departments: Actors,
Animators, Artists, Cameramen, Composers
and Sound Directors, Directors, Dramatists,
Editors, Film Critics)
Sofia 1504
Bulgaria
(+359 2) 946 10 69
www.filmmakersbg.org

JAPAN

Japanese Society of Cinematographers (JSC)
1-25-14 5F Shinjyuku, Shinjyuku-ku
Tokyo 160-0022
(+81 3) 3356-7896
www.jsc.or.jp/en

Appendix B

Glossary

The following is a list of insider terms and phrases you will hear on film sets.

ABBEY SINGER—the next to last shot of the night, named after an infamous Assistant Director who would make the crew believe that the *next to the last* shot was the *last* shot of the day

ABOVE-THE-LINE—descriptive for those in the movie business who are in the top creative or executive levels, typically the Producers, the Director, the Writers, and the Actors

ADR—Automatic Dialogue Replacement: actors go to a recording studio to reenact the scenes in order to record better audio than was originally recorded on set

ALLIANCE OF MOTION PICTURE AND TELEVISION PRODUCERS (AMPTP)—negotiates collective bargaining agreements for motion picture and television Producers with the entertainment industry's guilds and unions

APPLE BOX—a wooden box that the Grip Department uses for myriad purposes; there are full apple, half, quarter, and "pancakes," which are used to adjust the height of Actors and set pieces and as seats and platforms by the Camera and Grip departments

AVAILABLE LIST—a roster that many unions maintain for members to place their names when in need of work

B-ROLL—A standard news and documentary segment comprises two elements: interviews and "b-roll"; b-roll is the footage obtained of an event, activity, and/or insert shots of items relevant to the topic and spoken about in the interviews

BACKGROUND—any number of Extras who are placed in the background of a scene

BACK TO ONE—command given when the Director wants to do a take again, signaling everyone to reset to the starting positions

BASE CAMP—the location of the group of trucks and trailers brought together for equipment and cast needs

BELOW-THE-LINE—descriptive for employees in the movie business who are not at the top creative and executive levels

BLIMP—a soundproof box to place a camera into, typically used by the Unit Still Photographer (at present, the main supplier of these custom-made boxes is Jacobson Photographic Instruments, in North Hollywood, California)

BOARDS—see **STRIP BOARDS**

BOOKS ARE EMPTY—when all current members of a union are working or unavailable; this is the opportunity for new people to get their feet in the door and join the union

BOX RENTAL—a rental fee charged to the production by a crew member who is providing personally owned equipment to the project

BREAKDOWN, BREAKS THE SCRIPT DOWN—the process of going through a script to find all elements that are pertinent to a specific department

BROOM OUT—when all of the equipment used for a setup is cleared away so that a fresh scene can be rehearsed and blocked in the same space

BUMP UP—moving up to the next position in the chain of command for the day and getting additional pay for it

C-47—a slang name for a wooden clothespin; used mostly by Grips and Electricians to secure gels and diffusion to lights

CALL SHEET—a daily handout containing all scene information that is to be shot, who is supposed to be on set and when, and any special equipment needs

CALL TIMES—the start time each day for individual crew members

CANDY GLASS—special clear material that looks like real glass but allows Stunt Performers to crash through it safely

CANNED OUT—descriptive for exposed film that has been taken out of a film magazine and placed into a film can to be delivered for processing

CANS—slang term for headphones used by the Sound Department

CHECK THE GATE—The First Camera Assistant looks at the gate (the opening where the film is actually exposed inside the camera) to check for any debris that might have scratched the film during the last take

CLAPPER—another name for the Second Camera Assistant; also another name for the slate

CLOSED REHEARSAL—a rehearsal between the Director and Actors with no other crew on set

COMPANY MOVE—a packing up and transfer to a new location in the middle of the day, involving the entire crew, including trucks and trailers

CONTRACT SERVICES ADMINISTRATION TRUST FUND—a nonprofit organization that provides training and other services to the motion picture industry

COOGAN ACCOUNT—named for Jackie Coogan, a former child star, it is a special financial account required for all minor Actors to protect their earnings

COPY THAT—a response to a request, usually on the **RADIO**

COVERAGE—the pieces of a scene that are shot after the **MASTER**, usually close-ups or inserts

CROSSING THE LINE—the imaginary line that the camera should not cross as it moves around the set to shoot **COVERAGE**; crossing the line can result in mismatched editing when two characters who are facing one another appear to be looking the same direction when the film is edited together

CUTTERS—those who help create new wardrobe from scratch

DAILIES—the film shot the day before to be reviewed during production; sometimes called "rushes"

DAY CALLS, DAYPLAYING—instead of getting to work on a project every single day, you are called in to work just one day or sporadically on an as-needed basis

DAY RACK—an apparatus upon which the Costumer places the wardrobe that is needed each day

DEAL MEMO—a short contract that every crew member fills out that details the specifics of pay and responsibilities

DEPTH OF FIELD CALCULATOR—a small manual device (usually not electronic) to help the First Camera Assistant calculate how much of a shot will be in focus within given parameters involving the film stock and lens settings

DGA—Director's Guild of America; represents Directors (film and television), Unit Production Managers, First and Second Assistant Directors, Technical Coordinators, Associate Directors, Stage Managers, and Production Associates

DIGITAL INTERMEDIATE—the process of manipulating a film's color and contrast with a computer rather than chemically

DIRECTOR'S VIEWFINDER—a small self-contained lens used to line up shots

DOUBLE-DIPPING—booking and working two separate jobs for two different companies in a single day

DOWN CONVERSION—the process of enabling a **HIGH-DEFINITION** video image to be viewed on standard-definition monitoring equipment

EFP—Electronic Field Production; description of videotape production that emulates the working protocol for a film production but on a smaller scale

ENG—Electronic News Gathering; description of the working protocol for news production

EPK—Electronic Press Kit; videotape or DVD of behind-the-scenes footage and interviews given to the media to promote a project

EXPENDABLES—any number of disposable items used on set, such as tape or light bulbs

EXTRAS—secondary Actors in a movie who have no dialogue

EYE LINE—the direction that an Actor is looking, usually near the camera

FEBREZE—a brand-name cleaning product used by the Wardrobe Department

FEEDING THE CAMERA—getting everything necessary in front of the camera, generally referring to Actors

FILLS THE FRAME—when the Second Assistant Cameraman places the slate in the place in space in front of the lens that makes it appear to be the same size as the frame; this distance from the lens varies as the size of the lens changes

FILM BREAK—taking all the film shot up to a point in the day and preparing it for delivery to the lab

FINAL TOUCHES—the few moments before the cameras roll when the Costumer, Makeup Artist, and Hair Stylist double-check their work on the Actors

FIRST TEAM—the primary cast

FIRST UNIT—the primary shooting crew

FLASHING—whenever someone takes a still photo on set and the flash will fire, it is necessary to call out "Flashing!" so that the Electricians do not think that one of their units has blown out

FLYING IN—usually heard over the **RADIO** when something is asked for, such as "The C-stand is flying in," meaning that it is on its way

FORCED CALL—when your **TURNAROUND** just can't be met and you have to come to work early the following day; usually very expensive for a production, so it is avoided whenever possible

FOUL-WEATHER BAG—a soft duffel bag that you fill with additional clothing for inclement weather and keep on your truck or in your vehicle throughout production

FREELANCERS—independent contractors who are not employed on a permanent staff

FRENCH HOURS—the crew works for ten continuous hours and is not broken for an official lunch at any point, although a hot meal buffet is available throughout the day; usually happens when shooting day exteriors with limited time to complete the day's work

FURNEY PAD—shorthand for furniture pad; used for a variety of purposes on set, such as blacking out windows or wrapping up expensive equipment

GAFFER'S TAPE—cloth-based tape that comes in a variety of colors, used for a variety of purposes such as labeling camera, lighting, and grip equipment and cases or making marks on the floor for Actors to stand on

GENERAL CREW CALL—the start time at the beginning of the day when everyone should be on set and ready to get to work; some crew members have pre-calls a few minutes prior to the general crew call to give them time to prep their equipment

GENNY—shorthand for the generator that provides power to the set

GETTING BURIED—when another person or department intentionally or unintentionally creates a situation that makes doing your job difficult

GOLD, GOLDEN TIME—A normal crew deal pays straight time for the first ten hours, one-and-a-half time for the next two hours, and double time for every hour after twelve hours; that double-time pay is called "Gold" or "Golden time"

GOOD GATE—what the First Camera Assistant says when he finds no debris inside the camera body after a take

GREAT PROJECTS—the way Producers will describe small independent projects in which there is little to no money available to pay the crew

GROSS—the total amount of money that a movie takes in at the box office, as opposed to the **NET**

HALF-SPEED REHEARSAL—a rehearsal of the action performed at a slower speed than will be performed when the camera actually rolls; usually done during takes with stunts involved

HEADSHOT—an Actor's résumé, which has a large portrait photo on one side and the resume on the other

HIGH-DEFINITION—the newest video technology, which acquires images at very high resolutions

HONEYWAGON—portable toilet facilities built into a trailer that sits at **BASE CAMP**

HOT POINTS—usually when a Grip is carrying long items with potentially sharp or dangerous ends jutting out, such as dolly track or C-stands, he will call out "Hot points!" so that everyone around knows to watch out and not get in the way

IATSE—The International Alliance of Theatrical and Stage Employees, Moving Picture Technicians, Artists and Allied Crafts of the United States, Its Territories and Canada, AFL-CIO (American Federation of Labor and Congress of Industrial Organizations), CLC (Canadian Labor Congress): union representing the crafts (jobs and departments) that work together to make movies

INDUSTRY EXPERIENCE ROSTER—after you complete the requirements for joining your specific IATSE local, your name is placed on the Industry Experience Roster; Producers control the Roster but it is maintained by the **CONTRACT SERVICES ADMINISTRATIVE TRUST FUND**

IN THE CAN—a slang term describing a scene that is shot and finished

INSERT SHOTS—extra shots that are edited in between the main action, usually close-ups of items or of someone's hands performing a specific action

KILLS—an Actor can prevent the use of a percentage of the still photos that the Unit Still Photographer takes on set; the photos they choose to disallow are their "kills"

KIT RENTAL—see **BOX RENTAL**

LAST LOOKS—see **FINAL TOUCHES**

LAV MIC, LAVALIERE MICROPHONE—a very small microphone that is clipped onto an Actor

LIVE-TO-TAPE—a TV show that is edited while the show is in progress

LOCAL, WORK AS A—when you are asked to work in a distant location (from your own home) but are hired as a local, meaning that the production will not pay to accommodate you or pay per diem

LOCATION—the place where a movie is being shot when away from the main sound stage

LOCK UP—keeping all unwanted activity and noise from interrupting a take

LOCKED THE PICTURE—when the final edits on the movie are approved and no more changes will be made

LUNCH—the meal period six hours after general crew call, not necessarily at the normal "lunch time" someone has at home: if call time is at 7:00 A.M., then lunch is at 1:00 P.M.; if call time is at 2:00 P.M., then lunch is called at 7:00 P.M.

LUNCHBOX—an electrical distribution box used on set to provide power from the generator to lights and other equipment on set

MAGS, MAGAZINES, FILM MAGAZINES—a removable part of the camera in which to load raw film stock

MAGIC HOUR, GOLDEN HOUR—the few minutes (approximately twenty minutes) just prior to the sun setting below the horizon

MAKES THE DAY—completes all of the work that was scheduled for the day

MARKING REHEARSAL, BLOCKING REHEARSAL—rehearsal done to place tape marks on the floor for specific blocking after the Director and Actors finish the rehearsal for performance and character

MASTER (SHOT)—generally a "wide" shot of the entire action shot before going in for "tighter" **COVERAGE**

MARTINI—the last shot of the day, so named because, in theory, after the shot the crew can finally relax and enjoy a martini

MASTER TAG—used in Wardrobe to identify clothing for specific talent and scenes

MacGyver—slang term in reference to a 1980s TV program that featured a character who could invent any number of ingenious contraptions from very ordinary items

MEAL PENALTY—like a library fine, an amount of money paid to the crew if they are not broken for lunch on time, usually six hours after crew call

NABET—National Association of Broadcast Employees and Technicians-Communications Workers of America: a union that primarily represents workers in TV broadcast rather than film production (which is represented by IATSE)

NEGATIVE, SHOOT THE BEST—the goal of exposing the film so that a minimum of postproduction work has to be done to make it look better

NEPOTISM—the practice of offering employment to family and friends before considering anyone else

NET—the amount of money a project earns after expenses are deducted

NETWORKING—the process of creating a web of relationships that can lead to employment

ON A BELL—The First Assistant Director announces that "we're on a bell" to signal that everyone should be quiet. Generally the Sound Mixer pushes a button that rings a bell once to signal that everyone should be still. After a take is completed, the bell is rung twice to signal that everyone can make noise again.

ONER—when a scene can be filmed in just one shot instead of the typical master/coverage scenario

ONE-LINER, ONE-LINE SCHEDULE—a summary of the entire shooting schedule throughout production; as production progresses and plans change for one reason or another, revised one-line schedules are created and distributed to the crew

ON THE DAY—slang term in reference to when a shot actually will take place, as in "On the day, the cameras will actually move over there"

OSHA—the U.S. Department of Labor Occupational Safety & Health Administration, which exists to help promote a safe working environment

OUT-TIME—the time placed on the time card when someone is actually done working for the day, which is usually several minutes or more after the First AD calls wrap

PAINTER, STAND BY—a member of the Art Department on set who literally stands by in the event that something needs to be painted or touched up due to damage, such as a set wall

PER DIEM—an amount of money paid to the crew on location to cover living expenses, such as food (off set) and laundry, in addition to their normal salary

PRACTICAL LOCATION—when shooting occurs at a real location as opposed to a constructed set on stage

PRELIM—set slang for "preliminary call sheet," which is a rough draft of tomorrow's call sheet; created by the Second AD and distributed to all department heads during the course of the day in case any corrections or concerns need to be addressed before the final **CALL SHEET** is approved and printed

PRESS JUNKET—typically taking place over a weekend, an event for entertainment reporters from around the world to conduct very short interviews with the movie stars

PUSHED CALL—when the Assistant Directors have to adjust the call times after having already printed out the following day's **CALL SHEET**

PRINT, PRINTED—Many takes of a shot are done, but only a few are good enough to keep; the best are printed on film from the negative for review at dailies the following day

PRODUCTION—a term used to describe any film or TV project

PRODUCTION REPORT—a legal document prepared by the Assistant Directing Department that records exactly who worked each day, what equipment was used, and what was accomplished, as well as any significant problems, such as accidents

RADIO—a shorthand term for walkie-talkie

REALIES—a slang description for **FIRST TEAM**

RESIDUALS—in addition to the normal salary, SAG, DGA, and WGA members can receive income every time the project (movie, TV show) is exhibited

REVERSE, SHOOTING THE—After the action is shot in one direction, the camera turns around to shoot the other direction; for instance, after the camera has shot all of the dialogue for one Actor in a master, a medium shot, and a close-up, the crew will set up the reverse to shoot the same kinds of shots for the other Actor in the scene

RUBE GOLDBERGIAN—descriptive for an overly complicated invention created to perform a simple task

SAFETY MEETING—a quick meeting called on set prior to a major stunt or special effects sequence that may present danger to cast and crew, to inform everyone involved of what is planned and how to avoid trouble

SCHMOOZING—the act of being friendly to another person with the intention of improving your career

SCREEN ACTORS GUILD, SAG—guild representing TV and film talent, including stunt players

SAG CARD—the proof of membership into the Screen Actors Guild. One way to get the card is to work as an Extra and earn vouchers, one for every day you work. Accumulate three and you are eligible to join the union. Another way to get your SAG card is to be given a line of dialogue to say onscreen, in which case you are considered a principal Actor. A third way is to be in a commercial and be recognizable for around eight seconds, long enough that a viewer can tell that it is you. Or, if there is a stunt to do and you are the only person qualified and/or available to do it, you can be "**TAFT HARTLEY**'d" in. Once you do any of these things, you are eligible and *must* join SAG to continue to work on union projects. Contact the **SCREEN ACTORS GUILD** for additional information.

SECOND MEAL—union rules require a meal break every six hours. The first meal, known as "lunch," happens six hours after general crew call. The next meal is required six hours after the crew has been called back after lunch. Normally, the production will not break for a Second Meal and instead will just pay the meal penalties.

SECOND TEAM—the Stand-ins for the Actors while the set is lit and prepared for shooting

SECOND UNIT—an additional crew that normally shoots anything other than dialogue with principal Actors, such as stunts, effects, and inserts

SET—where the scene is being shot, either indoors on a practical location, on a sound stage, or outdoors

SETUP—every new shot in a film requires new camera angles, lenses, lighting, and blocking; it can take many individual setups to shoot the **MASTER** and all of the necessary **COVERAGE**

SHOOTING THE REHEARSAL—on occasion, there is a decision to roll cameras without first running a rehearsal; the idea behind this is to capture great performances on film instead of having them only seen by the crew on set

SHOW—term used by crewmembers to refer to any type of movie or TV production

SIG ALERT—a traffic alert posted in Southern California when an incident will close two or more freeway lanes for two-plus hours; named after 1940s radio reporter, Loyd Sigmon

SOUND EFFECTS—enhanced sounds added to the soundtrack in postproduction

"SHAKE THEM UP" (SHINY BOARDS)—when shooting outside, sometimes the Director of Photography will use large reflectors instead of powered lights; because the sun is moving across the sky, every few minutes the Grips are asked to adjust the reflectors (shiny boards) to keep the light shining in the correct direction

SHOPPER—a Costumer in the Wardrobe Department who goes out to retail stores to purchase appropriate clothing

SIDES—shrunken pocket-size copies of the script pages that will be shot that day.

SLATE—the white board with attached wooden sticks that the Second Assistant Cameraman claps together before each take; the visual of the clap on film is used in conjunction with the sound of the clap recorded by the Sound Mixer to sync the picture and the soundtrack

SLATE, TO—the act of hitting together the wooden sticks that are on the slate

SMART SLATE—a battery-powered slate with electronic time-code numbers that are used to sync with the time code recorded by the Sound Mixer

SOFT—when the First Assistant Cameraman (Focus Puller) misses focus for part of a shot

SPECIAL EFFECTS UNIT—a separate crew that only shoots elements that are needed to create special effects on set, sometimes used in conjunction with Visual Effects

SPLITS, SPLIT DAY—when half of the shooting day is done in the daytime and the other half at night

START PAPERWORK—all of the necessary forms for salary, tax, and safety that each crew member fills out prior to beginning work

STEADICAM—a body-mounted camera stabilizer

STREAKS AND TIPS—a brand name temporary hair color spray that is used instead of paint to age items or set walls

STICKS—another name for the wooden part of the slate that is clapped together, as in "hit the sticks"; also another name for a tripod, as in "get the sticks"

STINGERS—slang term for electrical extension cables

STRIKING—said just before a large light is turned on to warn and protect anyone who might be looking right at it

STRIP BOARD—created by the AD Department, used to plan out the entire movie schedule. They were formerly created manually with colored cardboard or plastic strips but are now mostly done by computer. The First AD breaks the script down into individual elements (like Actors and locations) that are needed and each is assigned a distinct color. The Second AD refers to this board when creating the daily call sheets. Changes are frequent and occur throughout production.

STUDIO ZONE—a thirty-mile radius from the intersection of Beverly Boulevard and La Cienega that helps determine pay rates and travel and accommodation requirements for union crew

STUNTMEN'S ASSOCIATION—an organization of the highest caliber Stunt Coordinators, Stunt Performers, and Second Unit Directors, which promotes quality work and safety

TAFT HARTLEY—an alternative in the SAG membership requirements that allows a Producer to hire a non-SAG Actor for a role; an Actor can receive up to three roles this way before being required to join SAG

10-100—old CB radio shorthand that means you need to go to the restroom ("I'm 10-100")

TAIL STICKS—when it is difficult or impossible to clap the slate prior to the take, the Second Assistant Cameraman will put the slate in front of the lens after the Director calls, "Cut!"

TAKE THE BULLET—take the blame for something you did or didn't do

TALENT—anyone appearing on-camera

TEAMSTERS—the International Brotherhood of Teamsters represents transportation professionals in all industries, but it is Local 399 that specifically represents Drivers in motion-picture production; also represents Animal Trainers, Auto Service Personnel, Casting Directors, Chef Drivers, Couriers, Dispatchers, Location Managers, Mechanics, Warehousemen, and Wranglers

TEAR SHEETS—a portfolio of conceptual costume sketches drawn by the Costume Designer

THROUGH-THE-WORKS—the process of getting Actors into the proper wardrobe, having their makeup done, and having their hair styled correctly for the scene

T-MARK—two pieces of colored tape placed on the floor in the shape of a T by the Second Assistant Cameraman to mark the spot where an Actor is supposed to stand

TOP STICK—a brand name adhesive used by the Wardrobe Department

TRADES—magazines specific to the motion-picture industry, such as *Daily Variety* and the *Hollywood Reporter*

TREATMENT—a quick synopsis describing the main elements of a story; most movies begin this way before advancing to the screenplay stage.

TURNAROUND—the amount of time required between wrap and call time the following day; for instance, SAG Actors must have a twelve-hour turnaround

TURNAROUND, TURNING AROUND—Generally when shooting a scene, all of the action that faces one side of the set is shot first; when everything looking that direction is finished, the cameras move and turn around to shoot the action that faces the other side of the set

TURNING THE KNOB—a slang phrase that describes how the First Assistant Cameraman adjusts, or "pulls," focus

VANITIES, THE—a slang description for the Hair, Makeup, and Wardrobe departments

VIDEO VILLAGE—the area just away from the main action on set where the video monitors and directors' chairs are placed; the Director, Script Supervisor, Producers, and anyone else who is not working on the shot itself can view the take from here

WALKAWAY—when you can literally turn off your equipment and go home because you'll return to working in that exact spot the next day

WESCAM—a camera stabilizer, usually mounted on a helicopter

WALKING MEAL—when the crew is not broken for lunch but food is available for them to have while they keep on working

WRITER'S GUILD OF AMERICA, WGA—a labor union representing writers for TV and theatrical features

WILD WALLS—one or more removable walls built into an interior, facilitating camera and lighting setups

Appendix C

Additional Resources
BOOKS

When you are ready to learn more about a specific job or department, here are suggestions for further reading:

Stunts

Anderson, Jameson. *Stunt Double (Atomic)*. Chicago: Raintree, 2007.

Bondurant, Bob. *Bob Bondurant on Police and Pursuit Driving (Bob Bondurant On)*. Osceola, WI: MBI, 2000.

Boughn, Jenn. *Stage Combat: Fisticuffs, Stunts, and Swordplay for Theater and Film*. New York: Allworth Press, 2006.

Ware, Derek. *Stunt Performers (Living Dangerously)*. Ada, OK: Garrett Educational, 1992.

Wiener, David Jon. *Burns, Falls and Crashes: Interviews with Movie Stunt Performers*. Jefferson, NC: McFarland & Co., 1996.

Wolf, Stephen A. *A Day in the Life of a Stunt Person (Day in the Life of)*. Mahwah, NJ: Troll Associates, 1991.

Wolf, Steve. *The Secret Science behind Movie Stunts & Special Effects*. New York: Skyhorse Publishing, 2007.

Props

James, Thurston. *The Prop Builder's Molding & Casting Handbook*. White Hall, VA: Betterway Publications, 1989.

Wilson, Andy. *Making Stage Props: A Practical Guide*. Malborough, UK: Crowood Press, 2003.

Wardrobe

Anderson, Barbara, and Cletus R. Anderson. *Costume Design*. Belmont, CA: Wadsworth/ Thompson Learning, 1999.

Covey, Liz, and Rosemary Ingham. *Costume Designer's Handbook: A Complete Guide for Amateur and Professional Costume Designers*. Portsmouth, NH: Heinemann, 1992.

La Motte, Richard. *Costume Design 101: The Business and Art of Creating Costumes for Film and Television*. Studio City, CA: Michael Wiese Productions, 2001.

Landis, Deborah Nadoolman. *Costume Design (Screencraft) (Screencraft Series)*. Burlington, MA: Focal Press, 2003.

Makeup

Graphic-Sha. *A Complete Guide to Special Effects Makeup: Conceptual Artwork by Japanese Makeup Artists*. Tokyo: Graphic-Sha, 2007.

Kehoe, Vincent. *Special Make-Up Effects*. Boston: Focal Press, 1991.

Kehoe, Vincent. *The Technique of the Professional Make-Up Artist*. Boston: Focal Press, 1995.

Musgrove, Jan. *Make-Up and Costume for Television (Media Manuals)*. Oxford, UK: Focal Press, 2003.

Thudium, Laura. *Stage Make-Up: The Actor's Complete Guide to Today's Techniques and Materials*. New York: Back Stage Books, 1999.

Vinther, Janus. *Special Effects Make-Up*. New York: Routledge, 2003.

Production Assistant

Alves, Jeff and William-Alan Landes. *The Production Assistant's Handbook*. Studio City, CA: Players Press, 2005.

Carboni, Tiffany. *The Hollywood Food Chain: A Comically Real Look at Hollywood through the Eyes of Production Assistants*. San Jose, CA: Writer's Showcase Press, 2000.

Production Management/ Assistant Directing

Patz, Deborah S. *Film Production Management 101: The Ultimate Guide for Film and Television*

Production Management and Coordination. Studio City: Michael Wiese Productions, 2002.

Cleve, Bastian. *Film Production Management.* Burlington, MA: Focal Press, 2005.

Singleton, Ralph S. *Film Scheduling: Or, How Long Will It Take to Shoot Your Movie?* Beverly Hills, CA: Lone Eagle, 1997.

Singleton, Ralph S. *Film Budgeting: Or How Much Will It Cost to Shoot Your Movie.* Beverly Hills, CA: Lone Eagle, 1996.

Directing

Katz, Steven. *Film Directing: Cinematic Motion.* 3rd ed. Studio City, CA: Michael Wiese Productions, 2004.

Katz, Steven. *Film Directing: Shot by Shot: Visualizing from Concept to Screen.* Studio City: Michael Wiese Productions, 1991.

Kingdon, Tom. *Total Directing: Integrating Camera and Performance in Film and Television,* Los Angeles: Silman-James Press, 2004.

Proferes, Nicholas. *Film Directing Fundamentals: See Your Film Before Shooting.* 2nd ed. Burlington, MA: Focal Press, 2004.

Schreibman, Myrl A. *The Film Director Prepares: A Complete Guide to Directing for Film and TV.* Beverly Hills, CA: Lone Eagle, 2006.

Vineyard, Jeremy. *Setting Up Your Shots: Great Camera Moves Every Filmmaker Should Know.* Studio City, CA: Michael Wiese Productions, 2000.

Weston, Judith. *Directing Actors: Creating Memorable Performances for Film & Television.* Studio City, CA: Michael Wiese Productions, 1999.

Wilkinson, Charles. *The Working Director: How to Arrive, Survive and Thrive in the Director's Chair.* Studio City, CA: Michael Wiese Productions, 2005.

Script Supervision

Miller, Pat P. *Script Supervising and Film Continuity.* 3rd ed. Woburn, MA: Butterworth-Heinemann, 1998.

Rowlands, Avril. *Continuity Supervisor (Media Manuals).* 4th ed. Oxford, UK: Focal Press, 2000.

Camera/Lighting

Alton, John, *Painting with Light.* Berkeley, CA: University of California Press, 1985.

Box, Harry. *Set Lighting Technician's Handbook: Film Lighting Equipment, Practice, and Electrical Distribution.* 3rd ed. Burlington, MA: Focal Press, 2003.

Brown, Blain. *Cinematography: Image Making for Cinematographers, Directors, and Videographers.* Oxford, UK: Focal Press, 2002.

Brown, Blain. *Motion Picture and Video Lighting.* 2nd ed. Burlington, MA: Focal Press, 2007.

Elkins S. O. C., David E. *The Camera Assistant's Manual.* 4th ed. Burlington, MA: Focal Press, 2005.

Hart, Douglas. *The Camera Assistant: A Complete Professional Handbook.* Newton, MA: Focal Press, 1996.

Jackman, John. *Lighting for Digital Video & Television.* 2nd ed. San Francisco: CMP Books, 2004.

Krasilovsky, Alexis. *Women behind the Camera: Conversations with Camerawomen.* Westport, CT: Praeger Paperback, 1997.

Lowell, Ross. *Matters of Light & Depth.* New York: Lowel-Light Manufacturing, 1999.

Malkiewicz, Kris and David M. Mullen. *Cinematography.* 3rd ed. New York: Fireside, 2005.

Malkiewicz, Kris. *Film Lighting.* New York: Prentice-Hall, 1986.

Mascelli, Joseph, V. *The Five C's of Cinematography: Motion Picture Filming Techniques*. Los Angeles: Silman-James Press, 1998.

Schaefer, Dennis. *Masters of Light: Conversations with Contemporary Cinematographers*. Berkeley, CA: University of California Press, 1984.

Uva, Michael. *The Grip Book*. 3rd ed. Burlington, MA: Focal Press, 2006.

Viera, Dave, and Maria Viera. *Lighting for Film and Digital Cinematography*. Belmont, CA: Wadsworth Publishing, 2004.

Sound

Altman, Rick. *Sound Theory, Sound Practice (AFI Film Readers)*. New York: Routledge, 1992.

Holman, Tomlinson. *Sound for Film and Television*. 2nd ed. Focal Press. Burlington, MA: Focal Press, 2001.

Kenny, Tom. *Sound for Picture Edition: The Art of Sound Design in Film and Television (Mix Pro Audio Series)*. Vallejo, CA: MixBooks, 2000.

LoBrutto, Vincent. *Sound-On-Film: Interviews with Creators of Film Sound*. Westport, CT: Praeger Paperback, 1994.

Weis, Elisabeth, and John Belton. *Film Sound: Theory and Practice*. New York: Columbia University Press, 1985.

Yewdall, David Lewis. *Practical Art of Motion Picture Sound*. 3rd ed. Westport, CT: Focal Press, 2003.

Special Effects

Fielding, Raymond. *Techniques of Special Effects of Cinematography (Library of Communication Techniques, Film)*. Oxford, UK: Focal Press, 1985.

McCarthy, Robert. *Secrets of Hollywood Special Effects*. Newton, MA: Focal Press, 1992.

Pinteau, Pascal, and Laurel Hirsch. *Special Effects: An Oral History-Interviews with 37 Masters Spanning 100 Years*. New York: Harry N. Abrams, 2005.

Rickitt, Richard. *Special Effects: The History and Technique*. New York: Billboard Books, 2007.

Production Design/Art

Helton, J. R. *Below the Line*. San Francisco: Last Gasp, 2000.

LoBrutto, Vincent. *The Filmmaker's Guide to Production Design*. New York: Allworth Press, 2002.

Olson, Robert. *Art Direction for Film and Video*. 2nd ed. Woburn, MA: Focal Press, 1998.

Preston, Ward. *What an Art Director Does: An Introduction to Motion Picture Production Design*. Los Angeles: Silman-James Press, 1994.

Rizzo, Michael. *The Art Direction Handbook for Film*. Burlington, MA: Focal Press, 2005

Woodbridge, Patricia. *Designer Drafting for the Entertainment World*. Burlington, MA: Focal Press, 2000.

Index

About the Author

Brian Dzyak began his career as an Editor, Videographer, and Producer at WBGU-TV27 in Ohio. Since 1987, has had experience around the world in just about every type of film and television production that exists. As a member of IATSE Local 600 in Los Angeles, Brian worked as a motion picture Camera Assistant for over a decade on feature films, episodic television, music videos, and commercials. He currently works as a freelance Cameraman, primarily capturing behind-the-scenes footage and interviews for television and DVD use.